ND TRAILS

MISSOURI

RIVER

KOTA

od

d City

TH DAKOTA

CLOUD AGENCY

ourt House Rock

LEGEND
HISTORIC PLACES_____ ▪
LANDMARKS _____ ▲
TRAIL ROUTES_____ ∿

0   50   100   150

miles

N

Ash Hollow

Loup R.

Omaha

Plattsmouth

Platte   River

Big

Nebraska City

Lower
California
Crossing

Blue R.

Nemaha R.

Brownville

FORT
KEARNY

Little   Blue R.

St. Joseph

er

nia
ing

NEBRASKA

Atchison
Leavenworth

KANSAS

Marysville

Kansas   R.

Kansas
City

Smoky   Hill   River

River

Nebraska State Historical Society

PUBLICATIONS

VOLUME XXVI

NEBRASKA STATE HISTORICAL SOCIETY

Publications

Volume XXVI

FROM THE MISSOURI TO THE
GREAT SALT LAKE:

An Account of Overland Freighting

By

WILLIAM E. LASS

PUBLISHED BY THE SOCIETY

1972

To Garner

who appreciates the West

From the Missouri to the Great Salt Lake

by William E. Lass

Foreword

This study relates to an area of Nebraska and western history that has long been the subject of a variety of individual reports or studies. The January 10, 1900, meeting of the Nebraska State Historical Society was designated "Old Freighters Meeting," with many of the men who made freighting history present to record their recollections. Despite the years of interest, this publication by Professor Lass is the first comprehensive study of freighting to be published for the Missouri River frontier.

The research has been aided by a Woods Fellowship grant administered by the Nebraska State Historical Society from funds donated by the Woods Charitable Fund, Inc. Funds for the publication were provided by the Nebraska State Historical Foundation. The study "The Great Platte River Road" by Merrill J. Mattes, published by the Society in 1969 as Volume XXI of the *Publications* series, was the first in the series of Woods Fellowship studies.

MARVIN F. KIVETT, *Director*
Nebraska State Historical Society

Preface

In the history of the Great Plains, the period prior to the construction of the Union Pacific Railroad was characterized by a massive westward migration by wagon—a migration of thousands of frontiersmen seeking the fertile lands of Oregon, the gold of California and the Rockies, and the refuge of the Great Basin. Most of these migrants passed through the Platte Valley, but some of them settled in eastern Kansas and Nebraska, choosing the more certain gold of corn and wheat rather than that promised by distant El Dorados beyond the plains. Thus, in the mid-nineteenth century, the frontier was developing in a haphazard fashion, with the Indian-occupied Great Plains left as a barrier between the far western areas and the farming frontier along the Missouri and lower Platte rivers.

To the man bound for California or Oregon, the Platte Valley was merely an area through which he must pass, since the land along the Pacific was supplied by way of the ocean, not by overland trails. But the man in Utah or Colorado realized that the valley was his link with the supply centers on the Missouri River; thus the day of the commercial freighter in the Platte Valley came with the movement of people into the Great Basin and the Rockies.

When one visualizes the central Great Plains, without a navigable river and without a railroad, the importance of wagon freighting can be imagined. For nearly two decades thousands of wagons loaded with goods of every description were drawn through the valley of the Platte. Every wagon that moved westward carried goods. Settlers on their way to the Columbia hauled their possessions; so did the California-bound miners and the Mormons. But these people were not freighters. The freighter was the man engaged in commercial wagon transportation. Most freighters carried goods for a fee for someone else. Some of them, however, were merchants whose primary interest in the wagon trade was transporting their own merchandise. Though they dominated, freighters never monopolized plains commerce. Their business, by its very nature, was slow and methodical; consequently, they did not command the trade of light items that had to be moved quickly. The stagecoach companies with their express service handled much of the trade in light goods.

During the years 1849-1867 overland freighting was essential to the economic growth of the central Plains. Many hundreds of individuals profited from it, and much of the derived capital was later instrumental in financing towns, railroad lines, and businesses. The freighting trade itself had many attendant effects. Merchants in the river towns traded in a hinterland stretching hundreds of miles to the west. Farmers and millers of eastern Kansas and Nebraska marketed their corn and flour to the forts and mining areas. Farmers also sold thousands of work cattle to freighters, and many farmers worked part-time in freighting.

Throughout its history overland freighting depended heavily on the government, which generally used civilian contractors to supply frontier garrisons and expeditions. In fact, the central Plains freighting began because of the government's decision to fortify the overland route through the Platte Valley. For a time Fort Leavenworth was the base of the western trade and then, with the creation of Kansas Territory, the towns of Leavenworth and Atchison soon assumed importance as supply points for the expanding military trade and the civilian trade with Utah. Freighting through the Platte Valley experienced its first real boom during the Mormon War of 1857-1858 when the government decided to use Nebraska City as an additional rendezvous point for the Utah-bound supply trains.

Supplying the Utah army was a business of short duration, but it was soon followed by an active trade to the gold regions of Colorado. The needs of the miners opened the way for extensive freighting from Omaha, making it a sharp rival of Nebraska City.

During the early Civil War years, a time of depressed trade, Nebraska City was the foremost freighting town. In 1864 and 1865 a variety of factors—the Montana gold rush, the expansion of the military frontier, and the construction of the Union Pacific—contributed to an unprecedented boom in freighting with Nebraska City, Atchison, Plattsmouth, and Omaha the principal centers.

The building of the Union Pacific through the Platte Valley ended overland freighting's long hauls. There was, however, a sharp but brief revival of the business during the Black Hills gold rush. Freighting from Sidney, located on the main line of the Union Pacific, to the gold mines of Dakota Territory was good for five years; then it succumbed to westward-advancing Dakota railroads.

The purpose of this study is to present a clear, concise history of overland freighting in the Platte Valley based on available evidence in both contemporary accounts and later writings. The story is arranged chronologically in order to show the fluctuating fortunes of overland freighting and to relate freighting to the significant economic and political developments in the West. Hopefully this synthesis will contribute not only to the historical literature of the Platte Valley, but also toward a better understanding of overland freighting on the Great Plains.

WILLIAM E. LASS
Mankato, Minnesota
October 5, 1971

Acknowledgments

I take this opportunity to thank those who facilitated the preparation of this study. First of all I wish to express my appreciation to the Woods Charitable Fund, Incorporated, of Lincoln, for providing funds for a Woods Fellowship in Nebraska History, which made the study possible. I also appreciate the work of the Nebraska State Historical Society in administering the fellowship program.

The staff of the Nebraska State Historical Society was most interested and cooperative. I especially thank Donald F. Danker for his assistance in locating materials and talking through some aspects of the work with me. I also thank Marvin F. Kivett, the Society's director, for his interest and cooperation in seeing the work through to its final form. William D. Aeschbacher, former director of the Society, provided much assistance during the early stages of the research, as did John B. White, former librarian of the Society. I am grateful to numerous staff members of the Library of Congress, through whom I was able to obtain many newspapers and books. Personnel in the Bureau of Indian Affairs and Old Army Sections of the National Archives were most cooperative in locating transportation contracts, and Mrs. Enid T. Thompson, librarian of the Colorado Historical Society, provided invaluable assistance in obtaining Denver area newspapers and other materials. I also thank Harold Williamson and J. Alvin Rodgers of the Mankato State College library for their enthusiastic assistance in locating and obtaining source materials.

My wife Marilyn deserves particular mention. She not only provided encouragement throughout but assisted in all phases of the project.

xv

Table of Contents

List of Maps

List of Illustrations

LIST OF ILLUSTRATIONS (continued)

List of Tables

From the Missouri to the
Great Salt Lake

I

Outfitting and Operating Wagon Trains

Each spring, in the years prior to the coming of the Union Pacific Railroad, the freighting towns along the Missouri River teemed with activity. Animals, wagons, and drivers filled the streets and crowded the pastures outside of town. These milling masses exemplified the inherent nature of overland freighting—a business that demanded much equipment and great preparation to move comparatively small quantities of goods. Over 300 oxen, 26 wagons, and 30 men were needed to run a single train hauling sixty to seventy-five tons of goods. Big operators, especially military contractors, talked in terms of hundreds of wagons and men, and thousands of animals. Weeks of preparation were needed to dispatch trains. Oxen had to be assembled from miles around, additional wagons often had to be brought in by steamboat. Drivers were sometimes recruited from great distances. Though freighters usually solved their own problems, they owed much to Russell, Majors, and Waddell, whose experience in large·scale freighting provided much information, ranging from the most desirable types of animals and wagons to the practical techniques of managing a train on the trail. Out of the experience of the many freighters and the example set by Russell, Majors, and Waddell evolved a fairly standard operating procedure.

Once the spring assemblage of animals, wagons, and men was completed, yet more intensive work began. Animals had to be broken, wagons prepared, and the men trained before the wagons could roll. Freighters who kept diaries or later wrote reminiscences invariably dwelled on these topics.

The challenges of moving vast distances with heavy loads required freighters to use an animal that was both hardy and strong, and the necessity of using numerous wagons forced the freighter to look for an animal that was available in quantity at reasonable prices. Horses, which were commonly used in Conestoga wagon freighting east of the Mississippi, did not meet western needs. They were too scarce and consequently too costly, and they could not do heavy work when fed on grass and forage alone. Space was dear to the freighter; he felt it unreasonable and uneconomical to attempt to carry grain for draft animals during normal operations. For these reasons horses were used in the overland trade but sparingly. If an individual did use them, he usually commanded a short notice in the local newspaper remarking upon his uniqueness.

Thus mules and oxen were the work animals of overland emigration and freighting. There was never universal agreement as to the superiority of one over the other, and freighters who worked the year round in both short and long distance hauling found it advantageous to use both. Each animal had its virtues and faults. Oxen were reputed to have more endurance than mules. Alexander Majors, who did more than anyone else to popularize oxen, claimed that if properly handled they could travel 2,000 miles a season.[1] Randolph B. Marcy, an army explorer who had ample opportunity to observe both oxen and mules, likewise noted that the oxen endured better on long marches.[2] Oxen were always more numerous and less costly than mules, and they could generally be obtained on the frontier, usually from farmers in the region of the freighting towns. Their availability must be credited, in part, to the lack of demand for them as work animals by farmers and the military. Anyone using a single team or even two teams to a vehicle found horses and mules much more manageable than oxen. The army almost exclusively used mules since much of their work was on-post drayage, where maneuverability—backing and turning short—was necessary. Oxen simply did not have this ability. During periods of military crisis such as the Mormon War and the Civil War, mules were scarce on civilian markets. During the Civil War especially, those who wanted to use mules could secure them only at considerable difficulty and expense. At war's end, however, the army sold thousands of mules. During the fall of 1865, some eight thousand were to be put on the market at Fort Leavenworth alone.[3] Despite fluctuations in supply, mules always cost more than oxen. Normally bringing about $100 each, though price varied according to the size, age, and training of the animal, they brought prices as high as $200 each during the 1865 boom in spite of the large number of army mules on the market.[4] In comparison, oxen usually cost from $40 to $75 a pair, once again, the price being influenced by the size, age, and gentleness of the animal, as well as by local supply and demand. During 1865 when freighting reached unprecedented proportions, yokes were reported to be selling for $160.[5] Not only were oxen less expensive than mules, but they cost far less to outfit. Their equipment consisted basically of yokes that sold for about $3 and chains that sold for around $2.50, while mules had to be outfitted with harnesses.[6]

Oxen were also valued for their docility and their unlikeliness to stampede. In emergencies they could be butchered and eaten while there seems to have been a popular aversion to mule meat. Freighters believed that another advantage of oxen was that they were not desired by Indians, who much preferred stealing and riding mules or horses.[7]

Despite their many assets oxen were far from being the perfect draft animal. Their biggest fault was their ponderously slow pace. Mules, while hardly rapid, were considerably faster than oxen. Mules pulling loads walked just over two and a half miles an hour, while oxen under comparable road conditions and load walked at a pace of only two miles an hour.[8] The daily advantage of mules could easily amount to five or six miles. When carried out over a trip from the Missouri to Denver, this amounted to a considerable time saving. Mule trains commonly made the trip in about a week less than oxen-drawn wagons. Whenever possible, freighters sent light items that were much in demand and subject to severe price fluctuations by mule train because a few days advantage in reaching the market could mean the difference between profit or loss. In these situations the added expense of mules was easily justified by the possibilities of tapping a booming market. Likewise, the speed of mules made them desirable for winter freighting where quick passage was the principal aim. In the winter regardless of the type of animals used, grain had to be carried, since it was impossible even for oxen to subsist by grazing for short periods on dried grass while working hard. Thus, in winter the oxen had no advantage at all over mules. In fact, mules were almost always used by those who ran winter trains.

Since most overland freighting consisted of moving heavy goods great distances in no particular hurry during spring and summer months, oxen were used much more extensively than mules. There were some who praised mule teams for their lively step and uniform color; their smart appearance was often highlighted by flashy harness decoration. Close investigation would undoubtedly bear out that those freighters who used mules primarily did so because the animals' speed was an economic consideration to them, not because they were flashy. There is no particular mystery about Alexander Majors holding that oxen were best suited for overland freighting. Majors engaged primarily in military freighting, where the market and price were assured. If he had freighted during the winter or in a highly competitive market, he would have shed some of this great regard for oxen.

The most desirable oxen were large, well matured, four- to seven-year-old beasts. It is unlikely that many of these work cattle died of old age. Some succumbed to the rigors of the business on the first trip and veterans of even several seasons were scarce. The average use of a yoke of oxen would probably not be any more than a single freighting season. Most of the oxen were purchased in the region about the freighting towns and were classified as native cattle. They came in virtually every color and color pattern and were generally horned, though freighters sometimes dehorned their oxen. Texas and Cherokee cattle were always available, and some of them were used on nearly every train. The Texas longhorns were in demand because of their rangy frames and toughness.[9]

All oxen were branded, usually with the first letter of the owner's surname. Livingston & Kinkead used a large *K* and Russell, Majors & Waddell an ox yoke, which was considered to be the firm's private brand. There evidently were no brand books or registration of brands, but rather there seems to have been a common understanding that each freighter would use a distinguishing mark. Freighters were evidently never plagued by the loss of cattle to their rivals, and the entire trade appears to have been comparatively free of cattle stealing, even when herds were wintered on the open range. Drivers oftentimes named their cattle and would speak of them by name rather than merely as the off leader or nigh wheeler. Thaddeus S. Kenderdine, a bullwhacker for Russell, Majors & Waddell during the Mormon War, observed that most of the names were prosaic such as "Roan," "Nig," or the like. Kenderdine, mainly to puzzle his companions, used Biblical names. Samson and Goliath were his wheelers. His fellow whackers showed something of their taste by dubbing a particular yoke Tom and Jerry.[10]

A wagon carrying 5,000 to 6,000 pounds was usually pulled by six yoke of oxen, sometimes five if the cattle were very large. The cattle were designated as leaders, wheelers, pointers, and swing cattle. The two leaders were the best broken animals and were usually lightweight, long-legged, Texas longhorns. They actually pulled little of the load but instead set the pace and started any turning of the team. Leaders were usually trained to respond quickly to commands of "gee" and "haw." The smoothness and rapidity of the corralling movement and other maneuvers depended heavily on the nature and training of the leaders. The rather common impression that all draft oxen were longhorns probably derives from the use of the Texas longhorns as leaders and the prominent position of the leaders in trains. Wheelers, like leaders, needed to be well trained. Hitched directly to the wagon, wheelers were always the heaviest and strongest animals since they pulled more than any other yoke.[11]

The pointers, just ahead of the wheelers, were next in size and training and the second hardest-working pair on the team. In cases where more than six yoke were needed, additional pointers were used. Between the pointers and leaders there were two or three yoke of swing cattle, usually identified as the first, second, and third swings, numbering from the pointers forward. These were wild steers, untrained and even unbroken before their maiden trip. Young and unruly, these steers were the bullwhackers' continual irritant, but their position in the team between trained animals made them manageable, at least when on the move. Each yoke had an "off" or right ox and a "nigh" or left ox, designations earlier used with Conestoga horse teams. Probably they were so called originally because the "off" animal was the farthest from the driver, who normally stayed to the left of the team.[12]

If time permitted, animals were taught to stand and become acquainted with the feel of the yoke and to respond to the usual commands, "gee," "haw," "giddap," and "whoa." Usually, however, animals and men were not assembled long enough before rolling out to permit the luxury of training, and animals were hitched only a few times, then broken in while working on the trail. Hitching was many times a new experience to both oxen and bullwhackers, who were introduced to it in a general melee. Hitching even on the trail with well-broken cattle was sometimes hectic.

The oxen, 300 for a full train, were contained in a corral formed by placing wagons in an ellipse about fifty by thirty yards. Then the twenty-five drivers, each with a forty- to fifty-pound yoke slung over his right shoulder, a bow in his left hand, and keys in his teeth, plunged into the mass of flesh, hoofs, and horns to find and yoke his off wheeler. This was the moment of truth for the neophyte. A single twist of a longhorn's head was sufficient to stab a man. Crushed toes and bruised legs were normal occupational hazards, and many a driver suffered the humiliation of being knocked down on manure-splattered turf, especially when the ground was slippery from rain. Yoking was the worst part of the bullwhacker's never easy day. A lost key, a dropped yoke, a brush with a steer, or a lost animal—any one was sufficient to evoke the bullwhacker's most expressive verbiage, for which he was famed throughout the plains.

Among shouts, curses, and bellows, the off wheeler was located and yoked. First the yoke was laid across his neck; then the hickory bow was pushed through two holes about two inches in diameter and fastened in place either by iron keys or wooden pegs that were pushed through a small hole near each end of the bow and secured by a short piece of rawhide tied around the bow. The off wheeler was then faced into and sometimes tied to a wagon wheel, and his partner was pulled, pushed, or beaten into position and yoked. The same procedure was followed in locating and yoking the leaders. The swing cattle and pointers were then brought up in order behind the leaders. Swing cattle, pointers, and leaders were hitched together by sections of log chain that ran from yoke ring to yoke ring and were secured with clevices. The wheelers were then hitched to the tongue, and while they held it up the rest of the team was driven in a looping circle so as to brush past the wagon and wheelers and come into position with the pointers just ahead of the wheelers. Then these two yokes were chained together and the team was ready to go.[13]

Depending on the skill of the bullwhackers and the gentleness of the steers, hitching could either be casual or hellish. Wild animals usually kicked, foamed, and twisted violently, sometimes to the point of snapping their necks. Once yoked, the unbroken beasts were not freed from their wooden burden or their partners until they were completely submissive. They worked, grazed, and slept as yokes for at least several days and sometimes for two weeks or longer.[14] If the animals were tame, the men trained, and lost keys and twisted chains kept to a minimum, hitching could be accomplished speedily. Majors recalled timing men on one of his trains who yoked and hitched all twelve animals on every wagon in only sixteen minutes. Kenderdine claimed the feat of a train once yoking and hitching in only five minutes, but this record is hard to believe.[15] William Henry Jackson, who bullwhacked from Nebraska City to Utah in 1866, believed that Majors had coached expert bullwhackers intensively in order to make the sixteen minute mark. He noted that "after many weeks our outfit never did better than thirty-five or forty minutes—and we considered that an excellent job."[16]

Hitching and driving oxen and hitching and driving mules were different skills. The muleskinner needed more know-how than the bullwhacker, and his animals had to be better trained. As a result, muleskinners were less numerous and commanded higher wages. The size of the team determined the method of hitching mules. One or two spans were driven with reins attached to the bit rings of each animal. Such teams, however, could not pull enough to justify their use in overland freighting, and more animals than this could not be easily handled with reins. Three or more spans were usually driven by a "jerk line." This method was introduced to the West after being used for years with six-horse Conestoga teams east of the Mississippi. The jerk line could be easily used on ten or more spans if the occasion required. Three spans were the usual team, however, since mules were generally used in fast freight service employing light wagons.[17]

The jerk line, usually a cotton rope, ran from the left bit ring of the near leader back through rings in the collars of the near

mules to the skinner, who rode either on the saddled near wheeler
or on the wagon box, or else walked alongside the near wheeler.
The leaders were attached by a broom-handle-sized jockey stick,
which forced the off leader to follow the movements of his mate,
the best trained animal in the entire team. Some near leaders were
taught to respond to "gee" and "haw," but most reacted only to
the pulls or jerks on the line. A steady pull on the rope naturally
forced the near leader's head to the left, which pulled on the
jockey stick and brought his mate along. A series of short jerks
caused the rope to slap on the neck of the near leader, which made
him throw up his head to the right, thereby pushing the stick toward the off leader and turning him out, since the stick was chained
to his outside bit ring. Sometimes straps attached to the left and
right sides of the two leaders' bits were used instead of the jockey
stick, but the signals were the same as those used with the jockey
stick—a steady pull drew on the left straps and head jerks pulled on
the right straps.[18]

Mule harness was essentially that used on a work horse. It consisted basically of a collar and hames and heavy traces (or tugs)
made of leather, or else chains covered with leather which were
held in place on the animal's flanks by a saddle piece and belly
band, and a spine strap that ran down the back and across the
rump.[19] The muleskinner harnessed each animal, usually while it
was eating, and then bridled it. A trained person could easily
harness an animal in two to three minutes or even less.

In hitching, the wheelers—heavy, well-broken mules which had
to initiate any backing or holding back on downgrades—were fastened to the tongue by singletrees attached to a spreader, colloquial-
ly called an "evener" since it kept the two singletrees an even distance from the tongue. The spreader was fastened on the tongue
near the wagon box with a pin or bolt. The tongue was held up
by passing the end of it through a ring in the neck yoke supported
from the hames of the wheelers. The succeeding spans of swing
mules and the leaders were hitched by singletrees and either
spreaders or support chains to a long heavy chain that ran from
the pole ring at the end of the tongue between each span.[20]

Most western wagons used before and during the Civil War
resembled their common predecessor, the Conestoga wagon, which
had dominated the trans-Appalachian frontiers for over a century.

The main Conestoga features were evident: the sway-bottomed box, the outwardly inclined end gates, and the great canvas or osnaburg cover projecting over the wagon ends and supported by arching bows.[21]

There has been a tendency historically to use the names "prairie schooner" and "Conestoga" interchangeably. This is no doubt due to the similarity in size, shape, and color which the western wagons bore to the Conestogas. Close observation, however, shows that plains freight wagons were definitely not Conestogas but rather only resembled them. The first western wagons differed only slightly from the Conestoga, but constant experimentation brought about the evolution of particular types and styles of western wagons suitable to particular western purposes.

Like the Conestoga, western wagons were uniformly finished in the national colors. Mud and dust were less likely to show against the red wheels and blue box, and the white cover provided protection from both sun and rain. The Conestoga wagon makers had chosen practical colors; there was no need to change them for western wagons. Other features of the Conestoga, however, were modified. The western wagons had a less exaggerated sway to the floor of the box. In fact, many smaller wagons had flat boxes. The ends tended to be less inclined and the end bows more erect, with the result that the covers were less poke-like in appearance. The wheelbase was reduced somewhat to facilitate sharp turning in hilly and mountainous terrain. Occasionally lighter materials such as cottonwood were used in part of the wagon's construction because the supply of good seasoned hardwood was often limited on the plains.

Western wagon makers produced many different models even within the same company, thereby differing from the tradition-bound wagon makers of southeastern Pennsylvania, who produced but one type of Conestoga wagon at dozens of different sites. Of the many kinds of wagons used the most popular were those produced by Joseph Murphy, H. & C. Studebaker, and Louis Espenschied. Most freighters seemed to prefer the "J. Murphy," probably because of its reputation for sound construction and its availability from St. Louis, where it was made. Joseph Murphy, an Irish immigrant, flooded the plains with wagons of all sizes, ranging from a light, one-ton-capacity vehicle to the heaviest wagons, which could hold well over three tons. Murphy constructed his wagons according to the customers' desires so there was no common shape even among wagons of the same size, but all were clearly marked with the name of the maker. The Studebaker, manufactured in South Bend, Indiana, was highly regarded and was said to be the easiest running wagon. The Studebaker brothers carried on the family tradition. Their father John had been a wagon maker first in Pennsylvania and then in Ashland, Ohio. Like Murphy, the Studebakers made many different models which varied in both size and shape. Espenscheids, commonly used by the army, were produced in St. Louis. These were high boxed with very erect ends, giving the wagons the appearance of being considerably larger than they actually were. They were heavily used immediately after the Civil War, when hundreds became available as war surplus, and were usually described merely as "U.S." wagons due to this identifying mark on the sides.[22]

There were many other brands. Schuttlers made in Jackson, Michigan, were commonly used. The Wilson made in Philadelphia was used to some extent. In the 1850's Hiram Young, a free Negro of Independence, Missouri, made the large, high-boxed Young wagons. The Kansas Wagon Manufacturing Company of Leavenworth turned out many wagons, and the town of St. Joseph, Missouri, had nine wagon factories by 1867. Other wagons were produced in Chicago.[23]

Nebraska City freighters paid dearly for wagons since they had to be shipped in by steamboat disassembled, and then assembled, which was both costly and time consuming. Nebraska City boosters long tried to get a wagon factory established there, but numerous advertising pleas to attract "a good mechanic with a capital of five or ten thousand dollars" who would "make a fortune" proved fruitless.[24]

Most freight wagons were massively impressive. Boxes were commonly sixteen to eighteen feet long, four and a half feet wide, and four to even six feet high. All box sections were removable so the sideboards could be adjusted to the desired height, with spread chains used on high boxes to hold the top boards firmly in place. Desirably, boxes and all other wooden parts were made from well-seasoned hardwoods which would not react to changing weather, but unseasoned wood was not unknown by any means.

Wood, to become thoroughly seasoned, had to be kept in a dry place for as long as three to five years. Sometimes the demand for wagons far outstripped the supply of seasoned wood. Kenderdine recalled that during the Mormon War twenty-two of the twenty-six wagons in his train did not make it through to Utah because they were made of unseasoned wood. In like situations most trains would have made every effort to repair the wagons, but since Russell, Majors & Waddell had many empty eastbound wagons on the trail, the faulty vehicles were simply exchanged for these as the opportunity presented itself.[25]

Special care was taken in the construction of the axles and the wheels. Axles were normally made from hardwood such as hickory, but sometimes iron was used although it never proved popular. The big difficulty with the iron axle was that if broken there was no way of repairing it on the trail, whereas wooden axles could be replaced without great difficulty by stripping an abandoned wagon or fashioning a new axle from an extra pole carried under the wagon as a precaution. Plains wagons are oftentimes described as "thimble-skein" after the style of the axles which were first used about 1850. The tapered axle ends were sheathed with an iron cover or thimble that revolved in the skein—the metal hub interior. This thimble, which reinforced the wooden axles and made breakage much less likely, was a considerable improvement over the preceding strap skein axle, which was reinforced by strips of metal rather than a solid sleeve. On some models the wheels were held in place with a linch pin and on others with a threaded bur. Wheels had to be made with special care since they were the most fragile part of the vehicle. Felloes, spokes, and hubs were all made from choice hardwoods and had to be fitted together securely and properly to retain the dishing and strength of the wheel. The size of the wagon's wheels and the thickness of the iron rims were related to the weight of the wagon. Light wagons of about one-ton capacity usually had a three- to four-inch rim. Large freight wagons commonly had rims from six to eight inches or even more to keep them from sinking into the prairie sod.[26]

Large wagons generally were loaded with 5,000 to 6,000 pounds. The load, however, varied according to the condition of the road. Frontier newspapers commonly mentioned "fifty-five hundred" or "sixty hundred" wagons. On a dry, firm road it was possible to carry much more for a short distance. J. H. Hill, using only two mules and four horses, once performed the extraordinary feat of running a wagon loaded with 7,300 pounds from Brownville to Fort Kearny.[27]

Loading wagons efficiently demanded both experience and patience. Everything had to be tightly packed and secured to mini-mize jostling and breakage on the trail. A carelessly packed, top-heavy wagon was particularly dangerous; thus the main aim was to get heavy items on the box floor, where the weight was directly supported by the bolsters and axles. The commonest trade items, sacked corn and flour, could be easily and effectively packed, but some items presented special problems. Because bacon melted easily, it had to be tightly packed in heavy cloth sacks or boxes and then surrounded by bran in the bottom of the wagon, the coolest area. This special handling accounted for the extra allowance for trans-porting bacon in military contracts. Butter was preserved by boil-ing it and then skimming off the top scum, leaving a clear, oily product. It was then shipped in sealed canisters. Sugar had to be water-proofed with India rubber or gutta-percha sacks. Apples, much in demand in mining areas, especially during the winter, were usually packed in bran. Light, floppy buffalo robes were folded once, stacked and tied firmly with ropes, while wool was usually shipped in bulk and handled much like hay. Long, heavy objects such as saloon bars or boilers for quartz mills were carried on flat wagons. Wagons were stripped of sideboards and endgates and the extra long load extended over the sides and ends. Sometimes they were carried on stripped wagons in tandem.[28]

There were other instances where it was necessary or desirable to resort to tandem wagons. It had long been standard practice for empty wagons on the the return trip to be coupled together and drawn tandem. This was necessary because many times drivers were discharged at western destinations and animals sold. The prairie schooners, however, were hard to couple. They weighed as much as two tons even when empty, and they had too long a wheel base for sharp turns. In 1860 Solomon Young experimented with light wagons on a trip to Salt Lake City. His train was composed of forty wagons coupled in twenty pairs with each unit pulled by six yoke of oxen. He was of the opinion that a pair of light wagons was easier to handle than a single heavy one.[29] They were easier to load and were more maneuverable, and by driving them tandem he needed but one driver and the same number of animals as for a single heavy wagon. While Young did not say so, his trial was probably caused by the shortage and comparatively high cost of large freight wagons and the availability of light farm wagons. On another occasion Stebbins & Porter of Atchison tried 2,500-pound-capacity wagons, each pulled by a single yoke of oxen with one driver to every three wagons. The *Rocky Mountain News* of Denver philosophized that "you can calculate yourself, if you have any sort of analytical mind, or a thinking machine in intelligent order, the peculiar advantages and saving effected by this new and rather novel fashion of freighting."[30] Evidently the *News* misjudged either the advantages of the method or the intelligence of its readers, or else it was merely joshing Stebbins & Porter. This method was never widely imitated. In the meantime coupling (usually done by shortening the long tongue of any horse or mule drawn wagon by about half and fastening it to the rear axle of the lead wagon) had become very popular. Eugene F. Ware noted that Omaha freighters in 1863 had a way of coupling even heavy freight wagons together and using approximately a dozen yoke of oxen. Coupling as applied to heavy wagons saved manpower, but otherwise it was impractical because of the sloped end of the wagon box and the overhangs of the wagon covers. The rather obvious solution, two or sometimes three or more short, straight-ended, flat-bottomed, light wagons specially designed to be hooked together as a rolling unit, was apparent by 1866. Jackson recalled that his train had Studebakers and Murphys but also some of the "latest Jackson 'back-action' wagons" (made in Jackson, Michigan) consisting of two light sections in tandem. These "back-actions" were undoubtedly a Schuttler product, another indication of the manufacturer's response to customer demands. The short, erect-ended sections were easier to handle on grades and turns than conventional wagons and were easier to load, and two sections could carry as much as a single wagon without increasing the bull power. Any further sections, however, necessitated a like addition of oxen. Thus, enormous teams of ten or even twelve yoke were used on three or more sections. The introduction and popularization of the revolutionary boxlike units in the few years following the Civil War meant the end of the prairie schooners, and they were gradually replaced as they wore out. The abandonment of the Conestoga-type wagons did not occur until after freighting's boom, but all subsequent freighters, such as the suppliers of the Black Hills, were affected by the change.[31]

Overland freighting's labor force, the bullwhackers and mule-skinners, represents the least-remembered Great Plains frontier type. While the mountain men and the cowboys have been idolized in story and song, the lowly bullwhacker has remained on the shadowy edge of historical remembrance. This is understandable. The bullwhacker was never in the mainstream of frontier life. The writers and journalists who covered the West traveled by stage and caught only glimpses of the laboring oxen and whackers as the stage sped by. There were no outstanding heroes among the bullwhackers. The business did not produce Kit Carsons, Bill Codys, or Jim Bridgers. The bullwhackers seem to have lacked the articulate spokesmen who tall-storied the mountain man into a lasting niche in the nation's memory. As a group the bull-whackers were probably the least literate frontiersmen. Examples of bullwhackers' orthography were commonly scrawled on wagon covers. Various wagons in one train were labeled with "Home A Gain," "Bown for Fort Kurnay," and "Hurray for thee Waggun Boys."[32] Some men wrote interestingly of their experiences as bull-whackers. William Henry Jackson, later a well-known artist and photographer, William Chandless, an observant Englishman, Thad Kenderdine, and Julius Birge have left good accounts of their com-rades. All of these observers, however, were one-trip bullwhackers, not professionals. Writings by long-standing bullwhackers are vir-tually non-existent.

The casual observer's first impression was that bullwhackers were all alike. The bullwhackers' dress practically amounted to a professional uniform. Most wore red or blue plaid or checked flannel shirts, which were reputed to be warm in winter and cool in summer. Trousers supported by a broad belt were tucked into high boots, and on nearly every waist there was a great bowie knife and a revolver. The long, greasy, sometimes matted hair would be topped by a wide-brimmed felt hat which could be twisted into a variety of shapes.[33] Moustaches and beards were commonplace and personal hygiene neglected. On the trail drivers were continually plodding in dust clouds and sleeping on the ground and were necessarily dirty, a condition to which they became so accustomed that they had little inclination to be otherwise. The sweat-soaked, sometimes vermin-infested hair and clothing of bullwhackers helped earn them their low position on the plains social ladder. No one, except possibly buffalo skinners, had as much opportunity to become physically repulsive.

Bullwhackers may have seemed all of a kind to the outsider, but actually the men came from practically every region and trade. Probably the greatest single group was composed of farm boys from Missouri, but there were also Mexicans who came northeast with the Santa Fe trade and other young men recruited from points throughout the Midwest, East, and South, although men from Dixie were rare during the Civil War. During the Mormon War, Russell, Majors & Waddell, through agents, hired many farmhands in Indiana and Michigan to serve as bullwhackers.[34]

Jackson remembered his companions as a "Foreign Legion in miniature." There were several Civil War veterans, four or five middle-aged professionals, and a dozen or so lads, several of "good address" and "some education." A few had been farmers, several others clerks, three were former steamboat roustabouts, another a French-Canadian, and still another " 'a genuine jack-of-all-trades from Boston.' "[35] Kenderdine recalled such men as "Irish John," an old Indian campaigner, "Dutch Bill," a German raised on the borders of the Black Forest, "Bentley, a deserter from the regulars," "Kaintuck," "Yank," a New Yorker, and "Missouri Bill."[36] Chandless' mess group of ten consisted of "four Germans, always called Dutchmen in the West, two Irishmen, two Americans, a Mexican, and myself, the solitary Englishman of the whole camp. . . ."[37]

While most of the bullwhackers and muleskinners had some familiarity with livestock, many had never driven long ox teams. Then there were some who had never driven anything and whose credentials were nothing more than youth, muscle, and determination. Bullwhacking was not intended for physical weaklings. These men had to be strong enough to handle ox yokes with ease, wrestle bulls into position, and withstand consuming fatigue. Not many men stayed with bullwhacking for long. Hundreds of bullwhackers entered the business for the sole purpose of financing their way west. Owners realized this and capitalized on it by offering higher wages to those who would agree to be discharged at the western

destination. On nearly every wagon crew there were a few professionals who had crossed the plains time and time again. These were
usually older men in their forties and fifties who had been smitten
with the business and undoubtedly regarded it as being just as desirable as farm work. Wagonmasters in all cases were plains veterans,
and there were trains in which only the wagonmaster and his assistant were experienced. Bullwhacking was not a particularly complicated art, and any willing greenhorn could become a passable
driver in a few days.

The social behavior of bullwhackers was much like that of other
foot-loose frontier males such as itinerant cowboys or fur traders.
Many imbibed excessively, gambled, and patronized women of the
streets. These were free spirits, away from family and hometown
controls and uninhibited by custom and law, both poorly defined
in wide-open frontier towns and even less so on the trail, where
wagonmaster and brute strength alone limited conduct. The free
frontier environment contributed to a lively social scene, but it
did not *make* the man. It is doubtful that frontier hell-raisers had
ever been guilty of exemplary conduct, whereas the non-drinker
and non-swearer commonly carried these traits through his frontier
experience. John Bratt said of his fellow bullwhackers, "a few were
good, some medium, and others very bad." As the only one of thirty-
three men who "did not drink, swear, play cards, smoke or chew
tobacco," he was classified by some as a " 'goody-goody' " and by
others as a "fool."[38]

Kenderdine's mates included "odds and ends of human driftwood"[39] who stole anything movable, bullied the weakest drivers
out of the choice animals, settled most differences by fighting them
out, and then, finally, deserted. Desertion was common, especially
before trains left the supply point, but also after outfits had been
advanced. Newspaper advertisements of which the following is
typical often carried: "WARNING: I hereby warn all freighters and
others against employing the following named boys, who I employed
to accompany my train as teamsters, i.e. DAVID ARCHER AND
JOHN ARCHER, they each having obtained outfits from me and
then deserted my train.—Jim Adkins."[40]

Drinking was the bullwhacker's main recreation. Liquor was
easily obtainable, not only in towns where round-the-clock bars
were the most common establishment, but at all road ranches as

well. Liquoring and brawling were understandable releases for men who had spent long, hard weeks on a dirty trail, and bull-whackers established a solid reputation as imbibers. Their drinking habits were undoubtedly no worse than those of cowboys and frontier soldiers; indeed, the bullwhacker was to the freighting towns what the cowhand was to Abilene or Dodge City. The bull-whackers' proclivity for whiskey was easily exaggerated. Sir Richard Burton, the English explorer, stereotyped bullwhackers as social scum who drank practically anything wet; they were said to be unable to do anything without their liquor, which they affection-ately called "tarantula-juice, strychnine, red-eye, corn-juice, Jersey-lightning, leg-stretcher and 'tangle-leg'!" Tangle-leg was supposed to consist of diluted alcohol, nitric acid, pepper, and tobacco.[41]

The first step in the making of a new bullwhacker was to issue him an outfit from a company store or outfitting house. Outfits always included blankets and clothing, and oftentimes raincoats and weapons. The matter of weapons was handled in various ways. Some bullwhackers were expected to pay for their own revolvers or rifles and ammunition and to have them before moving out on the trail; others were issued company weapons, but only when well out on the trail where Indian attack was likely. Outfits cost from $30 to $50 depending on whether the individual bought a raincoat and one or two weapons. They were charged to the driver's account and deducted from his wages when he was finally paid off.[42]

Wages, like everything else affected by frontier inflation, were considerably higher than those paid workers and farmers in settled areas. They fluctuated with the rising and falling fortunes of freight-ing. Wages were quite good during the Mormon War, fell during the early Civil War recession, rose to an all-time high during the boom period, but fell sharply in 1866.

In 1858 Russell, Majors & Waddell paid its Utah-bound freighters $26 monthly if they made the round trip, but $40 per month if they accepted discharge in Salt Lake City or Camp Floyd. The company held out the larger inducement because it intended to sell many of its wagons and animals in Utah and so would have less than normal need for teamsters on the return trip. Teamsters were, of course, furnished food; the economy of not having to feed men on the return trip helped make the higher rates for one-way trippers possible. In spite of these higher rates, those discharged on the western end of the trip did not have much cash in hand after the cost of their outfits was deducted from their salary due. The practice of paying one-way teamsters more than round-trippers existed throughout the history of freighting. The difference usually amounted to about $10 a month.

In 1859 bullwhackers in Nebraska City were getting about $25 and wagonmasters $75 to $100 per month. In 1863 Henry Dosch was paid only $20 a month for an Omaha to Salt Lake City trip. Atchison bullwhackers were being paid $25 by late June of 1863, a sharp increase over the $8 to $15 paid earlier in the season when teamsters had been more numerous. The 1865 boom, coupled with the Indian scare, created new demands and drove bullwhackers' wages up to $60 and $65 monthly for the round trip, and $75 one way. Muleskinners were given $10 a month more. By the next year wages had fallen. Jackson, who accompanied one of the last Nebraska City to Salt Lake City trains before the effects of the Union Pacific were fully felt in 1866, got only $20 per month. Wagonmasters were paid approximately three times as much as drivers, while night herders received only slightly more than the drivers.[43]

Once outfitted, drivers were taken to assembly areas which stretched several miles out from the edge of town. Here cattle were pastured and broken. After weeks of preparation animals, wagons, and men were finally brought together as a working unit, small enough to be managed by a wagonmaster and his assistant and large enough to form corrals and insure trail safety. In the jargon of the trade, a "full train" consisted of twenty-five freight wagons and one mess or supply wagon. This was the number of wagons needed to form a sufficiently large, tight corral, and the oxen required for a train of this size could usually obtain water and grass near the campsite. Large companies ran full trains when possible, but it was not uncommon to find trains of fifteen, twenty, twenty-two, or sometimes as many as thirty or forty wagons. The shotgun freighters who had only a few wagons did not corral unless they were able to cooperate with several other small units. Newspapers often reported trains of several hundred wagons; what observers were actually seeing were many trains closely following each other. During the rush period trains often closed in on each other and gave the appearance of being a single, massive operation. Ranchemen told of seeing lines of wagons ten to fifteen miles long with as many as 800 to 900 wagons passing a ranche in a single day when traffic both ways was counted. What travelers and townspeople did not see was that at dusk the great caravan would carefully break into small units which corralled as trains far enough from their neighbors to assure adequate pasture and fuel.[44]

Every train had some loose stock, usually the equivalent of about 10 per cent of the required work stock. Thus, a full train using six yoke per wagon would have about three hundred head of oxen working at any given time and about another thirty head driven alongside to be used as replacements for the infirm, lame, and dying. The loose bulls or "calfyard" (apparently a corruption of the Spanish *caballada*) were tended by the cavvyard or "cavvy boy," usually a fourteen- or fifteen-year-old boy who assisted the night herder.[45]

In addition to the bullwhackers the train personnel included a wagonmaster and his assistant, a night herder with one or two assistants, and, infrequently, a cook and a clerk. The wagonmaster desirably was familiar with every phase of the operation. He supervised the loading and repair of wagons and the breaking of animals. He also selected campsites and arbitrated quarrels. In fact, as one bullwhacker put it, the wagonmaster was "responsible for everything."[46] Wagonmasters were like Bratt's bullwhackers, "good, medium, and bad." Chandless remembered that he could not have wished for a better man than his boss Carril Hughes. Jackson's wagonmaster was sound and patient, but Bratt apparently worked under a tyrant and knave. George W. Beehrer reported that his much-hated supervisor was later gunned down by one of the bullwhackers. Clerks were sometimes used to keep records of the contents of each wagon, including the size, weight, nature, and destination of all items, so their work came mainly at the beginning and end of a trip. Most often the functions of the clerk were performed by the wagonmaster or assistant wagonmaster or both. The necessity of keeping records required the wagonmaster to be a cut or two above bullwhackers educationally.[47]

A wagonmaster was responsible for a major investment considering the combined value of the livestock, wagons, equipment, provisions, and cargoes. His employer had to spend thousands of dollars in order to outfit a train, with the greatest outlays going for livestock and wagons. The cost of both was naturally influenced by fluctuations of the trade, and there was a considerable range in the value of a full train between good times and bad times. During the years 1855–1857, Russell, Majors, and Waddell's wagons had an average value of about $190, amounting to $122,550 for the 645 wagons they used in 1857. In 1858 and 1859 when oxen in Atchison were normally selling for $70 a yoke, wagons were usually valued at $200 each, meaning that the owner of a full train of 300 oxen and 26 wagons would have had $10,500 invested in cattle and $5,200 in wagons. However, during 1860 values declined to $130 for wagons and $50 per yoke of oxen, but prices rose sharply during the boom of 1865 when wagons in Atchison were reported to have an average worth of $300 and oxen a value of $160 a yoke. The report of the 1865 trade from Nebraska City listed costs considerably lower than those of Atchison. Wagons were said to be worth $225 and oxen equipped with yoke and chains were placed at $150 a pair. The Atchison reports indicated that the expenses per full train for provisions for the men and equipment (yokes, chains, extra wagon bows and tongues, tools, etc.) in 1860 and 1866 were about $900 and $1200 respectively.[48]

Obviously, the wagon prices reported by newspapers were a mean figure that did not take into account variances in size and age. There was a rather lively trade in used wagons since the vehicles normally lasted for many years and quantities of second-hand wagons were peddled each spring, especially if one of the major government contractors lost the business. Russell, Majors & Waddell, for example, sold hundreds of wagons to its successor, Irwin, Jackman & Company, and in 1862 A. W. Street of Nebraska City advertised to sell 200 wagons of the defunct company at "low" prices.[49]

Whether the wagons were new or used and the livestock expensive or cheap, the fact is that the freighter had to be either a man of means or a debtor of some proportions to put even one train on the road. The veteran army contractor Alexander Caldwell recalled that the "investment in a single train of twenty-six wagons was about $35,000."[50] Caldwell's estimate was doubtlessly based on maximum costs and probably included bullwhackers' wages and interest on borrowed capital. Even during the comparatively poor year of 1862, Irwin, Jackman & Company was said to have a $10,000 to $15,000 stake in each train. The final value of any train was determined by its cargo, a figure that varied considerably because of price fluctuations and the nature of the goods, but the freight frequently drove the total worth of a normal-sized train to $60,000 or $70,000.[51]

A fully assembled train moving ponderously out upon the sea of grass was an impressive sight. The bright wagons and loud-shirted bullwhackers striding alongside colorful teams stood out against the endless green background broken intermittently by prairie flowers. The wagonmaster rode ahead of the procession, usually on a mule but sometimes on a horse; the assistant wagon-master rode at the rear, and the "calfyard" was guided at a flank or the rear. Freighters of private goods sometimes assigned num-bers to wagons to provide organization and ready identification of contents, but they did not always mark the number on the wagon itself. Any military freighters, however, were required to assign a number to every train, and each wagon within the numbered train had to be prominently marked with its number on a large sign attached to the sides of the box. Some owners used cards or marks on the box or cover bearing their name and place of origin. The lead wagon might have been marked "Frost, St. Joe" or "Munn, Nebraska City." Certain other vehicles were dubbed according to the whims of drivers. Chandless reported such names as "Polar Star," "Clipper No. 2," "City Hotel," and "Excelsior," the last in-terpreted by its assigner to mean "Regular go-a-head and no mis-take."[52] Certain wagons in another train were the "Constitution," "President," "Great Republic," "King of Bavaria," "Lola Montes," "Louis Napoleon," "Dan O'Connell," and "Old Kaintuck."[53]

On the trail there was a terrible sameness as day blended into day. Distant destinations seemed no more real than Xanadu. The oppressive sun, unrelenting wind, choking dust, and mercilessly end-less space were the bullwhacker's lot. Nearly every day he followed the same procedure—up before dawn, hitching, driving, resting and eating, driving again, and then finally going into night camp.

Men were roused before dawn by the unmistakable roar of "Roll Out! Roll Out!" from the wagonmaster and his assistant. Hooker remembered being awakened by a singing night herder, but the usual reveille of the plains, said Kenderdine, was "Roll Out!" followed by some expletives meant to warm up the laggards. It was the night herder who roused the wagonmaster. At first light, he would bring the bulls into the corral and waken the wagonmaster and his assistant, who in turn rousted out the men. Bulls were hurriedly yoked and hitched in semi-darkness with the aim of getting on the trail before other outfits. Sometimes there was time to gulp a cup of coffee and wolf down a piece of bacon or bread, but most outfits started off on empty stomachs and had "breakfast" after the morning drive.[54]

The train started moving to any one of several commands— "Pull Out," "Roll On," "Stretch Out." The morning drive varied according to the availability of grass and water and the condition of the cattle, but it usually lasted to about 10 A.M., when the train was corralled to permit the cattle to rest and graze during the hottest part of the day. Usually something more than half the day's distance was covered during the morning drive, which was slightly longer than the afternoon drive because the bulls were fresher. Distance covered varied considerably from train to train depending on the road and the condition of the oxen but roughly averaged about fifteen miles for each day of travel. Kenderdine's train, plagued by heavy roads early in the trip and an uncommon loss of stock and vehicles, averaged only eight miles a day. Jackson, however, recalled an average speed of fourteen miles, and Rolfe remembered a sixteen to eighteen mile average.

Wagon trains were usually led by the oldest and most experienced drivers, who were given the best animals, partially in keeping with their seniority but also to give observers a good impression of the train. Being in the lead or close to the front was a matter of some concern to the bullwhackers. Those in the lead ate the least dust; also, being in the lead was advantageous in case of a breakdown. Oftentimes lagging wagons which had trouble were ignored by the advance units. In some trains positions were altered from day to day, but in others the place of any given wagon was fixed for the entire trip.[55]

Drivers had to pay almost constant attention to their teams. About the only diversion was picking up buffalo chips and pitching them into a convenient "chip sack" on the wagon box. The trail was sometimes dusty, sometimes muddy, the roadbed a hard packed thoroughfare in some places, in others nothing more than two deep ruts. When the trail was bright and clear, some bullwhackers appreciatively noted the plants and flowers, the wild animals, and the changing terrain. But there were other days when the great thoroughfares were fouled by decaying carcasses of animals and the air filled with nauseating odors. When the road was fast and hard, the drivers could sneak short rides on the tongue out of sight of the wagonmaster, who was well ahead, but usually the bull-whacker strode alongside his charges, encouraging them with word, goad, or whip. Nearly everyone had the proper words, and anyone could use a goad to jab unwilling beasts, but the whip, the bull-whacker's trademark, was mastered only after frustrating weeks of apprenticeship. Its great length, necessary because of the stretch of the ox teams, made it difficult to handle. The stock, usually of hickory or some other hardwood but sometimes made of tarred rope, was anywhere from eighteen inches to three feet long. Attached to it was a long lash, normally ten to fourteen feet but sometimes even twenty feet, that gradually swelled to a thickness of about an inch and a half a quarter of the way out from the stock and then tapered in again. The lash was tipped with a popper or cracker, an eight- or nine-inch piece of rawhide which swiveled freely. A greenhorn always wondered if all this could possibly be controlled by a two-handed mortal!

There was a special technique for handling the whip. The stock was held in the left hand, the lash coiled in the right and held lightly by the left index finger. Then both hands were moved rapidly in circles above the head. Within this movement the whip was cut loose straight out and then quickly jerked. Experts, of whom there were few, were said to be able to draw blood from the tough-est bull. For show purposes, a whip thrown in the air could be made to snap nearly as loud as a revolver report. Young claimed that the real experts would bet a tenderfoot they could cut out a small piece of his trousers with the whip at twelve feet without disturbing the flesh, then accomplish the feat nine times out of ten.[56] Hard knots in the popper made the whip more vicious, and stories were commonly told of animals being cruelly abused. As a final irony, the hides of bulls which succumbed on the trail were used for making new poppers. Whips, goads, and clubs were not always sufficient prods for the drivers. Sometimes beasts were slashed or stuck with knives, or their eyes gouged. The ox may have been a patient beast but some of his keepers were not.

Drives were not always routine. The monotony of the days was sometimes interrupted by broken equipment, approaching Indians, a sudden thunderstorm or tornado, mired wagons, steep descents, or stream crossings. Muddy roads were particularly troublesome near the eastern edge of the plains, and wagons sometimes sank to the axles after heavy rains. Such a condition as this evoked varied reactions. Alexander Caldwell, the military contractor, recalled passing a freight wagon that was mired to the axle. Caldwell's companion sympathetically remarked to the driver, " 'Well, my man, you are in a bad fix.' 'Oh no,' " shot back the unruffled bullwhacker, " 'I am all right, but there are two wagons below mine, and those fellows down there are having a h—l of a time!' "[57]

To free a mired wagon, another team of six oxen would be hitched to it. If this double-teaming did not work, more oxen were added; ultimately, twenty yoke or more might be used. If a straight pull did not succeed, there was a last resort guaranteed either to move the wagon or pull its tongue out. Dirt before the front wheels was spaded out, the wagon partly unloaded, and a great double file of oxen placed in a rough "S" formation. This formation permitted the animals to get up momentum before they felt the weight of the wagon. All along the line men beat the beasts and the lead and middle yokes were practically running when the jerk was finally relayed to the wheelers; hopefully the wagon was lifted out. Otherwise there were forty oxen dragging a loose tongue.

Braking was sometimes troublesome, too. On short, gradual descents the regular brakes consisting of two wooden shoes held against the hind wheels were sufficient, but these friction brakes were not adequate for heavily laden wagons on long, steep grades. Furthermore, such descents caused excessive wearing of the shoes, and there was always a chance that the brake mechanism would malfunction. Thus, teamsters often supplemented the regular brakes by chaining the rear wheels to the wagon box. The friction brakes and the chains caused the rear wheels to skid, and the prolonged use of them caused excessive rim wear and could result in flat wheels. Such wearing was sometimes prevented by placing a "rough lock," a metal skid or chain, around the contact point of the rim and felloe and holding it in place with a chain attached to the box.[59]

The descent of sharp grades in the bluffs and mountains could not be managed with friction brakes and chains because dragging wheels were simply not adequate to restrain the plunging wagon.

For these situations a western expedient, the "Mormon brake," a long, heavy log dragged behind the wagon, was often used. The rear axle was raised and the front of the log securely lashed to the center pole. Thus, when the rear end was lowered, the rear wheels were off the ground and the weight of the wagon bore down on the log. This was a very effective drag since the wagon was really held back by its own weight, and it was a simple matter to discard the log once it had served its purpose.[60] There were places, however, such as Windlass Hill at the head of Ash Hollow, with declines so step that large logs, even if they had been available, would have been insufficient to restrain the wagons. The usual recourse in such situations was to lower the wagons by ropes.[61]

Fording creeks and small rivers was normally not difficult and the regular number of animals was used, but fording the Platte was another matter. It was not always necessary to ford the Platte, and fortunately most outfits that did ford it had to do so only once. All perishable goods were placed at the top of the load, and the strongest oxen were broken into several eighteen- to twenty-yoke teams, creating a double file a hundred or so yards long. Usually heavy freight necessitated even more elaborate preparations. Thomas Creigh, bound for the Montana mines, recorded that one of the boilers carried on his train was forded at the Upper California Crossing with twenty-six yokes of oxen and fifteen men, and another boiler with forty-eight yokes and twenty-one bullwhackers. In all crossings, once the stream had been reconnoitered and the ford determined, the animals were whipped furiously so they would be running when they hit the water. The aim was to keep the wheels rolling, for any halt would permit the wagon to sink into the soft river bed, perhaps past the point of recovery. Sometimes the heaviest men rode the lead bulls to weigh them down in the water and force their feet to the bottom when deep water was first encountered. Other men, partially clothed or sometimes nude, struggled alongside whipping the animals. When there were deep channels, the great length of the team was its salvation. While some animals were swimming, others would be pulling the load. The perilous 800 to 1,000 yard passage of the Platte at either the Lower or Upper California crossings could easily take as much as two hours and was a frightening experience. Many outfits lost animals and sometimes men. Whenever possible, any crossings of the Platte or other streams were made before making camp in order that a sudden rise caused by a shower miles upstream would not impede the advance.[62]

Some trains drove daily, but many stopped on Sunday. Some freighters like Majors laid over for religious reasons, but others stopped simply because they knew that well-rested animals could do as much in six days as tired ones in seven. Some were governed entirely by the circumstances. If they had tired, sore-hoofed oxen on a particular Sunday they would stop, whereas the next week they would not.

Near the end of a morning drive, the wagonmaster scouted ahead for a likely campsite near water and grass, preferably on a rise somewhat removed from timber, hills, depressions, and deep creeks and rivers. In this way the camp could not be surprised by Indians, or, if it were attacked, the men would not be trapped against a barrier. Such points also assured that the herd was in view at all times, minimizing stampedes and theft. Corrals afforded the only practical protection from Indians and also served as an invaluable enclosure for controlling lively stock during hitching and unhitching. It is quite likely that corralling would have developed on the plains as long as unbroken animals were used even if there had been no Indians. The circled wagons also afforded some protection from sweeping winds and violent thunderstorms.

The corralling method depended on the organization of the train. Most full trains had two sections or "wings" designated as right and left, each headed by a captain who had supervisory duties on the trail and was responsible for leading his wing into the corral. If the trail was narrow and if there was no particular concern about Indians, the train would travel in single file with the wings alternating the lead from day to day. Just before corralling, the file would be closed up and the corral started from a point designated by the wagonmaster. The lead wagon of the first wing would swing either right or left depending on its assignment in the train, and all wagons in the wing would follow it to form a semicircle. Then the following wing would form an opposite semicircle so the lead wagons of each wing would come close together, facing each other at the head of the corral.

Trains with wings oftentimes corralled from double files, which were commonly used when the road was broad and dry. By running the two wings parallel, the train was more tightly organized and the rear drivers were subjected to much less dust. During times of imminent Indian threats, double filing was standard procedure unless a particular section of road absolutely prevented it. Freighters believed that Indians were most likely to attack as corrals were being formed because this was the time when the animals were the wildest and the drivers least prepared to defend themselves. Corralling from double files with the two wings forming opposite semicircles simultaneously could be accomplished in about half the time of single file corralling, so such trains could easily form an oval if Indians approached.

Trains that did not use the wing system usually corralled from a single file with wagons swinging out alternately to form the semicircle. When conditions permitted or demanded, they would, of course, corral from double files.

In positioning wagons within the corral, the usual practice was to bring a following wagon up so that the outside front wheel was placed against the inside rear wheel of the wagon ahead with the tongue lying inside the corral. In this way all stock was inside as soon as the corral was formed, and yokes or harness, as the case might be, were merely dropped on the ground. Some trains corralled with the wagon tongues to the outside. Usually these were either outfits with well-trained oxen or mules which did not need to be corralled to be controlled or else small trains where the corral would not be large enough to hold the stock. Most corrals had two openings or "gates," one at the front and one at the rear for easy access to the stock, but some had only the front gate. All gates were closed with heavy log chains, and in many instances all wagons were chained together so the corral became a real bastion almost impossible for poorly organized, lightly armed Indians to take.

Rapid corralling, like any of the maneuvers involving the wagons and oxen, was the result of long practice. Well-disciplined crews were able to form a corral in just the time their wagons needed to move the length of the oval. Cattle often bcame unruly when they recognized signs of the long awaited halt and had to be held back or they would break into a run.[63]

Once stopped, the animals were quickly unhitched and driven to water and pasture by the herder and several bullwhackers. The remaining crew set about preparing breakfast, which was usually eaten just before noon. Only rarely did trains have full-time cooks, so food was prepared by the men themselves, who were divided into messes of normally six to eight. Within the mess there was a "cook," who was usually sentenced to a week's duty, but sometimes he was quickly replaced by one of the chief gripers. In other instances he would last through the entire trip. The cook, in order to last, had to have a hide as thick as that of a bull. This quality was certainly just as important as any culinary ability. There were some advantages in being cook, since he was excused from day and even night guard and also workaday tasks such as carrying water or greasing wagons. The mess arrangement was really the most practical because a single cook for a train could not have prepared meals rapidly enough. Besides, the talents of a professional cook would have been wasted in light of the limited provisions carried by the wagon train.[64]

Messes were the social units of the train and represented a sort of plains caste system. The old bullwhackers grouped together, as did immigrants and newcomers. In order to work, the mess had to be well coordinated and cooperative. As the cook started the meal someone else would dig the fire trench (camp stoves were used but not commonly), another would fetch water, and others would bring fuel. Dry wood was the most desirable fuel. Driftwood was sometimes caught and dried by carrying it under the wagon for several days.[65] Sometimes completely green wood was all that was available, and in many sections buffalo and bull chips, identified by some with the French term *bois de vache* (wood of the cow), had to be used. Freighters and travelers referred continually to buffalo chips, but actually after a few years trail leavings of the oxen had replaced the buffalo chips. Jackson wrote that before the cooks began their meal preparations, there arose a "mighty chorus" of "Bull chips! Bull chips! Bull chips!" as they relished their brief moments of command over the chip gatherers. Jackson was careful to explain that the plains version of the cry was "a touch more robustly Anglo-Saxon than I have indicated."[66] Well aged and completely dried chips were good fuel, and a bank of live coals could be maintained in the fire trench long enough to bake bread. The tendency was to carry dry wood into treeless areas and use it only on damp days when chips were not combustible. No wood and wet chips left the men no choice but to eat raw meat or left-overs. To meet such emergencies, no food was thrown away but was carried along in a dusty, fly-ridden wooden box on the rear of the mess wagon.[67]

Breakfasts and evening meals were invariably bread, bacon or side pork and coffee. Dough was raised either by saleratus, which made the loaves sponge cake yellow, or by soda and then baked in a Dutch oven until "done." This was oftentimes determined by the impatience of the appetites rather than the condition of the bread. Most often it was undercooked. Chandless wrote of eating "warm dough," and Birge remembered it as sometimes having the "consistency of putty." Loaf substitutes such as flapjacks and "fat cakes" were made when green wood or wet chips prevented banking hot coals for baking. Fat cakes were blobs of bread dough fried in bacon grease. All meals were delayed while the dough was rising; then as the loaves baked, bacon, occasionally rancid in summer, was fried in a skillet and strong coffee boiled. The bitter, black coffee was the standard beverage in regions where men did not dare drink the water. Bags of unroasted coffee beans were carried along in the mess wagon, and each evening a quantity was browned in a skillet and then ground with a coffee mill just before brewing.[68]

These staples were sometimes supplemented with fresh meat such as antelope, buffalo, deer, grouse, and jackrabbit, and during layovers near streams men sometimes caught fish. As a general rule, however, drivers had little time for hunting, and game had to be procured close to the trail or not at all. Baked beans, sugar, corn meal, dried fruit, and molasses or sorghum syrup were sometimes part of the diet, but beans demanded much preparation and were not used unless someone was willing to stay up into the night boiling them for the next day's breakfast.

Each man was equipped with a tin cup, tin plate, and knife, fork, and spoon, but all well knew that fingers were made before forks. Water was a precious commodity; no one wasted it for frivolities like washing dishes. The usual recourses were "sanding"— grinding all cooking and eating utensils into loose soil, preferably sand—or "grassing."[69]

There was usually an hour or two between breakfast and the beginning of the afternoon drive, which may or may not have been a relaxation period, depending on the condition of the wagons and animals. Wagons had to be greased daily. This involved smearing the interior of each hub liberally with thick, black axle grease carried in a bucket hanging from each wagon. Sore-footed oxen were usually shod during the daytime halt when the light was good. Oxen were seldom shod before a trip, but a quantity of the small cleats was taken along and tender-footed animals treated as the occasion demanded. Each ox required eight cleats since the toes were shod separately. Because the cleats were small, they could be fitted by cold hammering. Normally this chore fell to the wagon-master, his assistant, and the veteran drivers whose experience qualified them for this task.[70]

Aside from the normal daily maintenance, wagons many times demanded special handling because wooden parts, especially wheels, shrank during dry periods. Loose rims were tightened when possible by simple expedients such as driving metal or wooden wedges between the rim and felloe, securing the rim with rope or rawhide, and soaking the wheel overnight. These, however, were all temporary solutions, and if difficulty persisted the rim had to be reset either by a ranche blacksmith or else on the trail if the crew included a smithy. In resetting, the rim was removed and heated and the felloe wrapped with several thicknesses of heavy, wet cotton duck. The red-hot rim was then replaced and quickly doused with cold water to prevent the cloth and felloe from burning. As the metal cooled it would shrink into a tight fit. Severe aridity could cause the spokes to shrink faster than the felloes and become too short. Packing the holes or wedging or nailing the spokes would sometimes work, but in extreme cases the only recourse was to reduce the circumference of the wheel by cutting small sections from opposite sides of the felloe so as to retain the original dishing. This would solve the problem of loose spokes, but then the felloe had to be covered with strips of wood cut from the wagon bows or barrel hoops in order to make the rim fit securely.

Loose wagon boxes were wedged with pieces of soft wood or cloth, and a broken tongue or axle had to be replaced either with a spare that had been slung under the wagon or by cutting a new one, something that was impossible in many areas.[71]

Once necessary tasks were completed, there was some time for cards, dice, napping, singing, and perhaps nipping and dancing at a near-by ranche. "Stag dances" in which "the boys were proficient" were sometimes held, but those they enjoyed most were those which included women from emigrant trains.[72]

Singing was a favorite pastime, and many bullwhackers chorused their favorite lyrics during rest periods or even on the trail. Among the common songs were those originated during the California gold rush. "Joe Bowers," which tells the story of a Missouri boy from Pike County who went to California, was said to be a favorite of the freighters.[73] Another ballad, "Root Hog or Die," was very popular among freighters and versions of it have come to be known as "The Bullwhacker."[74] A song with many variations, it probably originated among the ginseng diggers of upstate New York, who may have meant "Root Hog or Die" quite literally. It was subsequently chorused across the land and even New England sailors worked out a version.[75] Bullwhackers, apparently borrowing only the tune, improvised lyrics which poked fun at Majors' profanity ban and told of their trade.

> Oh! I'm a jolly driver on the Salt Lake City Line,
> And I can lick the rascal that yokes an ox of mine;
> He'd better turn him out, or you bet your life I'll try
> To sprawl him with an ox-bow—root hog, or die.
>
> Oh! I'll tell you how it is when you first get on the road:
> You've got an awkward team and a very heavy load;
> You've got to whip and holler (if you swear, it's on the sly)—
> Punch your teams along boys—root hog, or die.
>
> Oh! it's every day at noon there is something to do.
> If there's nothing else, there will be an ox to shoe;
> First with ropes you throw him, and there you make him lie
> While you tack on the shoes, boys—root hog, or die.
>
> Perhaps you'd like to know what it is we have to eat,
> A little bit of bread, and a dirty piece of meat;
> A little old molasses, and sugar on the sly,
> Potatoes if you've got them—root hog, or die.
>
> Oh! there's many strange sights to be seen along the road,
> The antelopes and deer and the great big sandy toad,
> The buffalo and elk, the rabbits jump so high,
> And with all the bloody Injuns—root hog, or die.
>
> The prairie dogs in Dog-town, and the prickly pears,
> And the buffalo bones that are scattered everywheres;
> Now and then dead oxen from vile Alkali,
> Are very thick in places, where it's "root hog, or die."

Oh! you've got to take things on the plains as you can,
They'll never try to please you, "or any other man";
You go it late and early, and also wet and dry,
And eat when you can get it—root hog, or die.

Oh! times on Bitter Creek, they never can be beat,
"Root hog, or die" is on every wagon sheet;
The sand within your throat, the dust within your eye,
Bend your back and stand it, to root hog, or die.

When we arrived in Salt Lake, the twenty-fifth of June,
The people were surprised to see us come so soon;
But we are bold bull-whackers on whom you can rely,
We're tough, and we can stand it, to root hog, or die.[76]

Once the afternoon drive was underway, the train proceeded for four or five hours before evening corral. The length of the drive depended in large part on the temperature. Moderate temperatures usually permitted a drive of from four to six hours, but excessively hot days could mean the drive would not get underway until well past mid-afternoon and then run to sundown. Evening camp generally consisted of repeating the breakfast break activities; most of the men were then soon abed in a wagon or underneath on the ground until daybreak—unless they had night duty. Each night two shifts of guards, which changed at midnight, assisted the night herder. The guards were usually from the same mess, and the second shift was regularly routed out by the first shift. These men soon developed a knack for telling midnight by the lay of the Big Dipper in relation to the North Star.[77] But soon "The Bulls are Coming" and "Roll Out, Roll Out" would signal the end of night and the beginning of the daily cycle all over again, an experience repeated numberless times during the saga of the freighter.

II

Beginnings of the Trade, 1848-1856

The valley of the Platte River has been one of the foremost highways in American history. The route along this sand-choked, island-studded stream was an essential part of the famed Oregon Trail. The river itself is impressive because of its peculiarities. Jeeringly described as being "a mile wide, and an inch deep," it held no promise for navigators of large boats. At times the channel might be two feet deep, sometimes more, other times much less. In some places there was one channel, in other places a myriad of channels that ran unsystematically around and about wooded islands.

During a dry spell the waters of the Platte oozed lazily through endless stretches of quicksand. Rains or melting snows, however, would quickly turn the lethargic stream into a raging torrent that might in places run six feet deep or more and fill a channel a mile or more in width. The gradient of the river—six feet per mile— while not great, was enough to create considerable velocity during periods of high water. The tremendous force of the rushing current did not cut a deep channel; it only moved the sand about, eroding in one place, depositing in another. Because of this constant process of filling in its own channel, the river maintained the characteristic shallowness for which it was named.[1] Perplexed migrants who wanted to cross the Platte claimed that the river "could not be forded since it had a quicksand bed, that it could

35

not be bridged because one could not find a bottom for piers, and that it could not be ferried for want of water."[2] Others said that the Platte was "too thick to drink, too thin to plow, too shallow to sail on, too broad to shoot a rifle across."[3]

Since the Platte could not easily be crossed, it became a clear demarcation for the North Platte area and the South Platte area. Because of that stream, two major trails developed, the Oregon Trail south of the river and the Mormon Trail to the north.

While the river was useless for boats, its valley was indispensable for wagons. This trough across the semi-arid plains was the link between the navigable Missouri and the Rockies. It provided the essentials for overland travel—water, fuel, and grass. These items were not necessarily abundant at all times, but certainly they were in relative abundance along the stream as compared to the open prairie. The silt-filled water of the Platte was not good, but migrants and their animals preferred the river water to that of stagnant, mosquito-laden ponds. The trees on the banks and islands, mostly cottonwood, box elder, and willow, provided the fuel for many thousands of campfires during the period of overland migration. The favorite camping places were in or near the best tree stands, but always the supply of the desired dry wood was rapidly depleted; hence, it became common for emigrants to carry wood with them when they found it. Timber stands on the river banks were quite plentiful from the river's mouth through the Grand Island, but farther west trees were found irregularly—only around springs, along creeks, in canyons, and on islands.[4]

Because the river bottom attracted a variety of animal life, particularly buffalo, it also attracted the Indians, and they in turn attracted the fur trade. Fur traders considered the Platte Valley not only a source of furs and robes but also a route to and through the Rockies. The significance of the Platte route was increased by the activities of the Rocky Mountain Fur Company after the mid-1820's, especially after the company started trading through South Pass into the Green River area. The supplies for the annual rendezvous of the mountain men were normally hauled along the Platte. Some years of experimentation by fur traders, first of the Rocky Mountain Fur Company and then of the American Fur Company, resulted in an overland trail that connected the Missouri River and the Columbia River. These fur traders were followed by Oregon-bound missionaries and then, beginning in 1841, by land seekers.

The Oregon Trail, as this great overland route came to be called, started from points on the great bend of the Missouri where the river turned sharply northward. The first settlements there were outfitting places used by Santa Fe traders, who had to leave the river before it looped north away from their destination. The first town was Independence, founded in 1827 on the right bank of the Missouri below the mouth of the Kansas. But the capricious Missouri meandered away from Independence, and a new steamboat landing, Westport Landing, was located ten miles upstream on a stable bank immediately below the mouth of the Kansas. Because of Westport Landing the nearby village of Westport, platted in 1833, developed as Independence's great rival and soon succeeded the older town as the mistress of the Santa Fe trade. Independence and Westport were the first bases of routes that ran hundreds of miles into a vast hinterland.[5]

The original Oregon Trail ran west along the south bank of the Kansas River to about present-day Topeka, where it broke off from the Santa Fe Trail and crossed the river by various fords. The north bank was followed for a time, but then the trail left the river and proceeded northwestward to present Bigelow on the Big Blue. From there it traced up the Big Blue, which was forded in the neighborhood of Marysville. From this ford it was only a short distance to the Little Blue, the avenue to the Platte.

Upstream from Westport a number of feeder routes which intersected the Oregon Trail near Marysville were established. The first of these was the route west from Fort Leavenworth, a military post started in the same year as Independence. Later such places as St. Joseph in Missouri and still later Leavenworth and Atchison in Kansas also became important ports for spur lines leading into the main trail.

The Oregon Trail entered Nebraska while following the well-timbered Little Blue River. It ran generally northwestward over sometimes level, sometimes gently rolling land to a point in the neighborhood of present-day Leroy, where it left the Little Blue.[6] Between there and the Platte the route crossed a low range of sand dunes, "the Coasts of Nebraska" as they were called, which lay parallel to the river. The Platte was reached somewhere near the head of the Grand Island. The nature of the country permitted great lateral movement; thus the Oregon Trail was not strictly confined to a single set of tracks or even to several. In fact, the trail reached the Platte at many places near the Grand Island. Ultimately, however, a main trail developed.

West from the Grand Island the trail lay on the bottomland between the Platte on the right and a range of bluffs on the left. To the eye this bottomland was flat, but actually it inclined upward to the west at roughly the gradient of the river. While the ascent was gradual, men and animals moving west were conscious of working up a slight grade. The sandbar-studded river stretched like a great finger across an expanse that became increasingly more arid. The usual distance between the bluffs and the river was about three miles, but in a few places the hills pinched to within a mile of the river. Near the Grand Island the sandhills were very low—only about fifty to sixty feet higher than the river—and gradually sloped. They were usually covered with buffalo grass, but occasionally a sand bank was visible where the vegetation had been eroded away.

Westward from the Grand Island vegetation along the river became more and more stunted, and the bluffs became ever grander. About a hundred miles upstream the bluffs were about five or six times higher than those at the Grand Island. Below the forks of the Platte near Cottonwood Springs were some sharp cliffs and deep ravines lined with red cedar, cottonwood, and brush. The ravines, usually at right angles to the river, were deeply shadowed when the sun was low. And so the trail moved west, with the travelers hemmed in between the hills and the river—fixed guides which made it almost impossible to stray.[7]

When the trail reached the forks of the Platte, the South Platte tapered off to the southwest and ultimately to the Colorado Rockies, while the North Platte reached out to the northwest in the direction of South Pass, Oregon, and California. The main task for Oregon- and California-bound travelers after this point was to cross the South Platte and then trek over the divide to the south bank of the North Platte. While emigrants were understandably anxious to cross the South Platte, marshy lowlands and numerous channels prevented the development of good fords just above the forks. Consequently, they usually continued along the river for some distance and had to contend with O'Fallon's Bluffs, one of the most formidable barriers of the entire route. These bluffs, about twenty-five miles above the forks and just southwest of present Sutherland, extended to the very edge of the river, and the traveler's only recourse was to climb up the steep, crumbly road to the summit, cross the bluffs, then descend into the valley again. Crossing these several miles by wagon could easily take an entire day.[8]

Emigrants forded the South Platte at the first place they found a shallow current and a comparatively solid bottom. Between the forks and Lodgepole Creek, nearly one hundred miles above, many fords were used. Continual experimentation, however, led to the development of two main crossings. The first, the Lower California Crossing or Lower Ford, was about sixty-three miles above the forks just west of present Brule. Here the Platte was about a half mile wide and the entire valley two to three times wider than the river. To the northwest lay long sloping hills patchily covered by sagebrush and buffalo grass; beyond these and over the divide separating the two Plattes about twenty five miles from the crossing was Ash Hollow, a precipitous ravine that led down to the valley of the North Platte. Mainly because of the perilous precipices at Ash Hollow, a second crossing, more popular than the first by the early 1860's, was developed about thirty-five miles above the Lower Crossing. This, the Upper California Crossing, or Upper Ford, was just west of the mouth of Lodgepole Creek, near present Ovid, Colorado. The scenery here was typical of the South Platte. South of the river the bluffs, somewhat lower than those east of the forks, swept off and up for three or four miles at about twenty to thirty degree angles. North of the river the trail followed Lodgepole Creek up long ridges and then over an undulating plateau across the divide. At the point where the creek swung west the road left it and continued north, finally coming out on the North Platte east of Court House Rock.[9]

The scenic trail along the North Platte was but a preview of the geologic majesty of the West. Here, where the Platte drove hard from the mountains to the plains, the Wildcat Hills lay parallel to it. The main range was visible from the trail, but the primary attractions were the monuments which stood between the hills and the river—Court House Rock, Chimney Rock, and Scott's Bluffs. These sandstone marvels were products of many thousands of years of erosion which had eaten away all but the most resistant strata. Court House Rock and its smaller neighbor Jail Rock were to the east; then came Chimney Rock, which was just that—a tall spire rising from a conical hill. While lower than the hills to the south, it stood alone and was visible for some thirty

to forty miles. Massive Scott's Bluffs about twenty miles above
Chimney Rock suggested the grandness of the unlimited West.
This great loaf-shaped extension of the Wildcat Hills, looming
800 feet above the river, initially forced the trail south. Between
its face and the river was a series of deeply cut ravines, the bad-
lands of Scott's Bluffs, which made passage there impossible. For
many years the trail ran south around Scott's Bluffs by way of
Robidoux Pass, but Mitchell Pass in Scott's Bluffs became the
more popular route after a roadway was graded through it in
1851.[10]

Beyond Scott's Bluffs the trail rose noticeably, first past Horse
Creek, then over the Laramie River, which it crossed at Fort
Laramie. Soon after leaving Fort Laramie the eastern foothills of
the Laramie Range, called the Black Hills until the 1870's, were
encountered. The trail lay along the North Platte until the river
turned southward near present Casper, Wyoming. From here the
route ran mainly along the Sweetwater and then through South
Pass and beyond.

The Oregon Trail was the main route for those who passed
west through Nebraska with one major exception—the Mormons.
Partially to avoid Missouri because of the bitter heritage of
Mormon difficulties there and partially to avoid Missourians on
the Oregon Trail, Brigham Young led the pioneer band of Mormons in 1847 out over a trail north of the Platte. This North Platte
route was followed until it reached Fort Laramie, where it joined
the Oregon Trail.[11]

The overland migrations through the Platte River Valley were
but a part of the westward impulse in the 1840's. This was a decade
of decisions affecting the western frontiers; Texas was annexed
and the Oregon area was acquired. A decisive war was fought
with Mexico and gold was discovered in California. There was a
great rush westward. America was expanding from ocean to ocean.
United States expansion into Oregon and California depended
upon the safeguarding of the Oregon Trail. The need to fortify
this route to protect emigrants and encourage further emigration
was realized by 1845. Fittingly enough, the first advocates of fortification were two outstanding champions of Manifest Destiny—
President James K. Polk and Senator Thomas Hart Benton.

Polk, in his annual message to Congress, December 2, 1845,
called for suitable stockades and forts manned by Mounted Rifle-

men to be located on the trail. Benton of Missouri, as chairman of the Senate Military Affairs Committee, embodied the Pesident's suggestion in a bill proposed on December 30. The act providing for the establishment of these installations was passed on May 19, 1846.[12]

Soon after, the federal government became desperately short of troops because of the Mexican War; hence, fortification of the trail was postponed until the military outcome of the war was certain. During the war Missouri Volunteers did construct a blockhouse and establish a camp near the mouth of Table Creek on the west bank of the Missouri about one hundred miles above Fort Leavenworth. This location, where Nebraska City later developed, was selected because it was a crossing place for some of the Oregon emigrants. However, this post, the first Fort Kearny, was obviously well off the main trail and did not fulfill the congressional intention of protecting the route.[13]

While the posts on the main trail were not founded during the war, the War Department carefully studied the problem of site selection. One of the most significant reports on this topic was written by Thomas Swords, an army quartermaster officer who accompanied Stephen Watts Kearny's troops from California to Fort Leavenworth by way of South Pass and the Platte route. Swords, on the basis of his 1847 observations, believed that the most desirable places for posts were "on or near Grand Island, in the Platte River, about ninety miles below the junction of the north and south forks; at Fort Laramie, about one hundred and seventy miles above the junction, and perhaps a site might be found for a small post on the north fork, higher up."[14]

The site for the easternmost post was chosen by Lt. Daniel P. Woodbury in the fall of 1847. Woodbury, carefully taking into account the availability of timber for construction and fuel, concluded to locate the post near the head of the Grand Island at the southernmost sweep of the great Platte bend and seventeen miles west of the point where the main Oregon Trail route reached the Platte. The new fort was started the following spring when the garrision was transferred from the Table Creek camp, which was then abandoned and has since been known as Old Fort Kearny.

Three temporary buildings were erected in 1848 and the next year construction of permanent quarters was undertaken. It was first called "Grand Island Post on Platte River, Oregon Route," then briefly "Fort Childs," but on December 30, 1848, the War Department ordered the designation of "Fort Kearny." Its setting between the sand bluffs and the Platte was 310 long miles from Fort Leavenworth, and the intervening area, then part of the Permanent Indian Frontier, was barred to white settlement.[15]

Fort Kearny was small, like most frontier outposts. It was first garrisoned by two companies of Mounted Riflemen with an aggregate strength of 137. After its first two years and until the Sioux difficulties of 1854, Fort Kearny was manned on the average by about one company of seventy men.[16]

In 1849 the War Department determined to locate the second post on or near the site of the old American Fur Company trading post of Fort Laramie, a little adobe quadrangle on the left bank of the Laramie River about a mile from its juncture with the North Platte. As a trading post Fort Laramie had been a significant way station on the Oregon Trail since its beginnings in 1834. It was, moreover, a major hub for a trade route connecting the country of the South Platte and the Yellowstone region.

Maj. Winslow F. Sanderson, who was to command the fort in the Laramie area, decided the best choice was Fort Laramie itself, 337 miles from Fort Kearny. Because of the ready availability of wood, water, and grass, he asked Woodbury, Fort Kearny's founder and fiscal agent for the acquisition of sites on the trail, to purchase the post from Pierre Chouteau, Jr. & Company. Woodbury did this for the modest price of $4,000.[17] The army soon changed the appearance of the fort by constructing new buildings. Like Fort Kearny, Fort Laramie was mainly occupied by Mounted Riflemen, and up to 1854 the two posts were roughly comparable in strength.

The importance of Fort Kearny and Fort Laramie was underscored by an unprecedented migration following the Mexican War. To the lure of Oregon and Utah was added the gold of California. This first major strike of ore in the United States tripped off a rush of many thousands of Argonauts, who moved by both land and sea. The overland trails were flooded with wagons, people, and stock. Maj. Osborne Cross, on his way to the Columbia River area in 1849, described the scene at the Lower Crossing: "The banks of the South Platte seemed to be lined with large trains, moving on both sides of the river, and over the divide which separates the North and South Forks. They could be seen as far as the eye extended." Cross estimated the total seasonal migration at

35,000 persons, 8,000 to 10,000 wagons, and nearly 100,000 animals.[18]

The migration of 1850 over the Oregon and Mormon trails was even larger than that of 1849. By June 3, 11,443 men, 119 women, 99 children, 3,188 wagons, 10,000 horses, 3,588 mules, 3,428 oxen, and 233 cows had passed Fort Laramie. The register at Fort Laramie up to August 14 showed 39,506 men, 2,421 women, 609 children, 23,172 horses, 7,548 mules, 36,116 oxen, 7,323 cows, 2,106 sheep, and 9,927 wagons. The total emigration for the year has been estimated at about 55,000 people, most of them bound for California.[19] This movement of thousands each year through the valley of the Platte continued throughout the decade.

Forts Laramie and Kearny served many purposes other than military. To the tired emigrants they were rest stops and mail stations, and they had blacksmith shops for civilian use. They served as stores, since it was possible for emigrants to purchase goods from the army. The creation and maintenance of these Oregon Trail posts was the first reason for the start of commercial freighting north of the Santa Fe trail.

The two forts were supplied from Fort Leavenworth, which was the base of the military trade both southwest along the Santa Fe Trail and northwest along the Oregon Trail. The extension of the frontier army onto the plains after the Mexican War gave Fort Leavenworth a new importance—that of a frontier depot for military goods shipped from St. Louis by steamboat. Posts established before the war were generally located on or near navigable streams and could be supplied by steamboat. After the war the plains posts were sometimes many hundreds of miles from a navigable river and were often located in agriculturally unproductive areas. Practically everything used at the Santa Fe and Oregon Trail posts had to be shipped great distances by wagon. The isolation of these frontier stations accounts in large part for an abrupt increase in army expenditures for transportation of troops and supplies, from $130,053.52 in 1845 to $2,094,408.51 in 1850–1851.[20]

Fort Leavenworth was not initially equipped for its new role as intermediary between the steamboats and the wagons. It did not have a steamboat landing, nor did it even have warehouse facilities. Maj. E. A. Ogden, assistant quartermaster at the post, reported that "from the tops of the rocks at the river side it was necessary to haul all the supplies up a steep hill and store them wherever an imperfect shelter could be found in decaying stables, company quarters, a nine-pin alley, and two leaky blockhouses."[21] In 1850 Ogden supervised the construction of two stone warehouses on the river bank. The largest one, 40 by 100 feet, was a split level three stories high with a graded landing to its front and a dirt bank at its rear. Steamboat freight was taken in at the lower level, and wagons picked it up at the third story on the other side.[22]

While the quartermaster was responsible for handling goods at Fort Leavenworth, the actual transporting was done by civilian contractors who obtained the business through competitive bidding. The army regarded it as economical to use commercial transportation rather than freight its own goods, the reasoning being that since continual use could not be made of the wagons and animals, it would be costly to care for them. Up to 1855 the quartermaster at Fort Leavenworth made transportation contracts for individual posts. Normally, the Fort Kearny and Fort Laramie business was done by different parties. These contracts did not give the freighter a monopoly of the trade to any given destination. The quartermaster could, and sometimes did, make contracts with several different parties to supply the same post. The contracts were always expressed in terms of the freighter agreeing to transport such goods as might be turned over to him.

These first freighters over the Oregon Trail were men who had already had some experience in the Santa Fe trade. Supplying the Oregon Trail posts was but an addition to their business. The first contracts for supplying Forts Kearny and Laramie were for the year 1849. John Dougherty, who had been an Indian agent at Bellevue, agreed to carry the Fort Kearny freight for $6 per hundred-weight, with the exception that bacon would be charged at $6.30. David Waldo was given a Fort Laramie contract at a rate of $8.91 per hundred.[23] These rates were for the entire distance from Fort Leavenworth to the respective destinations.

During the fiscal year ending June 30, 1851, Fort Kearny was supplied by Jones Creech, David Hunt, and John Dougherty. Fort Laramie supplies were freighted by David Waldo and A. Dawson. The Fort Kearny goods, amounting to 195,278 pounds, were carried as forty-three wagonloads of about two and a quarter tons per wagon. The Fort Laramie freight was 237,333 pounds, hauled as forty-seven wagonloads. While this trade was small compared with the business of later years, it was rather significant to the freighters when considered as an addition to their Santa Fe business. Most of the military freighting in 1850–1851 was done to New Mexico destinations. The total business from Fort Leavenworth amounted to over 3,000,000 pounds, with about one-eighth of this sent to Forts Kearny and Laramie.[24] Table 1 shows the freight rates for the period 1849–1854.

TABLE 1

MILITARY CONTRACT RATES FROM FORT LEAVENWORTH TO FORTS
KEARNY AND LARAMIE, 1849–1854

Year	Fort Kearny	Fort Laramie
	per 100 lbs.	per 100 lbs.
1849[a]	$6.00	$8.91
1850[b]	4.47	7.74
1851[c]	3.80	6.80
1852[d]	3.80	6.80
1853	—	—
1854[e]	3.80	7.90

[a]*House Exec. Doc. 38*, 31 Cong., 1 Sess. (Serial 576) pp. 19, 24.
[b]*House Exec. Doc. 23*, 31 Cong., 2 Sess. (Serial 599) p. 15. *Senate Exec. Doc. 1*, 32 Cong., 1 Sess. (Serial 611) pp. 295–97.
[c]*Ibid.*
[d]*Senate Exec. Doc. 12*, 32 Cong., 1 Sess. (Serial 614) p. 20.
[e]*House Exec. Doc. 68*, 33 Cong., 2 Sess. (Serial 788) p. 11.

The transportation contracts of 1854 were supplemented by grain contracts. Shrewsbury, Woodward & Company, which had the transportation contract to Fort Kearny, also had contracts to deliver 2,000 bushels of corn to Fort Kearny for $2.40 a bushel and 1,000 bushels to Fort Laramie at $4.47 a bushel. Alexander Majors, who had the Fort Laramie transportation contract, was to deliver 1,000 bushels of corn there at $4.89 per bushel.[25] For these prices the contractors would purchase the corn, usually in western Missouri, and then deliver it to the posts. In 1854 the grain contracts alone amounted to nearly a quarter million pounds, or fifty to sixty wagonloads.

Freighting on the Oregon Trail through 1854 was relatively light because army operations in the area were quite routine. There was nothing of note to disrupt the normal garrison and patrol duties. The indigenous tribes, the Pawnee, Teton Sioux, and Northern Cheyenne, frequently intimidated emigrants by their presence, but they did not commit any overtly hostile acts. During the migration season there were, of course, many Indians, particularly Teton Sioux, camped on or near the trail. The attraction of the Great Medicine Road, as the Sioux called the Oregon Trail, stemmed in large part from the opportunities to beg, trade, and steal. Also, under the provisions of the Laramie Treaty of 1851, the western Sioux were to obtain annuities each summer someplace in the Fort Laramie vicinity. Thus, they were naturally attracted to the Platte just when thousands of whites were moving through. In view of the many contacts each season between whites and Indians, it is amazing that there were not a great many serious incidents before the unfortunate Grattan' episode.

In August, 1854, a large body of Teton Sioux—Brule, Oglala and Minneconjou—were camped eight miles east of Fort Laramie awaiting their agent and their annuities. A lame cow belonging to a Mormon emigrant hobbled into the sprawling tipi city of 2,000 Sioux, where it was rather summarily butchered and eaten. Lt. John L. Grattan, accompanied by twenty-nine men, attempted to arrest the Indian who had killed the cow. Misunderstandings, perhaps caused by Grattan's interpreter (who had a particular hatred for the Sioux), and some foolish vanity on both sides tripped off a shooting scrape since called the Grattan Massacre. Grattan and his command were annihilated and the head chief of the Brule, The Bear, died as a result of wounds.[26]

The Grattan incident ended the peaceful period on the trail. After this time life was less secure and Indian-white relations were uncertain and many times hostile. The immediate effect of the affair was to cause great concern over the safety of Fort Laramie, which was soon reinforced by two companies of infantry, bringing its strength to 171 men. Over the winter of 1854–1855 the government decided that the Sioux should be punished for their hostile act, and plans were formulated to send out an expedition headed by Gen. William S. Harney.[27]

The flurry of military activity in 1854–1855 promised to tax the supply system. It was quite obvious at that time that freighting demands would be greater than in the past and also obvious that the freight would have to be delivered with greater dispatch. These new military demands caused the quartermaster to initiate a new contracting policy in 1855. The old system of letting many contracts was replaced by a new one of contracting with one firm giving it a monopoly of the trade along an entire route. Also, the contract rates were expressed in figures of so much per hundred pounds per hundred miles. This change was caused by the fact that the military forces were mobilized. In a situation involving Indian campaigns, it was quite likely that supplies would have to be transported to temporary camps or from one post to another. The effect of the new rate system was to make transportation transactions more flexible.

On March 27, 1855, Maj. E. S. Sibley, quartermaster at Fort Leavenworth, made a contract with the newly organized firm of Majors & Russell for the transportation of stores for the period 1855 and 1856. This two-year contract specified that the company would carry "such military stores as may be turned over to them by the officers of the quartermaster's department at Forts Leavenworth, Laramie, Riley, Union, and Kansas [City], Missouri, and to deliver them at any posts or depots that are now or may be established in Kansas and New Mexico (including El Paso and vicinity) Utah and Nebraska Territories."[28] The total quantity in each year was to be from 50,000 to 2,500,000 pounds. The contract rates, scaled upward as the season progressed—and grass and water became scarcer and operating costs higher—ranged from $1.14 to $2 per hundred pounds per hundred miles to Fort Union, New Mexico, and destinations east of it; $1.40 to $1.80 for posts beyond Fort Union; and $1.30 to $2.15 for the Oregon Trail and Utah destinations. This contract amounted to a monopoly of the transportation of military stores on both the Oregon Trail and Santa Fe routes. This did not necessarily mean that Majors & Russell carried everything used at the posts. The partners had the transportation contracts for goods owned by the military, but they did not have all the grain contracts. In 1855 S. Fernandes had a contract to deliver 5,000 bushels of corn to Fort Laramie for $5.08 a bushel. This amounted to a 300,000 pound item not covered by the transportation contract.[29]

The contract for 1855–1856 was the largest single military transportation agreement made for the plains up to that time. It was instrumental in Majors & Russell's expansion of operations in both the shipping of military and civilian goods to the southwest and the northwest. The firm of Majors & Russell was actually a combination formed by William H. Russell and William B. Waddell of

Lexington, Missouri, and Alexander Majors of Westport. Russell, the planner of the trio, before entering large scale overland freighting had operated a retail store in Lexington, speculated in town lots, served as postmaster, and had been involved in many civic activities. While continuing merchandising, he entered the Santa Fe trade in 1847 and three years later formed a partnership with John S. Jones to transport military supplies. Offices and ledgers, not wagons and animals, were Russell's real interests. His role in freighting was essentially that of financier. Waddell, the silent partner, before entering the partnership had spent two decades in Lexington operating a wholesale and retail business dealing in produce, grain, and hemp. He knew Russell very well, and in 1852 the two formed a merchandising partnership and contracted to carry military supplies the next year.

Majors, raised on a Missouri farm, abandoned the soil in favor of the Santa Fe trade in 1848 when he was thirty-four. He entered the trade independently, running just a few wagons. Majors soon earned a reputation for his ability to handle men, animals, and wagon trains. His talents nicely complemented those of Russell and Waddell when he joined them in 1855. The firm did well in both 1855 and 1856. According to Majors, the company showed a profit of about $150,000 in each of these years.[30] The original firm name of Majors & Russell was retained through 1857, but beginning with the 1858 contract the more famous one of Russell, Majors & Waddell came into being.[31]

The determination of the government to punish the Sioux for the Grattan affair was satisfied by Harney's smashing victory at the Battle of Ash Hollow, fought September 3, 1855. In addition to Harney's campaign, the military asserted itself by sharply increasing the strength of Forts Kearny and Laramie. The Adjutant General's report of November 27, 1855, showed that Fort Kearny was garrisoned by 178 men and Fort Laramie by 439. This was about three times greater than the normal garrison at Kearny and about seven times greater than the usual garrison at Laramie. The reinforcement of these posts obviously increased the freighting of military supplies. While the immediate effect of Harney's campaign was to move the Sioux back from the trail, it did not bring calm to the plains. In 1856 the Cheyenne were very troublesome in the Grand Island area. When they killed some people in a Mormon party north of the Platte, cavalry units were put in the field against them in August and September. Many of the military needs of 1855 were carried over into 1856, adding to the importance of the posts and enlarging the problem of adequately supplying them.[32]

While the military trade was developing, so also was that to the Mormon settlements in Utah. Brigham Young's decision to isolate the Mormons from populated areas resulted in their settlement in the far-off area around Great Salt Lake. Into this area of the Great Basin about twelve hundred miles from the Missouri, Young led his pioneer band in 1847. During the next few years thousands of the faithful turned their backs on civilization in favor of the new Zion. By 1850 the population of Utah Territory was 11,380, over half of whom lived in the immediate Salt Lake City area. During the next decade this population nearly quadrupled, increasing to 40,273. In 1860 Salt Lake City with 8,236 inhabitants was the only place of more than 1,000 people in the entire territory.[33]

The Mormons had all of the usual frontier problems, complicated by their extreme distance from supply centers. Experiments in communitarianism and irrigation resulted in a comparatively successful production of grain and vegetables, but the Mormons still needed manufactured products such as machinery, tools, and cloth, and food items such as sugar, coffee, and spices. The Mormons longed to be free from the Gentile world, but they could not effect a self-sufficient economy because they had neither the capital nor the skill to establish local industries other than those related to the processing of agricultural products, such as flour milling. Hardly an issue of the *Deseret News* passed without a plea to the believers for the skilled craftsmen to come forth and establish textile mills, brick kilns, or mercantile companies. While the church made heroic efforts to convert and recruit the necessary craftsmen, it met with extreme frustration.

The Mormon's world was discovered by many Forty-Niners who passed through Utah enroute to the California gold fields. While this invasion disturbed Mormon privacy, it also provided some opportunities for trade since the migrants were usually willing to exchange dry goods and bulky food for such things as fresh eggs or poultry. Some, in fact, carried extra goods so they could sell them in Utah, and some California-bound merchants had stocks valued up to $10,000 out of which they traded liberally before moving on. This random trade helped, but it was not sufficient.

The Mormons, who so desperately wanted to divorce themselves from the hostile East, were forced to accept contact with it once more.

The first regular Utah trade originated with Gentile merchants who traded through Independence, Westport, Weston, and St. Joseph. As a general rule they freighted their own goods. Howard Livingston and Charles Kinkead were the pioneers in the trade to Utah. In 1849 they brought into Salt Lake City goods valued at $20,000 and set up business in an adobe house. During 1850 a number of other merchant-freighters became active in the Utah trade, including Ben Holladay, Thomas S. Williams, and John and Enoch Reese. The enterprising twenty-six-year-old Holladay, later internationally known as the "Stagecoach King," traded out of Weston, Missouri, where he had lived for some years as a saloon-keeper, mill operator, and land speculator. Holladay's early transportation experience came during the Mexican War, when he had a contract to carry supplies for Kearny's expedition to New Mexico. At war's end he purchased much surplus war material from the government, including wagons and oxen. Holladay undertook his Utah venture equipped with a letter of recommendation from Gen. Alexander W. Doniphan, who had become well acquainted with Brigham Young during the Mormon difficulties in Missouri in 1838. Holladay's mule train of fifty wagons got underway on May 1. Like other trains in the 1850's it followed the Oregon Trail through South Pass southwestward to Fort Bridger, then to Salt Lake City, arriving after two months on the road. Because many of his teams failed, Holladay had pushed ahead of his train to Salt Lake City to procure assistance. The Mormons, anxious to cooperate, helped deliver the goods.[34]

On July 3 Holladay, under the name Holladay & Warner, opened a store managed by William H. Hooper, who had been brought along for this purpose. Theodore F. Warner, Holladay's Missouri partner, had reportedly financed the purchase of the supplies. During its five years of business in the city, the firm dealt in general merchandise. The contents of their first shipment is indicative of the kinds of goods freighted into Utah. It was advertised as a "complete and general assortment" of goods including "Staple and Fancy Dry Goods, Ladies and Gents Boots & Shoes, Mens & Boys Hats & Caps, Ladies Bonnets, Parasols, etc., Also Oysters, Sardines, Pepper Sauce, Lemon syrup, Tobacco, Peas, Rice, etc." A second train was to bring in "Groceries, Hardware, Glass, Nails, Oil, Paints, Leather, Stationery, etc." It arrived late in August.[35]

Holladay and Warner, as Gentiles, had an awareness of both Mormon ethnocentrism and frugality. The *Deseret News* of July 6 announced that they had come to Salt Lake City "with a view to a permanent location and it is their intention to do business upon that fair and liberal scale. . . ." The opportunistic Holladay was said to have indicated an interest in converting to Mormonism.[36]

Although Holladay & Warner's first shipment of 1850 arrived very early in the season, this was unusual. Throughout the Utah trade most of the Missouri River trains did not arrive until August or September, and oftentimes as late as October or November. The trip from the Missouri River towns took about two months, if there were no serious delays, and sometimes up to three months. Sometimes freight was delivered in May, but this was usually goods that had been stockpiled somewhere along the trail over the winter. Livingston & Kinkead had two trains which arrived in September. The first of sixty wagons carried the standard run of general merchandise, including groceries, queensware, leather goods, clothing, hardware, glass, dye-stuffs, and paints. Rather than winter their oxen and return them to the Missouri the next spring, this firm sold them.[37] The transportation season ended in late September with the arrival of the Williams and Reese trains, and the retail market was quite active for a brief period. Then the market languished until the following July.

Since goods originated in St. Louis, it was quite common for Utahans to compare St. Louis and Salt Lake City prices. St. Louis sugar cost 6¼¢ a pound and coffee was 16⅔¢. The Salt Lake City prices charged by Livingston & Kinkead were 40¢ for both commodities, while Thomas S. Williams charged 37½¢ for coffee and 33⅓¢ for sugar. The freight on these items, Utahans said, was not over 15¢ a pound, and the *Deseret News* left the impression that merchants were profiteering at the expense of the Mormons, who desperately needed consumer goods. The newspaper was not only the constant defender of the Mormon goals of honesty and frugality but was an advocate of an extremely narrow interpretation of the fair price principle as well. Why, inquired the editor of the *News,* when sugar cost 10¢ a pound less in St. Louis than coffee, should Utahans pay nearly the same price for the two commodities, in spite of the fact that they were of comparable bulk for freighting purposes? What the *News* seemed to want was that merchants sell each commodity at a price scarcely more than the St. Louis price and freighting costs combined.

The merchants, for their part, had to be concerned with the entire business rather than the price of individual items. They pointed out that they had many expenses other than freighting, such as that of maintaining stores in Utah. They also had to consider their unusual risk in transporting thousands of dollars worth of goods across hundreds of miles of unsettled country. Some of them undoubtedly had interest payments on borrowed capital. These Gentiles, in an effort to allay the mistrust of the Mormons, gave assurances through advertisements that they were fair and that their goods were of the best quality. Some went so far as to claim that they intended to become permanent residents of the Mormon community.[38]

It is quite unlikely that the merchants were making any more than 10 or 12 per cent profit, which in their minds must have seemed very reasonable. It is certainly understandable, however, why the spokesmen of a comparatively poor society would regard this as excessive. Although the Mormons and the outside merchants had different economic views, they nevertheless needed each other.

As the population of Utah increased in the 1850's, so also did the demand for the consumer goods of the Salt Lake City mercantile houses. Holladay & Warner shipped in about 150 tons in 1851 and Livingston & Kinkead had about 100 tons equally divided between two trains. In 1854 Livingston and Kinkead sent six trains to Salt Lake City. In early July they, along with J. Needham, H. R. Robbins, L. Stewart, and W. Mac, were said to have had goods valued at $1,000,000 on the trail. These merchants hastened in before their trains in order that the arrival of the much anticipated freight could be properly advertised. Many of the freighters brought newspapers and letters for parties in Salt Lake City, a much appreciated gesture.[39]

Beginning in 1855 most Utah freight originated in Leavenworth, Kansas Territory, rather than the Missouri towns. One of the immediate effects of the Kansas-Nebraska Act, which opened the area west of the Missouri, was the creation of a number of new towns, each of which aspired to become a metropolis of western trade. Leavenworth was the first town to benefit from this shift of civilian freighting to west of the river. It was advantageously located adjacent to Fort Leavenworth, so that anyone engaged in the military trade which began at the fort could easily use the town as the starting point for civilian goods. Also, the town being west of the Missouri eliminated the ferrying problems faced by St. Joseph or Weston traders. Leavenworth could compete easily with Independence and Kansas City for the Oregon Trail trade since it was located thirty miles northwest of them. This thirty miles could be covered by a steamboat in a matter of hours, but it was a two-day trip by wagon. A freighter bound for Utah would probably favor Leavenworth, 1,172 miles from Salt Lake City, over Kansas City, 1,202 miles from the Mormon capital.[40]

Leavenworth boomed quickly. Within five months after it was first platted, about one hundred buildings had been constructed and the population had climbed to 300. When only a year old, it had 1,600 inhabitants, 300 buildings, and boasted a lively economy based on the steamboat-wagon trade. Prophecies that Leavenworth "is bound to become the great Commercial Emporium of Kansas Territory" were expressed by the *Kansas Weekly Herald* of February 23, 1855, when it announced that two traders had already decided to outfit at Leavenworth. The major boost, however, came when Majors & Russell decided to make Leavenworth its base for both its Oregon Trail and Santa Fe trade. Company men erected shops for assembling and repairing wagons. They built complete blacksmith facilities, mainly for their own use but also to serve the public, and they opened a general merchandise store that was specially equipped to outfit plains travelers and farmers.[41]

The wagon trade, which was reportedly employing about twelve hundred wagons, a like number of teamsters, and over ten thousand oxen by early June, brought new steamboat business to Leavenworth. The town was well situated with a rock-bound shore, assuring it of comparatively stable port facilities. During the trading season the levee was a scene of great activity. At one time 150 tons of goods were unloaded in a week. This freight, first stacked in huge piles near the river, was moved by drays, carts, and light wagons back from the wharf and stockpiled. It was later packed into freight wagons. One steamboat could have carried the 150 tons of goods unloaded at the levee, but about sixty wagons and over seven hundred oxen would have to be used to move it across the plains.[42]

During 1855 Majors & Russell, Leavenworth's most important freighting firm, used 500 wagons, 1,700 men, and 7,500 oxen to carry out its military contract, which amounted to 1,600 loads, totaling over 8,000,000 pounds. The company's seasonal steamboat freight bills alone came to over $26,000.[43] Leavenworth's extensive Utah trade would have to be added to this business in order to determine the grand total of the Leavenworth–Fort Leavenworth business.

The Utah trade of 1855 was recorded by Brigham Young, who hoped to use his statistics to persuade steamboat men that this was so extensive a trade that they should experiment with navigation of the Platte and even the upper Yellowstone and Green rivers in order to cut the overland distance to the Great Basin. While Young failed to attract steamboat men with such lofty aspirations, his study of the freighting for the year was valuable. The freight of T. S. Williams & Company, Livingston, Kinkead & Company, Gilbert & Gerrish, Snow & Company, Blair & Company, and W. S. Godbe amounted to 513 tons, which was transported at 17¢ per pound for a total freight bill of $174,420. The biggest shippers were Williams & Company with 185 tons and Livingston, Kinkead & Company with 160 tons. These freighters used 304 wagons and 3,210 oxen, 722 of which they lost on the trail. At least one train arrived after Young's report. This was a Williams outfit that did not pull into Salt Lake City until December 17, probably delayed by heavy snow in the mountains northeast of the town.[44]

Leavenworth in its early years was relatively more important than at any other time in its history. During this time it was a base for freighting operations carried southwest to the Rio Grande and northwest to the Great Basin. As the metropolis for most of the plains the town was much envied by potential rivals, all of which had ambitious promoters who wanted to boost their towns as outfitting and freighting centers. As the businessmen of Leavenworth were soon to find out, nothing was more fleeting than an economy based on freighting.

III

Nebraska City and the Mormon War

Nebraska City was created during the speculative rush that dominated the first territorial years. Optimistic promoters thronged to desirable sites on the Missouri River and laid out the metropolises of the future. Backers in every struggling village and even some paper towns had aspirations of their city's becoming the great springboard for westward movement. Ambitious men gave these towns what they vitally needed to boom the economy—a newspaper, a bank, and a few buildings. Would-be lot buyers were advised to buy in Omaha, or Nebraska City, or Brownville because these were the towns of the future. Normally, the voice of the town, the newspaper, was the voice of the townsite planners.

Through the paper and other advertisements overeager speculators created an image of great prosperity by ballyhooing the value of town lots and adjacent farmland. Wild speculation was stimulated by easy money from local banks. The wildcat banks, hastily chartered by the sympathetic Territorial Legislature, solved the typical frontier currency shortage through the simple expedient of printing their own notes, which were usually accepted at face value only in the immediate locale.[1]

During this brief boom Nebraska City, on the Missouri at the site of Old Fort Kearny near the mouth of Table Creek, held great promise. According to its spokesmen the city bids fair to become the most flourishing city in Nebraska. . . . Already some thirty-five or forty good buildings have been erected in the place, also a large and commodious hotel. Some eighty lots have been sold to persons, who have bound themselves to build in four months. Contracts have been made, for making the present season a million and a half brick, and this time next year it is believed some three hundred buildings will be put up in the town. There is a good Steam Ferry Boat opposite the town, with good roads leading to it. Nebraska City, will be a great point for outfitting for the plains, and is on the direct route for the great body of the travel north of Hannibal, for California and Oregon. Nebraska City is now the largest town in the Territory, and improvements going ahead daily. Men of capital have located there, who are determined to push the place ahead.[2]

The Missouri River frontier was shattered and sobered by the Panic of 1857. The failure of the Ohio Life Insurance and Trust Company touched off the panic that had been in the making through almost a decade of overexpansion and overspeculation. The crash was particularly disastrous in frontier areas of little money, where faith was a major ingredient of business. The series of demands, foreclosures, and bankruptcies that swept the northern states affected Nebraska by late fall. Here wealth proved to be as ephemeral as Law's Mississippi Bubble. Banks closed. Land sales stopped. Merchandise sales stagnated. Life was suddenly a stark contrast to what it had been. The economic salvation of Nebraska City and the southeastern part of the territory came from an unexpected source—the Mormon War.

The bloodless Morman War, the major military activity between the Mexican and Civil wars, was one of the most controversial actions of the very controversial Buchanan administration. Peace between the United States and the Mormons had always been uneasy. When Utah Territory was formed in 1850, Congress had flaunted Mormon preference by naming it after the Ute Indians rather than retaining the Mormon name of Deseret. It is difficult to overemphasize the misunderstandings between official Washington and Salt Lake City. Normal administrative matters were complicated by great distance and poor mail service. Events in Utah were never readily known and certainly never understood. When army engineer Capt. John W. Gunnison and his small surveying party were exterminated by Utes in 1853, there were widespread rumors that official Mormondom was implicated. Then too, the determination of the Pierce administration to extend the federal judicial system into Utah caused a clash of authority between the federal judges and the Mormon church, which had its own court system. Another major complication was caused by a running battle between Garland Hurt, the United States Indian agent, and the Mormons over his handling of the Utes.

In early 1857 the federal appointees, who fled from Utah, carried with them stories of Mormon disregard for federal authority. While these tales were undoubtedly exaggerated, the administration—contrary to its usual policy—moved decisively, sending military units into Utah as a show of federal might. The suddenness and official secrecy of the military movement have contributed to a long-standing question over the motives of the federal action.[3]

President Buchanan did not mention Utah in his inaugural address of March 4. Yet, in the next few weeks he and his cabinet considered sending in troops. The final decision came "on or about May 20."[4] Any experienced freighter or soldier would have concluded that this was quite late for troop movement because of the great distance to Utah. The administration persisted in its aim despite the wise counsel of the army's commanding general Winfield S. Scott, who preferred to wait until 1858. Gen. William S. Harney was named to head the Utah army.

The Utah-bound army of about twenty-five hundred men was assembled at Fort Leavenworth in June and early July. This was a relatively large force, as the total strength of the entire United States army was only 15,764. The frontier military needs were swelled still further by Col. E. V. Sumner's Cheyenne Expedition of nearly seven hundred men then operating along the Platte and Arkansas River routes. Thus, in 1857 over one-fifth of the army was committed to special assignments west of the Missouri.[5]

While the troops were assembling, the army quartermaster in St. Louis worked feverishly to purchase and forward supplies to Fort Leavenworth. Up to July 4 the quartermaster had purchased 302 horses, 234 mules, 325 wagons complete with harness for a like number of six-mule teams, 5,750 tons of quartermaster and commissary stores, 15,000 bushels of oats, and 70,000 bushels of corn. The value of the quartermaster stores was estimated at $700,000 and the commissary stores at $328,000. This preparation was said to have resulted in the expenditure of from $1,200,000 to $1,500,000 in Missouri alone. Speaking for the depression-ridden state, the *Missouri Republican* aptly noted that "such a depletion of the treasury, for supplies to be found at our doors, cannot help exciting a beneficial influence upon the pecuniary affairs of this state."[6]

The army planned to use mule trains to carry its own provisions during the march to Utah, but it was not deemed advisable that the military should attempt to transport the supplies needed for an army of occupation. Thus, the emergency caused by the Utah crisis led the army to prevail on its regular contractor, Majors & Russell. The advertisement for the regular transportation contract of 1857 was circulated in January, well before even the government had anticipated an expedition to Utah. Obviously no contract provision had been made to cover such a contingency as the Mormon War. Bids were accepted to January 21 on two routes covering the trade to the southwest and the northwest. On February 27 Majors & Russell signed a one year agreement with Capt. Thomas L. Brent at Fort Leavenworth to carry the freight on both of these routes. The quantity of freight for the year was anticipated at 50,000 to 5,000,000 pounds. The rates, like those in the 1855–1856 contract, were graduated according to the time of year, becoming increasingly higher as the season progressed. (Although rates varied from month to month, only the prevailing rate for the month in which goods were dispatched was applied to a particular train.) The contract specified that freight to Fort Kearny and intermediate points would be transported for from $1.25 to $3.55 per 100 pounds per 100 miles. The rate to Fort Laramie and intermediate points beyond Fort Kearny was to be the same, but to Great Salt Lake and intermediate points beyond Fort Laramie it would be $1.29 to $3.55. The government obligated itself to give the contractors notice ranging from ten days for shipments of less than 300,000 pounds to sixty days for those over 2,500,000 pounds.[7]

The contractors already had their trains on the road by the time they received a request from Brent on June 19 to transport an additional 3,000,000 pounds. Russell, who realized that the season was late and the risk high, first contended that compliance with the request would ruin his firm, then unwisely consented to transport the freight without going through the formality of drawing up a new contract. So Majors and Russell, on the oral assurance that the government would pay them, quickly expanded their operations by adding hundreds of wagons, oxen, and men.[8]

The emergency caused by the Mormon campaign stimulated an inflationary run that greatly advanced cattle prices and bull-whackers' wages. In recruiting drivers the contractors had to compete with the army, which was in the process of hiring 160 mule-skinners for its trains. Both the army and the contractors in recruiting drivers through public notices held out the inducement that this was a good way for men to get to California, as they would be paid off and released in Salt Lake City. Trained teamsters were not available to meet the greatly expanded needs, so greenhorns, many of them handling oxen and mules for the first time, were hastily gathered from "all trades and occupations." The army soon learned that these men, so indiscriminately recruited, were unruly, hard to handle, and destructive of public property. There is no reason to believe that the men hired by Majors & Russell were of any different character.[9]

By the time the first troops embarked from Fort Leavenworth on July 18, the quartermaster and the contractors had decided to establish supply depots at Forts Kearny and Laramie, along the route to be used by the army. The freighters' lead trains reached Fort Laramie in late July and South Pass by late August. Meanwhile, Col. Edmund B. Alexander of the Tenth Infantry had led the advance units over the plains and through the mountains. Alexander was a frustrated man. He was in the vanguard, but there was some question as to how quickly he should proceed to wherever he might be going. Part of the confusion stemmed from the change in command. In August, Harney, probably because of his reputation as a fighter rather than a diplomat, was replaced by Col. Albert S. Johnston, who did not leave Fort Leavenworth until after September 10. The administration, in the meantime, recognizing the need for troop accommodations in Utah and desperately hoping for a peaceful occupation, dispatched assistant quartermaster Capt. Stewart Van Vliet on a fruitless mission to negotiate for supplies and campsites with Brigham Young.

Young not only refused to cooperate with Van Vliet but expressed a strong determination to resist the advancing army. Probably because Young convinced him and probably because he was impressed by mountains white with snow on September 16, Van

Vliet concluded that the army could not possibly move toward Salt Lake City during the fall or winter.[10]

To consolidate the straggling army, Alexander established Camp Winfield on Ham's Fork of the Green River about thirty miles northwest of Fort Bridger. The first troops arrived there on September 28, and within a few days some of the freight trains of Majors & Russell had come into the vicinity. Meanwhile, mainly as a result of Young's proclamation that Utah was being invaded, units of the Mormon militia had advanced northward to harass the federal forces. In view of Young's exhortations to the faithful, it is amazing that considerable bloodshed did not occur. As it was, the apparently well disciplined Mormons harassed only the supply trains and avoided any shooting fray with the army.

On the morning of October 5, Mormon units, notably the one led by Maj. Lot Smith, destroyed three contractor's trains—two on Green River and one on Big Sandy Creek east of the Green. The bullwhackers and their personal belongings were spared, but the wagons and all supplies were burned and the oxen were taken. The wagons and oxen were private property but the supplies, amounting to well over 300,000 pounds, were government property. Included were food items badly needed by the army: 2,720 pounds of ham, 92,700 pounds of bacon, 167,900 pounds of flour, 270 bushels of beans, 68,832 rations of desiccated vegetables, 7,781 pounds of hard bread, and quantities of coffee, tea, and sugar. Only a small portion of the supplies, 13,333 pounds of soap, 800 pounds of candles, and 6 lanterns, was not food.[11]

The destruction of the three trains was but a part of the contractor's loss for the year. The firm lost about nine hundred oxen to a pillaging band of Mormons who boldly struck only ten miles from Camp Winfield. The freighters also lost cattle to marauding Cheyenne. Majors and Russell had a contract to supply the army with beef. Above Fort Kearny their herd of 800 was attacked by the Cheyenne, who killed one of the herders and made off with the stock, some of which was later recovered. Majors and Russell's performance in 1857 bolstered their firm's reputation as an efficient freighter. They had sent out fifty-nine full trains to various destinations on the Santa Fe and Oregon trails and to Utah. But for so extensive a business the firm incurred losses of $493,553.01.

Ironically, its greatest performance was accompanied by financial failure.[12]

The disappointment of the freighters was perhaps exceeded only by that of the administration and the army. After nearly a year in office Buchanan could review nothing but a succession of failures highlighted by the Panic of 1857 and the Kansas and Utah troubles. The Utah army by year's end was tenuously situated in snowbound Camp Scott and at Fort Bridger. While the demoralized troops sulked in their isolation, a hostile Congress demanded to know the reasons for the Mormon War. The administration, committed to an unpopular war, could only push the campaign to a decision in 1858.

By January 11, 1858, the Utah forces amounted to about one-third of the entire army. There were 2,588 troops in the Fort Bridger area and orders had been issued for over 3,000 more men to be marched from Fort Leavenworth in the spring. The freighting demands of 1858 promised to be much greater than those of the preceding year. The only concern capable of handling this volume was Russell, Majors & Waddell.[13]

On January 16, 1858, Russell, Majors & Waddell entered its two transportation contracts with Q. M. Gen. Thomas Jesup. The larger of the contracts pertained to the Oregon Trail and Utah trade and the other to the Santa Fe trade; both were to run through 1858 and 1859. The Oregon Trail–Utah contract rates per 100 pounds for 100 miles for the first 10,000,000 pounds were as follows:

> To Fort Kearny and intermediate posts from $1.35 to $4; to Fort Laramie and posts beyond Fort Kearny, from $1.35 to $4.50; to Great Salt Lake City or depot, in Utah, and points beyond Fort Laramie, from $1.80 to $4.50, according to the month in which transportation is furnished; with 25 per centum additional for the next 5,000,000 pounds; and for all over 15,000,000 pounds, 35 per centum; also 10 per centum additional allowed for transportation of hard bread, bacon, pine lumber, and shingles; and $5 per day for each and every team unnecessarily detained by public agents over two days.[14]

The increased rates for freight in excess of 10,000,000 pounds undoubtedly were made because of expenses incurred by the contractors when they expanded their operations to meet the military needs. The detention provision was apparently a reaction to numerous incidents in the 1857 campaign when the progress of the freighters had suffered because of uncertain troop movements. Russell, Majors & Waddell was required by the government to post the unusually large bond of $250,000. The anticipated Santa Fe business, while considerably smaller than that of the northern route, was expected to be as much as 10,000,000 pounds. The firm of Russell, Majors & Waddell was faced with an assignment considerably larger than that of the previous year.

The Utah and way-points freight was to be started at Forts Leavenworth, Riley, and Laramie and other "designated points," a provision that was included to enable the development of an alternate depot upstream from Fort Leavenworth. Realizing the immensity of the expanding business, Majors recommended an alternate starting place because of the impossibility of handling all freight in one place and the inability to procure grazing land for thousands of animals within a reasonable distance of town if only one depot were used. Furthermore, both the contractors and the army were somewhat disenchanted with the long route from Fort Leavenworth to the Platte. This portion of the trail was very often muddy in the spring and crossed many unbridged tributaries of the Kansas River. A second depot would not only make the contractors more efficient but would also reduce the distance to Fort Kearny and thereby lower government transportation costs.[15]

For several weeks after the contract negotiation Majors and an army quartermaster, Lt. Beekman DuBarry, examined several possible sites along the Missouri north of Fort Leavenworth. On February 27 the *Nebraska News* of Nebraska City proclaimed to all, and particularly to Omaha, that Nebraska City had been selected. In bold headlines the *News* announced "NEBRASKA CITY SELECTED AS A MILITARY DEPOT AND A POINT FOR SHIPPING THE SUPPLIES FOR THE ARMY OF THE WEST!" It appeared that the depression-stricken town was to be revived with a business worth several hundred thousand dollars. Triumphantly the *News* noted:

> Fraud located the Seat of Government of Nebraska at Omaha and gave that place a temporary advantage over all others in the Territory; but the shrewd judgement of sagacious and careful businessmen derived from a personal examination of its geographical position and natural advantages, has finally secured for NEBRASKA CITY a prominence and prospects for the future unquestionably fairer than those of any other point in the Territory.

The *Nebraska Advertiser* of neighboring Brownville, obviously sympathetic to her South Platte neighbor and apparently indignant about Omaha's political power, judged that the military trade for Nebraska City would "add greatly to her importance, and be worth more to her really than the Capitol of the Territory."[16]

Omahans, recognizing the value of Nebraska City's prize, were keenly disappointed. W. W. Wyman, the editor of the *Times,* in commenting on the selection of Nebraska City and the future of Omaha raised a provocative query:

> But what will Omaha do? Ah, there is a hard question, we can ask it, but cannot answer. She is not on hand when anything really important is to be got. We all know that this is decidedly a better point from which the munitions of war for the Utah army should be shipped, than either Fort Leavenworth or Nebraska City. We all know that the route north of the Platte is superior to the South. We have men of capital, and influence, and yet when we all knew that a point was to be selected for a military depot, Omaha had not a friend at Court; she was not represented, and the result we have seen.

But all was not lost. Nostradamus-like, Wyman foresaw that "the greatest struggle is yet to come, the Railroad policy of the Territory is yet to be fixed. . . . What will Omaha do?"[17]

There are many reasons why the practical Majors chose Nebraska City as a depot. It was the principal settlement south of the Platte, and he undoubtedly wanted to stay on the south side of the river. If he had started from Omaha, he would have committed himself to fording some of his wagons across the hazardous Platte near Fort Kearny. Nebraska City came within a mile and a half of being due east of Fort Kearny, a fact often pointed out by the town boosters. This advantage was purely hypothetical however, since the road did not run as the proverbial crow flies.[18] Majors realized that the established trail from Nebraska City to Fort Kearny was sometimes muddy and quite circuitous, but he evidently considered it to be superior to other routes.

Aside from route considerations, the contractors desired to locate in an area where they could purchase many thousands of oxen and hire hundreds of men. Nebraska City, connected by ferry to Iowa, could easily tap the farmlands of the southwest portion of that state. Too, it was centrally located so as to command the trade of the Nebraska farming area that lay along the Missouri.

Majors and his partners regarded the political climate of Nebraska City as favorable. All three men were slave owners and because of this had been subjected to sharp attacks from abolitionist critics—particularly Northern and Eastern newspapers. Countless charges that the Buchanan administration had pro-Southern leanings were partially based on the well-known slave sympathies of its chief contractors. Russell particularly was controversial because of his role as treasurer of a pro-slave group in Leavenworth when "Bleeding Kansas" dominated national attention.[19] Nebraska City was controlled by an element of ex-Missourians who regarded slavery as an established institution rather than a moral issue. The *News* staunchly defended slavery and slaveholders against attacks by abolitionists, whom it labeled "self-righteous nigger-worshippers."[20] It is unlikely that these men could have found a town where they would have been more in accord with local thinking than Nebraska City.

Russell, Majors, and Waddell wanted to work from a place that would give certain assurances about levee repair, prohibition, and road building. Nebraska City was such a place. S. F. Nuckolls, the town founder and leader, was perfectly willing to make any agreement for the moment, and apparently just as willing to forget it after it had served his purpose. He curried the contractors' favor and was instrumental in formulating certain resolutions which were accepted at a public meeting on February 22 before Majors had formally named Nebraska City as the depot. The first resolution called for the repair of the levee, which was to be finished by the opening of navigation. This was one stipulation that the community probably wished to honor, since a good levee was vital to its business regardless of government freighting; but levee improvement was still an issue two years later. At the insistence of Majors, who had long been known for his moralism, a resolution was accepted that called for the suppression of all liquor shops, since they were likely to interfere with the moral program of the contractors, who put their employees under oath to refrain from imbibition. Apparently, no one felt there was any harm in indulging Majors in this way. He had been a spokesman of the good life through a decade of freighting, and nothing akin to the Great Awakening had as yet swept over the plains. The prohibition policy was to be executed by a committee of thirteen who were to use "moral suasion if possible, and that failing—every lawful and honorable means."[21] But alas, frontier habit proved to be stronger than moral suasion and honor, and Nebraska City failed to become a model community.

Majors, who was not satisfied with the existing oxbow trail, extracted a pledge that a committee of three would be appointed to collect subscriptions to survey and improve a direct route to Fort Kearny. This project was never realized during the period when Russell, Majors & Waddell had the military contracts.

The enormous responsibility of sending from 800 to 1,000 wagons from the new depot caused Majors himself to move to Nebraska City. He came in grand style, accompanied by wife, children, and several slave servants. As the most important man who had ever set foot in Nebraska City, he was received with much deference. His acts and judgments were venerated by the local press, which used his presence and work as irrefutable proof that Nebraska City was superior to any other point in the territory. From the start he was the central figure in town society. Public gatherings commanded his presence, and he was invariably asked to speak. While not particularly penetrating or reflective, his reasoning and logic were sound, and he always impressed observers as the very epitome of the man who had pulled himself up by his own bootstraps. He was Nebraska City's version of the great American success story.

Despite the public attention lavished on him, Majors remained modest and unassuming. He was frank, honest, and affable. Free from guile, he communicated with a wide range of humanity and was liked by government officials, army officers, merchants, and even his own bullwhackers. While many of them did not agree with Majors' moralizing, they did not doubt his sincerity. He lived what he taught, abstinence from liquor and tobacco, reliance on the Bible, and observance of the Sabbath. While the critic of slavery may have seen something hypocritical about this man holding slaves, Majors was so matter-of-fact that he accepted slavery without question because it was an established institution.

Basically Majors was a man of action. As an entrepreneur he was more at ease with bellowing oxen, moving wagons, and unwashed bullwhackers than with desks and ledgers. He could and did talk to his men. He worked with them, ate with them, and rode with them. Despite the proverbial hazards of familiarity, he was re-

spected by his employees. While the trains were on the move,
Majors frequently rode out and supervised by moving from train
to train on horseback and talking to wagon bosses and bullwhackers.
This love of the trail enabled him to understand trail problems.
He undoubtedly knew more about trail methods than any other
freighter, and his formulation of certain trail rules affected all who
followed him.

As preparation for the expected increase in steamboating to
Nebraska City, the deputy quartermaster in St. Louis, Lt. Col. G. H.
Grossman, signed a contract with W. M. McPherson, president of
the Pacific Railroad Company, to carry supplies from St. Louis to
points as far up as Nebraska City. The company was to be able to
move as much as 150 tons per day by steamboats during the navigation season of 1858. For this service the government agreed to pay
not over $1 per hundredweight for Leavenworth freight and the
regular current rates for freight above Leavenworth. The Nebraska
City goods were probably carried at $1 to 1.25 per hundred. The
company also agreed to transport troops to Leavenworth: officers
for $12 and enlisted men for $6.[22] The army constructed warehouses near the Nebraska City levee and let a special contract for
drayage from the steamboat landing to the warehouses, where the
supplies would be kept until wagons were available to haul them
across country. The drayage contract was given to J. W. Peannan
of Nebraska City at 50¢ a ton.[23]

Meanwhile, Majors swung into action. Wagons were shipped in
by steamboat, but additional oxen and men had to be obtained
locally. Majors hired as an agent Kinney & Holley of Nebraska
City, which purchased oxen by advertising in area newspapers and
by touring farms. The firm wanted from 600 to 800 yoke, for which
it offered to pay $75 a yoke. The oxen were to be "good working
cattle, from four to seven years of age," and were to be delivered
to Nebraska City between April 15 and May 15. Russell, Majors &
Waddell expected to spend about $600,000 for oxen but did not
have ready cash. Farmers were asked to accept notes variously due
in 60, 90, or 120 days.[24]

Public notices soliciting teamsters mentioned that the firm
wanted 1,500 men in Nebraska City by April 15. The men, who
were to be paid $25 a month, were to be in good health, and the
advertisements clearly stated that "none but men of good habits

need apply; as drinking intoxicating liquors, card playing, and profane language will not be permitted while in employment."[25] In addition to the teamsters, forty wagonmasters, who were expected to come well recommended, were to be employed. When Russell, Majors & Waddell hired the train bosses and bullwhackers, it supplied each of them with a Bible and a hymn book. Each man was made to sign a pledge in which he agreed "not to use profane language, not to get drunk, not to gamble, not to treat animals cruelly, and not to do anything else that is incompatible with the conduct of a gentleman."[26] The bound man finally agreed to accept discharge without pay if he violated any of the rules. The *Nebraska News,* with tongue in cheek, expected "to see two thousand teamsters of temperance, principles and habits, a spectacle of moral grandeur which we believe no human eye has as yet rested upon."[27] Alexander Caldwell twitted Majors for not realizing that the bullwhacker was a "hard citizen," and that profanity was so much a part of his nature, the cattle pulled "in proportion to the energy and fluency with which the driver delivered himself of his most familiar expressions."[28]

While Majors' scruples seemed unrealistic and childish to his contemporaries, it is very unlikely that he was completely naive. He probably never expected that his code, a combination of morality and frugality, would ever be observed by many, but it could be an ideal for all. Even if he kept one bullwhacker from tippling he achieved a moral victory, and if he persuaded another from maltreating an animal he attained an economic goal.

With his thousands of oxen and hundreds of wagons and men, Majors created a hubbub of activity that quickly transformed dreary Nebraska City into a teeming hive. Shouts, bellows, and dust filled the air, but the villagers swallowed it all and consoled themselves with their new-found prosperity. Extensive facilities were required to outfit the wagon trains. The contractors bought 138 lots in the west end of Nebraska City, where they erected their headquarters. Majors also acquired 600 acres of land five miles west of town, which he immediately broke preparatory to planting corn. On its town land the company constructed a storeroom, a blacksmith shop, a wheelwright shop, and a house for Mr. Thorne, the overseer. The three-story storeroom was thirty by eighty feet, as were the five-furnace blacksmith shop and the wheelwright shop. The contractors employed sixty or seventy carpenters, ten to fifteen blacksmiths, ten to fifteen wheelwrights, and "a number of grounds keepers, plasterers, masons and others." Among contemplated projects was a stable large enough for 600 to 800 horses.[29]

A grove on the land provided a shaded park enclosed by a board fence. This was the site of the Sabbath observance, where Majors as well as local ministers sermonized and read from the Bible. The Sabbath, according to Majors' rules, was a rest day both in camp and on the trail.

During 1858 Nebraska City trains had two principal destinations, Fort Kearny and Utah. The fort was again a supply depot for the Utah-bound army. The reinforcements, sent to Utah in May and June from Fort Leavenworth, consisted of 3,658 men organized into fourteen different units. The first wagons bound for Fort Kearny left on April 27, several weeks before the Utah ones were dispatched. By late May trains were leaving daily for Kearny and Utah. The Kearny trains made the return to Nebraska City, but for the Utah wagons it was a one-way trip. The trip to Kearny and return took nearly a month, about twenty-five days of actual travel and four of stoppages caused mainly by heavy roads and swollen streams. The trip out consumed an average of eighteen days traveling time, but the return trip, downgrade with empty wagons, took only eight days.[30]

During the season Russell, Majors & Waddell dispatched thirty-four trains, mostly in May and early June. All went as far as Fort Kearny, and about half went all the way to Utah by way of the South Pass route. The trail west of Fort Kearny was actually better known than the route between Nebraska City and Kearny. This road, a feeder of the Oregon Trail, had been used previously by army units and emigrants, but it was tested by heavy freight wagons for the first time during the Mormon War.

For the first forty miles, from Nebraska City to Salt Creek, the route ran northwestward through hilly terrain composed of alternating prairie openings and timber stands. Cabins and cultivated land, unmistakable signs of the white man's westward advance, were usually within view until Salt Creek, the "Jordan of our route," as one freighter expressed it, was reached.[31] Weeping Water Creek, which had to be forded first, was crossed about midway between present Elmwood and Weeping Water, and Salt Creek was easily forded at present Ashland on a limestone outcropping that made the approaches and stream bottom practically as firm as a paved road. Just east of this ford the Plattsmouth and Nebraska City roads merged.[32]

Beyond the ford were two trails that did not merge until Elm Creek, a small stream southeast of Columbus. The left-hand or southernmost path was slightly longer than the other, but because it was dryer and firmer it was more popular and was considered to be the main trail. It snaked northwestward along ridges on the divide between the west fork of Salt Creek and Wahoo Creek, running through present Swedeburg; it then passed about three miles north of present Brainard and two north of present David City before crossing Elm Creek about four miles from the Platte, nearly opposite the mouth of the Loup Fork. This sixty-mile stretch was well drained with an abundance of grass and water, but wood was usually carried from Salt Creek. The right-hand road lay northwestward from Salt Creek along Wahoo and Cottonwood creeks before coming out in the Platte Valley near present Linwood. It then ran through the valley only about twenty miles before joining the southern trail.[33]

Wood was found at Elm Creek about midway between Nebraska City and Fort Kearny, and some was normally carried ahead by those who wanted to avoid going into the muddy bottom lands. Five miles west of Elm Creek the road forked again, and the north and south branches ran several miles apart for about thirty-five miles before finally blending as a single trail about sixty miles east of the fort. The north branch stayed quite close to the river, where wood could be easily obtained. But in the spring trains often had difficulty with the mud and sloughs in the bottomland, so the dryer path was developed. It first lay along the base of the bluffs several miles from the river, then ascended to the hilltops, following along near the crest through sandy ridges broken by ravines leading down into the valley. After the roads joined, the trail stayed in the bottoms near the river, merging with the Oregon Trail about seventeen miles east of Fort Kearny.[34]

Because the trail forked twice, because some freighters and emigrants improvised shortcuts, and because still others had to detour from the trail to obtain fuel, the distance from Nebraska City to Fort Kearny was variously reported. Majors said it was 200 miles, which was undoubtedly the shortest possible distance and did not take into account the branches and detours. Some emigrants' guides agreed with Majors, but others reported the distance to be as much as 225 miles. In fact, one exceptionally wayward group reportedly covered 250 miles in moving from Nebraska City to Fort Kearny. These varying distances pointed up one of the great disadvantages of the route. It was undependable. In any event, the oxbow route, which appeared on maps as an exaggerated northern loop, was only about two-thirds as long as the Fort Leavenworth way to Fort Kearny.[35]

Nebraska City controlled only a portion of the military trade in 1858 because the contractors also started trains from Leavenworth and Westport. Only goods for Utah and way points were sent from Nebraska City, whereas Leavenworth and Westport were depots for both the Utah and the Santa Fe trade. Russell, Majors & Waddell's trade for the year was about one hundred trains, nearly double that of 1857. Some of the business, particularly that from Westport, was handled by subcontractors, who sent out at least twenty-five trains. The subcontractors, including E. C. Dyck & Company, Arnold L. Winion, and Chouteau, Polk & Company, transported Utah freight the full distance for $19.60 per hundred. They gathered their own drivers and oxen, but Russell, Majors & Waddell sold them wagons, ox yokes and chains, and food for the bullwhackers. The subcontractors were not required to pay interest on the credit extended by Russell, Majors & Waddell. Realizing that the Mormon War would be of short duration, Russell, Majors & Waddell did not care to drastically overextend itself with equipment which it would have to sell at a loss after the emergency was over.[36]

The bulk of the Utah trains had just gotten underway when the Mormon War suddenly ended. Buchanan, disgraced by the straggling army, decided to try diplomacy. His peace commissioners met with Brigham Young in mid-June and effected an agreement that Johnston's army would enter Salt Lake City without resistance. Without incident the troops passed through the city and established Camp Floyd about forty miles to the southwest. This large encampment nearly an equal distance from Salt Lake City and the territory's second major town Provo was the main base of the occupation army, but other troops were assigned to Fort Bridger. On November 30 there were 2,322 men at Camp Floyd and another 274 at Fort Bridger.[37]

Because of the many troops stationed in Utah, the end of open hostilities did not bring an end to freighting needs. The trade to Utah was never easy, and the normal problems of distance and drouth were complicated by hostile Indians in 1858. West of Fort Kearny the Sioux and Cheyenne harassed trains by surrounding them and demanding a tribute of goods. Despite the strength of several combined trains, the Indians had a fairly effective toll system. On one occasion in August, 800 marauders exacted tribute from a massive train of over 100 wagons. While the Indians were not highly destructive, they were enough of a nuisance to delay freighting.[38]

Further delays were occasioned by loss of oxen, which succumbed in great numbers to drouth, alkaline water, and fatigue. One freighter estimated the seasonal losses as high as 5,000 cattle with individual trains losing up to 120. The inexperienced subcontractors were said to have suffered the heaviest losses. As late as mid-October many trains were still 100 miles or more from Salt Lake City and were making but little progress through fifteen inches of snow. Five miles a day seems to have been the best accomplishment. The snow and shortage of stock meant that wagons had to be moved by combining teams, temporarily abandoning one wagon while another was pulled a few miles ahead, and then retracing steps to retrieve the first vehicle. This double-tripping accounted for the poor daily progress. Despite these difficulties most of the trains reached Camp Floyd in November. By this time Majors was on hand supervising the discharge of many of the teamsters, since the contractors did not intend to return very many of their wagons to the Missouri.[39]

While Russell, Majors & Waddell was engaged in fulfilling its military contract, the merchant trade to Utah expanded. To their normal business the merchants added sutlerships for the many Utah army units. Most of this private freighting started in Atchison, Kansas Territory. This little town was advantageously located twenty-five miles northwest of Leavenworth on the westernmost point of the Missouri River bend that arcs into northeastern Kansas and was near the Leavenworth road to the Oregon Trail. Freighting from Atchison was reportedly started by Livingston and Kinkead in 1855 after they discovered that one of their Leavenworth trains took four days to reach a point only five miles west of

Atchison. Atchison stagnated during the turmoil of "Bleeding Kansas," but by 1858 it was ready to fully benefit from its geographic advantage over Leavenworth.[40] Private shippers were attracted to the town partially because freight started there took several days less than freight from Leavenworth, Independence, or Westport. Then too, the military trade of 1858 so exhausted the resources of the military depot towns that private freighters, who had to compete in procuring men and animals, found it advantageous to use a point not preempted by the military contractors.

Anticipating an active Utah trade, private freighters thronged to Atchison in the spring of 1858. There was great demand for goods in Utah because little freight had gotten through the previous year when the trails were blockaded. The Atchison business was all directed west to the Big Blue, then along the Oregon Trail through the Platte River Valley and South Pass. First on the scene were various sutlers of the Utah Expedition including Livingston, Kinkead & Company, McShotan & Polk, and R. H. Dyer & Company. In early April much of their freight was delivered by four steamboats, then handled and stored by the mercantile houses of G. W. Bowman & Company and L. C. Challiss. Like other freighting stations, Atchison experienced its greatest activity in May and early June. During the last week in May, five trains amounting to 138 wagons, requiring 229 men, 1,770 cattle, 41 mules, and 17 horses, and carrying 681,000 pounds were outfitted.[41]

Heavy June rains made the trail virtually impassable but did not dull Atchison's enthusiasm for her major business. All other towns, at least as reported in the *Freedom's Champion*, were second rate in comparison to Atchison. Neighboring Leavenworth, an object of particular scorn, was depicted as the beginning of what must have been the muddiest, slowest trail in the West. During wet June, trains from Atchison were reported taking two or three days to reach Lancaster only ten miles out, but the government trains from Leavenworth were said to take twelve to sixteen days to reach that point.[42] On the full trip to Utah, Atchison wagons "invariably beat those which started from Leavenworth by ten to thirty days."[43] Why would any sensible person start from Leavenworth? "Simply because Government is swindled and cheated by men who have large interests in Leavenworth, and pays exorbitant prices for shipping goods from disadvantageous points, to reward her partisans."[44] The river between Leavenworth and Atchison was in excellent condition, but that portion between Atchison and Nebraska City was "uncertain and hazardous," and the little distance gained by shipping through Nebraska City "is no compensation for extra charges and freight."[45] Atchison trains were claimed to have a two- or three-day advantage over Nebraska City trains on trips to Fort Bridger.[46]

During the season Atchison had the trade to back up the ballyhoo. Twenty-four trains totaling 775 wagons carried 3,730,905 pounds of freight away from the town. These trains used 1,114 men, 7,963 oxen, 1,286 mules, and 142 horses. Most of the freight, 472 wagons making up twelve trains, was taken to Salt Lake City. The owners of these trains for the most part were merchants in Salt Lake City as well as sutlers. The largest shippers in the Salt Lake trade were R. H. Dyer & Company, Livingston, Kinkead & Company, and C. A. Perry & Company. Livingston, Kinkead & Company, the pioneer Utah mercantile firm, did not freight its own goods but hired various freighters from Independence.[47]

The second greatest amount of freighting was done by mail contractors, particularly Hockaday, Burr & Company, which was to deliver the Salt Lake mail. John M. Hockaday, the senior member of the firm and an experienced stagecoach operator, planned to establish a chain of station stores on the mail line from Atchison to Salt Lake City. These stores were intended to bring about faster service by supplying the mail trains, thereby relieving them of the burden of carrying their own provisions. Also, the mail stations were intended to sell provisions to emigrants. To equip the stations, Hockaday dispatched four trains totaling 182 wagons. One of these was proclaimed "the largest train, started by private enterprise, that ever crossed the plains."[48] It was composed of 105 wagons, 80 drawn by oxen and 25 by mules, and the train carried 465,500 pounds. This single train utilized 225 men, 200 mules, 1,000 oxen, and 50 horses. One small train of twelve wagons carried the freight of George Chorpenning, the mail contractor for the Salt Lake–California mail, who was to establish stations on that route. Some freight for the Fort Kearny and Fort Laramie sutlers also started from Atchison.

Two of the trains dispatched from Atchison had Kansas destinations. One went to Palmetto and the other to Marysville. The

Indian traders of the upper Platte and Green River areas also freighted from Atchison. C. Martin sent a small train of seven wagons to Green River; and Bisonette and Lazinette, the traders at Deer Creek eighty miles above Fort Laramie, used thirteen wagons to carry goods to their post. These Deer Creek traders were responsible for the only eastbound freight through Atchison. It consisted of over two thousand buffalo robes, nearly three hundred wolf skins, and over two hundred pounds of beaver pelts. In previous years the fur traders had evidently shipped through Leavenworth or Independence.[49]

Most of the Atchison freighters had previously resided in Independence or Weston, and their move to Atchison was the beginning of a town upsurge that was directly dependent on overland freighting. By 1858 Atchison was clearly the most important point for the shipment of private freight in Kansas, and its boosters claimed that "every pound of freight, for Utah, not shipped by Government, starts from Atchison."[50]

There is little doubt that the Mormon War was the proper tonic for the economic ills of both the Missouri River area and Utah. Q. M. Gen. Thomas S. Jesup reported that "the expenditures on account of the expedition to Utah, as far as can be ascertained, exceed five millions of dollars."[51] Most of this money, used for quartermaster and commissary goods, payrolls, and contractors' transportation costs, was funneled through St. Louis or Fort Leavenworth and benefited great portions of Missouri, eastern Kansas, southwestern Iowa, and eastern Nebraska. On hearing that $2,000,-000 was to be distributed through Fort Leavenworth in a single week, the *St. Joseph Gazette* concluded that "it requires neither a prophet nor the son of a prophet to forsee that the result must be a rapid expansion in trade, and a general easing of our fiscal affairs." The money was expected to "perform a thousand good offices in a brief period" and to accomplish "the fruition of the advantages which we promised ourselves from the movements of Uncle Sam in the West."[52]

Most of the federal expenditures initially benefited farmers, who in turn spurred merchant sales as their money was pumped into the channels of commerce. Most of the federal funds paid to Russell, Majors & Waddell were used for the purchase of wagons and oxen and the hiring of men. The contractors during the cam-

Trails to Fort Kearny

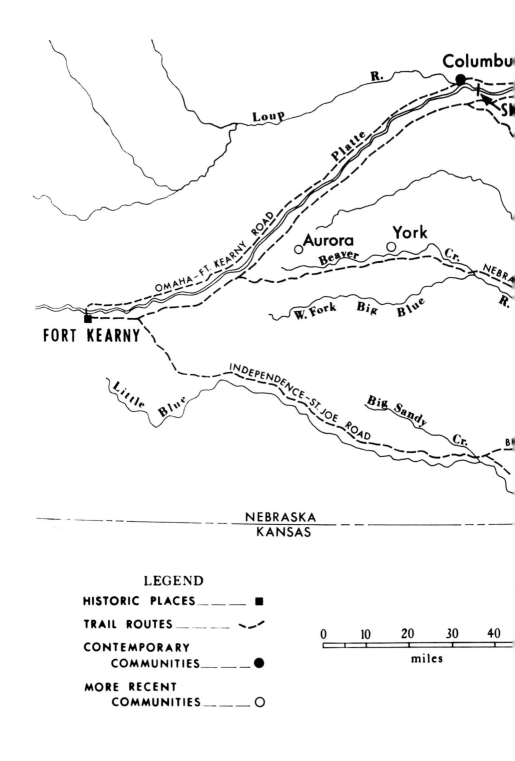

Columbu

R.

Loup

Platte

S

Aurora

York

Beaver

Cr.

NEBR

OMAHA—FT. KEARNY ROAD

W. Fork   Big   Blue

R.

■ FORT KEARNY

Little Blue

INDEPENDENCE—ST. JOE ROAD

Big Sandy

Cr.

B

NEBRASKA
KANSAS

LEGEND
HISTORIC PLACES _ _ _ _ ■
TRAIL ROUTES _ _ _ _ ⌣
CONTEMPORARY
   COMMUNITIES _ _ _ ●
MORE RECENT
   COMMUNITIES _ _ _ ○

0   10   20   30   40
miles

TRAILS TO

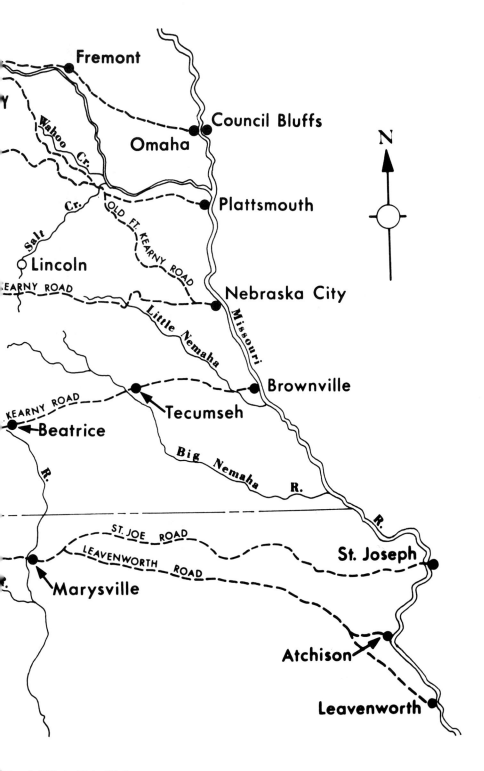

Fremont

Council Bluffs

Omaha

Plattsmouth

N

Wahoo Cr.

Salt Cr.

OLD FT. KEARNY ROAD

Lincoln

EARNY ROAD

Nebraska City

Little Nemaha

Missouri

Brownville

KEARNY ROAD

Tecumseh

Beatrice

R.

Big Nemaha R.

R.

ST. JOE ROAD

St. Joseph

LEAVENWORTH ROAD

Marysville

Atchison

Leavenworth

T KEARNY

paigns of 1857–1858 used 3,908 wagons, 46,856 oxen, and 33 mules to provision Fort Kearny, Fort Laramie, and the Utah army.[53] The trade in farm produce is reflected by a detailed report in the *Nebraska News* of September 25, 1858, which shows the amount of farm goods carried on the thirty-four trains sent from Nebraska City to be 283,778 pounds of flour, 195,626 pounds of bacon, 28,332 pounds of beans, 8,649 pounds of ham, 1,637,332 pounds of oats, 813,536 pounds of corn, and 231,170 pounds of barley. Aside from these government stores, the contractors used 136,000 pounds of bacon and over 2,000 sacks of flour for their men while enroute.

Most of the food carried on the Nebraska City trains originated in Missouri, but many of the oxen and mules were procured in the area of eastern Nebraska and western Iowa. Russell, Majors & Waddell reportedly spent $413,000 on oxen and $13,430 on mules for its Nebraska City trade. These were significant sums even though they fell short of the optimistic spring estimates.[54]

On the Utah end of the trade, Johnston's army and the merchants following in its wake sharply revived an economy that had languished during the wartime blockade. Eager merchants found a ready market in the long-isolated Mormons, in the troops, and in the freighters. Over 5,000 troops with the first opportunity in months to "live it up" lavished sums on traders' goods—particularly liquor. At Camp Floyd dissipation was said "to be the only recreation."[55] To this spending was added that of some 4,000 bullwhackers, many of whom were discharged in Salt Lake City, where they were paid for their season's work. While they may have helped business, some of the armed, unemployed teamsters seriously menaced the peace and safety of Salt Lake City. Despite a strong Mormon police force, "riot and dissipation" were said to be rife in what had been a clean and calm community.[56]

Before any trains reached the promising Salt Lake City markets they had to pass through the Provo Canyon toll road where a levy of $1 per ton of freight was exacted. The Mormons had spent heavily in carving the road through the rocky canyon and were determined to get their pound of flesh from the invading Gentiles. Even the wagons of Russell, Majors & Waddell, an integral part of the conquering army, were expected to pay the humiliating and costly toll. A dollar a ton applied to the freight carried by the contractors and merchants, possibly over 4,000 wagons carrying two to two and a half tons, would have amounted to $8,000 to $10,000.[57]

Another lucrative source of business, aside from merchant sales and tolls, came from the need to sustain the army. Many military supplies, particularly grain and hay, were purchased from Mormon farmers. While the government movement into Utah was bitterly resented and denounced by the Mormons, its effects on business were generally salutary. One veteran freighter recalled that the "arrival of the army had made business lively. Salt Lake had a real boom as a result of the war. One man said to me: 'The war has been a great thing for us. We have no crops this year and the arrival of this big army and plenty of food is all that saved us.' "[58]

The economic impact of the Mormon War was gratifying but fleeting. Newspapers of the Missouri River towns reflected an apprehension about the possible effects of a sudden end to the war. The *Nebraska News* throughout the spring of 1858 expressed joy over the new prosperity, but always there was uneasiness: What would happen if the campaign should quickly end?

Buchanan's decision to send out peace commissioners was not at all popular in the river towns. By late 1858 anxieties were somewhat soothed when it was generally realized that the government would occupy Utah and an active trade would continue in the foreseeable future. The administration pursued a policy of occupation through 1859, which resulted in the economic impact of the Mormon War lasting through that year.

The Utah garrison of 1859 was considerably smaller than that of the previous year but still large by frontier standards. The Adjutant General reported that as of June 30, 3,164 men were assigned to the Utah Department. Nearly two-thirds of these were stationed at Camp Floyd, with lesser garrisons at Fort Bridger and at Camp Clark, a temporary location in the San Pete Valley. Agricultural produce, particularly grain and flour, was obtained in Utah, but all other supplies had to be shipped in from the Missouri. The Utah-procured grain and flour greatly decreased overland freighting. For example, A. Gilbert, one of the grain contractors, agreed to furnish 40,000 to 100,000 bushels of wheat, barley, rye, oats, and corn for Camp Floyd.[59]

While the total trade was considerably smaller than that of 1858, it was Leavenworth, not Nebraska City, that absorbed the loss. If anything, the military business from Nebraska City was larger than the year before, mainly because Russell, Majors & Waddell used it almost exclusively. At one point in May, Majors announced that he would send about forty trains or 1,000 wagons from Nebraska City, but a week later this estimate was revised to from 400 to 600 wagons. Freighting prospects were again increased in late June with the announcement that all military freight to Fort Kearny, Fort Laramie, and Utah would be shipped from Nebraska City. With the exception of some goods sent from the nearby town of Wyoming in Nebraska Territory, Nebraska City apparently controlled the trade. Russell, Majors & Waddell had also stored many provisions over the winter in Fort Laramie warehouses. They were moved out in May by a number of wagons—definitely more than 50 and possibly as many as 100.[60]

The military trade of 1859 is not known except in general terms. A St. Louis newspaper reported that over 900 wagons were used to supply Fort Laramie, Fort Bridger, and Camp Floyd. The Kearny trade would have to be added to this. In August the contractors sent five trains from Nebraska City to the fort. These were evidently full trains, as they required 1,560 oxen and some 140 men. An 1860 report stated that Russell, Majors & Waddell sent out over 12,000 head of oxen from Nebraska City in 1859. This would suggest that the Nebraska City cargo may have amounted to as much as 1,000 wagonloads.[61]

Unlike the military business, the merchant trade to Salt Lake City in 1859 did not decline. It was about on a par with that of the previous year, despite less demand for goods. Many freighters, encouraged by the 1858 boom, entered the trade and glutted the Salt Lake City markets. The *Deseret News* of July 27, 1859, noted that "merchant trains have been coming in so thick and fast of late that their arrival has almost ceased to attract attention." The numerous trains were said to be loaded with "goods for the regular merchants, and others for transient traders, who are coming out here to pick up some of Uncle Sam's cash, which they supposed will be scattered about profusely."

Although Atchison remained the mistress of the Utah merchant trade, some of the merchant trains started from Nebraska City, which managed to attract a few Atchison defectors, notably Livingston & Kinkead. Livingston & Kinkead's goods, about 150 wagon loads, were hauled by Jones & Kerr, also an Atchison firm. Another freighting company, Windsor, Lyton & Ewing shipped about fifty tons through Nebraska City.[62]

Up to July 2, 3,019,950 pounds of freight had been sent from Atchison. About three-fourths of it went to Utah destinations— Salt Lake City, Camp Floyd, and Fort Bridger. The remainder was cargo for the mines and such places as Fort Laramie, Fort Kearny, Scott's Bluffs, and Bent's Fort.[63]

As a result of the Mormon War and its aftermath, Nebraska City had prospered because of the military trade and Atchison because of the merchant trade. The transformation of Nebraska City from a depression-plagued village to the most prosperous town in the territory was evident by late 1858, and the community's debt to Russell, Majors & Waddell was publicly acknowledged. The *News* of December 18, 1858, boasted that Nebraska City

> has about four thousand inhabitants, some of the finest buildings in the Territory, in addition to its having the Surveyor Generals Office for Kansas and Nebraska, the South Platte Land Office, the Military Depot, and being the grand entrepot of Russell, Majors & Waddell, who have during the past season SPENT OVER THREE HUNDRED THOUSAND DOLLARS HERE.

The military business after two years was said to have "made Nebraska City the foremost place in Nebraska—far beyond and above the contemptible malice of successful rivalry of any town in the Territory. It has given us a name and a reputation abroad worth millions of dollars to us."[64]

With each passing month of calm in Utah the prospects of the military trade became more and more uncertain. The 1860 trade was likely to be less than that of either of the two preceding years. Yet the local press did not reflect any of the dismal forecasts that had been so common in the summer of 1858. The trade winds were changing, and merchants and freighters looked hopefully to a new source of business in the recently discovered El Dorado across the plains.

IV

Freighting During the Colorado Gold Rush, 1859-1860

Between the Mormon War and the Civil War the most dramatic event on the frontier was the Colorado gold rush. "Pike's Peak" was a national cry in 1859, but it was not until the next year that Colorado freighting had increased to the point that it was more important than the declining Utah trade.

The 1859 Colorado population offered only limited opportunities for freighters. Most of the prospectors used simple equipment—pans and sluice boxes—in their placer operations. A good many of them were discouraged by initial failures and left the mining areas. But by 1860 the situation had improved considerably for both miners and freighters. The population stabilized greatly with the discovery of paying, high-altitude lodes, which created an immediate need for heavy equipment, particularly quartz mills to process the gold-bearing rock.

In one respect Colorado was like other mining frontiers. There was a considerable time lapse between the knowledge of gold and its "official" discovery. Age-old rumors about the wealth of the Rockies were given some foundation in 1850 when a party of California-bound Cherokee panned traces of gold on a branch of the South Platte. This strike was not fruitful, but eight years later the depression and the eternal hope of an easy solution sent two groups of prospectors into the Rockies. Their long labors produced meager amounts of gold, but it was enough for people who knew what to make of it.[1]

79

Newspapermen living in Missouri River towns more than 500 miles from the Rockies knew little about gold but a great deal about gold rushes. These promoters, faced with the prospects of a dwindling Utah trade and an end to the wartime prosperity, began conjuring up a gold rush. The little dust brought to Kansas City in August was liberally mixed with bold headlines and misleading verbiage that converted every rumor into gospel truth. This skillful admixture of fact and fable was soon steady fare for the reading public.

The Kansas City *Journal of Commerce* opened the journalistic campaign on August 26, 1858, by proclaiming a discovery of "THE NEW ELDORADO ! ! !"[2] This phrase, obviously suggestive of Cortez rather than Coronado, was soon echoed by the news sheets of every river town. Leavenworth was quickly afflicted by the "Pike's Peak 'Mad' " which threatened to carry off a number of its residents.[3] The *Nebraska News* of September 4 reported that some men had dug over $600 worth of gold per week and foresaw "a rush for the Western Gold Fields as was only witnessed in the grand rush for the rich placers of California. What destinies it will carve out for the Great West beyond the valleys of the Mississippi and Missouri, time alone can determine." Atchison, Omaha, and St. Joseph schemers, not to be outdone by rivals in this race to advertise their towns as the best starting place for the mines, contributed more of the same.

The verbal spawn of the Missouri could not be contained. It swept rapidly to the East and great sections of the land experienced an excitement comparable to that of a decade before. Within a few weeks of the discovery, hundreds of people east of the Mississippi were speaking knowingly of Pike's Peak and Cherry Creek. The *Nebraska Advertiser* of September 30 announced: "Already companies are forming themselves in St. Louis, Chicago, and other important cities, and their vanguards are now en route for the mines. The rush has commenced."

The lateness of the season prevented anything more than a modest exodus. Several hundred men drifted into the Cherry Creek area and laid out Denver and Auraria, collections of straggling huts and tents that were portrayed as meccas for the anxious pilgrims of '59. Throughout the long winter the prospects of the "Cherry Creek mines" were played up in the newspapers of Nebraska and Kansas. Merchants suddenly became expert in outfitting miners and advertised long lists of requisites for the venturers.

The rush of 1859 was probably even grander than its creators anticipated. Would-be miners by the thousands thronged through Missouri, Kansas, and Nebraska towns and crowded the trails to Cherry Creek. Most were poor and ill-equipped. They were generally ignorant of the plains and of prospecting. Most were understandably gullible and so were victimized by the rumor and ballyhoo. The gold was waiting for those who got there first, and many fortune-seekers embarked across the great desolation between the Missouri River and the mountains in March and April, well before there was grass for their animals. The St. Joseph ferry reported a business of 359 wagons, 1,428 horses and cattle, and 3,096 passengers for the week ending April 25.[4] Many emigrants were far out on the trail before winter had played its course. Severe storms in the Fort Kearny area that produced three feet of snow detained thousands, who were reported to be "suffering terribly." Corn at Fort Kearny was selling for $4 a bushel, about ten times the Nebraska City price, and "hundreds and thousands were destitute of any, or of means to purchase with."[5]

"Pike's Peak or Bust," inspired by hazardous trails, could validly have been rephrased as "Pike's Peak and Bust." To many prospectors the problem was getting to the mining area. To many more the problem was finding gold. Thousands of amateurs were bitterly disappointed when large nuggets were not readily found in stream beds. Prospecting turned out to be work rather than discovery. Failure, frustration, lack of supplies, and inadequate funds to survive in the inflationary economy caused the dejected, amidst charges of "humbug," "fraud," and many stronger utterances, to turn their backs on the new El Dorado. By late May hundreds were counter-rushing through the Missouri River towns.

The disbelievers who abandoned the search for gold and returned home soon heard new cries of gold, and this time they were true. Bands of diehards, having abandoned the area at the base of the Rockies, followed the streams to the higher elevations west of Denver and there found rich veins. During 1859 and 1860 mines were opened both in the area of Blackhawk west of Denver, and California Gulch and Tarryall in the South Park region southwest of Denver.[6]

The rush was resumed in 1860, and perhaps many of those who

left the year before were back for another try. With the wisdom of a year's experience, the gold seekers of 1860 traveled somewhat later in the spring. There was grass for their animals, and ample provisions were on hand in Denver when they arrived. The emigration was apparently heavy. The *Rocky Mountain News* of Denver reported on April 25 that "the emigration is coming in at the rate of over one hundred men each day, and constantly increasing. . . . Covered wagons are hourly passing in front of our office, and canvass tents dot the valleys along Platte river and Cherry Creek."

How many participated in the rushes of 1859 and 1860? The 1860 census showed 34,277 in Denver and the mining areas.[7] While this is an indication of the population at a given time, it does not show those who had come and gone. It is quite likely that the number of people who had spent some time in the region was considerably higher than this figure. If so, the market potential of the mining area was undoubtedly something more than the census figures would indicate.

Mining areas had a marked lack of self-sufficiency. There were prospectors and miners, saloonkeepers, camp followers, and merchants, but a vital lack in the mining community was the manufacturer and the farmer. The very nature of the terrain itself precluded any possibility of agricultural production sufficient to meet the needs of the miner and his attendant professions. As contrasted to Utah, where the Mormons lacked manufactured goods, the Colorado miner lacked both manufactured goods and farm produce. Thus, this mining frontier was much more dependent on established markets than was Utah.

And where were the logical supply points? Some produce might be obtained from New Mexico and perhaps some from Utah, but obviously the bulk of supplies had to come from the Missouri River. For the first time in the history of mining, a frontier was opened that could be logically supplied by way of the plains. The interdependence of the Missouri River frontier and the mining frontier was taken for granted from the start.

What did the mining areas need? Virtually everything. Quartz mills, steam sawmills, hardware, clothing, drugs, and food. In time there was a sufficient number of quartz mills, and in time the sawmills turned out enough lumber to obviate the need of transporting it by overland means, so the need for staple items—food, clothing, and drugs—provided the real long range basis of the trade.

Two of the commonest items in the Colorado trade were flour and liquor.

Which town was the best freight depot on the Missouri? Each town was obviously the "best." Every community between Omaha and Kansas City aimed to share in the Colorado trade both as a freighting point and outfitting place for emigrants.

Gold rushers moved on three main routes, the Arkansas, the Smoky Hill, and the Platte. The trail along the Arkansas River that served Kansas City was in reality for the most of its distance the old Santa Fe Trail. It followed this historic route to Pueblo, Colorado, where it turned north along the eastern base of the Rockies. While this route was reputed to be good with regard to timber, grass, water, and firm, level ground, it was considerably longer than any other route. Kansas City as a freighting center generally controlled the trade of the Southwest, but it could never overcome the disadvantage of distance in the contest for the Colorado trade and was always secondary to the towns north of the Kansas River as a freighting and outfitting center for the mines. The Smoky Hill route, a promotional brainchild of Leavenworth, was used briefly by emigrants but was not at all attractive for conventional freighting. A contemporary critic penned the gist of the Smoky Hill limitations:

> Leavenworth, in her struggle to prevent her lamp of life from going out, has discovered a panacea for her ills in the opening of the Smoky Hill Route, which to use the expression of one of the property holders of that city "runs plump into Leavenworth, and nowhere else." The road is no doubt a good one, and shorter than the Platte, but the scarcity of water on some parts of the road, and the too great abundance of Kiowas and other reptiles, militates against its popularity.[8]

The Platte route, because of the great migrations over it to California, Oregon, and Utah, was nationally known and very popular. However, since portions of it were woodless and sandy, the other routes were more attractive to some. The confused traveler was advised that " 'the Platte is the best known, and the most sandy; the Arkansas is the longest, but the firmest, and the Smoky Hill had the most claimed for it, but is, as yet, a *via incognita*. 'Choose ye for yourselves which ye will follow.' "[9]

Towns that used the Platte, or the "Great Central Route," never missed an opportunity to criticize the distance of the Arkansas or the dryness of the Smoky Hill route, but they saved their strongest venom for each other. The bickering revolved around the question of which was the best trail to Fort Kearny, where all of the feeder routes merged. Beyond Fort Kearny the road stayed south of the Platte and then curved southwestward beyond the forks, following the sweeping South Platte to Cherry Creek. It was 356 miles from Fort Kearny to Denver by the river trail, but sometimes a cutoff in the westernmost section was used.[10]

Excessive sandiness beyond Beaver Creek, particularly in late season after the road was badly cut by many wagons, caused the development of the cutoff which left the South Platte about fifteen miles west of the creek, where the river meandered to the north, and near the point where Fort Morgan, Colorado, now stands. Some called it the Beaver Creek Cutoff and others referred to it as the Bijou Creek Road. This is understandable. Beaver Creek was the last prominent stream crossed by westbound travelers, and the cutoff started a short distance east of Bijou Creek. In any event this beeline trace of about seventy-five miles saved approximately fifty miles over the curved river route and ran over firmer ground, but it was generally arid and quite devoid of timber and grass. Anyone who was willing to carry fuel, risk scant pasturage and water, and travel quickly could afford to use the cutoff. The cautious and slow-moving, including all ox trains, were advised to follow the river trail.[11]

East of Fort Kearny there were three basic trails. Farthest to the south was the Oregon Trail, which was used by Leavenworth, Atchison, and St. Joseph traffic. The northernmost route was the North Platte or Mormon Trail starting at Omaha and Council Bluffs. In 1858 it passed north of the river through recently settled farmland to points opposite Fort Kearny, where the Platte was forded. In a central location was Nebraska City's oxbow route.

While one town naturally competed with all others, its keenest rivalry was with its closest neighbor. Therefore, Leavenworth and Atchison fought for the trade funneled through the great western bend, and Omaha and Nebraska City locked horns over the trade channeled through the area near the mouth of the Platte. Since Omaha and Nebraska City had been rivals in so many things, such as the capital fight and the struggle for the land office, the battle of the trails became a part of the broad North Platte–South Platte contest led by these two towns.

Omaha loudly proclaimed the advantages of her 180-mile trail to Fort Kearny. It was the shortest. It was the most improved. It offered security and provisions because it ran through settled areas. Omahans claimed, and rightly so, that they had an advantage of over 100 miles over Leavenworth, but their claim of a 75 mile advantage over Nebraska City was a fabrication. Considerable portions of the trail had been improved by army engineers in the period 1856–1858. The Elkhorn River, Big and Little Papillion creeks, and many lesser streams had been bridged, and some of the more troublesome sloughs had been handled by grading roadbeds through them or else constructing trestles over them. From Omaha to Grand Island the trail ran through a well settled area, where shelter and produce could always be obtained at farms and in villages.[12]

Omaha's best testimonial was the use of her route by gold seekers and Mormons. The greatly criticized Saints suddenly became seers of all things geographic because of their use of the North Platte route. The *Omaha Times* reported, "Mormons, like Buffalo and Indians, always choose the shortest and best route. To those who are at all acquainted with the admirable organization and perfect order which prevails among them, this adage needs no support." Brigham Young, the selector of the route, "exercised great sagacity and prudence, which only a thorough knowledge of the country would enable him to bring into use."[13]

And so it went. Through editorials, advertisements, and testimonials, Omaha constantly kept her trail before the public. Hardly an issue of the weekly papers passed without some mention of the glorious trail. Table 2, published in the *Omaha Nebraskian* April 9, 1859, is a good example of the type of emigrant guide that frequently appeared in Omaha papers.

TABLE 2

TABLE OF DISTANCES FROM THE CITY OF OMAHA TO THE GOLD FIELDS
OF NEBRASKA

From Omaha City	Miles Total	Remarks
Elkhorn City	20	Cross Elkhorn River by bridge; station of Western Stage Co.; large settlement; plenty of grass, timber and grain.

Fremont	10	30	Stage station; heavy settlement; grain, timber and grass.
Columbus	45	75	Route from Fremont here through thickly populated country, several small towns intervening. At Columbus cross Loup Fork by ferry; several companies have boats here; ferry charges reasonable; county seat of Platte county, heavy settlement, hay, grass, grain, wood and water abundant.
Prairie Creek	13	88	Bridged; wood, water and grass.
Lone Tree	29	117	Mail station; wood, water, grain and hay.
Grand Island City	25	142	Large German settlement, plenty of grain, water, wood and grass.
Mendota	7	149	Stage station; cross Wood river by bridge, grain, water and hay.
Ft. Kearny	32	181	Ford Platte river; water from 6 to 18 inches deep; ford in constant use by Government and attaches of Fort. The road leading from Nebraska City, 250 miles; from St. Joseph 290 miles, from Leavenworth 313 miles, all converge here. Those who prefer to continue up the north side of the Platte will find excellent camping places, with plenty of grass, fuel and water, and can cross at upper ford, near the mouth of South Fork of Platte River. At Ft. Kearny are stores, wagon and blacksmith shops, hay, grain, wood, water and grass in profusion.
Plum Creek	33	214	Stage station and trading post; grain, hay, wood, water and grass.
Brady's Island	39	253	Heavy timbered island in Platte river; wood, water, and grass.
Cottonwood Springs	13	266	Trading post, wood, water and grass.
Junction of Platte	25	291	Wood, water and grass in abundance.
Old Ford	15	306	Wood, water and grass.

O'Fallon's Bluffs	18	324	Trading post; stage station, plenty of hay, wood, water and grass. Up to this point the road—ALL THE WAY—is within a short distance of timber, and with plenty of water and grass.
Crossing S. Platte	15	339	Road to Utah via Ft. Laramie crosses the South Fork of the Platte river here, by an excellent ford; water and grass.
Lodge Pole Creek	41	380	This creek comes into the Platte on north side; water, grass and timber.
Lieut. Bryan's Trail	50	430	Lieut. Bryan's trail in 1856 to Ft. Leavenworth via Republican Fork, water and grass.
Beaver Creek	19	449	Large stream with low banks; very shallow with gravelly bed and fordable at all times. Road for last 100 miles over plains, with timber from 3 to 5 miles off. Camping places are good, water and grass plenty, and road at this point comes into the timbered country again.
St. Helen's Island	19	468	Timbered island in Platte; wood, water and grass.
Cache la Poudre	34	502	A mountain stream 100 feet wide, flowing with a swift current over a rocky bed; comes into the Platte on the north side; round, or shot gold has been found on it, and the best diggings are said to be here. From this point a road leads to Medicine Bow and North Platte river; wood, water and grass.
Thompson's Creek	7	509	Small mountain stream; gold has been found here, and many miners are now camped on it.
St. Vrain's Fort	3	512	At this point the mining settlements are centered.
Auraria	25	537	Heaviest mining settlement; situated at the mouth of Cherry Creek, over 100 buildings already built and occupied.

Total distance from Omaha City to Auraria	....	537 miles
"	"	" Iowa City	"	"	....	800
"	"	" Chicago	"	"	....	1036

Obviously, a persuasive trail guide could not mention such trivia as muddy sloughs, inadequate ferries, and the sometimes difficult crossing of the Platte. These problems were not easily solved. Mud made doubletripping quite common through many of the unimproved sloughs. Engineers had not bridged the Loup Fork, primarily because of the cost, which was estimated to be about $85,000. The width, swiftness, and depth of this stream made fording hazardous, and most had to cross on a rope ferry located just west of the infant village of Columbus. Limited capacity of the ferry occasioned long, frustrating delays. Many travelers complained about excessive ferriage fees, which, they charged, were in excess of the allowable rates in the ferry company's territorial charter. Two dollars was the charge for a wagon and one yoke of oxen, and 50¢ for each additional yoke.[14] O. P. Hurford of Omaha, after acquiring the Loup Fork ferry charter in 1860, tried to restore public confidence by assuring "a safe crossing . . . which will be uniform in charges, as fixed by law, and FREE FROM VEXATIOUS DELAYS."[15]

Delays at Columbus were aggravating, but the main concern was the sometimes disastrous fording of the Platte. For those going to Colorado there was no avoidance of the problem—the Platte had to be crossed. Of course, it was possible, as Omaha advertised, to stay north of the river and proceed to the mines by way of Fort Laramie, where the North Platte was forded. This route by way of Fort Laramie, however, was not only seventy miles longer than the one by way of Fort Kearny but was out of the area of effective military protection, and it did not have mail stations or the road ranches whch were sometimes vital to emigrants and freighters. So naturally most chose to ford the Platte and pick up the South Platte route at Fort Kearny.[16]

There were several fords in the vicinity of the Grand Island. The first was near the foot of the island, but the most popular was near the head at a point directly opposite the fort. Here there were eight channels separated by ribbon-like wooded islands. Since fording during the spring crest was impossible, most would try to ford in May and June after the water had receded somewhat. Even then there were problems, but by doubletripping, lightening loads, and using lines, fording was usually accomplished. Sometimes a wagon, but more often supplies, would be lost to the current. It was not uncommon for trains to use an entire day or even two to reach Fort Kearny after it was first sighted from the north bank.[17] The easiest way to cross the Platte was to wait until winter and cross on the ice. Unfortunately for Omaha, winter was not the best traveling season.

An important variant that avoided both the Loup Fork ferry and fording was provided by Shinn's Ferry about twelve miles east of Columbus. Moses F. Shinn of Omaha began operating the rope ferry in April, 1859, a year before he obtained a charter from the Territorial Legislature. The trail to Kearny by way of Shinn's Ferry was the same distance as the route north of the river. Many continued to use the old route across the Loup Fork, but apparently Shinn's Ferry was heavily used. In the space of a few months in 1860 it had been used by 2,200 wagons. As a result of this ferry, one branch of the Omaha trail followed the South Platte route for about two-thirds of the distance to Fort Kearny. No one in Omaha cared to admit that this was the same frequently denounced, muddy, grass-less trail used by Nebraska City freighters.[18]

When the gold fever was rising in the fall of 1858, the *Nebraska News* prophesied that the North Platte route would be "one of the awfulest muddiest roads that was ever traveled in any country. It will be next to impossible to get through at all, much less with a heavy load."[19] This criticism was often seconded with the advice that the Omaha road crossed "the Papillions, the Elkhorn, and Loup Fork, three large and bad streams, and a great number of smaller ones, *and the Platte the worst river to ford in the West*."[20] The fact that the first two "large and bad" streams were bridged did not seem worthy of mention in *Nebraska City* newspapers.

Competition from Omaha in 1859 brought home to Nebraska City freighters something Majors had preached from the start—the oxbow route was not satisfactory. It ran through much muddy bottom land and was overly long, considering that Nebraska City and Fort Kearny lay practically on the same parallel. In order to take advantage of this "airline" distance, a new road had to be laid out. Location of the direct road had been a matter of great concern in Nebraska City since the arrival of Russell, Majors &

Waddell. In 1858 a short route to Fort Kearny was reconnoitered
and measured. Ward B. Burnett, surveyor general of the United
States Land Office in Nebraska City, who traveled over the route,
wrote on January 11, 1859, that he expected the new road of about
180 miles to be in use during the following season. The proposed
trail as described by Burnett was practically the same as the road
that was finally established in 1860.[21] Burnett's expectations were
not fulfilled in 1859 as trail marking was postponed from month
to month. There was some aversion to using a route that did not
lie along a prominent stream where water, grass, and fuel were
abundant, and there was also criticism that the proposed route,
running only from Nebraska City, would be so isolated that it
would be an inviting target for marauding Indians.[22] However,
the main deterrent was strictly economic. Who would pay for the
fords and bridges necessary on Salt Creek, the Big Blue River,
and numerous smaller streams? Russell, Majors & Waddell had
received positive assurances from leading citizens that Nebraska
City would locate a new route, so the contractors naturally assumed
that any improvement cost would be borne by the community. The
town leaders, in turn, tried to obtain federal aid, which was not
forthcoming because the government had not only designated the
North Platte route from Omaha to Fort Kearny as the military
road but had improved it in places and, logically, could not justify
two government roads to the fort.[23] Lack of federal support seemed
to leave Nebraska City no choice. The road would have to be
located and improved through local enterprise. However, continued
procrastination by town leaders forced Majors to take the initiative
in organizing public support.

On Saturday, February 11, Majors, at a public meeting in Nebraska City, repeated much of what he had said two years earlier.
The town needed to improve the levee. It should be roomy enough
for teams to turn and should be macadamized so that it would
be an all-weather facility. The second great need was to improve
the trail from the river to the high ground about fifteen miles west
of town. Majors suggested that Nebraska City buy land flanking
this fifteen-mile stretch of trail to prevent farmers from tilling and
fencing the adjacent prairie. He well realized from experiences at
Leavenworth that many farmers located along the trail were detri-
mental to the freighter who had quantities of stock to graze. If

Nebraska City would do these things, Majors asserted, it could command a trade of as much as 20,000,000 pounds in 1860.[24]

Evidently Majors had much greater success in convening public meetings than he did in stimulating public action. Since the community would not act, he hired August F. Harvey, the city engineer, to survey and mark a direct route to Fort Kearny. Harvey, following almost the same route Burnett traveled in 1858, succeeded in marking a trail that saved about twenty miles but more importantly provided firmer passage than the oxbow route. It did not realize the local ideal of an "airline," but it was considerably straighter than the old route. From Nebraska City to Olathe on Salt Creek, forty-six miles west, there was an established trail—the farm-to-market road of scattered homesteaders. (This trail ran past present Dunbar, Syracuse, and Palmyra to Saltillo, Olathe's successor, about six miles south of Lincoln.) It lay through an undulating prairie of long, grassy slopes that extended from the divide between the Platte and Kansas rivers. Occasional woods nestled in broad draws at the base of these hills. The entire area was broken by many little creeks and coulees. While not wide, these cuts were quite deep and steep and could not be readily crossed. To take advantage of higher ground and to avoid washouts, the trail was moderately serpentine, wending along the sides of the long ridges. Where creeks had to be crossed, it was necessary to make fords or construct bridges. This improvement was done generally by settlers along the Little Nemaha and Salt creeks, who were first of all interested in their own transportation but who also intended to benefit by selling provisions to travelers. The Salt Creek ford was made by filling the creek and its deeply cut banks with ten feet of rock and stone.[25] Harvey's real work started beyond Salt Creek where there was no well defined trail and settlers were the exception rather than the rule. Harvey must have had Burnett's survey or at least knowledge of it, but he still had to make his own measurements and markings. The nearly 100 mile section of trail from Salt Creek to the Platte was marked by a single furrow ripped by a breaking plow drawn by a four-mule team that followed along after the surveyors.[26] From Salt Creek the road was marked almost due west to the Big Blue River, which was crossed about midway between present Milford and Crete. Here just north of the forks a rock ford was laid, and the road then followed along the north side of the North Fork to near the mouth of Beaver Creek, which was forded near the spot where Beaver Crossing was later located. For nearly forty miles it paralleled the creek, touching it only on the southernmost meanders of the stream, coming just about a mile south of present York and then tapering off slightly to the southwest. It passed about four miles south of present Aurora, where it left the headwaters of Beaver Creek, before finally coming out in the Platte Valley and joining the old road opposite Grand Island about forty miles northeast of Fort Kearny.[27]

The *People's Press* introduced the route on March 30, 1860, with screaming headlines: "THE NEW ROAD TO THE MINES! A STRAIGHT ROAD! SEVENTY-FIVE MILES SAVED!" It is noteworthy that the *Press* thought it necessary to use Omaha's exaggerated measurement of the old road in order to magnify the significance of the new one. Interestingly enough, the road was not ready for use when the first proclamations were issued. Early trains did not follow it, but hurried improvements enabled it to be used within a month. The Little Nemaha, which had been no problem for light farm wagons but which promised to be a barrier to heavy freight wagons, was bridged in one place and partially filled in another spot to provide a ford. Some more grading was done at the Salt Creek ford, and several little creeks between the Big Blue and the Platte were bridged.[28]

As marked by Harvey and his crew, the road measured 182 miles from Nebraska City to Fort Kearny. Subsequent bridging and straightening of loops during later years reduced this by a few miles.[29]

In 1860 the trail was heavily used and began to assert its supremacy over the North Platte route. In Nebraska City it was billed as the best road in the West. Oddly enough, the great noise about the cutoff emanating from south of the Platte was not heard in Omaha, where the press still matter-of-factly reported their old "official" distance from Nebraska City to Fort Kearny as 250 miles. The Nebraska City newspapers, while presenting the trail as the best, nevertheless were concerned that the apathetic citizenry would not finish the improvement of the route. At the end of its first season, the Airline Route (frequently called the "Great Central Airline Route" by Nebraska City newspapers) still lacked bridges over Salt Creek and the Big Blue River and had some unnecessary sinuosities. The *Nebraska News,* especially, kept the road issue alive between freighting seasons by making very definite recommendations for bridging and straightening the trail.[30]

Once the direct road to Fort Kearny was open, Nebraska City was able to compete effectively for the Colorado trade. Until 1860 freighting from Nebraska City was heavily dependent on government contracting. Despite its boastfulness, Nebraska City was not equipped in 1859 to be an outfitting place for the mines. It lacked a good levee. There was a definite shortage of wholesale merchants and outfitters, and the trail was not particularly advantageous over that of Atchison, or even Omaha. Russell, Majors & Waddell did some freighting to the mines in 1859 as did S. F. Nuckolls, but the great burst of activity came the next year.

While the wagon road to the interior was vital to Nebraska City, so also were transportation links to eastern supply points. A major development occurred in February, 1859, with the completion of the Hannibal & St. Joseph Railroad across northern Missouri. This provided a connection between the Missouri River and Chicago and points east, and for the first time St. Louis had some serious competition for the Missouri River trade. By railroad St. Joseph was within eleven hours of the Mississippi. It was not uncommon for St. Louis steamboats to take over a week to reach St. Joseph. The overall effect of the railroad was to make steamboat rates competitive, so goods shipped from St. Louis to St. Joseph by steamer were carried for about the same rate as St. Louis freight that went by way of Hannibal and the railroad. Shortly before the railroad was finished, some St. Joseph businessmen organized the Hannibal & St. Joseph Railroad Packet Line. Their purpose was to work in connection with the railroad by running a regular packet service to Council Bluffs, nearly 250 miles above St. Joseph. Nebraska City, slightly less than 200 miles above the railhead, benefited greatly from the packets. Two days was normally considered good time for the upstream trip, but the *William Campbell* once made it in twenty-two hours and fifty minutes.[31]

During the active season of 1859, from May through November, 212 steamboats laid down 9,280 tons of freight in Nebraska City. Most of this was undoubtedly transshipped to Utah by Russell, Majors & Waddell. The combination of this business and the prospect of a lively Colorado trade caused the city to engage a large number of men for repairing and macadamizing the levee.

This work was in progress when the first boats arrived in March, 1860. Before the season was out, the value of competitive transportation was clearly evident. Freight rates from St. Louis to Nebraska City, either by river or the combination of river and rail, were 30¢ to 50¢ per hundred, or only about a third to a half of what they had been two years earlier.[32]

Nebraska City, with its improved levee and improved transportation links, in 1860 made good its claim to be one of the best outfitting points for miners and emigrants. Russell, Majors & Waddell, with its great experience and capital, was in a position to plunge energetically into the Colorado trade. Its business was augmented by that of many other merchants and wholesalers. In April, 1860, Nebraska City had nine general merchandise firms, two hardware wholesalers, four drug and medical supply stores, and three boot and shoe stores. All of these depended in part on the Colorado trade, and all billed themselves as both retail and wholesale outlets.[33]

The opportunities offered by the expanding West can nowhere be better seen than in the activities of Russell, Majors & Waddell. During 1859–1860 what had once been a freighting concern was transformed into a complex of allied businesses that operated stores, express lines, and mail services. Because of the Colorado miners, the company established in Denver a general merchandise store managed by R. B. Bradford and called R. B. Bradford & Company. Opportunities to carry passengers, light freight, and mail to the mines caused Russell and a Leavenworth associate, John S. Jones, to start the Leavenworth & Pike's Peak Express Company. Russell, always scheming, bought the contract of John M. Hockaday which called for mail transportation from the Missouri River to Salt Lake City. Initially, the stages ran over the Republican River route, but by late June, 1859, after but a month's operation, Russell decided to use the Platte River route. This allowed him to combine his Denver and Salt Lake business. All of the Leavenworth & Pike's Peak Express Company stages started from Atchison. The mail coaches followed the same route to Julesburg, a newly established stage station near the Upper California Crossing, but from this point the Denver mail went by way of the South Platte route and the Utah mail by way of Fort Laramie and South Pass.[34] Due to heavy expenditures for equipment, livestock, and wages, and an unexpectedly poor business, the Leavenworth & Pike's Peak Express was bankrupt by late 1859. Russell and his associates organized a new company over the winter—the Central Overland California & Pike's Peak Express. The COCPP, which began operations in 1860, simply absorbed the defunct company. The cumbersomeness of the chartered name caused people to refer to the company as the Overland Stage. In addition to taking over the Denver and Salt Lake businesses, the Overland Stage mail transportation was extended from Salt Lake City to California when the company purchased that mail contract from George Chorpenning.[35] The stagecoach business of 1859–1860 added considerably to the freighting activities of Russell, Majors & Waddell because materials and supplies for the numerous way stations were transported by freight wagons.

Not content with freighting, merchandising, and expressing, the imaginative William Russell conceived the idea of a really fast Missouri River to California mail service. The result was the short-lived Pony Express, which began operating along the Platte and South Pass route in 1860. The Pony Express was one phase of Russell, Majors & Waddell's activities which benefited American romance rather than the purse of its originators.[36] These new activities of Russell, Majors & Waddell changed the nature of Nebraska City freighting in 1860. For the first time it was essentially a non-government business. Most of the freight was goods for the firm's store in Denver and corn and supplies for the Overland Stage and Pony Express lines. The freighting itself was not done by Russell, Majors & Waddell but instead by Majors alone, who owned wagons and oxen which were independent of the company. Although Majors operated his own freight line, he still supervised the freighting of military supplies from Kansas City for the company of Russell, Majors & Waddell. Because Majors spent so much time in Kansas City, his Nebraska City business was handled by Peter Byram, who had been the Nebraska City agent of Russell, Majors & Waddell in 1859. Byram and his brother Augustus, who worked with him, had been two of the most trusted lieutenants of Russell, Majors & Waddell, but after 1859 their association was with Majors rather than the firm. The relationship of the Byrams and Majors is somewhat uncertain. Local newspapers variously referred to Peter Byram as "superintendent" and "agent." Other times the Byrams were said to be "connected" with Majors, and on occasion they were called "sub-contractors." Several news items infer rather strongly that the brothers were operating their own business. In all likelihood the Byrams independently owned and operated some trains while managing Majors' business. Because of this duality, it would have been virtually impossible for newspapers to distinguish clearly between the Byram freight and the Majors freight. In summaries of the year's business the papers simply classified it all as having been shipped by Majors.[37]

Majors' trade was crammed into the early part of the season. By mid-July sixteen of the twenty trains sent out that year were on the road. During May and June, Byram dispatched at least one train a week and sometimes more. The trade was about equally divided between the express stations and the mines. The bulk of the freight for the express stations was corn for the horses and mules used in this business. The goods for Denver were the typical assortment—food, liquor, stoves, hardware, clothing, etc. Some of this was carried for R. B. Bradford & Company and some for various Nebraska City and Colorado merchants. Apparently Majors worked closely with the Hannibal & St. Joseph Railroad Packet Line. Through the Byrams he had an arrangement to accept freight in St. Joseph and forward it to the mines by way of Nebraska City. The Byrams advertised that they would deliver St. Joseph freight in Denver one week sooner and just as cheaply as shippers using any other route.[38]

From April 25 to October 13, 1860, Majors forwarded 2,782,258 pounds of freight from Nebraska City using 5,687 oxen, 515 wagons, 72 mules, and 602 men. While Majors was the biggest single freighter, he shared the trade with many other merchants and freighters.[39]

One significant aspect of the gold rush was that it encouraged numerous merchants to operate stores in both the Missouri River towns and the mining communities. They realized that by having two stores they could not only outfit the transient but the resident miners as well. Many of these merchants had sufficient capital to enable them to transport their own goods. The small merchant probably would not have had the wherewithal to buy wagons and oxen and hire men, so he generally had to depend on the commercial freighter. But the major wholesalers could very well afford to have their own trains and carry their own goods.

Several Nebraska City men became important in both freighting and merchandising. Outstanding in this group was S. F. Nuckolls, the pioneer banker, speculator, and merchant. After a slow start in 1859, Nuckolls greatly expanded his business the next year. In partnership with Robert Hawke, he established a store in Mountain City where he wholesaled and retailed "Provisions, Groceries, Foreign and Domestic Liquors, Hardware, Mining Tools, Iron, Steel Nails, Tinware, Cook Stoves, Heating Stoves, Dry goods, ready made clothing, Hats and Caps, Boots and Shoes, Queensware, Glassware, Stationery, etc."[40] With their first merchandise train they sent out a steam sawmill and "the most complete Quartz Mill yet designed and prepared for the Rocky Mountain country. It has twenty stamps and is propelled by an engine of thirty horsepower."[41] The partners' sawmill was soon turning out pine lumber and was reported to be "coining money fast," but they met with less success with the quartz mill.[42] At one point they were said to be planning to send out sixty wagons loaded with supplies and groceries. They advertised that by the end of September they would have hauled 250 tons of merchandise to Mountain City with their own teams.[43] A rough estimate culled from numerous newspaper references is that Hawke & Nuckolls sent about one hundred wagonloads of supplies to the mines and various way points, which seems to bear out their claims.

Two other Nebraska City firms, John Bueter & Company and Goodlet & Gregg, established branch stores in the mining area and supplied them with their own wagons. Another company, Bailey & Hollister, transported goods to the mines and sold them during the summer and fall.[44] The partners' experience was that their venture was "not altogether unprofitable."[45] The frequency with which this type of business was repeated indicates that it could prove to be very profitable for a man willing to take many risks—physical as well as economic.

Expanding demands for goods caused a number of small-scale freighters to enter the trade. They sometimes carried goods for hire, but more likely than not they engaged in speculation, purchasing supplies, particularly flour, in Nebraska City and attempting to resell them in Denver or nearby towns. During the Mormon War very little flour was milled in the Nebraska City area, but by 1860 quantities of this locally produced commodity could be purchased in Otoe and Cass counties for as little as $2.50 per hundred pounds. The Colorado price of $15 to $17 per hundred was enough to cause an active flour trade even during the winter months. In January, 1860, a Mr. Carpenter took two wagonloads of flour to

Denver and sold it rapidly at $15 a hundred.[46] Jonathan Raley and a Mr. Jacobs commonly bought flour and other foodstuffs in Nebraska City and then struck boldly across the plains. Jacobs conducted a regular shuttle. By mid-June he had made four round trips, with the first being completed in the dead of winter. D. C. Corbin hauled powder to the mines; Thomas Chivington, J. H. and H. C. Cowles, and John McMechan, Jr., freighted hardware and food. These men may have accounted for a total trade of about fifty wagonloads. While their business was not extensive in 1860, it did contribute to the overall economy of Nebraska City, and their success encouraged other small operators to enter the trade.[47]

While Nebraska City freighters were taking advantage of the new direct road, their Omaha rivals were struggling to establish their city as a major freighting point north of the Platte. The city was advantageously located with regard to Chicago and points east, and by the beginning of the Colorado gold rush a railroad had been extended as far west as Iowa City. This railhead was more in line with Omaha than with any other city.

Omaha, as the northernmost outfitting point on the Missouri, logically commanded much of the emigrant traffic that came by way of Chicago and Iowa City. Because of its reputation as a starting point for the Mormons and the California miners, Omaha was nationally known and attracted great numbers of Colorado miners. These people were vitally concerned with, among other things, starting from a place where they might be conveniently and economically outfitted. Omaha and Council Bluffs, twin towns on opposite banks of the Missouri, had more to offer in this respect than any place north of St. Joseph. It was the Omaha and Council Bluffs merchants who pioneered freighting along the North Platte route.

Freighting from Omaha in 1859 was practically non-existent, but legitimate gold discoveries which assured some stability for the new mining area caused Council Bluffs and Omaha merchants to become interested in supplying Denver and the mining towns. Like Nebraska City, Council Bluffs and Omaha were supplied by river, either from St. Louis or the railhead at St. Joseph. Council Bluffs freighters were somewhat handicapped by being on the east bank of the river. Sometimes they crossed wagons on the ice before the spring break-up, but in most instances their freight was ferried during the navigation season.

The major Omaha freighter of 1860 was the merchandise firm of Lacey & McCormick, headed by Jesse H. Lacey and John Mc-Cormick. These dealers in groceries, provisions, liquors, and general outfitting goods sent out at least four trains loaded with provisions for the sutler at Fort Kearny and the mines. J. J. and R. A. Brown sent one small train to their branch stores in Denver, and the merchandising firm of A. H. Blair outfitted at least one train. F. Smith of Smith, Parmalee & Company also sent a train to Mountain City.[48] At one point Omaha merchants reported an inability to fill orders from the mines because they did not have enough teams or wagons. This opened the way for some small freighters, including W. Martin, James O'Banion, James Creighton, and King & Wood, to buy supplies in Omaha for resale in Colorado.[49]

Lacey & McCormick was closely rivaled by the Council Bluffs general merchandising firm of Pegram & Warner, which sent one large train loaded with fifty tons of flour and a smaller one loaded with general provisions. Pegram traveled to Denver with the first train and established a branch store there. Only one other Council Bluffs company was in the trade. This was the flour mill of Baldwin & Dodge which carried some of its own product to Denver.[50]

By Omaha standards the 1860 freighting was lively. During the year about 150 to 200 wagonloads of goods were sent to the mines and way points. This was such a sharp increase over previous years that perhaps The *Republican* should not be judged too harshly for being presumptuous. Omaha was said to be "fast assuming the precedence over all other points on the river as a place for freighters to purchase their goods and start their trains for the mines."[51] Certainly Omaha had no more than a fraction of the trade Nebraska City had. It was likewise in the wake of Atchison and even of Leavenworth. It would have to be said for Omaha that it was the major and only freighting point north of the Platte, but it did not measure up to its South Platte rivals.

The Colorado trade from Atchison and Leavenworth followed the pattern of the Nebraska City business. In 1859 it was clearly subordinate to the Utah business, but in 1860 it was the staple of freighting. Of the 709 wagons started from Atchison in 1859 only 46 were sent to the mines. In 1860 about 70 per cent of the season's total freight of 1,773 loads amounting to 8,220,883 pounds was sent to Denver and the mining towns.

Most of these wagons were outfitted by three large Atchison mercantile firms, A. S. Parker & Company, Home & Choteau, and D. W. Adams. Atchison had more freighters than any of its serious rivals for the Colorado trade. About three dozen different parties engaged in freighting during the year. The largest businesses were those of D. D. White and Jones & Cartwright.[52]

Leavenworth, in comparison with Atchison, had a small business and very few freighters. In fact, the great bulk of the business was done by two firms. Leavenworth had benefited from the military contracting in 1858 but had lost this business to Nebraska City in 1859 and to Atchison in 1860. Without the military freighting there was some question as to the business stability of Leavenworth, which was the largest town in Kansas Territory. Fortunately for Leavenworth, the local general mercantile firm of Jones & Cartwright chose to do most of its freighting from its home town. John S. Jones and Dr. Joseph L. Cartwright established a branch store in Denver in 1859 and supplied it with over 100 wagonloads of nearly three tons each. With their greatly expanded operations of the next year they sent twenty-two trains to Denver. These were all large trains, varying from twenty to twenty-eight wagons, so their business must have amounted to well over 500 wagonloads. Three of the trains were sent from Atchison and the remainder from Leavenworth. Only one other firm, Marshal & Company, was very active out of Leavenworth. Marshal had sent out 122 wagons by mid-June. The combined business of Jones & Cartwright and Marshal & Company was practically the sum total of Leavenworth freighting. Between the two firms Leavenworth probably had about one-third of the amount of Atchison's freight. One of the major items in the Leavenworth trade was quartz mills. Jones & Cartwright acted as agent for St. Louis foundries, and Leavenworth also had its own quartz mill manufacturer in Maison, Wilson & Company. By June 1, 159 quartz mills had been shipped from Leavenworth, Atchison, and St. Joseph. Twenty of these had been manufactured in Leavenworth.[53]

Freighting to Colorado tended to be much less seasonal than freighting to Utah. It was only half as far from the Missouri to Colorado destinations as it was to points in Utah, and the Colorado markets were not separated from their supply sources by the mountain barrier. The comparatively short distance and the absence of a major geographic barrier had two important effects. First of all, several trips were possible during the course of a season. Depending on the size of the load, type and condition of animals, and firmness of the trail, the average freight train took slightly more than a month to reach Denver from Nebraska City or Omaha. The return trip, normally made with empty wagons and possibly a few passengers, was negotiated in about half this time. So a freighter using oxen could start early in May when the grass was sufficiently high and still easily work in two round trips. Secondly, since the mountains did not have to be crossed, it was possible to make winter trips. The winter trade was never great compared to that of the spring and summer, but after 1858 there was always someone willing to risk blizzards and cold to take advantage of a demanding market. These winter expeditions were possible because the trail was generally open on the plains, something which was not true of the mountain route to Utah.

The relative proximity of Denver caused many little freighters, so-called "shotgun" freighters because of their express service, to engage in the business. A man with two or three wagons was easily led to believe that he could cover 500 miles quite rapidly without trouble. When one considers the thousands of wagons on the Platte River route during the spring, it is unlikely that the two-wagon man was ever out of sight of other freighters or emigrants. Also, the general passivity of the plains Indians in 1859–1860 may have encouraged the small freighter to attempt the Denver trade. The freighters of little means were characteristic of the Denver and way points trade. They did not engage in the Utah business because they did not feel equipped to cope with the distance and the mountains. Of course, if Utah had had a gold rush comparable to that of Colorado, there might have been shotgun freighters bold enough to attempt even this distance.

The Colorado business also raised the problem of wintering stock. In Utah freighting, oxen were very often sold at Salt Lake City or were even driven to California and sold. But since Colorado did not have a population that needed numerous cattle for draft purposes and miners preferred meat other than ox steak, there was little opportunity to sell the stock if they were on the western end of the trail at season's end. Furthermore, oxen were not used in the winter trade, so thousands of them had to be wintered. In Colorado the cattle were commonly herded on the public domain along the Cache la Poudre River in the north and the Arkansas

River in the south. On the eastern end of the trail the normal
practice was to distribute oxen among farmers for wintering. This
proved to be quite a good business for farmers in the Nebraska City
and Brownville area, where ample hay was available. Most of the
cattle wintered in Colorado were herded to the Missouri in late
winter or early spring. Some were used to haul back the empty
wagons.⁵⁴

The major freight destination in Colorado was Denver. Nearly
all wagons went to or through it. Advantageously located at the
eastern base of the mountains, Denver soon became the great outfitting point for the mountain towns and camps. Heavy freight
wagons could reach it with comparative ease, and most of the big
merchants had stores there. Since the roads into the mountains
were narrow and treacherous, goods were sometimes transferred
at Denver from heavy to light wagons. Many times, however, the
heavy freight wagons went on to such places as Blackhawk or
Mountain City. Usually the entire train would go through Denver,
where some of the wagons were unloaded, thereby making available ·
the extra oxen needed to pull the mountain-bound wagons up
steep grades.

The costliness of outfitting trains, the distance to Colorado,
frontier inflation, and the lack of serious competition from other
markets kept freight rates high from the Missouri River to the
mines. Within this characteristically high range there were sharp
fluctuations caused by the supply and demand on the Denver
market. Basically there was a seasonal price change. During the
winter and early spring when few goods were available, market
prices and freight charges were considerably higher than those of
late summer and fall after the markets had been replenished.
Within any given season, however, there were day-to-day changes
because the amount of imports could not be accurately foretold.
An arrival of a large shipment of flour, for example, would cause
a decline in the market price, which in turn would soon reduce
the freight charges since they were essentially determined by the
price differential between the Missouri River and Denver market
prices. The mercurial market was many times affected by emigrants
who dumped any surpluses they might have on the Denver market.
Since the shortages of Colorado were well known, many emigrants
carried extra goods with the design of selling them. The Denver
market was said to be so touchy that it changed with the arrival

of each train. The *Rocky Mountain Herald* of May 12, 1860, stated that the market might be "bare of certain articles to-day, and glutted with them in a week." In 1860 before the large trains arrived, flour per hundredweight commanded $20 to $22 on the Denver market, an advance of $6 to $7 over the previous fall. But by July, 1860, the price had declined to $14 to $15, where it held throughout the late summer and fall.[55]

When flour was bringing up to $22 a hundred, the freight rates from the river were $12 to $15 a hundred, but when flour fell to $15, the rates dropped to $8 to $10 per hundred. Rates were figured with Denver as the destination and extra charges were added for transportation to the outlying mountain towns. For example, in May, 1860, it cost $3.50 to $4 per hundred to ship goods from Denver to Mountain City only thirty-five miles away and $8 for the eighty-mile trip to Tarryall. This meant that the freight charges from the river to Tarryall amounted to about $28 to $30 a hundred. As the season advanced, the Denver to mountain town rates declined in proportion to the decline in the river to Denver rates. By September, when the rate from the Missouri River to Denver was $8 to $10, the Denver to Tarryall rate was $5.[56] Rates reported in the Denver newspapers were undoubtedly rough approximations; not all supplies were carried for the same rate. Freighters always made a distinction between heavy and bulky goods, with the higher rates applied to the latter. Any commodity of great density such as shelled corn or flour would be classified as heavy goods. Such goods could be easily handled and tightly packed. Items such as glassware and furniture, while not particularly heavy, took much space. Thus, at any given time the rates on furniture might be as much as three times those on flour. It should be kept in mind, however, that the preponderance of freight was heavy goods. It is likely that the rates reported in Denver papers applied primarily to heavy freight. Table 3 illustrates the differences in rates for heavy, compact freight and light, bulky freight.

A very important effect of the Colorado gold rush, and one which contributed immeasurably to freighting, was increased business along the main trails to Denver. Many of the gold seekers were poorly provisioned and had to purchase supplies, food, and even animals and wagons enroute. Even those who planned carefully often required the services of blacksmiths and wheelwrights. Unlike the earlier movement to California, Oregon, and Utah,

TABLE 3

ATCHISON TO DENVER FREIGHT RATES*

Commodity	Rate per Pound	Commodity	Rate per Pound
Flour	9 ¢	Crackers	17 ¢
Tobacco	12½	Whisky	18
Sugar	13½	Glass	19½
Bacon	15	Trunks	25
Dry goods	15	Furniture	31

*Frank A. Root and William E. Connelley, *Overland Stage to California* (Topeka, Kansas, 1901), p. 303.

the Colorado traffic was two-way because thousands of miners returned to the East for the winter. This traffic created an unusually heavy need for road stations. Many miners stopped at these stations only for emergencies or to replenish provisions, but those who traveled by stagecoach had to obtain meals and lodging along the trail.

Soon the great thoroughfare was dotted with trading posts called ranches, the same term used to designate way stations along the Santa Fe Trail. The ranches were situated some distance from each other. Quite often this was a day's travel for those moving with ox teams. Ranchemen, whenever possible, preempted the choicest sites near timber and springs, but some ranches had no particular advantage other than distance from a competitor.

The usual ranche was a small dwelling with an attached stable and corral, but a few were much more extensive and some even evolved into small villages. Ranche buildings came in a variety of sizes, ranging from small dugouts to Jack Morrow's two-and-a-half story, sixty-foot-long house. The typical ranches were made of logs heavily chinked with clay and mud. Some were made of sod, others of adobe. The roofs were always made of clay. Poles were intersticed with willow brush, and then covered with grass and six to ten inches of clay; it was then tamped down hard and left to bake in the sun. The final product was an impervious, concrete-like roof.[57] Interior walls were often lined with skins, robes, and cloth, and the floors were "oftenest such as nature offers only."[58]

Ranches were many things, depending on the needs and desires of the customer. They were first of all grocery stores. Some of the larger ones also handled general merchandise. They all peddled liquor by the bottle or by the drink. Invariably they were mail stations and stage stops. They were also restaurants, and the reputations of good and bad houses were soon widely known; stages tried to stop for meals at the best places. To the stage passengers, ranches were either "swing stations," where only teams were exchanged, or "home stations," where meals were taken. The staples of ranche meals, wrote Samuel Bowles, were bacon, eggs, hot biscuits, tea, coffee, dried peaches and apples, and pies. While describing the food as "very good," he was somewhat grieved that "each meal was the same; breakfast, dinner and supper were undistinguishable save by the hour."[59]

The better houses kept chickens and served fresh ranche eggs in preference to imported, or "State," eggs. There were, of course, exceptions to the general diet. Beef was sometimes served, and Capt. Eugene Ware recalled being treated to a "regular pioneer banquet" by rancheman Jack Morrow. It included broiled antelope heart, baked buffalo hump, fried beaver tails, and champagne served in tin cups.[60]

Overnight accommodations were hard to find at ranches and were usually makeshift. Only a few of the large ranches had rooms. Quite commonly stage passengers bedded down on the floor or in the stables. Even though emigrants with their own transportation did not put up at ranches, they normally clustered near them in the belief that they were much less likely to be menaced by Indians there than on the open prairie.

Ranchemen always had work stock on hand for sale or trade to emigrants and freighters. Quite often sore-footed oxen were taken in on trade. The usual deal was to take two lame animals in exchange for one sound one. The ranche operator would merely put the lame beasts out to pasture and allow them to rest and graze. Many times, as soon as the beast lost its limp, he would trade it off as good stock. There were naturally complaints about ranchemen peddling seemingly sound animals that gave out in a few days. Sizeable herds were built up in the two-to-one trading, and oftentimes there were chances to sell animals at high prices if travelers had lost stock. John Bratt claimed that Jack Morrow gained a "hard reputation" for his lively business in selling oxen for exorbitant sums. Many trains were suddenly victimized by Indian thieves near his ranche. Naturally their only recourse was to purchase animals from Morrow, who always seemed to have some on hand.[61]

Many freighters had their own replacements for lame stock and wanted only to leave the injured animals at ranches. In these instances where no trade or sale was involved, the rancheman charged a fee for caring for the animal. Charles McDonald, operator of the Cottonwood Springs Ranche, kept a very detailed account book, and the following are typical entries covering the care of cattle:

> November 13, 1862; Philip Gomer of Denver left a large red ox to be ranched at the rate of $2.50 per month.
>
> . . . .
>
> October 27, 1863. Received of I. S. Remick one blue steer belonging to A. & P. Byram to be kept at the rate of $2.50 per month.[62]

McDonald performed other services for freighters. He stored quantities of grain and then released them to the wagonmasters of the depositor upon demand. If the original depositor sold grain, then McDonald handled that transaction. He also stored freighters' supplies and equipment, including wagons and ox yokes. Although freighters were more independent than stage lines or emigrants, they still welcomed the system of ranches and made extensive use of them.[63]

After two years of gold rush there were, according to one emigrants' guide, forty-four ranches between Fort Kearny and Denver. Most of the small ones were nondescript affairs and made little impression outside of their locale, but some of the larger ranches were known "from Omaha to sunset." Major ranchemen continually advertised in Nebraska City and Omaha newspapers, and were usually singled out in press notices as rather prominent personages when they came east to purchase supplies. There were, of course, ranches along all routes, including the rather well settled North Platte trail from Omaha, but ranches had their greatest impact in the comparatively isolated country that had not yet been touched by farmers.[64]

Dobytown was the first point beyond Fort Kearny where migrants could stop, but it was not a desirable layout. This cluster of adobe shacks, only two miles from the fort and just off the western edge of the military reservation, was by all accounts a lecherous place

Northern
Trails
To Denver

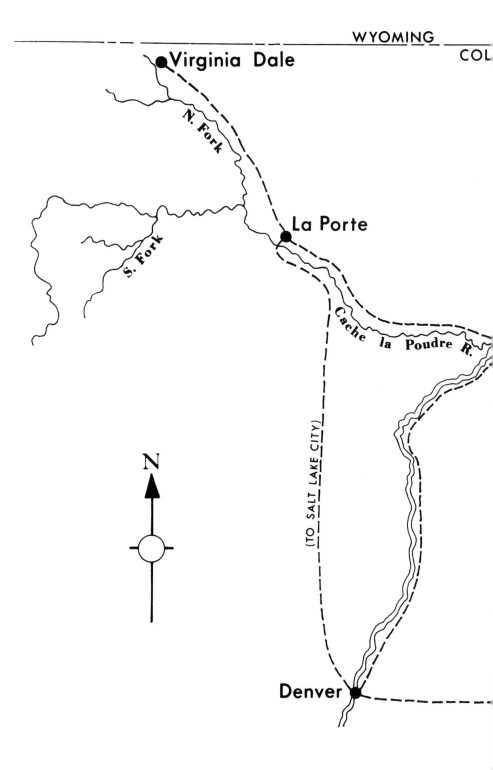

WYOMING

COL

Virginia Dale

N. Fork

La Porte

S. Fork

Cache la Poudre R.

(TO SALT LAKE CITY)

N

Denver

NORTHERN

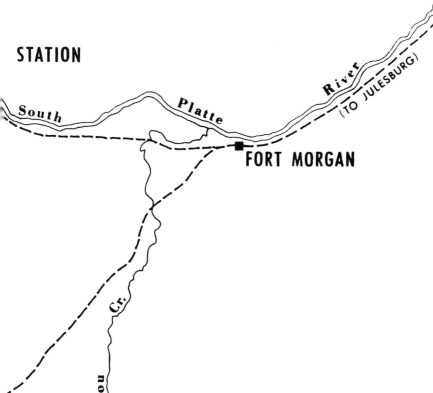

NEBRASKA

LEGEND
HISTORIC PLACES___ ___ ___ ■
TRAIL ROUTES___ ___ ___ ‿‿

0   10   20   30   40
miles

STATION

South   Platte   River

(TO JULESBURG)

■ FORT MORGAN

Bijou Cr.

TO DENVER

Bullwhackers and muleskinners represent one of the least-remembered frontier types, yet their service in the West was of heroic proportions.

—from an old sketch
Nebraska State Historical Society

Atchison, Kansas, a Missouri River port, became a major depot for overland freighting after 1855. Photo shows Commercial Street in the early 1860's.

—Kansas State Historical Society

Leavenworth, Kansas, never a great factor in private freighting operations, was important due to the nearby Fort Leavenworth quartermaster depot. Photo is of entrance to the fort about 1872.

—Kansas State Historical Society

Nebraska City, because of its favorable location, was chosen in 1858 as base of operation for the famed Russell, Majors & Waddell freighting firm. Sketch by Alfred E. Mathews is of Nebraska City street scene in 1865.

—Nebraska State Historical Society

The Outfitting Building, a brick structure used by Russell, Majors & Waddell in Nebraska City during its operations in the 1860's, later was remodeled and served as a school building by Nebraska College and Otoe University.

—Nebraska State Historical Society

NEW ADVERTISEMENTS.

ARMY OF THE WEST!

16,000 YOKE

OF

GOOD WORKING CATTLE,

From Four to 7 years of age, wanted at

NEBRASKA CITY,

for hauling freight from this point to Utah, for which SEVENTY-FIVE DOLLARS per Yoke will be paid. Notice will be given through the newspapers of the time they are to be delivered, but suppose they will be wanted about the first of May.

FIFTEEN HUNDRED MEN

Wanted for teamsters who will be found and paid Twenty-five dollars per month out and back.

None but men of good habits need apply; as drinking intoxicating liquors, card playing; and profane language will not be permitted while in employment. Each man will be presented with a Bible and hymn book. Forty Wagon Masters wanted who must come well recommended and who will be paid the usual wages.

A number of houses will be rented in Nebraska City, and one large store room. Apply to
RUSSELL, MAJORS & WADDEL.
by KINNEY & HOLLY, Agents.   Mr 20-4

Russell, Majors and Waddell used the newspapers to advertise for teamsters and draft animals for their freighting trains. Advertisement is from the Nebraska City News, *March, 1857.*

—Nebraska State Historical Society

The St. Louis Wholesale and Retail Store was operated by Kalkman & Wessels in Nebraska City from about 1858 to 1868.

Plattsmouth, Nebraska, during peak years of trade in the 1860's, gained a significant share of overland freighting. Photo of the Missouri River waterfront was taken by the Burlington & Missouri (about 1872) after wagon trains had been replaced by the railroads.

Herman Kountze

Alexander Majors

Edward Creighton

James R. Porter

Eugene Munn

James H. Pratt

Prominent figures in the central Plains and mid-Rockies.

Fort Kearny was located midway across Nebraska where trails from the Missouri River converged. Its garrison was important in patrolling the Oregon Trail. Photo by C. E. Mills is of parade ground and officers' quarters in 1858.

Gold dust mined in Colorado was transported from Denver eastward by overland stage. This receipt, issued in August 1862 to John B. Kuony, was for gold valued at $19.50. The shipment was sent to E. H. Warner in Omaha via Fort Kearny.

Fort Cottonwood (Fort McPherson after 1866) was located near the confluence of the North Platte and South Platte rivers about 100 miles west of Fort Kearny. The trail divided west of here, the south branch entering Colorado, the north moving toward Wyoming. Maj. George M. O'Brien made this sketch in 1864.

—Joslyn Art Museum, Omaha

Chimney Rock, located south of the Platte River near present-day Bayard in western Nebraska, became the most famous landmark on the Plains section of the Oregon Trail. This photo, taken in 1966, presents an eroded spire significantly smaller than that seen by the traveler a century ago.

—Nebraska State Historical Society

inhabited by liquor peddlers, gamblers, thieves, and prostitutes—all of whom had but one real business—bleeding troops, emigrants, and freighters.[65]

The first important ranche beyond Fort Kearny was Hopetown at Seventeen Mile Point. This was maintained by Moses H. Sydenham, a native Englishman who had spent some time as a seaman. After drifting West he acquired a number of interests. He first worked for the Fort Kearny trader and then was appointed postmaster at the fort, a position he retained throughout his ranche days. The Gilman brothers, Jerry and Jud, kept a large ranche about seventy-five miles from Fort Kearny or fifteen miles east of Cottonwood Springs. Jerry, the older, was a widely known trail character. He had, it was said, participated in one of Wee Willy Walker's Caribbean filibustering expeditions. Later Gilman tried moving overland to California, but his team broke down, so he stayed on the spot to become a rancheman. The Gilmans kept large stocks of supplies—sometimes, they claimed, as much as $50,000 worth.[66]

The Cottonwood Springs Ranche was one of the largest. It was located near good springs and unlimited supplies of timber and was also at the celebrated Indian portage of the Platte. The grandest ranche both in size and notoriety was only twelve miles uptrail from Cottonwood Springs. This was Junction Ranche, just south of the confluence of the two Plattes, owned and operated by Jack Morrow, whose name was known throughout Nebraska and Colorado. Morrow was part man and part legend. Everyone knew him, but no one seems to have known much about his past. He was rumored to be exceptionally rich. He was said to be untrustworthy. It was claimed that he had two Indian wives. It was widely believed that he had a quick gun and had killed several men. It was claimed that he had no equal in poker. He enjoyed a great reputation as an Indian trader, and his livestock holdings caused one contemporary to picture him as "one of the cattle kings of the great Platte valley."[67] Morrow played his part as a frontier character well. When John Bratt met him, the noted rancheman was wearing a diamond thought to be worth $1,000 on a badly soiled yellow shirt. Another bullwhacker, Julius C. Birge, pictured him as a powerful, athletic man with a brace of revolvers on his waist. Eugene Ware saw Morrow as a "tall, rawboned, dangerous-looking man, wearing a mustache, and a goatee on his under lip."[68]

There was no doubt about Morrow's stature near the junction. He was the lord of the region. Ware reported that Morrow held a virtual timber monopoly because he had cut great quantities of cedar in the canyons south of the ranche and prevented anyone else from doing so. According to Bratt there was no way to avoid Morrow's place. All trains were forced to pass right by the ranche because it was located between a canyon on the south and a specially constructed irrigation ditch on the north which prevented wagons from passing between the ranche and the Platte. Morrow, who must have been one of the richest men on the trail, claimed to have $100,000 in buildings, cattle, and supplies.[69]

The main ranche west of Jack Morrow's was the Williams' Ranche at the west edge of O'Fallon's Bluffs, the last timbered place for many miles. This was operated by Bob Williams, a veteran Indian trader, and his brother W. C., a former Nebraska City photographer. Like other ranchemen in the buffalo country, the Williamses did a considerable robe trade with the Sioux and Cheyenne in addition to their regular ranche business.[70]

It would be impossible to establish explicitly the quantity of the ranche trade, but there can be no doubt that it was quite important to both Missouri River merchants and overland freighters. The ranchemen sometimes hauled their own supplies, but the usual pattern was for them to depend on freighters for the heavy goods and stagecoaches for the light freight.

Colorado and ranche freighting surpassed but did not supplant other types in 1860. The old destinations of the military posts and Utah, while not nearly as important in the total trade as in the past, were still significant. Troop reassignment and the phasing out of most of the Utah army caused changes in the amount and nature of the military trade. Most of the troops at Camp Floyd, some 1,400, were transferred to forts in New Mexico. On June 30 Col. Edwin V. Sumner, commander of the Department of the West, reported the combined strength of Camp Floyd and Fort Bridger to be slightly over 800. The two other posts in Sumner's department, Fort Kearny and Fort Laramie, had garrisons of 206 and 333 men, respectively.[71]

Supplying this reduced but still rather large army was attractive to freighters and resulted in serious competition to Russell, Majors, & Waddell and broke the monopoly it had held in the military trade through five years. In July, 1859, the army, through newspapers in Missouri River towns, advertised for bids for transporting army supplies for 1860 and 1861 over three numbered routes. Route 1 was the Oregon Trail and Utah areas, Route 2, the Santa Fe Trail to Fort Union, New Mexico, and Route 3, forts in New Mexico to be supplied from Fort Union.[72] Russell, Majors, and Waddell wanted the entire business, but they were successful only in the competition for Routes 2 and 3. The Route 1 trade went to the newly organized company of J. C. Irwin and Allison White, called J. C. Irwin & Company.

The end of the monopoly came about because of the strengths of the new firm and the weaknesses of the old. J. C. Irwin of Kansas City and Allison White of Atchison were men of means and experience. Irwin, originally from Pennsylvania, represented a group of Pennsylvanians in the company who had extensive available finances from Philadelphia banks—particularly Jay Cooke & Company. While the new company lacked the practical experience of Russell, Majors & Waddell, there seemed to be no reservation about its finances or ambitions. Apparently the government regarded it as a promising concern, an estimate borne out by its subsequent successes.

It is unlikely that Russell, Majors & Waddell at this time had the equipment or the money to handle the entire business. The company had sold many wagons and oxen after the Mormon War. Its 1857 claim against the government for transporting extra supplies during the Mormon War had not been honored, and other ventures such as R. B. Bradford & Company and the Leavenworth & Pike's Peak Express had ended as financial failures. Even if the company had been completely solvent, there is a good possibility that the government would have shied away from giving it the entire business—particularly when a competent rival existed. Russell, Majors, and Waddell had suffered considerably in public esteem by 1859. Already stigmatized by their association with slavery and with the unpopular Mormon War, they further incurred public censure by foolishly violating the spirit of a government flour contract. They were to supply Camp Floyd with St. Louis flour, but instead they substituted Utah flour and collected freight charges from the Missouri River on flour that they had not actually transported. This affair was widely broadcast by Horace Greeley, then on his overland tour. Through the *New York Tribune* and his later travel account, Greeley frankly spoke of this alleged swindle.[73]

The loss of the Route 1 business ended Russell, Majors & Waddell's freighting through the Platte Valley. As the partners were soon to find, their misfortunes in 1860 were but the beginning of complete collapse.

The gist of the Irwin contract was publicly known by late October, but the actual agreement between Irwin and White and Maj. E. S. Sibley was not signed until February 14, 1860. It was drawn up like previous contracts—the rates were to vary from season to season, and a distinction was made between freight to Fort Laramie and way points and places beyond Fort Laramie. The rate provisions, expressed in hundred pounds per hundred miles, are shown in Table 4.

TABLE 4

Rates on Route 1 Military Freight—1860*

Rates	Jan.	Feb.	Mar.	Apr.	May	June	July	Aug.	Sept.	Oct.	Nov.	Dec.
To Ft. Laramie & intermediate destinations	2.00	2.00	1.75	1.45	1.19	1.19	1.19	1.19	1.50	1.75	1.75	1.75
To points beyond Ft. Laramie	2.00	2.00	1.75	1.45	1.34	1.34	1.34	1.34	1.75	1.75	1.75	1.75

*House Exec. Doc. 22, 36 Cong., 1 Sess, (Serial 1047), p. 23.

The *Nebraska News* of October 22, 1859, optimistically assumed that Irwin would ship from Nebraska City for the next two years, but in a few months this certainty had changed to the pronouncement that "we have information from a reliable source, that Messrs. Irving [sic] & Co., have determined upon doing a large portion, if not all of their freighting from this place."[74] And so it went—from the certain, to the uncertain, to nothing; early in April Irwin announced that Atchison would be his starting point.[75]

Most of the Irwin-carried freight went to Fort Laramie. Fort Kearny was the second destination and Utah the third. The total trade amounted to 444 wagons and 2,524,482 pounds of freight. Ten trains with a total of 312 wagons carried 800,000 pounds of goods to Fort Laramie, six trains totaling 106 wagons transported 598,000 pounds to Fort Kearny, and two trains with a total of 26 wagons carried 126,482 pounds of supplies to Utah.[76]

The sharp decline in military freighting to Utah was accompanied by a corresponding drop in the merchant trade. Both the end of the war economy and a new era of Mormon self-sufficiency were responsible. The drastic reductions of federal expenditures and manpower affected the Salt Lake City markets. C. A. Perry & Company, one of the main freighting and merchant concerns in 1858 and 1859, closed its doors in 1860 and assigned its goods to eastern creditors. The *Deseret News* of August 15, 1860, observed that "there are but very few merchants importing goods, into the Territory this season, and it is but reasonable to suppose that many of the mercantile establishments will close up their business soon, and try their fortunes in some other locality unless something transpires that is not now anticipated."

Withdrawal of many of the major Gentile trading companies resulted in a Mormon takeover of the trade in 1860. Mormon merchants cooperating with the church not only carried freight but escorted emigrants as well. These "church trains," as they were called, were usually assembled in Salt Lake City and sent east empty in the spring, particularly to Omaha and Florence. Merchandise was then purchased in Omaha, but the trains rendezvoused in nearby Florence, the assembly point for Mormon migrants. The church trains replaced the handcarts that had been used experimentally for several years. Capt. William Budge, in charge of a large emigrant company, led a train of 70 wagons and over 400 persons from Florence to Salt Lake City. Smaller trains were brought through by Capt. Joseph W. Young and Capt. E. D. Woolley.[77]

While the bulk of the business was done by these officially organized trains which had designated captains, there was some trade by private Salt Lake City merchants. Hooper & Eldridge, the successor of Holladay & Warner, prepared a train of twenty-five wagons at Omaha and Florence, and A. R. Wright, another merchant, outfitted ten wagons. The ability of Utahans to carry most of their own freight signaled not only a new plateau of economic achievement for them but definitely lessened their dependence on professional freighters based in the Missouri River towns. One Omaha firm, Porter & Duell, did send out a train of sixty wagons for Utah, but this was an exception to the general pattern in 1860. This new trade arrangement greatly benefitted Omaha, which became the chief outfitting point for Utah.[78]

Next to Omaha, Atchison was the main supply point for civilian Utah goods. Over 100 wagonloads, amounting to about 400,000 pounds, were sent from that point to Salt Lake City. Nebraska City did not have any great stake in the Utah business of 1860. Some sutler's stores for Camp Floyd were started there but evidently little else.[79]

During 1860, the major focus of overland freighting had shifted. Colorado had replaced Utah as the main destination. Missouri River freighters had very little competition for this mining market. In 1859 a few trains of provisions, particularly Mexican coarse-ground flour, were hauled into Denver from such places as Taos and LaJunta, New Mexico, but in 1860 the Denver newspapers did not mention the arrival of any New Mexican freight. There was a little business in hauling grain and flour from Utah to Colorado. The Salt Lake City firm of Miller, Russell & Company sent three trains amounting to seventy-seven wagonloads of these commodities from Provo and Salt Lake City to Denver in 1860. However, goods from Utah were no cheaper or more rapidly transported than those from the Missouri River towns, and such shipments were always an exception to the general rule of importing from the east. The Colorado market was contended for primarily by those Missouri River towns north of the Kansas River. The trade of Kansas City, then the leading freighting center on the river, was primarily directed to the south and southwest.[80]

At the close of 1860, Atchison ranked first as a freighting point for the trade to the west and northwest. With well over 8,000,000 pounds forwarded, she was far ahead of her closest rival, Nebraska City. Nebraska City did not publish a summary of the year's business. Evidence from many newspaper references would cause one to conclude that about 4,000,000 pounds of freight were sent out during the season. The Omaha trade can be estimated at 750,000 to 1,000,000 pounds.[81]

At this time Nebraska City in Otoe County and Omaha in Douglas County were nearly the same size. According to the official census of 1860, Nebraska City had 1,922 inhabitants and Omaha 1,883. They were the only settlements of more than a thousand people in the entire territory, which had an aggregate population of 28,696.[82] The superiority of Nebraska City in overland freighting is evident in the livestock statistics in Table 5.

TABLE 5

WORK ANIMALS IN DOUGLAS AND OTOE COUNTIES—1860*

County	Horses	Asses & Mules	Oxen
Douglas	264	15	206
Otoe	875	263	8496

Eighth Census of the United States: 1860. Agriculture, p. 172.

With the immediate past as his only guide, the freighter of 1860 who looked ahead to the next year could clearly see a rivalry of Nebraska City and Atchison over what was mainly a civilian trade to Colorado. Leavenworth, for two years without much of the military business, appeared to be dead. It seemed there was nothing that could seriously disrupt the Atchison trade and cause a sudden shift to Nebraska City.

V

Nebraska City's Dominance, 1861-1863

For well over a decade following the war with Mexico western frontiers boomed, but the great rush slowed perceptibly during the first years of the Civil War. Fort Sumter, Richmond, and Bull Run were the focal points early in the war, but the effects of the national schism carried far west into the frontier regions of Missouri and Kansas.

While the main Confederate units were fighting to save Virginia, their western guerrilla allies were raiding towns and harassing steamboats. The frontier phase of the war, even without major battles and large armies, was demoralizing and disruptive. Steamboats had difficulty reaching ports in western Missouri and eastern Kansas, and even when they reached towns there was no assurance that they could be unloaded without disturbance. The Hannibal & St. Joseph Railroad also was bothered by incessant raids which resulted in the destruction of bridges and track.

In 1861 especially, because of guerrilla activity along rail and river routes, Kansas was practically isolated. The leading freighting towns, Kansas City and Atchison, suffered greatly. Kansas City, largely because of contending Union and Confederate factions within the town, lost its military depot to Leavenworth. Atchison was practically devoid of business. Early in the spring the *Freedom's Champion* published enthusiastic predictions about prospects for the season, but they never materialized.

While Nebraska towns were affected by the trade disruption, they at least had local calm and enough civilian manpower to continue normal business operations. The overall freighting from Missouri River towns in 1861 and 1862 was down considerably from the immediate prewar years, but Nebraska City and Omaha business did not suffer. Instead, their trade actually increased because they gained much of what Atchison, Kansas City, and St. Joseph lost.

As the new center of the western trade, Nebraska City's main business was that of supplying Colorado and the road ranches along the trail. Nebraska City freighters also benefited by the transference of the overland mail line to the Platte River route. In addition, there was some military freighting and some trade with Utah. As trade increased in 1862 and 1863, Atchison recovered much of what she had lost, but this did not detract from Nebraska City because by that time freighting had again reached prewar proportions and several communities could prosper from it.

Nebraska City's eminence rested in large part on her favorable position and good trail. The northward trade shift raised again the controversy over the respective merits of the South Platte and North Platte routes. The trade of 1861 was contended for by Nebraska City and Omaha, without serious rivalry from the Kansas towns. Nebraska City could not claim any great advantage in distance over Omaha, so her case rested on the premise that the Airline Route was faster and drier than any other trail. Readers of the *Nebraska City News* were asked to keep a careful distinction in mind. The trail to Fort Kearny was wet enough to provide lush pasturage but just dry enough to provide firm footing.

Because Omaha freighters were continually faced with the problem of crossing the Platte, any high water year hurt the city's freighting. Heavy snowfall in the winter of 1860–1861 assured a full Platte the following spring. Two trains that left Omaha in March were reported to have been detained eleven days at the Loup Fork and another five days at the Fort Kearny crossing.[1]

As the emporium of the Colorado trade, Nebraska City never missed an opportunity to publicize her trail. The town's two newspapers, the *News* and the *People's Press,* through editorials, news articles, and testimonials, always kept the Airline Road in the public eye. Laudatory statements were eagerly solicited from freighters and emigrants. The papers were given a marvelous opportunity to publicize the trail in the summer of 1862 with the appearance of Joseph R. Brown and his steam wagon. Brown was interested in supplying the Colorado mines by steam wagon, a vehicle designed to obviate the need for the long-sought transcontinental railroad. It would seem that Nebraska City as a freighting town should have resented the appearance of this modernist and his terrible machine intended to replace the plodding ox and the creaking wagon. Not so—Brown was greeted enthusiastically and, probably much to his surprise, was promoted by the newspapers. The prominent Minnesotan, formerly a fur trader, Indian agent, and politician, was always "General" Joseph R. Brown in Nebraska City. The "General" assured the local population that he had selected Nebraska City as his departure point because it had the best trail to the mines. On the decisive day, Brown and his mechanics stoked the furnace and launched the puffing machine up the long, sloping main street and out along the trail toward distant Denver. As if realizing the enormity of the assignment, the wagon halted itself a short distance west of town. Brown stored his broken-down wagon in Nebraska City and left for New York to obtain the necessary repair parts. He would return, he said, and fulfill his dream.

However, Brown's immediate plans and for that matter his life were drastically changed by the sudden beginning of the Sioux Uprising in Minnesota. Brown hastened home, fearing for the safety of his family who lived close to the Sioux Reservation on the Minnesota River. He subsequently served in the punitive military expeditions against the Sioux and was reunited with his wife and children, but he never returned to Nebraska City. Any such intentions he may have had were undoubtedly undercut by the construction of the Union Pacific Railroad.

Brown's experiment had no great effect on the economy of Nebraska City and certainly did not revolutionize plains transportation. However, he left a legacy. Afterward, those inclined to accept intent rather than fulfillment called the road due west to Fort Kearny the "Steam Wagon Road."[2]

In addition to lending a new name to the trail, Brown indirectly stimulated improvement of the road to Fort Kearny. During preliminary conversations with city and county officials, Brown asked that the trail be made suitable for the operation of steam wagons. They were agreeable but pointed out that the long-sought bridges over Salt Creek and the Big Blue River would have to be completed. Such structures had been started in the spring of 1861 by W. E. Hill but were not completed due to lack of funds. Late in 1862, in the wake of Brown's memorable visit in Nebraska City, the people of Otoe County approved the issuance of $2,500 worth of bonds to improve the trail within the county. During the following winter and spring, some of this money was used to finish bridges over Salt Creek and the Big Blue, although these sites were well outside the county line. With the bridging of these streams there was no doubt that the Nebraska City to Fort Kearny trail was superior to all others.

The advantages and heavy use of the trail naturally led to the construction of frequent road ranches, most of which were started in the period 1861–1865. By the end of the Civil War there were no less than seventeen major ranches along the road, and a number of other places where travelers could find minimal accommodations. While most of the ranches were named for their proprietors, several were uniquely labeled, thereby contributing to the lore of the trail and the localities. One and one-half miles southwest of present Syracuse stood Nursery Hill Ranche, so-called because it was near the site of a nursery operated by Professor Rockwell Thompson, a botanist, and his partner. The ranche on Salt Creek was first called Olathe, but was renamed Saltillo after a city in Mexico at the suggestion of a Mexican War veteran. To the west of Salt Creek the operators of a ranche in Lancaster County gained a reputation as cheese makers, hence Cheese Creek and the Cheese Creek Ranche.[3]

The best evidence of the attractiveness of Nebraska City and her trail came from the many former Missouri and Kansas freighters who shifted part or all of their operations there. In 1861 a Mr. Frost of St. Joseph and Lansing & Alexander of St. Louis started shipping to Denver by way of Nebraska City. In 1862 a number of Atchison traders moved their operations to Nebraska City. Among these were Howe & Starr, a major Atchison merchandising firm, Jesse Taylor, William H. Chinn, T. Ewing, and W. A. Carter, sutler at Fort Bridger, who had reportedly always freighted from Atchison since his start in 1857. The most important new additions to Nebraska City's business community in 1863 were Lobb & Company, Carlyle Brothers, and Heth & Thomas.[4]

Nebraska City, like other Missouri River towns, was affected by guerrilla activity during the early war years. Guerrilla harassment in Missouri was a significant deterrent to navigation. In addition to this Union demands for St. Louis steamboats for operations on the Mississippi left boats for the civilian trade in short supply. In 1862 only two boats, the *Omaha* and the *West Wind,* were running in connection with the Hannibal & St. Joseph Railroad. Only a very few other steamers were reported operating on the river. The boat shortage caused most west-bound freight across Missouri to be shipped by rail to St. Joseph, where it accumulated for want of boats to move it upstream. The lack of steamboats to deliver necessary goods to Nebraska City brought about a new facet of the trade. Over the winter of 1862–1863 teamsters began carrying goods overland from St. Joseph to Nebraska City.[5]

Nebraska City's western trade involved many firms and individuals, but during the period 1861–1863 it was dominated by Peter and Augustus Byram, who probably transported as much as all other freighters combined. The Byram brothers were sometimes called the successors of Russell, Majors & Waddell. There is an element of truth in this. They had worked for the firm, and for the first time in 1861 they were completely free from it. The bankruptcy of the onetime giant enabled the brothers to move from semi-autonomy in 1860 to independence the next year. The Byrams undoubtedly bought quantities of oxen and wagons from their former employres. Unlike Russell, Majors & Waddell, the Byrams dealt primarily in the transportation of private rather than military freight. They carried goods primarily to Colorado and way points.

In April, 1861, the Byrams contracted to convey 10,000 sacks of flour from Nebraska City to Denver. Within a month they were sending out two to three full trains each week. The *Nebraska City News,* in its unceasing efforts to promote an emigrant traffic through Nebraska City, pointed out that emigrants could travel with the Byram trains and benefit from the protection of the thirty well-armed men who accompanied each train.[6]

The size of the Byram operation is indicated by the extensiveness of their livestock holdings. Over the winter of 1861–1862 they wintered 2,000 head of oxen in Colorado. With the return of these to Nebraska City, their total herd was estimated at about 5,000 head.[7]

Like most of the larger freighters, the Byrams extended their business from transportation into wholesaling. They had a warehouse in Nebraska City and a wholesale outlet in Denver managed by a Mr. Litchfield. In 1863 they had a new two-story fireproof warehouse constructed in Denver.[8]

There is no doubt that the Byrams during this period were the leading freighters in the Colorado trade, but it is impossible to determine who occupied the runner-up position. Alexander Majors freighted out of Nebraska City in 1861 and 1862, usually as a subcontractor for the Byrams. Majors was but a shadow of his former self; his interests, as a protection from creditors, were in the name of his wife Susan. His finances were managed by one of his associates and creditors, Samuel Poteet. During these years Majors was working with his men and animals and was frequently on the trail, where he loved to be. Despite his plunge from the ranks of the wealthy, Majors was still one of the most celebrated citizens of Nebraska City, an indication that his contemporaries judged him by his unpretentious personality rather than his pocketbook.

Nebraska City merchants continued their combined freighting-retailing business to the mines. Arnold F. Mollring and Herman H. Petring of the firm of Bueter, Mollring & Petring not only carried, bacon, butter, and eggs to Colorado but packed some of these supplies into isolated mountain camps where the best prices could be commanded. R. M. Rolfe, another of Nebraska City's major grocers, abandoned storekeeping in favor of freighting. After his start in 1862, he remained a freighter as long as Nebraska City had any trade.[9]

Small freighters were attracted to Nebraska City in part because it was a good place to secure equipment and wagons. Russell, Majors, and Waddell had left at their depot many wagons which they sold for considerably less than the market price of new wagons. As late as July, 1862, A. W. Street still had 200 of their wagons for sale.[10] Among those people who sent out several four- or five-wagon trains a year were Charles Otaway, Thomas Chivington, Alvin B. Daniels, John D. Clayton, and S. M. Freas. Infrequent traders, mostly Coloradans, who purchased goods in Nebraska City were A. Hanover, William Hayes, and J. B. Doyle.[11]

While Colorado remained a major market, its economy did not grow during the Civil War period. There was a war scare because of the Sibley Expedition in New Mexico, and hundreds of miners put aside their picks and shovels to serve in the territorial militia during the crisis of 1861–1862. Mining did not cease; in fact, gold production reached new highs. In 1862 about $3,400,000 worth was mined and a like amount in 1863. Compared with California and Nevada, however, this was a small return, and some regarded the Colorado gold rush a bust. Denver newspapers were continually countering claims that times were poor in Colorado. Perhaps no great advances were made, but at least the territory maintained its status quo.[12]

There was a good influx of freight into Colorado in 1861 because Nebraska City freighters competed sharply with each other and the trail was sound and free from Indian troubles. The *Rocky Mountain News* of September 25 reported that a "good many trains laden with goods are now arriving," and that the season had been very favorable for freighting. The heavy volume of imports directly affected freight rates to the advantage of the Coloradans. Through most of the season the rate on a hundred pounds from the river to Denver was $6.50 to $7. Even rates to outlying mining towns were affected. In May the rate to Tarryall, eighty miles from Denver was $5 to $7 a hundred; and the rate to California Gulch (present Leadville), 125 miles from Denver, was $6 to $8. By August these fell to $3 to $3.50 and $3.50 to $4, respectively. During the same period the rates to communities twenty to thirty miles west of Denver went from $1.50 or $2 down to $1 or $1.50.[13]

When the freight charges reached a new low, so also did the market prices. On one occasion in June, 1861, when Denver was jammed with forty loads of provisions, eggs fell to 20¢ a dozen, bacon to 15¢ a pound, and flour to $8 to $9 a hundred, which was a drop of $1 to $2 in about a month. Concern was expressed that these prices were too low for the freighters and merchants to make a profit, and that if the severe competition forced a further reduction they would be discouraged from importing into Colorado. The Denver market was always plagued by uncertainty and speculation, which caused the failure of a number of businesses in 1861. The editor of the *Weekly Commonwealth and Republican,* searching vainly for a solution, suggested that the river towns should conduct their trade on the basis of weekly trains so that wholesalers and freighters could better determine the amount of goods needed in Denver. Such a proposal was an anathema to the competitive frontier mind. For the freighter the solution was simple; all he had to do was beat his competitors to Denver.[14]

Denverites soon found that the low prices of 1861 were not resting on a permanent plateau. Light winter trade, high demand, and the heavy loss of cattle in spring storms caused prices to advance again. Relative inactivity during the winter was a constant factor, but such a thing as loss of cattle was one of those upsetting imponderables. Heavy snows in late April resulted in the straying of some 2,700 head of cattle, horses, and mules. Augustus and Peter Byram alone were reported to have lost nearly 1,000 head. Despite the recovery of many of these, the cattle market advanced and so did the cost of merchandise and freight rates. Freight went up to $8 to $10 a hundred, and flour in Denver was inflated to $20 per hundred pounds. In Central City, less than forty miles west, it advanced to $30.[15]

Increased trade during the late spring and summer of 1862 again reduced rates. The re-entry of Atchison freighters into the Colorado trade stimulated freighting, and by all newspaper accounts the trail and the trade were much more active in 1862 than they had been in 1861. One traveler reported that while returning from Denver he met an average of 100 wagons daily along the trail west of Fort Kearny. More and more flour was produced by Nebraska City mills, and on November 6 the *People's Press,* noting the trade of Nebraska City, observed that "immense trains of wagons freighted for the towns of Colorado are leaving almost daily."[16]

By June, 1862, the comparatively high early spring rates were down to $4 to $6. This was about all freighters could have been charging since flour in Nebraska City was selling for $1.75 to $2.50 a hundred and in Denver it brought $5 to $7.50 a hundred. Rates stayed at or below $6 until late November, when they advanced to $7.50 to $8. During the winter they advanced still further, to $9 to $10, but fell off to $5 to $6 the following summer.[17]

Coloradans, while realizing and acknowledging their dependence on towns to the east, particularly on Nebraska City, naturally yearned for economic independence. About the only way of accomplishing this would be to produce food close to the mines. Denver editors tried constantly to promote cattle raising, wheat cultivation, and flour milling. A long-anticipated and much-publicized local flour mill was finally put into operation in November, 1862. It symbolized local determination but did little to offset the heavy importation of flour.[18]

In spite of Colorado promoters' desire for economic independence, the area still depended almost entirely on the Missouri River towns for supplies, especially on Nebraska City. The extent of this trade cannot be fully determined from available evidence, but in 1862 the Byrams alone hauled more than 3,000,000 pounds of freight from Nebraska City to Denver. One estimate for the 1863 trade was that it would amount to at least 5,000,000 pounds.[19]

Nearly all of the Nebraska City trade consisted of commonly used commodities transported by wagon. But on at least one occasion the attractiveness of the Colorado market led to a novel experiment. In the spring of 1863 a poultry speculator passed through Nebraska City driving 850 turkeys before him with the expressed intention of walking them through to Denver.[20]

The second most important facet of the Nebraska City trade was the supplying of mail and stage stations on the trail to Denver and Salt Lake City. Nebraska City's gain was mostly attributable to a shift in the through California daily mail caused by the secession of Southern states. Early in 1861 as the Confederacy was being formed, it became very apparent to Congress that the Butterfield Overland Mail, which had followed the southern route to California, could not be maintained. The southern route lay partly in Texas and had been controversial since its inception in 1858. Reports of disturbances of the mail service in Texas convinced Congress that the route had to be shifted northward.

Under a new agreement negotiated in March, 1861, the Butterfield Company was to shift its operations to the Oregon Trail and to supply Denver and Salt Lake City with a tri-weekly mail. At the time the Butterfield Mail reached this agreement with the Postmaster General, it also sublet that portion of the mail service east of Salt Lake City to the COCPP Express Company. Under this arrangement all California mail had to be carried on the Oregon Trail, so inevitably stage traffic was increased.

The exact routes from the Missouri to Denver and Salt Lake City were to be determined by the COCPP Express Company. The company ultimately chose to follow the traditional path through South Pass, but only after considerable contemplation of two alternate routes farther south. Since both Denver and Salt Lake City had to be serviced, a direct route linking the two would have been cheaper and easier for the company to maintain. One possibility was a looping route that followed the old Cherokee Trail through Bridger's Pass. Another attractive possibility was a really direct route through the recently discovered Berthoud Pass west of Denver.

The company had not fully reconnoitered either of these routes by the time it was expected to begin service on July 1, so its only choice was to follow the South Pass route, where at least it had some stations because of its previous Salt Lake City mail contract and the Pony Express operation. Certainly the existence of the Pony Express on the northernmost route was a good reason to continue using it. If the company had shifted to one of the more southern routes in 1861, it undoubtedly would have had to shift the Pony Express, since it could not practically offer a mail service over two routes. Under the 1861 arrangement the main mail line ran from St. Joseph to the Oregon Trail, then along it to the Upper California Crossing, where Julesburg was located. Here the trail split, with the main route going on to Fort Laramie and beyond and the Denver route branching off to the southwest along the South Platte.[21]

The COCPP carried the overland mail through South Pass for only one year. The series of financial setbacks that had plagued Russell, Majors, and Waddell and their various associates since the time of the Mormon War came to a head in 1861 and 1862. The vaunted Pony Express, a complete financial failure from the start, ended its brief but dramatic career in the fall of 1861. The overextended COCPP was deeply in debt to Ben Holladay, who foreclosed in 1862, taking over the defunct company's equipment and business operations and embarking on a brief career that was to earn him the title of "Stagecoach King."[22]

In July, 1862, Holladay, both to avoid marauding Indians along the Sweetwater and to save distance, transferred the stage and mail service south to the Cherokee Trail. (This trail was so named after the party of California gold rush Cherokee who first used it.) The main line route to Julesburg was the same as before, but beyond Julesburg it followed along the South Platte to Latham Station, opposite and a short distance east of the mouth of the Cache la Poudre. From here a branch line ran to Denver, and the main route followed the Cache la Poudre to LaPorte, thirty-five miles upstream. From LaPorte it ran north through Virginia Dale

and on across the Laramie Plains before swinging west around the
northern end of the Medicine Bow range. After clearing these
mountains it ran roughly due west to Bridger Pass, where it merged
with the main path of the Oregon Trail.

Probably the most important point on the route was Latham
Station, where the Denver and through mail was separated. Initially, Denver's only service was provided by stages from this junction, but within a few months mail and passenger service was
extended and some of the Salt Lake City stages were sent through
Denver by way of LaPorte and the Cherokee Trail. Finally after
two years, all stages passed through Denver, and Latham Station
was abandoned because coaches used the cutoff route that ran
northeasterly from Denver to the South Platte. This change did
not alter the use of the Cherokee Trail. The only real trail changes
caused by the extension of the main line through Denver were the
abandonment of the short section from Latham to LaPorte and the
resultant use of the LaPorte-to-Denver trail and the cutoff road.[23]

The South Pass route continued to be used for several reasons;
the transcontinental telegraph was strung along it, and, also, some
emigrants and freighters preferred it because the route was less
arid than the Cherokee Trail. The Cherokee Trail, however, became increasingly important to the freighters because of the development of the new mail and way stations along the route.

During the period 1861–1863 the great bulk of the construction
materials for stage stations and the supplies to subsist men and
animals were carried from Nebraska City. Alexander Majors, while
a director of the COCPP Express Company in 1861, also acted as
its agent in Nebraska City. The freight contracts, however, were
handled by the Byrams. Early in the spring of 1861 the Byrams
sent out large amounts of pine lumber, doors, nails, and glass for
the construction of stations along the Platte. On May 11 the
Nebraska City News reported that the brothers had secured a
two-year contract to convey all corn and supplies to the express
company stations between the Missouri and Denver. The contract
was said to call for 40,000 to 50,000 bushels of corn and other food-
stuffs. The Byrams intended to use twenty to thirty full trains
each year. Since some of the trains could make two trips per season,
the freighters could handle this express business with 400 wagons,
4,000 to 5,000 head of oxen, about 70 mules, and probably slightly
over 400 men. The Byrams' operation meant a great deal to Ne-

braska City merchants. It was estimated that the freighters who carried supplies to the stage stations would annually use 37,400 pounds of bacon, 75,000 pounds of flour, 7,500 pounds of sugar, and 4,125 pounds of coffee, as well as quantities of dried fruit, beans, and tallow.[24]

In 1863 the contract to carry supplies for the Overland Stage Company went to Henry and Alexander Carlyle, who, like their predecessors, outfitted in Nebraska City. The brothers in the interest of speed used mule teams exclusively in the station trade. They used about seventy-five six-mule teams in 1863.[25]

Because of the Colorado and stage line trade, Nebraska City's freighting business was essentially private. Some government business was done from the town even though Nebraska City was not a designated military depot, but apparently only at times when the military goods could not be adequately handled in Leavenworth. For example, during June, 1862, the government consigned nearly 600,000 pounds of goods to Ashton & Tait, Nebraska City Forwarding and Commission Merchants. This firm handled the transfer of the freight in Nebraska City and then sent it out by various freighters. Also, in 1863 the sutler at Fort Laramie, Seth Ward, started hauling some of his goods from Nebraska City.[26]

Nebraska City's bitterest rival also progressed during the early war years, but the success of Omaha was more attributable to her role as an outfitting point for emigrants than as a freighting center. The advantage that Omaha had traditionally enjoyed because of her location relative to the major northern population centers was increased with the wartime disruption of river and rail transportation across Missouri. Few emigrants chose to hazard a trip across war-torn Missouri, the scene of much guerrilla activity, but instead stayed to the north and crossed Iowa by a combination of rail and stage facilities.

In the fall of 1861 the western termini of Iowa railroads were Marengo and Eddyville. The Western Stage Company carried passengers from these points to Council Bluffs in only forty-eight hours, and through the rail-stage combination Council Bluffs was but three days from Chicago. When the operations of the Hannibal & St. Joseph Railroad were temporarily suspended in September, 1861, the Iowa stages were said to have been crowded.[27]

Emigration during the early war years was considerably less than that of the immediate prewar years, but in May, 1862, J. Y.

Porter, a messenger for the U. S. Express Company, reported counting 872 emigrant wagons between Fort Kearny and Omaha, and an Omaha newspaper anticipated a movement of some 9,000 Mormons before the end of the season.[28]

The government, which had cut back its frontier commitment with the outbreak of the Civil War, felt obliged to offer some protection to emigrants as a way of encouraging loyal Unionists to move west, thereby lessening the possibility of any western secession plots. In May, 1861, Capt. Henry E. Maynadier with a force of about seventy men acted as an emigrant escort along the trail west of Omaha. During the next year the government was even more active in the escort service. Congressional appropriations made possible an escort force on the northern plains headed by Capt. James Liberty Fisk and one on the Platte River route commanded by Capt. Medorem Crawford.[29]

Omaha had a number of wholesale establishments that outfitted emigrants and supplied miners. They included William Ruth, W. C. Frederickson & H. G. Jackson, Hurford & Brother, John McCormick, J. J. & R. A. Brown, and James K. Ish & Company. Many of these merchants were also in the business of freighting to Colorado, and they sold many supplies to the numerous ranches which lay along the trail to Denver.[30] In addition to an aggressive business community, Omaha boasted good communications, particularly after the extension of the overland telegraph through the Platte Valley in 1861. Another valuable communications link was acquired in August, 1861, with the establishment of a daily mail service which ran from Omaha to Fort Kearny, where it connected with the overland mail.[31]

Though Omaha had the bulk of the emigrant business, some merchants wanted a larger portion of the freighting business. However, the old nemesis of the bridge-less Platte still confronted them. Unless the river was bridged, Omaha would suffer so long as the bulk of the freight was directed to Colorado destinations south of the Platte. "Bridge the Platte" was one of the standard preachments of Omaha newspapermen, but the project was never accomplished during the freighting period. Part of the reason was undoubtedly lack of local capital; but a stronger possibility is that many Omahans after 1862 were preoccupied with visions of a transcontinental railroad and could not convince themselves that lack of a wagon bridge across the Platte was anything more than a temporary inconvenience. Without such a bridge, however, Omaha definitely was a second-rate freighting center for the Colorado business, especially when compared to Nebraska City.

"Nothing is so necessary to the prosperity of this city," said a writer in the *Nebraska Republican* of May 5, 1862, with reference to bridging the Platte. The editorialist reminded readers that the Territorial Legislature at its last session had incorporated a company that was to build a bridge: Now "in our judgement it only requires a systematic, well-directed effort, to accomplish this important work." He estimated that such a bridge could be built for only $50,000 and would double Omaha's western trade. Nearly every time a Nebraska City or Leavenworth paper boasted of its Colorado trade some Omaha journalist would once again try to goad Omaha citizens into action. Some of the encouragement for the bridge scheme came from Denver, where the *Rocky Mountain News* greatly exaggerated the worth of the Colorado business. "The trade of Colorado" was said to be "no picayune affair. It amounts to millions of dollars annually, and each year increases it from fifty to one hundred per cent." Omaha readers were told that Nebraska City outstripped all others in the Denver trade and that Omaha and Council Bluffs should "grapple for your share."[32]

Another scheme to boom the Denver trade was the proposed operation of a ferry across the North Fork of the Platte at some point where it was still quite near the South Platte so that a trail could be developed from there to Denver by staying on the left bank of the South Platte. Hadley D. Johnson of Omaha planned to establish such a ferry, but only if he could obtain financial aid from Omaha businessmen.[33]

The lack of a bridge across the Platte caused Omaha freighters to develop most of their business to points other than Colorado. There was a little Colorado business, some Utah trade, a little freighting because of the construction of the overland telegraph, a considerable ranche trade, and by 1863 the beginnings of hauling to the Montana-Idaho mines. The first really big break for Omaha freighting came in 1863 when quantities of military supplies were sent from there to the western forts.

Most of the Omaha–Council Bluffs freight to Colorado originated with wholesalers in these towns. The merchants often transported their own goods, but there was also a small group of professional freighters. Particularly active and with a good local reputation was a small company managed by George Marshall and J. Shepherd. Marshall was a veteran Council Bluffs businessman, and Shepard was the General Western Agent of the U.S. Express Company. They sent out several small mule trains in 1861 and were often praised by Omaha journalists for their efficiency.[34]

Another firm which sent out several trains was Clopper, Reagan & Coffman. It generally used mule teams, and on one occasion in May, 1861, one of its trains returned from Denver to Omaha in twelve days. While this was with empty wagons going downgrade, it nevertheless was good time. One of these partners, J. F. Coffman, later worked with the wholesale grocery house of John McCormick & Company and offered to freight to any point on the plains. Other freighters were Wood & King, R. H. Willard, and A. E. and C. E. Tilton. The Tiltons' wagons were handled by J. E. Curley. Willard was unusual in that he used four-horse teams to haul part of his freight. One Omaha freighter in 1861 proposed to carry a number of cats to Denver. The animals were said to command a high price in the mining camps because of the prevalence of rats and because the cats made good pets for lonely miners.[35]

Large numbers of freight wagons left Omaha and nearby Florence for Utah in 1861–1863, but these wagons were nearly all operated by the Mormon church. The provisions carried by these trains, however, were purchased in Omaha. The 1861 migration consisted of 200 wagons and 2,556 emigrants. This movement was probably accomplished with three large trains. Capt. J. W. Young's train had eighty or ninety wagons, and one led by S. A. Woolley had about seventy wagons and a large number of Scandinavians. In 1862 the church trains totaled 262 wagons and 3,000 emigrants, and the following year this increased to 384 wagons and 3,646 new recruits for Zion.[36]

In addition to the church trains, some trains were organized by Mormon merchants. The most active of these was W. S. Godbe, who led several trains into Salt Lake City in 1861 and 1862. In May, 1862, Godbe and a single companion went east to Omaha by pack mule for the purpose of outfitting a train and returning to Salt Lake City before winter set in.[37]

There was some competition to the Missouri River towns as starting points for Utah freight from California. In June, 1862, the Walker brothers of Salt Lake City sent a train of agricultural produce to Carson, Nevada, and then crossed the Sierra Nevadas to pick up twenty-two wagonloads of Utah-bound goods at Folsom, California. After this time some Utah freight originated in the West each year, but Utah remained primarily dependent on Missouri River towns.[38]

Omaha's freighting business was stimulated briefly in 1860–1861 because of the construction of the transcontinental telegraph line. In 1860 Western Union, after obtaining assurances of a federal subsidy for a ten-year period, started the long walk of poles from the Missouri to the coast by extending their line from St. Joseph to Omaha and then out along the Platte. By early November the line had been strung to Fort Kearny. Meanwhile, Edward Creighton, general agent of Western Union, finalized plans to extend the line to the coast. After failing to secure a subsidy from Denverites for a direct connection, he decided that the line would be built through the South Pass route.[39]

In the spring of 1861 W. H. Stebbins, who had supervised the previous year's work, pushed the wires west to Julesburg. H. M. Porter, Stebbins' superintendent in Omaha, sent out twelve wagonloads of wire and insulators to the Cottonwood Springs area just east of the forks of the Platte, where quantities of cedar poles were cut in the adjacent canyons.[40]

Creighton, who desperately wanted to complete the line in 1861, organized an extensive work force in Omaha to extend the line from Julesburg to Salt Lake City, where it would meet one being built eastward from California. By late May, Creighton had received about 160 tons of material and was awaiting eighty wagons so he could move out. Some of his transportation had to be procured locally. He bought out the freighting concern of Baldwin & Dodge, paying about $8,000 cash for ninety yoke of oxen and fifteen wagons. In early June, Creighton dispatched two trains averaging nineteen wagons which were loaded to near capacity at 5,600 pounds each.[41]

With characteristic energy and determination, Creighton supervised the completion of the line to Salt Lake City by October 20, covering the great distance west of Julesburg in less than four months. Four days later the east and west wires were joined, and Nebraska and the nation witnessed a milestone in the modernization of the overland trail.[42]

The nature of overland freighting was changed as a result of the telegraph. It was no longer necessary to send dispatch riders scurrying out to relay instructions to wagonmasters. Trains could easily receive orders at any one of the telegraph stations and road ranches. After the completion of the line a fair amount of the freighters' business, particularly with the ranches, was conducted by telegraph. Alexander Majors would sometimes exchange telegrams with a rancheman to insure the well-being of even a single ox. It is difficult now to imagine the tremendous impact the telegraph had on the timelessness of the plains. With it, man could no longer be unaware of events in the world beyond the wagon trail.

While the telegraph and the overland mail service were making their impact felt in the Platte Valley, events were occurring in the distant Northwest which would also have an effect in the valley. New gold strikes were made in Idaho. Scant attention was paid in the river towns to the first discoveries in Idaho because they were too far away to be supplied from the east, but interest mounted as miners pushed eastward and discovered ore in present Montana.

Omaha newspapers as early as the spring of 1862 mentioned that some emigrants were passing through on their way to the Salmon River mines, but these migrants received nothing more than a passing nod. Idaho's first gold was discovered on the Clearwater River in 1860, but in a year this area was nearly abandoned because of new strikes on the Salmon River to the south. The Salmon River mines, in turn, were soon deserted because of new finds in the Boise Basin of southwest Idaho. While Idaho miners came from both the west and the east, the supplies came from the west by way of Columbia River steamers to Walla Walla and then by wagon or pack animal to the mines.[43]

Montana's first significant finds came in 1862 with gold discoveries at Bannack. These were followed the next year by strikes at Alder Gulch to the northeast, where Virginia City was to develop. The gold of Montana, like that of other mining frontiers, was known long before any organized rush. As early as 1852 a Red River half-breed Francois Finlay, also known as "Benetsee," found traces of gold in western Montana, and the next year some gold was found by the Isaac I. Stevens railroad survey party along a branch of the Hellgate River. Alexander Culbertson, the agent of Pierre Chouteau, Jr. & Company at Fort Benton, exchanged some provisions for gold in 1856 with a prospector named Silverthorne, who found his dust in the mountains southwest of the post. Despite the activities of Silverthorne and others, the fur traders did not publicize the suspected richness of the region, probably because they did not want a population influx that would alarm their native customers and disrupt their business.[44]

The Idaho strikes, however, set off a rash of hurried prospecting that called experienced miners into the Northwest from California, Nevada, British Columbia, and Colorado. Their push through Idaho and into the mountains of southwestern Montana was a natural result of a placer mining boom where any mountain stream was a logical source of nuggets or dust. The Bannack strikes fed the eastern fever, particularly in St. Louis, the logical starting point for those who ascended the Missouri; in St. Paul, the metropolis of any overland emigration on the northern plains; and in Chicago and points east, which would probably rely on the route through Iowa and the Platte Valley.

While there were many ways of traveling to Montana, there was really no good way. Both boat and wagon travel from the east were slow. Movement from the south by way of Salt Lake City had to go about 450 miles through an arid region, and the hopeful who came in from the west had to use a combination of the Columbia River and overland trails. Isolation was perhaps the key characteristic of frontier Montana. Since Montana was not really close to anything of note, the miners were continually plagued by an inefficient, seasonal freight service and, of course, exorbitant prices for any imported commodity. Before the completion of the Union Pacific Railroad, none of the overland routes could adequately compete with the Missouri River steamboats, but, despite the slowness and lack of capacity of their vehicles, the overland freighters did corner some of the Montana business. To the man who had freighted to Utah from the Missouri, supplying Montana was a perfectly sensible thing to do. Actually, the Montana business turned into a good thing for freighters. The government soon sent military personnel to guard the freighting routes, and the freighters naturally hauled supplies for these military posts as well as for Montana miners.

Omaha, because of her North Platte position, had roughly the same advantage in the Montana business that she had in the Utah trade. The city's business with Montana began slowly. Omaha freighters did some business with Bannack City in 1863, all on a roundabout route by way of Salt Lake City. Edward Creighton, who had gone into the freighting business, sent out two trains, the second being a large outfit of thirty ox-drawn wagons. George W. Forbes also sent a train of about thirty-five wagons to Bannack City by way of Salt Lake City. In all likelihood both Creighton and Forbes carried manufactured goods when they left Omaha and after unloading the Salt Lake City items reloaded some of their wagons with Utah agricultural produce for Montana delivery. The trail from Omaha to Bannack City by way of Utah was slightly over 1,600 miles. This trade in 1863 was the beginning of the boom that was to come with further gold discoveries in the Helena area, discoveries that coincided with a new westward sweep of emigration at the close of the Civil War.[45]

Though other phases of wagon freighting were slow in 1863, Omaha experienced a real boom in military hauling when the Route 1 military trade was ordered to start from there. The military business, while not nearly as large as in the period of the Mormon War, ranked second only to the Colorado trade during the first three years of the Civil War. This trade was monopolized by the new contracting firm of Irwin, Jackman & Company, successor of J. C. Irwin & Company.

Of necessity military contractors had to be able to operate on a grand scale. The army supplied all of its plains posts on three numbered routes; any contractor had to be able to handle at least all of the business for one route. Most aspiring contractors submitted bids for all three routes. The firm of Russell, Majors & Waddell is celebrated in large part because it was the first of a number of gigantic military contractors. Its uniqueness was not in its size but in its pioneer role in plains freighting. As the old company was dying in 1860–1861 a new one was rising in its place.

In 1860, the first year J. C. Irwin and his associates had the Route 1 (Oregon Trail and Utah) trade, they subcontracted to carry portions of the Route 2 (Santa Fe Trail to Fort Union) trade for Russell, Majors & Waddell, which was by then in serious financial trouble. In April, Irwin's company assumed a financial interest in the Route 2 contract equal to that of Russell, Majors & Waddell. In order to handle this and their Route 1 business, they acquired over 500 wagons and 5,000 oxen.[46]

The inability of Russell, Majors, and Waddell to assume full responsibility for the Route 2 trade was indicative of their overall financial difficulties. The Mormon War losses and liabilities incurred from the establishment of the Pony Express and the COCPP drove Russell and his partners to ruin. Russell, in desperation, prevailed upon a government clerk to loan him certain bonds so that he might use them as security in obtaining bank loans. The clerk did this partially because Russell, Majors & Waddell had a legitimate claim against the government, but mainly he was interested in saving Secretary of War John Floyd embarrassment for having signed acceptances in favor of Russell, Majors & Waddell without clear legal authority. At the time Russell received the bonds, he assumed the clerk had a right to loan them to him. He soon discovered, however, that he had been given Indian Trust Fund bonds that were not even government property. The bond scandal reverberated nationally when the story broke late in 1860. Russell was arrested, investigated by a Senate committee, and ultimately tried for having received stolen goods. Though legal charges against Russell were dismissed, the bond scandal burst the flimsy financial bubble on which one of the country's best-known companies had been floating. Numerous creditors foreclosed in 1861, and the former freighting barons were soon impoverished. None of the partners ever recovered financially. Alexander Majors, just forty-six at the time of the crash, struggled on for years in freighting but never achieved his former stature.[47]

While the firm of Russell, Majors & Waddell was disintegrating, Joseph Irwin moved in to fill the void in military freighting. Irwin was in business by 1861 as Irwin, Jackman & Company, a concern that included four Pennsylvanians, David K. Jackman of Lock Haven, H. S. Magraw of Lancaster, James Duffy of Marietta, and A. Welch of Philadelphia. In March, 1861, when it was obvious that Russell, Majors & Waddell was finished and would be unable to conduct any of the New Mexico business on its Route 2 and Route 3 (New Mexican posts beyond Fort Union) contracts, Irwin, Jackman & Company contracted with the quartermaster to assume the remainder of these contracts at a dime less per hundred pounds per hundred miles than the rates of the original agreement.[48] The assumption of these contracts combined with the Route 1 contract gave Irwin, Jackman & Company the much-desired monopoly of military freighting which it was to hold for three consecutive years.

On March 10, 1862, a somewhat reorganized Irwin, Jackman & Company secured a two-year contract for the 1862 and 1863 trade for all three routes. Irwin, Jackman, and Duffy along with a very important newcomer, Alexander Caldwell of Columbia, Pennsylvania, who managed the freighting operation, were the partners during this period. The company was expected to be able to transport a maximum of 20,000,000 pounds annually—half of which was for Route 1, the northern route. The rates which applied to the period April to September, inclusive, varied little. Beginning with this contract, the previous practice of graduating rates according to the season was discontinued. Freight for all months except July was to be carried at $1.20 per hundredweight for each hundred miles with the July freight going at $1.19. The contractors were expected to have an agent at the depot on the Missouri and a resident agent at Fort Laramie whose primary task was to relay and coordinate transportation requests from points along the western end of the trail. Fort Leavenworth was the only Missouri River depot specifically mentioned, but the government reserved the right to establish any additional or alternate depots on the west bank of the Missouri from Fort Leavenworth north to the forty-second parallel. The contract assured Irwin, Jackman & Company a monopoly of all military freight carried from any designated depot except that which might be carried by the government itself.[49]

The army to be supplied by Irwin, Jackman & Company along Route 1 was in considerable flux because of the Civil War, Indian disturbances, and re-routing of mail and stage routes. Early Civil War crises led to the complete withdrawal of the Utah garrison by mid-1861. The military stores accompanying the troops were hauled from Fort Crittenden (old Camp Floyd, which had been renamed because of John B. Floyd's Southern sympathies) to Fort Leavenworth by the experienced freighting firm of Gilbert & Bell. The firm was paid $25 per hundred for goods carried the entire distance and 7¢ a pound for forage and subsistence supplies while en route. The freight included at least 56,000 pounds of oats for Fort Leavenworth and 10,000 pounds of subsistence stores for points between Forts Bridger and Laramie.[50]

The garrisons of the two key trail posts, Forts Kearny and Laramie, were not reduced until late fall. In reports dated October 10, Fort Kearny had an aggregate strength of 200 and Fort Laramie showed 240 men, but in November the Fort Laramie garrison was reduced by nearly half, and the Kearny garrison was undoubtedly reduced substantially also.[51]

Indian difficulties along the Sweetwater River portion of the Oregon Trail forced the government to reappraise its military policy. During the spring of 1862, the hostiles struck stage and telegraph stations, threatening to disrupt vital transcontinental communications. Apparently, many Indians interpreted troop withdrawals of 1861 as a sign of government weakness. If so, they must have been surprised when the government reinforced the trail by ordering in troops from both the west and east. Col. William O. Collins led a battalion of Ohio Volunteer Cavalry to Fort Laramie in May. These men were soon distributed at key points from Fort Laramie to South Pass. In the fall Col. Patrick Edward Connor and his regiment of California Volunteers, who had been ordered east in July, established Fort Douglas on high ground overlooking Salt Lake City. Connor not only had the mission of protecting the overland route but was to ensure the loyalty of the Mormons, who were still hardly above suspicion by the Union.[52]

Despite these military reinforcements, Holladay shifted the stage and mail service to the Cherokee Trail, necessitating a further change in troop distribution. To protect the new route, the army constructed Fort Halleck during the late summer and fall of 1862. It was located at the north base of Elk Mountain (about thirty miles southeast of present Rawlins, Wyoming), where the trail swung off the Laramie Plains around the north end of the Medicine Bow Mountains.[53] The post was poorly located with regard to water and wood supplies, but it did serve as a significant trail bastion for several years until it was replaced by a post located at the point where the trail crossed the North Platte. To supply Fort Halleck, the military contractors shifted some of their freighting to the overland stage and mail route, sending wagons to Latham Station and then up the Cache la Poudre. An alternate freighting route to Halleck followed Lodgepole Creek northwest from Julesburg and out through the Laramie Range. This trail, while unprotected and quite arid, was sometimes used as a shortcut.

Some new military installations were started late in 1863, but they did not greatly affect freighting until the following year, so the major posts to be supplied in 1862–1863 were Forts Kearny, Laramie, Halleck, and Douglas, and several cantonments on the South Pass and Denver–Fort Bridger routes. The Irwin, Jackman & Company contract clearly provided that any military supplies for Utah would be taken by the South Pass route, but the location of Fort Halleck and the reinforcement of the trail west of there caused some of the Utah military freight to go by that route, which was not as well timbered or watered as the Oregon Trail.

Leavenworth was the first town to benefit from the Irwin, Jackman & Company monopoly. In the spring of 1861 the company shifted its Route 2 depot from Kansas City to Leavenworth and shortly thereafter transferred its Route 1 depot at Atchison to Leavenworth. The move away from Kansas City was necessitated by mob disturbances including a near takeover of the town by Confederate sympathizers. In part, the abandonment of Atchison was prompted by the possibility of secessionist guerrilla activity, but undoubtedly the company primarily wanted to consolidate its freighting operation near Fort Leavenworth, where communication with the post quartermaster officer would be convenient and where military protection for the depot or escorts for moving trains could readily be obtained.[54]

Irwin, Jackman & Company rented a brick building from Russell, Majors & Waddell and by early June, 1861, had sent out four trains and had indicated that it would average two full trains a week for the remainder of the freighting season. However, the firm was severely hindered by the wartime manpower shortage; it still lacked 150 teamsters as late as June. Finally it successfully recruited men from Missouri, many of whose loyalty was suspect; but, as the *Daily Times* of Leavenworth pointed out, about two-thirds of the freighters on the plains were from Missouri, and Missourians as such could not very well be excluded from the business of working for government contractors.[55]

Leavenworth recovered much of her past glory and trade when Irwin, Jackman & Company established itself there. Business was reported to have "improved wonderfully,"[56] and as the *Daily Times* later expressed its enthusiasm, "Leavenworth is enjoying the good times now, compared to what her recent experience has been. We hope for a speedy return of the 'palmy days' of '57–'58."[57] During each of the war years Leavenworth controlled at least a portion of the military business, much to the chagrin of jealous rivals who always complained that Leavenworth's success was due to political pull rather than superiority as a depot. The editor of the *St. Joseph Morning Herald,* lamenting the wartime slack in his town, advised his readers to:

Go into Leavenworth, and improvement is everywhere visible. Instead of being oppressed by the war, they have been enriched by it, and trade with them never was so lively as now. The town supports three large daily papers, and in their columns every man from the hod-carrier to the wholesale merchants, sets forth his inducements to patrons. Speculation and competition are rife, and the result seems to be, that all are acquiring wealth. No less than three theatres are supported, one of them almost equal to any institution of the kind in St. Louis or Chicago. We urge the people of St. Joseph to imitate the example of their most formidable rival.[58]

Omaha's emergence as a freighting depot came suddenly in 1863 when the army ordered its stores for Forts Laramie, Kearny, and Halleck to be started from there. This innovation, according to Omaha spokesmen, was in the interests of economy because the government could save about a dollar per hundredweight by starting freight from Omaha rather than Leavenworth. Leavenworth and Nebraska City interests simply would not accept this reasoning and entered formal protests when the transfer to Omaha became publicly known. The *Nebraska City News* passed the word that Omaha's selection was gained by Maj. Gen. Samuel Curtis, who was reported to be a one-twenty-fourth owner of the Omaha–Council Bluffs ferry and the owner of Omaha real estate. Omaha, contended the *News,* did not have the shortest and cheapest route, and for logical evidence pointed out that post sutlers at Kearny, Laramie, and Halleck preferred to ship their supplies through Nebraska City.[59]

Nebraska City and Omaha newspapermen never resolved the question of Curtis' possible conflict of interest, but E. B. Taylor, editor of the *Omaha Republican,* pursued the cheapest-route argument vigorously. The switch to Omaha, he said, was but a straw in the wind, and soon Nebraska City would lose her trade to the superior North Platte route. "Our friend of the News should, however," said Taylor, "console himself with the reflection that if the 'Prairie Schooners' should be taken from him, he yet has the 'Prairie Motor'—the veritable 'steam wagon' that is to annihilate time and space, to fall back upon. That ingenious Yankee will be back one of these days, and replace that broken wrist-pin, and then it may be, the Government freight will be ordered back to Nebraska City.!"[60]

Omaha's supreme moment came when Irwin, Jackman & Company subcontracted a portion of the freight to Alexander Majors, the long standing symbol of Nebraska City's greatest business. The insolvent Majors had emerged with his reputation comparatively untarnished from the collapse of the Russell, Majors & Waddell empire. He was still extremely popular and deferentially treated as the epitome of the frontier freighter. Nebraska City hated to lose him even for as much as a season.

Majors sent out at least five full trains as part of his season's work. There were other subcontractors including Peck & Wood, which carried some goods to Fort Laramie. In addition to the Irwin, Jackman & Company contract freight, the army started quantities of grain from Omaha. Capt. J. M. Bradshaw, acting quartermaster at Omaha, advertised for 50,000 bushels of corn in sacks for Fort Laramie and 15,000 bushels for Fort Kearny. Starr & Howe of Atchison obtained the business with a bid of $3.46¾ per bushel for Fort Laramie corn and $1.23½ for Fort Kearny. Then they subcontracted the whole business to Majors, who shipped the corn from Omaha. There is a good possibility that Majors hired numerous farmers to haul their own corn, at least in the Fort Kearny business.[61]

Even the greatest Omaha boosters with a few moments of reflection would have had to admit that in spite of the military business Nebraska City was still first and Omaha was still in second place. While the respective giants of the South Platte and North Platte regions were the leaders, a fair portion of the freighting business was cornered by lesser towns such as Brownville, Plattsmouth, and Peru.

Through 1863 Brownville was Nebraska's third freighting town. Its trade began with the Colorado gold rush and always depended heavily on supplying Colorado and transporting grain to Fort Kearny. During 1858–1859 Brownville developed its own trail which joined the Oregon Trail at the mouth of the Big Sandy, approximately one hundred miles to the west-southwest. The trail ran to Tecumseh, on to Beatrice, and then through the northern part of Jefferson County before intersecting the main trail.[62]

Freighting to Colorado over this route was incidental until 1861, when David J. Martin & Company, an outfitting establishment that handled a complete line of groceries, clothing, and hardware, started transporting quantities of provisions for its branch store at Central City. By early March, Martin was loading the last of forty wagons that were to carry 110,000 pounds of bacon, butter, lard, and other groceries to the mining area. This was part of quantities of provisions that had been acquired in southwestern Iowa and northwestern Missouri over the winter and assembled at Brownville. Most of Martin's wagons started in March to take advantage of the traditional early spring shortages in Colorado, but by June he was quite active again, when he attempted to hire fifteen or twenty teams to carry freight to Colorado. There is a chance that by this time Martin did not have the capital to purchase necessary stock to freight all of his goods, and there is also a possibility that the Brownville area had a shortage of oxen by summer. Irwin, Jackman & Company had purchased several hundred head of oxen around Brownville for use in their military freighting from Leavenworth. Within a few weeks Martin solved his animal shortage and sent out a large, forty wagon train.[63]

After Martin showed the way, many others in Brownville realized the advantages of the Colorado business. The *Nebraska Advertiser* of May 1, 1862, announced that "Mr. J. G. Melvin, and others, are busily preparing to freight flour and produce to the mines. Many farmers are also deserting their farms for the same purpose." Melvin was probably the main freighter during the season of 1862. He operated a grist mill that produced from sixty to seventy-five sacks of flour daily, most of which was ultimately sold in Colorado and much of which was transported by Melvin himself. Melvin advertised that he was prepared to furnish freighters and any other citizen with flour, corn, cornmeal, and buckwheat flour. Among other things, Melvin did custom milling at one-sixth in kind per bushel. Melvin's operation was indicative of an increasing utilization of Nebraska's agricultural resources.[64]

Some of the other Brownville freighting firms were Crow & Barrett and Rogers & Brothers, which carried freight for the merchant company of Hoadly & Atkinson. There were undoubtedly many others who sent out a wagon or two but received no publicity. Many farmers who freighted during idle times or who transported their own produce to Colorado would use their own horses rather than specially outfit with oxen.[65]

There was also some Colorado freighting from Peru and Plattsmouth. Fifty to seventy-five wagons stretched out on the Peru steamboat landing in June, 1861, gave promise of two or three trains from that point.[66] Freighting from Plattsmouth was in the hands of small traders who conducted their business with a few wagons. The *Rocky Mountain News* commonly ran resumes of the arrivals at the Elephant Stable in Denver. A rather typical excerpt is: "Mr. Conner, one team, flour, Plattsmouth. Chaplin & Co., two teams, flour and corn, Plattsmouth . . . ."[67] The heavy freight wagon was the standard equipment, but there were a few innovators. One Plattsmouth train consisted of ten one-ox carts, each containing about 1,200 pounds of flour. This entire train was managed by only two men, who in all likelihood had had some experience with Mexican carts of the Southwest or the Red River carts of the North.[68]

After the meager season of 1861, when only two Atchison trains were sent to Denver, Atchison recovered her position as the ranking depot for private freighting in Kansas. With the end of guerilla raids in northern Missouri, regular rail service was resumed to Atchison, and by the spring of 1862 freighters and emigrants were again passing through the town. Most of Atchison's extensive business that year was directed to Colorado by way of the Oregon Trail, but some freighting was done to points on the Santa Fe Trail. The total trade for 1862 was a respectable 4,046,714 pounds, about equal to the 1859 trade but well behind the 1860 figure. Well over half of the 1862 freight was transported by Howe & Starr, a large forwarding and commission house headed by George W. Howe.[69] The bulk of the Colorado business was standard items— flour, hardware, clothing, etc.—but there was at least one extraordinary train consisting of fruit trees and vegetable roots. A Col. Kipp of the Atchison Nursery visited Denver during the summer and took hundreds of orders for trees. In November he was back with thousands of apple and peach trees and a variety of smaller bushes and plants such as strawberries, raspberries, rhubarb, and grape vines. In order to successfully transport the trees, Kipp wrapped the roots in moss and then packed them in wagons tightly sealed to exclude light, water, and wind.[70]

Atchison's trade in 1863 was also brisk. It was characterized by a continuation of the Denver business and a sharp revival of the Salt Lake business. For some reason most Salt Lake City merchants abandoned freighting and returned to hiring professional freighters. It is quite likely that they lacked both the capital and the time to make the long trip to the Missouri and back, although the church trains continued to operate efficiently. The *Deseret News,* that advocate of Mormon self-sufficiency, was rather sensitive about the return of the outsiders, who included such Atchison firms as the Perry Brothers and Stebbins & Porter. These freighters also engaged in the Denver business, but the leader in the Denver trade was Howe & Starr, which advertised regionally that it would send out trains from Atchison on the first and the fifteenth of each month during the year.[71]

Atchison's freighting in 1863 was constantly advertised by the *Freedom's Champion,* which often reported the size and tonnage of individual trains and once reported that "freighting was never more brisk in Atchison than at the present. Trains are daily arriving and going out." No statistical summaries were published in that year, but the trade was later reported to have amounted to 5,438,456 pounds. Business was definitely on the upswing when compared to the slack year of 1861, although freighting did not measure up to prewar proportions.[72]

Leavenworth's main business was with the military, but some private freight was started from there in 1861. Jones & Cartwright, owner of the Pike's Peak Transportation Line, dominated this business as it had before the war. Its agents in Boston, New York, Chicago, Cincinnati, and St. Louis offered through bills of lading to Denver and the mining towns by working cooperatively with various steamboat and railroad lines. Some freighting from Leavenworth to Colorado was also done by McGaugh, Byer & Company and by P. G. Lowe.[73]

Leavenworth's freighting to Colorado apparently suffered some with the revival of Atchison in 1862. The *Leavenworth Conservative* claimed that the trade of 1862 was not publicly known because it was in the hands of many individual merchants and freighters rather than in the hands of large companies as in the past. The editor admitted that it would be "very difficult to secure full statistics of this trade. We know that no week goes by without one or more trains leaving this city for Denver."[74] Even this generalization is probably an exaggeration. Denver newspapers referred constantly to Nebraska City and Atchison freight but only occasionally mentioned Leavenworth after 1861. Leavenworth spokesmen did not seem to have been alarmed by the declining trade; after all, they had the trade of the most important military depot on the river.

A few freighters, including George B. Skinner and a Mr. Frost, worked out of St. Joseph. Frost became one of the first of the winter traders when he took a mule train of twenty-five wagons to Denver in February, 1861. St. Joseph's main significance, however, was as a starting point for emigrants.[75]

Freighting was generally a one-way business. About all a freighter ever brought back from the west was an empty wagon, but occasionally there was some eastbound business. Most freighters returning in the fall were willing to sell passage to homeward-bound miners. If they had any cargo, it was likely to be buffalo robes. Notices of trains arriving with robes were fairly often seen in Nebraska City newspapers. Within the space of a few weeks during 1862, about 13,000 buffalo robes were brought in from Fort Laramie. In 1863 some wool was sent east from Colorado, and small amounts of cotton were shipped through Nebraska from Utah. The Mormon church began experimenting with cotton in the Washington County or "Dixie" area of southwestern Utah in 1861. This was but another part of its overall aim of self-sufficiency. Some of the cotton was processed locally, and some was sent to the East for sale or processing. Eighteen months after the beginning of the experiment about 74,000 pounds had been freighted to the Missouri River and a smaller amount sent to California. Cotton, however, was never anything more than experimental in Utah and did not have any lasting effect on Missouri River freighting.[76]

By 1863 the amount of overland freighting must have been roughly equivalent to that of the immediate prewar years. Statistics for the period are not comprehensive, but they do suggest certain conclusions. Taking the entire period 1861–1863 into consideration, Nebraska City was the ranking freighting center. In slightly less than a month early in the 1862 season, 632 wagons carrying an estimated 5,000 pounds each started from Nebraska City for Colorado and way points. For the year Nebraska City's trade was 7,853,910 pounds, which required the use of 1,357 wagons, 1,788 men, 8,912 oxen, and 1,156 mules. This was nearly double the sum of Atchison's freighting.[77] In 1863 Nebraska City had eighteen freighting firms; some ran as few as one train, some as many as four or five.[78] There is no reason to believe that the 1863 trade varied greatly from the 1862 business or that the relative importance of Nebraska City and Atchison had been altered.

At the close of the 1863 season, freighters had every reason to be optimistic. The Civil War was going well for the Union, and its end would surely result in more people, and consequently a bigger market, in the West. The Union Pacific and the inevitable end of wagon freighting was still several years away. The Indians of the Plains were becoming increasingly more troublesome, which would probably result in more military business. The wheel of prosperity was on the upswing, and the result would be a business boom of unprecedented proportions.

VI

The Freighting Boom, 1864-1865

Overland freighting reached unprecedented proportions in 1864–1865. During these years westward emigration resumed its prewar scope, and the provisioning of road ranches was a major item in the overland trade. Then too, there was a continuation of freighting to Colorado and Utah and an expansion of the Montana trade. For the most part, however, the boom was caused by the great increase in military activities along the Platte Valley routes when the government responded to actions by hostile Indians. The Indians disrupted trade and blocked the emigrant routes, but since they were the main reason for the reinforcement of the military frontier, they also stimulated freighting. Because of the hostiles, freighters were dependent on the military to keep the roads open, and in many instances the roads were kept open so the freighters could supply the army. Looking at the situation in a strict trade sense, one must conclude that these were good years. To the man who lost wagons or stock or risked his life, these were the bad years. Good business and high risks were so closely intertwined that freighters might well have appreciated Dickens' reflection on an earlier troubled time in history: "These are the best of times, these are the worst of times."

By the mid-nineteenth century the great question of who was to lose in the old struggle between white and red men had long since been answered. There was no longer a question of control of the continent but rather a series of lesser questions involving the destinies of particular tribes. The Indian, of course, with few exceptions had never comprehended the large struggle of abrasive civilizations but always showed concern for local issues. After the 1850's the Indians of the plains should have realized, or so many white men thought, that the old order had passed on and that military resistance to the whites was futile if not suicidal. Within each tribe some advocated an accommodation to, or an imitation of, the white man's way. There were others, however—the traditionalists or blanket Indians—who wanted to go back to the old days when there were more buffalo and fewer whites. This could not be accomplished through councils and treaties, but only through war.

During the Civil War various Indian grievances, some old and some new, touched off a series of skirmishes and raids popularly known as the "Indian War of 1864." Many of the Sioux and Cheyenne bitterly resented the harsh treatment meted out by Harney and Sumner and looked for a chance to avenge themselves. The Colorado gold rush presented a new peril to the buffalo-hunting natives. In the old days the Oregonians and Californians had simply passed through the country, but the gold miners came to stay in their hastily-built towns nestled on the western edge of the plains. As miners entrenched themselves, the farming frontier crept inevitably westward from the Missouri. This population boom was neither understood nor appreciated by the Indians. The whites in the East and those in the West were within 500 miles of each other and maintained contact on heavily trafficked trails that ran through buffalo country. Certainly this was a grave threat to the Indian, whose mind was in the past and who did not trust either frontiersmen or government.

Indians were generally present along the Platte route, partially because this had been their trail before the white man came and partially because they could obtain provisions from emigrants and freighters—sometimes by begging, sometimes by bartering, and sometimes by demanding. Coloradans generally did not believe that the Laramie Treaty of 1851, providing for a trail through Indian land, had gone far enough. The Indians, they thought, should have been pulled away from the trail, and for that matter away from the mining area, and placed on reservations where they could be subsisted by a beneficent government. A negotiated settlement with the Sioux, Cheyenne, and Arapaho was not realized despite efforts by the governor of Colorado Territory and the Sioux agent. Indians would either not attend conferences or else would not consent to banishment to reservations. While the plains Indians balked at the white pressures, they were shocked to hear of an Indian war from a completely unexpected quarter—Minnesota.[1]

The four Minnesota tribes composing the eastern or Santee Sioux had never caused any serious difficulty prior to the Sioux Uprising of August, 1862. They had relinquished most of their tribal lands in 1851 and had been moved onto narrow reservations along the upper Minnesota River. Nearly forgotten except by a few zealous reformers and the government, these Indians suffered through a series of disasters—reduction of their reservations, unpopular traders, an incompetent agent, crop failures, near famine, and ultimately the failure of the government to deliver annuities. Within a few days after rebelling, the hostiles had killed several hundred whites, most of them farmers who lived close to the reservations. Once the Sioux lost the element of surprise, they were placed on the defensive and soon forced westward by Minnesota militiamen. Most of the hostiles fled into Dakota Territory or Canada. Some reached the Missouri River and joined bands of Yanktonai and Teton Sioux, who were greatly distressed by the increasing river trade to the Montana mines.[2]

Of the 7,000 Santee Sioux probably 10 to 15 per cent could actually be called hostiles. When the blood was fresh, however, frontiersmen did not concern themselves with such distinctions as good Indians and bad Indians. No Indian was to be trusted. Stories of atrocities in Minnesota and raids in southeastern Dakota were soon carried to Nebraska, where fear of an impending Indian war ran high. Much of Nebraska's hysteria was due to a Sioux raid on the Pawnee reservation in September, 1862. This attack was the work of western Sioux and in no way related to the Minnesota war, but panicky settlers did not realize this at the time. Many fled into towns, apparently thinking that a general Indian war was underway. Nebraska's answer was to organize the Second Nebraska Cavalry for defense of the east and north and to request federal support for overland trail protection.

The uprising in Minnesota unnerved the Indians of the northern and central plains as well as the whites, particularly when the government dispatched two large punitive expeditions into

Dakota Territory in 1863. The strategy of trapping hostiles between the double envelopment of Gen. Henry Hastings Sibley's troops crossing the plains from the east, and Alfred Sully's army following up the Missouri failed mainly becaue of poor communications and the unnavigability of the Missouri. Sully finally fought a decisive battle at White Stone Hill in present southeastern North Dakota. According to some of the Indians, Sully showed no more concern for women and children than Harney had demonstrated at the Battle of Ash Hollow. Sully was ordered out again in 1864 on an expedition that carried him all the way from the upper Missouri to the Yellowstone.

The army's large expeditions into Dakota forced many of the Sioux to retreat southward and come in contact with the tribes of the Platte region, who had been experiencing their own difficulties with the whites. Naturally the emotions of the Platte Valley tribesmen were further aroused when they heard numerous stories about the army's harshness from their embittered, frightened kinsmen. The ever-increasing militancy of the Indians in the Platte Valley was perhaps a manifestation of concern for their own safety. What assurance did they have that the army would not be sent against them next? Their worries were compounded by the government's rather obvious suspicion of all Indians.

Increasing government mistrust of Indians soon became apparent after the Minnesota outbreak when the issuance of guns and ammunition to the tribes that received annuities through the Upper Platte Agency was discontinued. Because the government had traditionally supplied these items, the new decision, according to the Indians, was tantamount to cheating and stealing from them.[3]

Since these things happened during the Civil War, it is tempting to think in terms of Indians seizing on the war as an opportunity to strike against a weakened government. In light of the 1863 expeditions in Dakota and the reinforcement of the overland trail garrisons in 1862 and 1863, it is unlikely that many Indians regarded the government as being particularly weak. Nonetheless, there was among the natives a militant element that wanted to fight regardless of the odds and the chances for survival. These small bands of swiftly moving warriors did not intend to bring on engagements with United States troops but rather to raid and ambush in situations where they had surprise and probably numerical superiority on their side.

The "War of 1864" began in typical Indian fashion—random strikes scattered over an area of several hundred miles. On April 3, 1864, some Cheyenne reportedly stampeded about 170 head of oxen belonging to Irwin & Jackman on the Big Sandy east of Denver. The Cheyenne later claimed that the cattle stampeded because of carelessness on the part of the white herders, who, in an attempt to absolve themselves, started the story of the Indian raid. Uneasy Coloradans immediately moved to punish the guilty Indians. Units of the territorial militia were ordered into the Cheyenne country to the east and southeast of Denver. One detachment fought a sharp engagement with some Cheyenne near Fort Larned on the Arkansas River, with Indian casualties reported at twenty-five to thirty dead. This riled up the neighboring Kiowa as well as the Cheyenne, and freighters on the Santa Fe Trail were soon attacked. On June 19 Crow & Barrett's train bound from Brownville to Fort Union, New Mexico, was attacked by about 120 Indians near Fort Larned. The freighters lost eight men, thirty-one head of oxen, and about $4,000 worth of property including many wagons.[4]

Meanwhile, hostilities had been extended along the Platte. In early May a detachment of Colorado militiamen attacked a Cheyenne village north of the South Platte, killing twenty-six Indians and wounding thirty more. Later in the month a band of Oglala Sioux killed two whites while attacking a train on the north bank of the Platte opposite Fort Cottonwood (McPherson).[5]

Near panic reigned in Denver when the news of the Hungate murders reached town. The Hungates and their two children, who lived about thirty miles east of Denver, had been murdered by Indians on June 11. The scalped, badly mutilated bodies were carried to Denver and exhibited by aroused citizens. Rumors that an attack on Denver was imminent kept Denver and neighboring communities on the alert. The anticipated attack never came, but the Cheyenne continued raiding along the South Platte.[6]

Peace overtures by Brig. Gen. Robert B. Mitchell, commander of the Military District of Nebraska, and John Evans, governor of Colorado Territory, failed to stop the raids. Mitchell talked with some Sioux at Fort Cottonwood and asked that they withdraw from the Platte routes. This they refused to do. Evans' attempts to parley with the Cheyenne, Arapaho, and Kiowa during the summer met with failure. Because of raids and reprisals by both sides and the general notion that the other side was at fault, it was impossible for the contenders to confer.

The Sioux were initially peaceful, and their leaders remained officially peaceful throughout the time of hostilities, but some of the young militants could not be restrained from joining the Cheyenne and Arapaho, who were making a rather good thing of seizing freighters' supplies. The greatest Indian successes came during a four-day period in August when they shifted their attacks to the trail east of Julesburg. Cheyenne, Arapaho, and Brule Sioux slashed at ranches, mail and stage stations, and emigrant and freighters' trains. On August 7 and 8 all ranches and stations between Julesburg and Fort Kearny were struck. The first to be attacked, Plum Creek Station, less than forty miles west of Fort Kearny, was the hardest hit. Despite many casualties, the men at Plum Creek managed to send telegraph warnings alerting the other stations. The hostiles then swept to the area east of Fort Kearny, following the main line of the Oregon Trail along the Little Blue River. All ranches and stations between Fort Kearny and the mouth of the Big Sandy in Nebraska were devastated. Since the settlers along the Little Blue were off the telegraph line, they were caught completely by surprise. Alexander Majors was among those who took refuge in Fort Kearny during the raids. After the attacks it was reported that twenty people had been killed along the Little Blue and another twenty killed between Fort Kearny and Fort Cottonwood, most of them at Plum Creek.[7]

Freighters suffered heavily. Several large trains lost all their stock, and some others were entirely abandoned. The raiding Indians were said to have been well supplied with luxuries such as silk cloth and ladies' finery. In order to safeguard small trains, the army imposed a military-type organization on the private freighters. Troops halted all wagons at designated check points such as the crossing of the Big Blue on the Nebraska City–Fort Kearny trail and at Fort Kearny. Then the smaller trains were formed into a single large train with an elected train captain and other guard officers. The size and organization of these trains was reaffirmed at all subsequent check points.

Train organization was sometimes prescribed through the issuance of special military orders by post commanders. O. N. Humphrey, a train "conductor" who freighted from Nebraska City to Denver, was issued one such order in 1865.

Hd. Qrs. Post Fort Kearney
N. T. Oct. 5th 1865

Special Orders
No. 245

In compliance with Special Orders No. 41, C. S. Hd. Qrs. Dept. of the Mo. the trains now at this Post are ready to start West is [*sic*] hereby organized with a Company for mutual protection and the safety of the train. Mr. O. N. Humphrey is hereby appointed conductor and will be held responsible for the holding of the organization and train together.

In no case will he permit the train nor men under his charge to straggle along the road. He will camp as near Military Posts as possible and will report any insubordination among the men belonging to the train to the Comdg Officer of the Post nearest the place where such insubordination shall have arisen.

By Order E. B. Murphy,
Capt. 7th Iowa Cavalry
Comdg Post

H. P. Leland
Lieut and Post Adjt.[8]

These raids caused the abandonment of great sections of the Nebraska frontier. Ranchemen, station operators, and telegraph clerks along the Platte scurried to the safety of Fort Kearny or Fort Cottonwood. Farmers in the North Platte area, with the exception of some at Grand Island, fled eastward, and settlers on the Big Blue removed themselves to the Missouri River towns. All stage and wagon operators likewise sought safety at the forts. The Overland Stage service was discontinued and stock and stages were withdrawn from the route. Denver mail for the East was sent to San Francisco by stage and then to New York by way of Panama.[9] An observer at Fort Kearny wrote to the *Omaha Republican* that "this great overland route, for many years past alive with the excitement of business and traffic, is now a desolation."[10] During most of August and September the hostiles prowled at will along the Platte between Fort Kearny and Denver. Troops at Kearny were braced for the expected return of the warriors. They constructed breastworks and dug rifle pits to defend the post and its many refugee inhabitants. Citizens of nearby Dobytown built a round fortification with loopholes for muskets in the center of town. At the western end of the trail Denverites were faced with impending famine before the red man's barrier finally dissolved in late September, enabling the resumption of travel and mail service. The Indians withdrew to the south just as they had gained the upper hand along the Platte. Military pressure did not cause them to move, but instead they vacated in favor of the buffalo hunting area south of the Republican. With winter approaching, the Indians had to turn their attention to the chronic problem of subsistence. The luxury of war had to be abandoned.[11]

The tension of 1863 and the hostilities of 1864 caused the army to increase its troop commitment greatly and to add additional posts. Prior to 1863 the major installations supplied by freighters were Forts Kearny, Laramie, Halleck, Douglas, and Bridger and Camp Weld, a Colorado militia installation at Denver. Camp Weld, started in 1861 because of the Civil War, was the induction and organization center for the Colorado Volunteers, whose main concern during the early war years was the threatened Confederate invasion of Colorado. Troops stationed there were frequently used for overland trail protection during the Indian raids of 1864–1865.

Overland trail protection was increased in 1863 with the addition of three new posts, one in Nebraska, another in Colorado, and a third in present Wyoming. In the fall of 1863 units of the Seventh Iowa Volunteer Cavalry were ordered to start a post at Cottonwood Springs, about ninety-five miles west of Fort Kearny. This site on the south bank of the Platte was on flat land between the river and Cottonwood Canyon. Part of the reason for this selection was that Indians commonly crossed the Platte here and followed through the canyon to the plains beyond. Thus, the post actually was at an intersection of the Oregon Trail and a heavily used Indian trail. The fort was picturesquely situated with the Cottonwood Springs and a ranche nearby. Rugged bluffs and cedar-filled canyons formed the background to the south. The abundant stands of red cedar enabled the troops to construct most of the buildings with logs secured within a few miles of the post. Initially the place was called Cantonment McKean; then in 1864 the name was changed to Fort Cottonwood and in 1866, to Fort McPherson.[12]

While Cantonment McKean was being constructed in late 1863, a company of Colorado Volunteers had been sent to LaPorte, the stage station north of Denver. In May, 1864, these men were replaced by two companies of the Eleventh Ohio Volunteer Cavalry. On June 9 the Ohioans were flooded out by the rampant Cache la Poudre River. They relocated on higher ground and named their new site after their commander, Col. William O. Collins. This post was maintained until 1867, and in subsequent years the town of Fort Collins grew up on the site.[13]

The Platte Bridge Station was about 130 miles northwest of Fort Laramie on the south bank of the North Platte where the Oregon Trail crossed the river. This was not a new site. The crossing had been a key spot throughout the great overland migrations, and in 1847 a ferry had been established there. It was later replaced by a toll bridge. In 1858–1859 troops were stationed there to guard the crossing. In 1862 troops were again sent to the site for the purpose of escorting emigrants and guarding the bridge. In 1863 a permanent garrison was sent to the Platte Bridge Station. The name was changed to Fort Caspar shortly after the death of the heroic Caspar W. Collins (son of William O. Collins) at the Battle of Platte Bridge Station in July, 1865.[14]

Safeguarding the trail in 1864 was the responsibility of Brig. Gen. Robert B. Mitchell, commander of the District of Nebraska. After futile peace negotiations following the outbreak in August, Mitchell reinforced the trail at several points during the fall by ordering troops to the vicinities of Scott's Bluffs and Julesburg. A small adobe post was located south of the North Platte about three miles northwest of Scott's Bluffs. This was deemed necessary to protect travelers and the telegraph line along the great stretch of previously unprotected trail between Fort Cottonwood and Fort Laramie. Once construction was completed, the fort was named after Gen. Mitchell.[15]

A larger installation, Fort Sedgwick (first called Fort Rankin), was started near the stage and telegraph station of Julesburg at the Upper California Crossing. This large sod stockade, 240 feet by 360 feet with eight-foot high walls, was situated a quarter of a mile south of the South Platte opposite the mouth of Lodgepole Creek. Here the river valley was only three miles wide with great bluffs looming up on both sides. To the south these rugged, grassy hills were interrupted by numerous sharp canyons, which enabled Indians to approach unseen. Since the fort had the mission of protecting the junction, it could have been located in no other place; yet this very location made it so vulnerable that when Indians struck Julesburg the garrison at Sedgwick was trapped and could not go to the aid of the village.[16]

Fort building along the South Platte was completed in July, 1865, with the addition of Camp Tyler just east of the mouth of Bijou Creek, where the Junction Ranche was located at the start of the cutoff road to Denver. The name was first changed to Fort Wardwell and then in 1866 to Fort Morgan. This fort greatly strengthened the South Platte route, but it was situated in a poorly grassed, virtually untimbered region, so it was always expensive to support. Hay, wood, and even building materials had to be imported. L. T. Cornforth of Denver freighted building supplies from Leavenworth in 1865. As he recalled, the post at that time had three commissary buildings, six officers' barracks, and ten small enlisted men's barracks. Rifle pits had been dug around some of the buildings, and an earth embankment about five feet high encircled the entire installation.[17]

In order to control the highly mobile Indians, the army found it necessary to use the permanent posts as bases of operation and to distribute most of the garrisons at key points along the trail. Mitchell sent troops to telegraph stations such as Ficklin's Springs, southeast of Scott's Bluffs (near present Melbeta, Nebraska), and Mud Springs, eight miles southeast of Court House Rock. Maj. George M. O'Brien, commander of Fort Cottonwood, placed men at stage stations and ranches on about a one hundred mile section of the trail west of the post. There were sixteen to twenty men assigned to each place. Some were infantry, who were used for guard duty, and some cavalry, who were used for patroling, scouting, and escorting.[18]

While the army was reinforcing the trail, the calm of the fall of 1864 was dramatically broken by the Chivington Massacre. In southeastern Colorado some Cheyenne and Arapaho led by Chief Black Kettle had indicated a willingness to deal with the government. Hopes of negotiating were shattered when their camp on Sand Creek northeast of Fort Lyon was suddenly raided by Colorado militiamen led by Col. John M. Chivington. The Chivington Massacre, while completely unwarranted, was generally received on the frontier as a rather practical solution to the Indian problem. The unprovoked and brutal attack caused many of the neutral and even friendly Indians to join the hostiles. The Sand Creek episode forced the Indians to conclude that negotiating was futile.

There was great concern among the tribes for their own safety since they had no assurance that Chivington's attack was not the first phase of a great military offensive. Thousands of Sioux, Cheyenne, and Arapaho, no longer feeling safe south of the Platte, began the long trek north to the Powder River country during the winter. The recent wars and the brutality of Sand Creek created a strong desire for revenge, and the tribes wreaked their vengeance on Julesburg. This little village near Fort Sedgwick was a major stage and mail depot, and quantities of merchandise were stored there. The Indians sought not only vengeance but provisions as well.

About a thousand warriors struck Julesburg on January 7, 1865, after first decoying some troops into the hills south of town. The sacking of Julesburg was followed by a series of sudden attacks on stage and telegraph stations and the ranches in the vicinity. Once again eastern contacts with Denver were severed. The overland telegraph wires were cut in numerous places, and all travel west of Fort Cottonwood was suspended. The Indians lingered in the area long enough to raid Julesburg again on February 2. The town was again sacked and buildings burned. The soldiers were helpless against the massive Indian war party. As they moved toward the Powder River, the hostiles attacked the telegraph station and cantonment at Mud Springs and carried on running engagements with cavalrymen from Fort Laramie on the North Platte.[19]

After their withdrawal to the north, isolated bands of hostiles returned to raid along the South Platte in 1865. In May a stage messenger reported that several hundred head of cattle had been run off by a small band of Indians. In October a war party of 100 to 300 braves attacked a large train near Alkali Springs a short distance west of O'Fallon's Bluffs and succeeded in killing four drivers and destroying six wagons. At about the same time Henry T. Clarke, a well-known freighter of Omaha, lost eighty-seven head of cattle near Julesburg to a small raiding party. Even after the trail was heavily fortified and patrolled, freighters and travelers felt insecure.[20]

The government reinforcement of the trail in 1864–1865 was not sufficient to satisfy frontiersmen. Some Nebraskans had been bitterly critical of the government for neglecting the frontier during the Civil War. Opinion, as reflected in the Omaha and Nebraska City newspapers, was that there was a crying need for more troops.

After the first raid on Julesburg, an editorialist for the *Nebraska Republican* estimated that "at least 10,000 troops are needed in this district to deal with the confederated tribes now devastating the country with pillage, murder, and the torch."[21] After the raids of 1865 the *Nebraska City News* made the dire prophecy that the Indians had enough strength to again block the trail. In calling for a "vigorous prosecution" of the Indian war, the writer concluded that "a force of twenty thousand more troops along the roads will not be too large for the vast scope of country which requires protection."[22]

Frontiersmen and the government had conflicting views on how to solve the Indian problem. The westerners talked in terms of a military force large enough to remove the Indian menace permanently, perhaps with a Chivington-type solution. It is noteworthy that the frontier press generally defended Chivington and criticized Ben Wade, the chairman of the Congressional committee that investigated the Sand Creek Massacre. The government, at best, hoped only to keep the overland route open and comparatively safe. Emerging from the long, costly Civil War, it had neither the funds nor the desire to commit an extraordinarily large force to the frontier. As it was, those troops who were assigned to the frontier were generally demoralized, and the use of Confederate prisoners, the famed "galvanized Yankees," was criticized by frontier editors.

In 1864, with the outcome of the Civil War certain, and in 1865, with the war's end, the government assigned more troops to overland trail duty. On December 31, 1864, slightly over 3,000 soldiers were assigned to the trail between the Missouri and Salt Lake City, including the South Platte route to Denver. This was a little more than double the strength of a year before. By April 30, 1865, these routes were guarded by nearly 3,800 men, most of them cavalry. In addition to supplying the troopers, the army had to subsist thousands of horses. Supplies for both had to be transported from the Missouri River towns.[23]

As in previous years the transportation of supplies was handled by civilian contractors. The successful bidder for Route 1, which included trade originating at Fort Leavenworth and points north and destined for Denver, Salt Lake City, and all points on the Platte River trails, was Alexander Caldwell & Company. This new firm was the successor of Irwin, Jackman & Company. It included many of the personnel of the old firm, but there were some significant changes. Alexander Caldwell was the senior partner in a trio that included David K. Jackman and James Duffy. As of 1864 J. C. Irwin was no longer with the firm. The effects of wartime inflation were clearly shown in the Caldwell contract. The rates, $2.25 per hundred per hundred miles, were higher than they had been in several years. This contract signed on July 18 was to cover the period April through September. Evidently the contractors and the government had an understanding before the agreement was signed because the work had been underway for several months.[24]

The Indian difficulties and military preparation of 1864 caused a very lively competition for the expanded army business of 1865. Caldwell was in an advantageous position because he had the experience and the equipment to handle this great volume of freight. Many of his competitors undoubtedly hoped to obtain the contract and then make arrangements to handle the business. The Route 1 bidders included such well known freighters as Andrew Stuart, James R. Porter, John Kerr, and David A. Butterfield. Caldwell, fully realizing the rising costs and risks, bid $2.90 per hundred per hundred miles. All of the bids were higher than the 1864 rates, but H. S. Bulkley, the successful bidder, was willing to settle for an advance of only one cent per hundred over 1864.[25] Bulkley, a Leavenworth resident, did not have the necessary freighting equipment at the time he submitted his bid, but the quartermaster regarded him as "responsible." Bulkley purchased quantities of wagons and cattle from Caldwell and then hired Caldwell to manage the business for him. Bulkley bid on the contract as a speculation, but the army was still dealing with an efficient, experienced administrator.[26]

In addition to the general contracts for transporting supplies and provisions, the army let many contracts for supplying corn. In 1864 the largest corn contracts were made with Leonard T. Smith, who was to supply 45,000 bushels at Forts Collins, Laramie, and Halleck, and with George Clark, who was to supply 50,000 bushels for Denver. In 1865, in addition to the regular contract, Bulkley had two major corn contracts: one to supply Fort Laramie with 20,000 bushels and one calling for 25,000 bushels to be delivered to Denver.[27]

During the fiscal year ending June 30, 1865, alone, contractors carried about 36,000,000 pounds of grain, mostly corn, to military destinations in Nebraska and along the trails west. The corn contracts always called for the grain to be delivered at a particular place at so much per bushel. For instance, corn delivered to Fort Kearny brought $5.03, to Fort Laramie $9.26, and to Denver $10.05. These rates were roughly equivalent to the general contract rate of 1865, $2.26 per hundred per hundred miles. The cost of corn at any destination was a combination of the purchase price and the transportation charges. It was the contractor's responsibility to purchase the corn and then perhaps store it prior to shipment. The grain was normally bought in the farming areas of eastern Nebraska and Kansas and western Missouri and Iowa.

Protection of the overland trails was very expensive. During the fiscal year ending June 30, 1865, the government spent over $6,000,000 on transportation and grain for all of its posts on the three plains routes. The heaviest expenditures were for Route 1, where $2,526,727.68 was paid for delivered grain and $1,524,119 for provisions and supplies on the regular contract.[28]

All of the Missouri River towns benefited from the military trade of 1864 and 1865. Leavenworth was named as the main depot in all contracts other than grain, and once again there arose the widespread resentment of her rivals because she commanded virtually no private trade but somehow was selected as the entrepot of the military business. Nebraska editors attributed Leavenworth's success to the fact that Kansas as a state had much more political strength in Washington than did Nebraska Territory. Atchison's spokesmen credited Leavenworth's military business to Senator James Lane. The army quartermaster officers contended that Leavenworth was the logical depot because of the ample warehouse facilities there. Military freighting, especially in 1865, proved to be so extensive that it was impossible to handle it from any one place. Thus, Leavenworth's rivals were also designated as military depots. The major contractors Caldwell and Bulkley had agents and subcontractors in all towns, and probably more military freight was actually shipped through Nebraska points, especially Nebraska City and Plattsmouth, than through Leavenworth. The corn contractors usually bought grain near their home towns, so every major town had a share of the military grain trade.

While the government was expending great sums to control the hostile Indians, it was also sending annuities to friendly Indians who were living under treaty obligations. After the opening of Kansas, Atchison became the main depot for Indian supplies and controlled the trade through 1863. Nebraska City and Omaha were considered to be eligible depots, but Nebraska did not have any of the Indian trade until Julian Metcalf of Nebraska City bid successfully in 1864. Metcalf secured the contract for freighting about forty tons of provisions to the Upper Platte Agency, just east of Fort Laramie, and fifty tons to Fort Bridger and Salt Lake City. For the Upper Platte freight he was paid $1.39½ per hundred pounds per hundred miles from Nebraska City to Fort Laramie or a site named by the agent, presumably the agency. The freight carried beyond Fort Laramie commanded $1.47⅝ per hundred per hundred miles.[29]

In 1865 the supply contract went to William McLennan of Nebraska City. In addition to the Upper Platte and Utah freight, he was to haul about sixty tons to old Fort Atkinson, Kansas, and fifteen tons to Santa Fe and Maxwell's Ranch, New Mexico. McLennan's contract called for the total shipment of about 165 tons from Nebraska City. For all routes he was paid $1.97 per hundredweight per hundred miles.[30] McLennan's goods were probably hauled in seventy to eighty wagons. During the period when overland freighting was important, annuities were slight compared to later, after the buffalo had been nearly exterminated and the Indians placed on reservations.

During 1864–1865 the overall volume of freighting to Colorado increased. This was primarily due to the military's heavy corn shipments. It is unlikely that the civilian trade varied greatly from preceding years. In fact, it may have been somewhat less. Mining activity had leveled off by 1864 and gold production decreased sharply after that time. The Colorado economy stagnated until the 1870's, when railroads and new mineral discoveries ushered in a new boom.[31] The main accomplishment of the Coloradans during the Indian difficulties was to sustain themselves, and this took considerable effort because of the many interruptions of the trade routes. It is ironic that as the wealth of Colorado decreased the cost of living skyrocketed because of the scarcity of goods and the perilous nature of overland freighting.

To Denverites 1864 was a calamitous year. Before the Indian troubles the elements plagued them. Heavy snow during the winter of 1863–1864 delayed freighters so much that most of them took from fifty to eighty days to travel from the Missouri to Denver. The delay and the heavy loss of stock drove freight rates as high as $10 to $15 a hundred. Coloradans naturally anticipated that costs would decrease with the resumption of spring and summer freighting. However, costs did not decline. First freighters had difficulty with muddy roads and then Denver and most of the mountain towns were made almost inaccessible by a great flood of the South Platte and the mountain streams that fed it. The Denver flood of May 19 came suddenly as a result of heavy rains on the divide near the source of Cherry Creek. Aside from the immediate destruction it wrought, the waters washed out the bridges and mountain roads that led to the interior. Unfortunately, the flood was followed by more heavy rain which caused yet more damage to mountain roads. The impassibility of the mountain routes drove the price of flour to $40 a hundred in Black Hawk and Central City. The road to the Gregory diggings was reported to have been torn away for miles, sometimes to depths of ten feet. Denver prices, which normally fell off sharply in the summer, remained high. Flour was still selling for $18 to $20 in June, and speculators were reported to be going out and meeting wagon trains outside Denver in order to purchase incoming supplies and controlling the market.[32]

Colorado had not yet recovered from the snows and the flood before the Indian outbreak in August completely severed supply routes. Flour by September was $20 to $22 a hundred. However, not much flour was being freighted. When shipping had been resumed in the fall, many freighters carried machinery rather than provisions since there was less chance of losing it to the Indians.[33] Provisions were so dear by late fall that even green apples, described as "very green" and "diminutive and dwarfish," were being peddled on Denver streets for $20 to $25 a bushel, or about $3 a dozen.[34] Nebraska City freighters who had had little opportunity to deliver goods in the fall entered the winter trade.[35] The *Rocky Mountain News* of December 21 reported that "freight, by mule train, from the Missouri to Denver is up to from twenty-three to thirty cents. A few winters since it was easy at twelve to fifteen cents."

Rates were lowered during the spring of 1865, but not greatly. Butterfield's express freight from Atchison charged 20¢ per pound for mining machinery, and the price of flour during the fall of 1865 was only slightly lower than it had been the preceding fall. So, despite the Indians' shift to the north, the price hike stimulated by their actions prevailed through 1865.[36]

Utah during the boom years continued to offer less opportunity to the commercial freighter than Colorado because Mormons had achieved a higher degree of self-sufficiency. The relentless urge to realize an economically independent society caused the Mormons to continue the use of church trains and to experiment with a new supply route from California by way of the Colorado River. In 1864 the Mormons moved their Missouri River staging area from Florence to the little village of Wyoming, seven miles north of Nebraska City. The move was evidently inspired primarily by a desire to obtain an area that offered more room for assembling trains and pasturing cattle. Wyoming was the last Missouri River assembly point used by the Mormons. Church trains were assembled there in 1864 and again in 1866. No Mormon trains were sent east in 1865, but Wyoming still was used as a point of departure for Mormon emigrants that year. During 1864 and 1866 combined, twenty-two organized church trains were sent out from Wyoming. The total emigration with these trains was about sixty-five hundred. The trains of 1866 alone used over three thousand oxen, about five hundred men, and nearly four hundred wagons.[37]

Nebraska City benefited from the Mormon shift to Wyoming. Usually the church trains were made up in Utah, but in 1866 sixty-two wagons and some stock were purchased in the Wyoming area. Part of this was obtained from the Overton brothers of Nebraska City, who sold all of their equipment—ninety mules and fifteen wagons—to the Mormon emigrants. In a fit of disillusionment after a Denver trip, the brothers decided to get out of the freighting business. They had underestimated the depth of a stream and soaked hundreds of bolts of calico and muslin. In order to save their cargo, they had had to unroll thousands of yards of cloth and stake it on the prairies to dry, then re-roll and re-pack all of it. Apparently this incident was the last straw for the Overton brothers.[38]

The proximity of the Mormons and their trade in Nebraska City made Nebraska City freighters more aware of the Utah trade.

Isaac Coe and D. J. McCann, two of the city's major freighters, became active in the trade. Nebraska City also benefited when Siegels, one of the largest of the Salt Lake City merchandising houses, forwarded most of its goods through the town. Since the Utah trade did not increase appreciably during the boom years, it is obvious that Nebraska City's new Utah business was mostly drawn away from Omaha because of the Mormons' shift to Wyoming.[39]

Salt Lake City merchants continued to carry freight to Utah in their own wagons. W. S. Godbe, Hooper & Eldridge, Kimball & Lawrence, and Walker Brothers all combined freighting and merchandising.[40] Some of their provisions were shipped on to Montana as Salt Lake City developed as one of the supply sources for the miners to the north. During the fall of 1864 Howard Livingston advertised that he was prepared to "furnish transportation for any amount of freight, either by mule or ox teams" from Salt Lake City to points in Idaho and Montana.[41]

The Utah economy was always adversely affected by the isolation of the Great Basin and the resultant heavy expense of transporting freight from either the Missouri River or California by wagon. While Utahans depended heavily on the Missouri River towns, they always realized that the 1,100- to 1,200-mile trip was a serious impediment to economical trade. As early as 1857 Brigham Young became interested in the possibility of a quick California freight route which would combine steamship transportation to the mouth of the Colorado, steamboats to the head of navigation, and wagons from some point below the Grand Canyon to Salt Lake City. Seven years later concrete steps were taken to implement this scheme. Young, as leader of the church, commissioned Anson Call, a successful missionary, to establish a depot on the Colorado River. Late in 1864 Call located a landing, called variously Callville, Call's Landing, and Old Callville, on the right bank of the Colorado about fifteen miles upstream from the present Hoover Dam at a site now inundated by Lake Mead.

The church, in cooperation with a group of Salt Lake merchants called the Deseret Mercantile Association, constructed a warehouse at the landing, and plans were made to ship goods in 1865. The dreams of the planners ran well ahead of their realization. About one hundred tons of freight were sent by the Colorado route in 1865, and the next year the Walker Brothers brought several trains from the river to Salt Lake City. However, the river proved to be difficult to navigate, and the overland trail was rough and slow. Whether this way would ultimately have proven better than the trail from the Missouri is problematical. The rapid construction of the Union Pacific in 1866 so shortened the mileage from the Missouri that importation from the east became demonstrably cheaper and faster than that from the southwest.[42]

Unlike Colorado and Utah, which were fairly stable during the Civil War, Montana boomed. The lure of gold drew thousands to this distant land. While not as well promoted as the Pike's Peak rush, the Montana rush was considerably richer. The 1863 returns of $8,000,000 were doubled the next year and then reached a high of $18,000,000 in 1865. The population of Montana Territory by the fall of 1864 was reported to be about twenty-one thousand. Most of these emigrants came from the southeast, either by the Missouri River or overland. The itineraries of 1,474 emigrants who had reached Montana before 1865 showed that more than 1,300 had traveled either by the Missouri or across the plains from the Missouri. The remainder came from the Pacific Northwest, Canada, and Minnesota.[43]

Montana was virtually an American Siberia. It was close to no place. The miners were supplied from many sources, none of which alone was adequate to meet their demands. The Missouri River was the main trade artery. St. Louis–based steamboats plied the river nearly 3,000 miles to Fort Benton, the head of navigation, and freight was carried from there to the mines by wagon. Steamboating was normally possible only in the spring and early summer when the river was high, so Montanans had to depend, in part, on overland connections with the Missouri River towns to the southeast and California and Oregon towns to the west.[44]

Despite challenging distances and Indian disturbances, Nebraska freighters continued in the Montana trade in 1864. Some combined the Nebraska–Salt Lake City–Montana business; others went directly to Montana by taking the route through South Pass, then proceeding north by way of Fort Hall. Both routes were long and necessitated crossing the Continental Divide twice. First, the mountains had to be crossed at South Pass or Bridger Pass and then again before entering the mining camps from the west. Thus, the 1,600 mile trip from the Missouri commonly took freighters as long as four or five months.[45]

Freight rates from the Missouri River towns were usually 25¢ a pound, sometimes slightly less, other times higher. One freighter was paid 28¢ a pound for delivering a stock of drugs, liquor, and "store fixtures" from the Missouri River to Virginia City in 1864. These rates seemed high to Montanans, but actually they were not greatly different from those being charged at that time to Coloradans, who were over 1,000 miles closer to the freighting towns. It would seem that Montana rates should have been much higher; there are reasons why they were not. Montana freighters had passed through the Platte Valley before it was overrun by the Indians in 1864, so the hostiles did not have nearly as much impact on Montana as on Colorado. Also, freighters had no competition for the Denver trade and so at times may have charged what the traffic would bear, but Montana freighters were regulated considerably by competition from the Fort Benton–bound steamboats and overland freighters from the Pacific states.

Stagecoaches offered the fastest connection between the Missouri River and Montana. Under ideal conditions stages made the trip by way of South Pass in sixteen days of round-the-clock traveling, carrying passengers for $350 with each meal a dollar or two extra. Express freight commanded $2 a pound. While providing comparatively rapid passenger and express service, the stages could not transport heavy freight.[46]

Sidney Edgerton, the first governor of Montana Territory and a veteran of the overland trip, was fully cognizant of Montana's isolation and poor transportation facilities. In order to make the territory more accessible and attractive to emigrants, Edgerton proposed the opening of a new trail that would save many miles and avoid crossing the Rockies. The Territorial Legislature, fully sympathetic with the governor, petitioned Congress early in 1865 to establish a more direct route to Montana.[47]

Montanans were not really asking the government to reconnoiter a new route but simply to protect one that in fact already existed. The existence of a direct route that stayed east of the Big Horns and connected the Oregon Trail and Virginia City was well established by 1865. This route, which lay through Indian land, came to be popularly known as the Bozeman Trail.

During the winter of 1862–1863 John M. Bozeman, a young Georgian who had prospected in the western mountains for three years, made the long trek from the Bannack City area to the North

Platte by traveling east of the Big Horns. During the summer of 1863 and again in 1864, he led parties to Montana by this new way. Bozeman was not alone in seeking a more direct route. On April 24, 1863, the *Nebraska Republican* reported that a Maj. Graham, an old mountain man originally from Illinois, had explored a route from Fort Laramie to the Three Forks and Bannack City area. Then too, Jim Bridger, the almost legendary mountain man, used a trail that ran through and then west of the Big Horns. He led a wagon train to Virginia City over this trail in 1864.[48]

White penetration of the plains east of the Big Horns alarmed and angered the Sioux, who were determined to protect their vast buffalo hunting grounds. The federal government responded to Montana's call by deciding to clear the hostiles from the Bozeman Trail. This difficult mission was given to the Connor Expedition in 1865. Gen. Patrick Edward Connor, commander of the newly created District of the Plains, headed a three-pronged offensive that struck into the Powder River country. The eastern division started at Omaha and then marched to the Powder River by staying east and north of the Black Hills of Dakota. The middle division went from Fort Laramie to the west slope of the Black Hills, and the western division, headed by Connor, assembled at Julesburg, then proceeded to Fort Laramie and later picked up the Bozeman Trail and followed it northwest. The three units had a combined strength of nearly 3,000 men. Unfortunately, they were never able to coordinate and acted practically as unrelated movements. Nothing went right with the expedition. The troops were mutinous. Connor had virtually no intelligence of the country or the enemy. Supplies arrived late and were short. Nothing of note was achieved by the expedition, though several indecisive skirmishes occurred and Connor did establish a post, Fort Connor, on the Bozeman Trail near present-day Sussex, Wyoming.[49]

Some freighters first used the Bozeman Trail because of the Connor Expedition. Connor's quartermaster, Capt. H. E. Palmer, pressed freighters into service at Fort Laramie because the army had only eighty wagons. In this way he secured 105 more men, including forty from Edward Creighton and thirty from Tom Pollack.[50]

During 1865, despite the presence of the hostiles and the indecisiveness of the Connor Expedition, most of the Montana overland trade from Missouri River towns shifted from the South Pass route to the Bozeman Trail because the new route was 400 to 500 miles shorter than the old. These freighters followed the established Oregon Trail to the mouth of LaPrele Creek, eighty-two miles up the North Platte from Fort Laramie and about fifty miles east of present-day Casper. At LaPrele Creek they forded the North Platte and followed the trail pioneered by Bozeman to the mines. This road, lying through open country east of the Big Horns, ran slightly northwest past present-day Sheridan, Wyoming. It then swung west around the north end of the Big Horns and went on through present-day Bozeman, Montana, to Virginia City. Jim Bridger, who surveyed the route in 1866, reported the distance from LaPrele Creek to Virginia City as 526 miles. The total distance from Fort Kearny to Virginia City by way of the Upper California Crossing of the South Platte, noted Bridger, was 967 miles. Hence, Nebraska City freighters who went to Virginia City by way of Fort Kearny and the Upper Crossing traveled approximately 1,150 miles.[51]

Omaha claimed the shortest route because her freighters stayed along the Platte and North Platte all the way to the Bozeman Trail. The South Platte towns were disadvantageously located in the competition for the Montana trade because their freighters had to ford the Platte. Since they usually forded at the Upper California Crossing rather than at Fort Kearny, their route was also longer.[52]

Omahans, mainly because of the geographic advantage, easily led the way in the Montana trade of 1864–1865, and were probably a close second to Plattsmouth traders the next year. S. R. Brown, Edward Creighton, Henry T. Clark, and Boulware & Maxon all did some business with Montana. Their Montana freight was the usual provisions, and their eastbound business, if they had any, was returning miners. Montana mining, like that of Colorado, was quite seasonal and hundreds of miners came back east in the fall. Most of them made their way to Fort Benton and came down the Missouri by steamboat or mackinaw, since this was the fastest passage. It was also safest for those who had gold; about five-sixths of Montana's gold was reported to be shipped by this route. Some miners, however, preferred the wagon trip and paid the returning freighters for a wagon ride. Edward Creighton once brought back over 200 miners with one of his trains.[53]

While Omaha dominated the Montana trade, she did not mo-

nopolize it. All of the South Platte towns had some freighting to
Montana. Their position south of the river did not exclude them
from the Montana business any more than Omaha's position north
of the river excluded her from the Denver business, but it did make
it more difficult to compete.

During 1864–1865 overland freighting to Montana was a significant business, but in the overall Montana trade it was secondary
to Missouri River steamboating. The well-known journalist and
traveler Albert D. Richardson estimated that in 1865 "about one-
fifth of the supplies come overland from California and Oregon;
one-fifth overland from Kansas and Nebraska; and three-fifths up
the Missouri from St. Louis to Fort Benton."[54] The absence of
statistics precludes any possibility of either verifying or disproving
Richardson, but it is generally recognized that most of the supplies
came up the Missouri River, so his estimates would seem logical.

During the Montana boom Nebraska towns faced a new threat
from Sioux Citians who ambitiously promoted a road across northern Nebraska connecting Sioux City and Virginia City. Before 1865
there had not been any overland freighting from any Missouri
River point north of Omaha because the great western markets
could best be served by the Platte River routes. The Montana gold
rush and the far northern location of the new area caused Sioux
City boosters to think that the trade routes could perhaps be
shifted away from the Platte River. It was commonly recognized
that time and distance to Montana could be saved if overland
freight were shipped up the Missouri by steamboat as far as possible. By starting from Sioux City, a freighter would save at least 100
miles, which was the approximate distance from Omaha to Sioux
City. One hundred miles normally could be traveled by steamboats
in one or two days, whereas wagons would take six or seven. Sioux
City's main transportation interests had always been geared to the
steamboat business, particularly that of the upper Missouri. A
combination of steamboating and overland freighting would enable
Sioux City to dominate the business of Montana. Since the Missouri
turned northwestward at Sioux City, any major point above there
was a potential rival for the Montana business. Fortunately for
Sioux City, the country above was generally unsettled, and the
scheme by Minnesotans to establish a trade center at Fort Thompson, above Fort Randall, had failed. Yankton, Dakota Territory,
was the only town of note above Sioux City in 1865, and its leaders

chose to concentrate their energies on plans to open the Black Hills. Thus, Sioux City was the point farthest upstream on the Missouri that had any interest in overland freighting to Montana.

Sioux City merchants and promoters talked up a Montana road in 1864, when there was general dissatisfaction by miners, travelers, and the government with the South Pass route. Sioux City's request for federal aid, presented in Congress by Representative A. W. Hubbard of the Northwest Iowa Congressional District, coincided with the Montana petition calling for the protection of the route east of the Big Horns. As a result, Hubbard's proposal was received by the government as one of the possible solutions for the ticklish problem of improving connections with Montana. Congress provided $50,000 for the surveying, marking, and improving of a road from the mouth of the Niobrara to Virginia City, with branch roads from both Omaha and Sioux City to the Niobrara. Sioux Citians, particularly Congressman Hubbard, had much more interest in the road than did Omahans. Hubbard worked closely with the Interior Department in planning the opening of the road.

James A Sawyers, a Sioux Citian with some frontier military experience, was appointed superintendent of the project. He assembled a party at the mouth of the Niobrara in June, 1865, which included surveyors, a military escort, and the train of a private company, C. E. Hedges & Company of Sioux City. Thirty-six of the eighty wagons in the train were Hedges'. The road builders followed the Niobrara for over 300 miles and then struck northwest across the White River to the Big Cheyenne, which was followed into present-day Wyoming. From the Big Cheyenne they proceeded to Pumpkin Buttes and then to the Powder River, where they followed the recent trail of Connor's expedition to the place where it merged with the Bozeman Trail. They then took the Bozeman Trail into Virginia City, over 1,000 miles and four months from the Niobrara. The expedition was a grim undertaking. The escort of "galvanized Yankees" was unenthusiastic and inefficient. Sawyers and the escort commander did not get along. In the Powder River country the train was under almost continual harassment by the Sioux, who killed several members of the party and secured provisions from the others through threats. Omaha newspapers rarely missed an opportunity to report the expedition's troubles and the undesirability of the new northern trail.

The *Sioux City Journal,* the most vocal backer of the Niobrara road, was still enthusiastic after 1865. Sawyers took out a small party in 1866 to improve the trail, but he was faced with the growing realization that the government preferred the Platte River and Bozeman Trail routes. Military forces, already overtaxed by the necessity of fortifying the Bozeman Trail while still protecting the Oregon Trail, were drastically cut back in 1866 during the post Civil War economy move. The government had neither the men nor the desire to fortify yet another route along the Niobrara. Sawyers' second expedition was the last train to use the Niobrara–Virginia City road. The road was obviously well to the north of the main emigration flow and generally lay through more arid country than the Oregon Trail. Sioux City boosters had overestimated the ambitions and the abilities of their townsmen to take up overland freighting. The rapid extension of the Union Pacific dealt the final blow to the Niobrara–Virginia City road. Portions of the trail were later used by emigrants to the Black Hills, but as a road to Montana the route was a total failure.[55] Sioux City in no way detracted from the booming trade through the Platte Valley, where Nebraska City continued her dominance.

Nebraska City freighters had a share of all facets of the business but relied most heavily on military freighting and supplying Colorado and road ranches. Nebraska City was in the most advantageous position to seize on the boom because she had the men, animals, equipment, warehouses, merchants, and experience necessary to handle a rapidly expanding trade, a trade that ran well ahead of even monthly expectations throughout 1865.

The effects of increased overland freighting were reflected in the steamboat business. The *Press* of July 11, 1864, reported that steamboat arrivals were double those of any previous year. In 1865 Nebraska City was served by five boats of the Hannibal & St. Joseph Railroad Packet Line, six of the Merchants Line from St. Louis, five of the Atlantic & Mississippi Company's line that operated from New Orleans, and three independent boats. Levee receipts to the first of June were expected to average not less than 1,000 tons a week. By early May, 51 steamers had deposited freight on the Nebraska City levee amounting to over 8,500,000 pounds. During the winter, freight, as in the past, was carried by teams from St. Joseph to Nebraska City. This St. Joseph winter freighting in 1864–1865 was probably just as important as the winter trade across the plains.[56]

The boom and bustle of freighting was contagious. Nebraska City grew rapidly and prospered. The economy of the town was indicated by the United States Assistant Assessor in July, 1865. He reported among other things 16 blacksmith shops, 10 wagon shops, 1 carriage maker, 4 builders and contractors, 8 eating houses, 7 butchers, 8 cattle brokers, 7 harness makers, 7 livery stables, 23 physicians, 4 photographers, 12 lawyers, 6 hotels, 28 boarding houses, 48 retail liquor dealers, 57 retail general merchandise dealers, and 165 freighters.[57] It is not at all surprising that citizens complained of the clouds of dust raised by grinding wagons and throngs of animals. Near the end of the boom, Nebraska City had something over 6,000 inhabitants, 7 churches, 8 schools, 40 saloons, 10 billiard tables, 2 newspapers, and, reported the *News*, "a steam wagon."[58]

There were many familiar names among Nebraska City's dozens of freighters during the heyday of 1864–1865, including Thomas Chivington, Alexander Carlyle, and D. J. McCann. Notably absent were the Byrams, who had abandoned Nebraska City in favor of Atchison. Most of the boom period freighters, however, were recent arrivals in Nebraska City, including many who came up from Atchison. The Atchison transfers always commanded press notices, since they continued to be the best proof of the superiority of the Nebraska City route. A large number of freighters, particularly those who arrived in 1865, worked out of Nebraska City for only one season or part of it, so there are no local records of them. Most of these freighters were enticed to Nebraska City by the opportunities to subcontract for the shipment of military supplies, especially corn. The corn contractors were always short of teams. In April, 1865, a Nebraska City forwarding house, Hawley & White, advertised for 500 teams to freight corn to Fort Kearny and intermediate points.[59]

Nebraska City's freighting in 1864 broke existing records, and these, in turn, were greatly surpassed the next year. The 1864 business was first reported to be 18,000,000 pounds but was subsequently said to be 23,000,000.[60] The aggregate livestock holdings were estimated at 10,000 yoke of oxen and 2,000 span of mules. After the 1864 season the *Daily News* boasted that "we can send more freight hence to Denver, the mountains, Idaho and Utah than can be forwarded from any other point on the Missouri River."[61]

Despite inclement weather and bad roads, freighters were on the trail in numbers early in the spring of 1865. Most of them hauled corn for the government, and there was a certain urgency in forwarding this to the frontier cavalry. Some of the corn was purchased in eastern Nebraska, but much of it was brought to Nebraska City levees by steamboats. Corn was undoubtedly the largest single item in both the Missouri River and overland businesses. By July 10, counting poundage for only those trains of four wagons or more, slightly over 32,000,000 pounds of freight had been sent overland. Activity slowed considerably after July, which was always the case, but the year's total came to 44,023,598 pounds. The forwarding of this record amount of freight utilized 4,081 wagons, 3,040 men, and 35,850 oxen. The value of animals and equipment was estimated at over $4,000,000.[62]

Quantitatively, Nebraska City's trade increased sharply in 1864–1865, but her freighters were not relatively as important as they had been, because they controlled a smaller proportion of the total trade, especially compared to the 1861–1863 period. The trade of 1865 was so large that no single place could hope to dominate it; in fact, the major freighting centers of Atchison, Leavenworth, and Nebraska City combined could not handle it, because it was impossible to concentrate all of the animals, men, equipment, and goods in so few places. New depots had to be developed to handle freight.

A combination of heavy shipments and the riskiness of the North Platte route caused Plattsmouth to become a major freighting center overnight and to replace Omaha as Nebraska City's chief rival. Plattsmouth had not had much freighting before 1865— so little, in fact, that no sizeable warehouse had ever been constructed on the levee. Plattsmouth's rising fortunes were due, in part, to the decision of the army quartermaster to locate a depot there. During 1865 a Sgt. McMaken superintended the army's business at Plattsmouth by organizing trains to carry military freight.[63] Nearly every issue of the *Nebraska Herald* contained notices of the arrival of steamboats with corn and other goods and the departure of trains. In addition to the military freight, Plattsmouth did a lively civilian trade, especially with Montana-bound miners, who commonly transported quartz mills. This civilian

Military Posts Supplied by Missouri River Freighters, 1864-1866

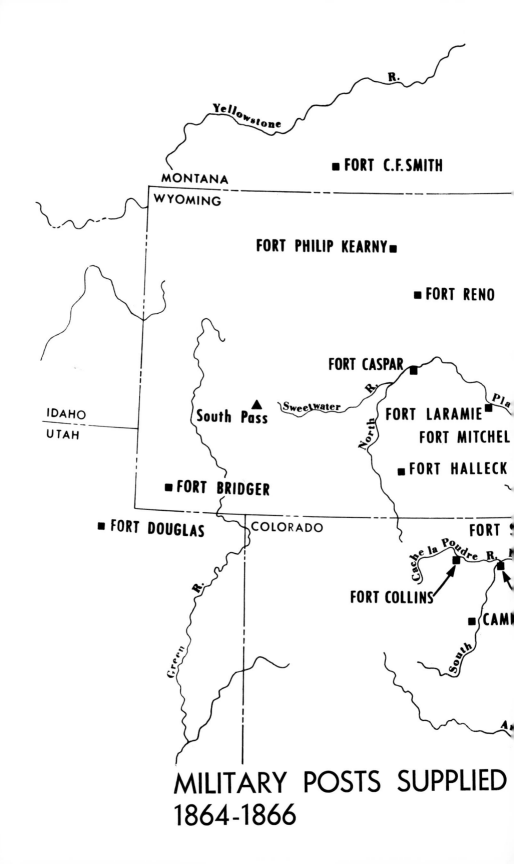

MILITARY POSTS SUPPLIED
1864-1866

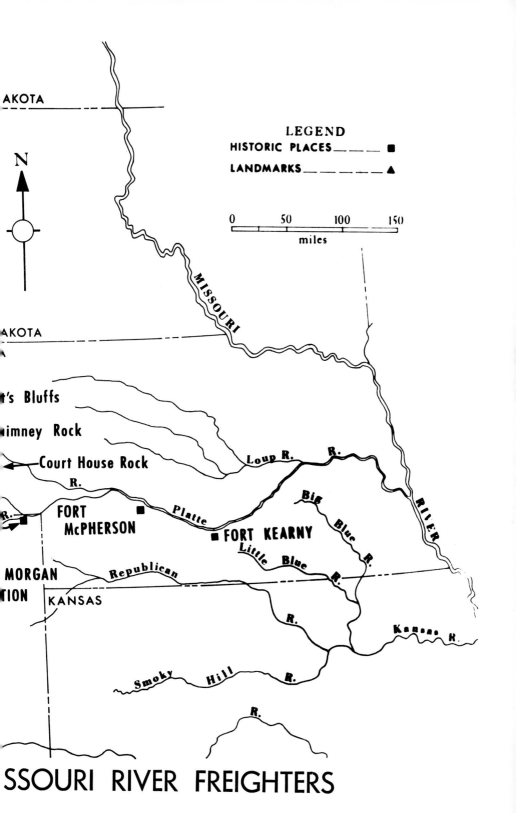

LEGEND
HISTORIC PLACES_____ ■
LANDMARKS_____ ▲

0   50   100   150
miles

SSOURI RIVER FREIGHTERS

trade, in part, was diverted from Omaha and the North Platte route because of the prevailing notion that the Indian threat was more severe north of the river. This idea was officially endorsed by the military, much to Omaha's distress. There were instances of freighters coming by boat from Omaha to Plattsmouth, either because of the Indian threat or the unwillingness of those who were bound for Colorado to cross the Platte. Plattsmouth was probably the major depot for the Montana business in 1865. Montana-bound parties are often mentioned in newspaper reports, much more often than by the press of Omaha or Nebraska City.

Plattsmouth's leading freighters were the Porter brothers, James R. and William B., of Plattsmouth, C. H. Parmalee of Council Bluffs, and John McCormick of Omaha. There were many others who were military subcontractors. These freighters and the many emigrant trains that passed through Plattsmouth used the trail along the South Platte, which was the old Nebraska City road beyond Salt Creek.

Plattsmouth was nearly as significant as Nebraska City in 1865. During one week in June, 500,000 pounds of freight were brought up by steamboats for western destinations, and during a four-day period in August, 400,000 pounds of corn were unloaded at the levee. An official statement issued by the town mayor reported 35,712,500 pounds freighted out in 1865, requiring 8,000 men, 53,526 oxen, 7,186 mules and horses, and 7,825 wagons. A report circulated in Colorado by J. M. Cavanaugh placed the figure at nearly 44,000,000 pounds. Plattsmouth's only year as a major depot was truly a remarkable one. What reputation the town has as a freighting entrepot is based almost entirely on the 1865 business.[64]

Omaha was less affected by the boom than either Nebraska City or Plattsmouth. An estimate of Omaha's trade has to be based on such generalities as "trains heavily laden with all kinds of goods, groceries and provisions, are leaving this city almost daily for Denver . . . "[65] rather than specifics since statistical summaries were not published. Omaha newspapers apparently preferred the generalities because any quantitative report would simply have confirmed the third-rate status of Omaha's freighting.

Omaha had even less military freighting in 1864 than the preceding year, because Leavenworth was again designated as the starting point for most of the North Platte freight. In January of

1865, Capt. S. H. Moer, the quartermaster officer, sent several trains from Omaha with supplies for Fort Kearny, but by spring most of this business had been shifted to Plattsmouth.[66]

Omaha's inability to maintain her relative importance as a freighting and emigrant staging center was caused partially by the well-known difficulty of crossing the Platte, which was necessary for those bound for Colorado. Indian troubles also left the North Platte road exposed, since Forts Kearny and Cottonwood were both south of the river and the military concentrated its efforts on keeping the Oregon Trail open. Because of these circumstances, even Montana-bound emigrants who started from Omaha might have found it necessary to travel part of the time south of the river. The question of bridging the Platte was lively again in 1865. Shinn's Ferry had been inoperative for long periods in the spring because of delays in securing new boats. It was not until June 16 that the *Nebraska Republican* could assure its readers that the ferry would be "in good order" within three days. In the meantime many freighters and emigrants had gone by way of Plattsmouth. O. P. Hurford of Omaha, who had long wanted a bridge at Fort Kearny, claimed that such a bridge was an absolute necessity if the people of Omaha wished "to recover and retain their trade with the West."[67] Hurford reported that he had the necessary $30,000 pledged in 1862 but could not obtain permission from the Secretary of War to construct a bridge touching the military reservation. Hurford believed that permission could be obtained in 1865, and he proposed that $20,000 be raised from private parties and the remaining $10,000 from the counties on the North Platte route between Omaha and the Fort Kearny crossing.[68] Once again Omaha citizens failed to respond to the plea to bridge the Platte.

The dangers of the North Platte trail became well known when Gen. Connor, prior to his expedition in 1865, sent the following telegram to Capt. S. H. Moer, the Omaha quartermaster: "If trains with fifty armed men desire to take the north side of the Platte, so organize them; notify them however that the Platte cannot be crossed on account of high water, and that I will not be responsible for their scalps, nor can they have any escort on the north side, as I have not the troops to spare. I can only protect one line of travel."[69] Connor's statement, while roundly denounced by the Omaha press, was seized upon by all downstream journals as authoritative testimony about the condition of the North Platte road. Traffic north of the river was not stopped, but it was certainly slowed by the unbridged Platte and the Indian menace.

Simply being located south of the Platte was not a guarantee of freighting success, as the village of Brownville realized. Brownville freighting during the boom of 1864–1865 was considerably less than in the early war years. Hoping to recapture some of their earlier prosperity, Brownville residents on November 25, 1865, held a public meeting for the purpose of raising funds to improve their connecting road to the Oregon Trail. Something over $1,500 was subscribed, but this was the year before the end of the freighting era, so their concern came a little too late.[70]

Kansas-based freighters, particularly those from Atchison, greatly expanded their business during the boom. Atchison maintained its reputation as the principal starting point for civilian goods, while Leavenworth relied almost exclusively on the military trade. The carriers of civilian goods who had a choice of starting places usually avoided Leavenworth because of the greater length of its trail and the increasing difficulty of maintaining a decent road because of encroaching farmers. Strange as it now seems, the government never visualized the overland trails as precursors of great national highways. The trails were not exempt from land surveys. When trailmakers had complete choice of terrain they naturally chose the high, dry ridges for wagon trails. With the advancing farmers came the systematic land surveys. When land was taken up, a farmer by fencing off an area could force the trail around his land. The over-all effect near Leavenworth was to increase the mileage and force the wagon routes into the low, wet ground which was the least suited for agriculture.[71]

Atchison was at least as well situated as Nebraska City to seize on the boom because she had location, experience, and equipment. Not only did the town have river transportation but it was the westernmost point to have railroad connections with the East. Some of the largest freighting firms in the West were based there. They included Stebbins & Porter and George W. Howe. These two firms were probably the most important in Atchison's freighting history, if the entire period is considered. During the boom some newcomers added to Atchison's importance. In 1864 the Byrams switched from Nebraska City to Atchison. The *Freedom's Champion* welcomed them as "men of capital, energy and great experience . . ." who were said to have realized profits to the amount of $50,000 annually for the past five years.[72] Atchison's most important newcomer, however, was David A. Butterfield of Denver, who established an express freight service between Atchison and Denver and forwarded goods to other western destinations. He offered through bills of lading from eastern sources to any major depot in Colorado, Utah, and Montana. During his first year Butterfield was actually a forwarding and commission merchant who subcontracted for the actual hauling.[73]

Atchison's freighting in 1864 was nearly three times greater than that of the previous year. From March 1 to November 1, 16,639,390 pounds of freight were sent to western destinations.[74] Atchison was clearly on the move, and enthusiasm ran high. The *Freedom's Champion*, long the leading publicist of Atchison's transportation business, noted with a neat piece of imprecision that "the great advantages Atchison possesses as a starting point for all places on the Great Plains, has concentrated nearly, not quite, all the freighting business here."[75]

As early as January of 1865 Atchison freighters anticipated a record year. Hundreds of wagons were accumulated at the town, and arrangements had been made to import freight by both railroad and a regular line of steamboats from St. Louis. By early spring hundreds of tons of freight had been stockpiled on the levee and at the depot.[76]

Through 1864 Atchison freighters to western and northwestern destinations used the Oregon Trail, but in 1865 the Smoky Hill route through Kansas was developed as a freighting road. This trail from Atchison to Denver was shorter than the Platte River route, but it had the reputation of being dry and subject to Indian attacks. It had been used by some emigrants during the Pike's Peak gold rush but had never attracted freighters, who feared heavy losses of stock on the arid trail. Interestingly enough, it was David A. Butterfield, the newcomer to overland freighting, who was willing to experiment and open the Smoky Hill Trail as a way for wagons and stages by providing way stations for the storage of grain and forage. Early in the season Butterfield had used the old route to Denver and had sent out 2,000,000 pounds of freight by June 1. He was reported to be planning on a total shipment of 35,000,000 pounds for the season.[77]

Opening the Smoky Hill route was a major undertaking. Butterfield's first train was accompanied by a military escort of 250 men and a number of engineers. The party improved the road as it went by removing obstructions and selecting sites for future trail stations. The vanguard of the expedition reached Denver on August 9. Later in the season Butterfield sent several large trains on the Smoky Hill Trail and began running stages over the route after some of the stations had been completed. Butterfield's Overland Despatch was soon famous throughout the West. There is no doubt that in 1865 Butterfield was the major carrier of civilian goods on the plains. He intended to establish express freight service by the spring of 1866 which would convey freight from Atchison to Denver in only eight days. Butterfield's great enterprise was hailed on both sides of the trail. Atchison's material gain was obvious, and Denverites looked forward to the first reliable system in their history.[78]

Since Butterfield's Overland Despatch was so novel and grand, it was the most newsworthy aspect of Atchison's business. However, many of Atchison's freighters to Colorado and Utah continued to travel the old route, and quite likely a greater proportion of Atchison's freight was sent through the Platte Valley than by the Smoky Hill Trail. The respective freighting over the two routes was never reported statistically by the newspapers. There is even some difficulty in determining the exact amount of freighting during what was Atchison's record year. The *Freedom's Champion* of January 4, 1866, reported an admittedly incomplete grand total of 21,531,830 pounds. This included the returns of only one of the major wholesale grocers and did not include freight sent to most Kansas destinations. Of the above total nearly 12,000,000 pounds went to Colorado, nearly 3,000,000 to Utah, about 1,500,000 to Santa Fe, about 600,000 to Montana, and the remainder distributed among the major military posts such as Fort Riley, Camp Collins, and Fort Laramie.

The freight of Nebraska City, Atchison, and Plattsmouth, combined with that of Leavenworth, St. Joseph, and Omaha, resulted in staggering new totals for overland freighting in 1864–1865. Albert D. Richardson reported that the station keeper at Fort Kearny recorded 6,000 freight wagons which had passed by within a six-week period in 1865—900 of them in a three-day period. Individual towns were primarily interested in reporting their own trade, but railroad promoters were vitally concerned with the size of the overall trade, since this was the best indicator of future railroad freight volume. Lt. Col. James H. Simpson, assigned to the Union Pacific project, reported on the basis of a prospectus of Butterfield's Overland Despatch that the 1864 freighting from all points on the Missouri from May to November totaled 63,000,000 pounds. He estimated that the 1865 trade might be 250 per cent larger. The *Nebraska Republican,* while reporting on the Union Pacific, claimed that the 1865 wagon trade on the plains was 200,000,000 pounds. This estimate evidently included the Santa Fe business. The figure is perhaps exaggerated, but probably not greatly so.[79]

The extent of freighting for 1865 can probably never be determined except in general terms. It was definitely unprecedented and clearly pointed out not only the need for railroads but also the desirability of rapid construction of them. There was every indication, with the increasing emigrant tide, that the 1866 western freight would reach new dimensions. It did, but it was the Union Pacific, not the wagon freighter, which benefited.

VII

Overland Freighting and the Union Pacific, 1866-1867

Freighters were always aware that it was just a matter of time until their business would be replaced by railroads. Overland freighting had developed during the years of Congressional debate over transcontinental railroads, then boomed after Congress in 1862 chartered the Union Pacific. The railroad was authorized by an optimistic Congress, which had taken upon itself the responsibility of making sweeping decisions affecting the West. The chartering of the Union Pacific and the Homestead Act of the same year were basic parts of an overall plan to link East and West. The opening of vast areas of the public domain in mid-continent began the closing of the last frontier. For a time the starting point of the railroad was in doubt, but when Omaha was chosen as the eastern terminus, Nebraska City and her freighters realized that this decision had determined which of the towns would become preeminent. However, the inevitable fate of overland freighting was delayed for a time.

Congressmen who had granted to the railroad generous portions of public domain to defray construction costs anticipated and expected rapid building. They were bitterly disappointed when lack of capital and manpower delayed the start of the road. The railroad was greatly talked about during the Civil War, but it never really got beyond the planning stage. Thus, the rapidly increasing trade of 1864–1865 was left to the overland freighters.

177

During 1865, the Platte Valley's greatest freighting year, the Union Pacific began laying track. The company had many problems to solve. Construction in a frontier area necessitated the importation of labor. Housing was scarce in Omaha, so the company had difficulty quartering its men. Most of the men were inexperienced, and it took time before they could be welded into tightly-disciplined, effective work forces. Ties were normally cut from timber on the Missouri River bottoms, but rails had to be imported from the East by steamboat because Omaha did not have an eastern railroad connection. The company during this first year completed only forty miles of track, and freighters took satisfaction in the calculation that it was a long way to the Pacific at that rate. They certainly never anticipated the decisiveness of the next year.[1] A favorable winter enabled the contractors to work much of the time. They put down side tracks and constructed a station house at Fremont and then pushed on. Before spring, however, they were delayed by a shortage of rail which persisted until the opening of navigation. By late March the arrival of rail was imminent, and the engineers announced a point opposite Fort Kearny as their December, 1866, goal.[2]

The state and prospects of the Union Pacific in early 1866 did not still the blatant optimism of Nebraska City spokesmen. Any fears they may have had were soothed by continual newspaper assurances of the bright outlook for the coming season. There was considerable justification for the freighting capital's view, since the government initially followed its customary overland freighting contracting procedure. The Route 1 contract, which was now expanded to include fortifications on the Bozeman Trail south of forty-four degrees north, as well as all posts along and near the Oregon Trail east of Salt Lake City, was awarded to Alexander Caldwell on March 12. Caldwell agreed to carry from 100,000 to 10,000,000 pounds at a season-long rate of $1.45 per hundredweight per hundred miles.[3] This low rate was indicative of the severe competition from other freighters for the military trade. Also, the decrease was in keeping with the general rate reduction after the Indians no longer threatened the trails along the Platte. Nebraska City freighters anticipated a great share of the military business, which, as per custom, was to start from Leavenworth and other designated points. This was the arrangement that had been followed in the past, and it had generally resulted in Nebraska City benefiting heavily, since it was selected as an alternate depot.

Nebraska City also continued to control what Indian trade existed. Harrison H. Moulton agreed to haul about fifty tons of Indian annuities to Salt Lake City and intermediate points at $1.78 per hundred per hundred miles. This business was considerably less than that of the preceding year, since it apparently did not include goods for Indians served by the Upper Platte Agency. These tribes were to be assembled at a peace conference at Fort Laramie later in the year, and separate arrangements were made to transport the provisions for this council from Omaha.[4]

In addition to this government business, Nebraska City anticipated a continuation of the Colorado, Utah, and ranche trade and a livelier Montana business. Freighting was evidently quite brisk in the spring and early summer, but then it fell off rapidly. As business declined the *Nebraska City News* began speaking in general rather than specific terms in describing freighting, which was in marked contrast to other years when statistical summaries were printed. The paper described only particular, large, single shipments or very active days. On one occasion 600 tons were said to be lying on the wharf awaiting transshipment; a later report was of 163 wagons leaving town in one day. Despite an obvious effort to pretend that nothing essential was changing, the references to freighting became less frequent as the season wore on, and it was obvious by late summer that Nebraska City was losing its hold on the transportation business.[5]

Plattsmouth, which had had only one really outstanding freighting season, did not have as much tradition to defend as Nebraska City, and so it was considerably easier for her freighters to accept the new order of things. The *Nebraska Herald* of April 11, 1866, frankly reported that "the spring, so far, has been very backward, and trade apparently dull. . . ." There is no reason to believe that conditions at Plattsmouth changed much during the season; if anything, they worsened. During the spring about 100 wagons a week loaded in Plattsmouth, but by summer a wagon train was an exceptional sight.

Nebraska City and Plattsmouth freighters felt the effects of the Union Pacific much earlier than they had expected. In early June tracks were laid to Columbus on the Loup Fork, and both the government and private parties concluded that they could effect a considerable saving of time and money by using this nearly ninety-mile portion of track. The army decided henceforth to ship most of its supplies from Omaha. This was done in part because Omaha had been named headquarters of the recently created Department of the Platte, but mainly because there were clear advantages to utilizing the railroad.[6]

This change was legally permissible in the military contract, but it drastically altered the freighting arrangement because it forced Caldwell and many of his subcontractors to shift their operations to Omaha. Leavenworth, which had benefited for years because Fort Leavenworth was the starting point for quartermaster contracts, was hit hard also. Her freighters either had to move to Omaha or get out of the business. In a short time some 300 wagons were transferred from Leavenworth to the end of the track. Some of the Nebraska City freighters who worked with Caldwell had to move to Columbus, much to their chagrin. A number of them were reported to have said that they would rather work out of Nebraska City for less money than make the move.[7] The economy to the government hardly proved to be one to the many individuals who had to accommodate to the new policy by moving their equipment and making new arrangements for pasturage and outfitting. Just as military expansion gave promise of a more lucrative trade, freighters were required to move to a new location, a location which considerably shortened their hauls.

The government's decision to fortify the Bozeman Trail greatly increased freighting opportunities along the route to the Montana mines. The army was sorely disappointed by the abject failure of the Connor Expedition of 1865. Many Indians, especially the Sioux led by Red Cloud, were as belligerent as ever, and the promise of Montana gold diminished with hundreds of hostiles occupying the area between the Oregon Trail and the Yellowstone. What was one of the Indian's last buffalo grounds was also the best overland route to Montana. Connor's failure and the continuing hostility of the Sioux caused the army to move decisively in the spring of 1866 in an attempt to regain some of its lost prestige and to curb one of the last remaining blocs of hostile Indians.

On May 19, Col. Henry B. Carrington started from Fort Kearny on the most difficult task of his career—to open and protect the Bozeman Trail. This proud man, disdainful of the savage opposition, was embarking on one of the grandest failures of the frontier army. Carrington had about 2,000 men, but only 700 were destined for the Bozeman Trail. Nearly two-thirds of the men were to be used to relieve troops stationed along the Oregon Trail and the South Platte route to Denver. Carrington was under instructions to start three new posts and to abandon Fort Connor, the only tangible result of the famed expedition of 1865. Instead, he decided to expand Fort Connor, which was renamed Fort Reno by order of the War Department. He then moved northwest and established the second fort in July. This was Fort Philip Kearny on the Little Piney, a branch of the Clear Fork of the Powder River (about twenty miles south of present-day Sheridan, Wyoming). The third post, C. F. Smith on the Big Horn River (about thirty-five miles southwest of present-day Hardin, Montana), was located in August.[8] These fortifications encouraged a heavy traffic by emigrants, who were assured at Fort Laramie that the route was open and safe. Red Cloud's Sioux never accepted the opening of the trail and immediately began a series of raids known as Red Cloud's War, a war relentlessly pursued until the government agreed to abandon the Bozeman Trail in 1868.

The isolation of these posts and their relative inaccessibility during the winter forced the army to stockpile huge quantities of supplies, grain, and forage. The grain was all shipped from the terminus of the Union Pacific. Rather than expand the Route 1 contract with Caldwell, the military opened a new contract to cover grain transportation. Herman Kountze, an Omaha banker and businessman who had had previous contracting experience with a Fort Halleck hay contract in 1863, accepted the responsibility of supplying the distant forts. He agreed to convey 1,680,000 pounds to Fort Laramie, approximately 500,000 pounds of grain to Fort Reno, 300,000 pounds for what became Fort Philip Kearny, and 300,000 pounds for what ultimately became Fort C. F. Smith. At the time the contract was signed only Fort Laramie was definitely established. Fort Reno was the only Bozeman Trail post referred to by name. The second post was simply described as the "new fort at Foot of Big Horn Mountains," and the third fort was the "new fort at head of Yellowstone." Kountze was to be paid $1.42 per hundredweight per hundred miles. The unknown distances were to be decided by agreement between the contractor and quartermaster officers. Five days later Kountze signed a second supply contract—to haul 25,000 bushels of grain (approximately 1,350,000 pounds) at $1.40 per hundredweight per hundred miles from the railroad terminus to Fort McPherson, the main post guarding the Union Pacific surveying and construction crews. The slightly lower rate in the second contract was undoubtedly stipulated because of the comparative security of the trail to Fort McPherson.[9]

As the season progressed, Kountze and all other freighters made increasingly shorter hauls as the Union Pacific crews pushed forward rapidly. In June, Kountze's wagons started from Columbus, which was 215 miles from Fort McPherson, 486 miles from Fort Laramie, and 825 miles from Fort C. F. Smith, the most distant destination. By July the wagons were starting from Lone Tree (present Central City), about 40 miles beyond Columbus, and by late August from the terminus at Kearney, over 100 miles west of Columbus. Military demands exceeded early season expectations, since Kountze transported about 200,000 pounds more than had been estimated in the contracts.[10]

As in the several previous years, the 1866 trade consisted mainly of grain for the ever-increasing frontier military. Caldwell and Kountze combined could not handle the military needs, and several other large grain contracts were let. J. P. Sears, Jr., had one to deliver 600,000 pounds of corn at Denver at $9 per hundred, and James Martin agreed to deliver 100,000 pounds of corn at Denver for $6.45 a hundred. D. J. McCann had a contract to supply Fort Caspar, which called for 207,000 pounds of shelled corn at $5 a bushel. As usual, the contract price was a combination of the cost of the corn and transportation.[11]

During the summer of 1866 the North Platte route became the main avenue for the many military contractors who worked in the shrinking space between the railroad terminus and the western forts. The North Platte road was the scene of feverish activity as the railroad construction crews pushed on and thousands of wagons carried goods from the terminus. Two great frontier dramas, the death throes of overland freighting and the birth of the Union Pacific, were enacted simultaneously. Most of the freighters acknowledged that this would probably be their last good year in Nebraska, as the Union Pacific was proving to be the master of distance in its relentless push toward the Rockies.

The railroad's goal for 1866 was attained in August, when track reached Kearney Station, one of the end-of-track section headquarters that survived as the nucleus of a later city after the crews moved on. Immediately the railroad opened a passenger and freight service from Omaha to Kearney. The 190 miles that had oftentimes taken freighters two weeks was covered in as little as fourteen hours. As Kearney boomed temporarily as the terminus and freighting center, the crews moved steadily west followed by a ragamuffin colony. The liquor vendors, prostitutes, card sharks, and unscrupulous merchants found easy prey in the lonely and rowdy construction hands. Many of these railroad camp followers had little cabins on wheels. The wheels were never removed, making their entire business portable, and they moved apace with the tracks. This "end-of-track" mass of wagons and tents even had an itinerant newspaper, the *Frontier Index,* whose publication was irregular due to the constant shifting.[12]

By the end of 1866, tracks were laid to a point 305 miles from Omaha, and construction slowed for the winter just beyond the mushrooming new terminus of North Platte, which had boomed from "untrodden prairie" to a village of 675 inhabitants in a space of a few weeks.[13] J. H. Simpson, president of the Union Pacific Board of Commissioners, who visited the town in December, reported that "where three weeks ago, there was nothing, are already some twenty buildings, including a brick engine roundhouse . . . a frame depot of the usual beautiful design; a large frame hotel, nearly finished to cost about $18,000."[14] The small village was served by four daily trains. North Platte enjoyed its terminal position until the following July when Julesburg, nearly ninety miles west, became "king." Then North Platte was described as a decaying place of "thirty or forty nondescript one-story buildings" and "a suburban belt of tents." Anything movable was off for Julesburg.[15]

While North Platte declined sharply, it nonetheless survived. Like many other former termini it had a difficult adjustment to make, an adjustment to a much less active and dramatic but more stable business—that of serving as a major depot. Like other places such as Kearney and Sidney that were section headquarters, the town grew with the railroad and the area. Some of the former boom towns were not so fortunate and were abandoned after a fleeting exposure to the light of history.

During its first few months North Platte was naturally Nebraska's freighting center, and it was for a time the transfer point for shipments by the Western Transportation Company, which well illustrates the interaction of rail and wagon transportation. The Western Transportation Company was promoted by Omaha businessmen, who, realizing that Omaha's future depended on railroads, made every effort to make railroad transportation as efficient as possible. One of Omaha's main drawbacks was that while the Union Pacific was being constructed the town did not have an eastern rail connection and so had to tolerate seasonal steamboat service. Anxious Omahans led by Augustus Kountze, Edward Creighton, and John McCormick decided not to await the arrival of the Chicago & Northwestern tracks at Council Bluffs but instead to form a company which would run wagons from the terminus of the Chicago & Northwestern to Omaha, transfer goods to the Union Pacific, and again run wagons from the Union Pacific terminus to various western destinations. This way they could offer through bills of lading and stimulate a winter trade through Omaha.

The company was organized in November, 1866, when the Chicago & Northwestern had reached Woodbine, Iowa, about forty miles east of Omaha. Edward Creighton, of telegraph and freighting fame, was president of the company, which included two well-known railroad engineers, Gen. J. S. Casement and Gen. Grenville M. Dodge, as directors. The Western Transportation Company was evidently the outgrowth of a freight line that Kountze, Creighton, McCormick, J. P. Peck, and J. W. Paddock had formed the previous spring to forward goods from Omaha to Denver.[16]

The company's express service that operated day and night began to function in December. Its first wagon reached Denver in less than five days from North Platte. The goal was to cover the distance from North Platte to Denver in five days, but this was sometimes done in four. Chicago freight was carried through to Denver in about ten days. The Iowa business of the Western Transportation Company ended in the spring of 1867 with the arrival of the Chicago & Northwestern at Council Bluffs, but a lively wagon business from Julesburg to Denver was continued for some time because the Union Pacific main line was constructed well north of Denver through Cheyenne. Julesburg was a significant freighting town until a railroad was completed from Cheyenne to Denver in 1870.

Although the Union Pacific lacked a decent crossing of the Missouri (it relied on ferries until a bridge was completed in March, 1872),[17] it was clearly the master of the western trade, as one of Nebraska City's greatest boosters finally admitted. J. Sterling Morton, editor of the *Nebraska City News,* visited Omaha in January, 1867, and came away convinced that "Omaha is the city of Nebraska. The streets were alive with people from all parts of the Territory . . . ." The only complaint of note was that merchants did not have goods enough to supply the great demand. The editor could only conclude that the "Pacific RR has performed wonders for Omaha."[18]

During 1867 freighters probably forwarded more goods in terms of pounds than in any previous year, but they were carrying it from North Platte, then Julesburg, and finally Cheyenne. Kansas freighters were likewise affected by the Union Pacific, Eastern Division (called the Kansas Pacific after 1869), which was operating as far as Fort Harker by June.[19] The total trade if thought of in ton-miles had actually decreased. The much shorter hauls meant that freighters could make several trips, sometimes many, during the course of the season, so there was less need for extensive numbers of men, wagons, and animals.

The bulk of this short-haul freighting was military supplies. Indian disturbances along the Bozeman Trail, highlighted by the Fetterman Massacre and the prolonged siege of Fort Phil Kearny, forced the government to reinforce all garrisons and to establish more posts. During the summer of 1867 Fort Fetterman, to be used as a base of operations against the Sioux, was built at the point where the Bozeman Trail left the North Platte, about fifty miles downstream from present Casper. Fort D. A. Russell, for the protection of the Union Pacific and the trails to Denver and Fort Laramie, was constructed on Crow Creek about three miles west of where Cheyenne was soon founded. With the addition of these posts the Department of the Platte included thirteen installations and approximately 5,000 men.[20]

The grandness of military freighting for 1867 was revealed when the army advertised that it would accept bids to transport up to 30,000,000 pounds on Route 1, which served the Department of the Platte. The projected business for this northern route was somewhat larger than that of the military business of the Santa Fe Trail and New Mexico combined. Since the government preferred to let a contract to a single bidder, the business demanded a contractor of considerable capital and equipment. Many of the major freighters and capitalists, including Alexander Caldwell, D. J. McCann, and Augustus Kountze, submitted bids[21] for this business, which was reported to exceed "by millions of pounds, that of any former years."[22]

Much to the disappointment of the experienced freighters, the contract went to the successor of Ben Holladay's Overland Stage, Wells, Fargo & Company. This company was well established in the East, first operating in the Boston to New York trade. It boldly moved into frontier areas with the purchase of Holladay's stage and express line. Within a short time Wells Fargo became a national byword as the company ran stages throughout the West and won fame for its service into mining areas. During its first full year of expanded operations, the company was the largest single freighting contractor in the West.

Wells Fargo was not at all equipped to handle the military contract with its own men and teams, and so throughout the year relied heavily on subcontractors. These were mostly Nebraska City freighters, who thronged to the railroad terminus mainly to haul goods into the dangerous Bozeman Trail country. While these subcontractors were advancing the fortunes of Wells Fargo, the Union Pacific construction crews moved on out of Nebraska. With them went the overland freighters.[23]

The year 1867 was a memorable one for Nebraska. It lost overland freighting, but it gained the Union Pacific and statehood, two great symbols of progress. It is perhaps fitting that wagon freighting and territorial status, representing frontier beginnings, gave way at the same time to a more advanced technological and political status.

The Union Pacific drastically changed the fortunes of Omaha and Nebraska City. One has only to look at the relative development of the two places after the frontier period to realize this. It is perhaps fruitless, but nevertheless tempting, to speculate on the nature of Nebraska's development had the Union Pacific commissioners chosen Nebraska City instead of Omaha as the starting point for the railroad.

Nebraska City freighting declined abruptly in 1866 but still was a long time in dying. There were scattered items in the *News* of the spring of 1867 about freighters loading and departing, but the old braggadocio was missing. Phrases like "extensive preparations" gave way to references such as "twenty head of mules being dressed up with new harness."[24] The new statistics showed the new place of freighting. A few, but very few, die-hards hung on into the next year. As late as August, 1868, a Mr. Perry set forth, from Nebraska City with a wagon train for Utah, explaining that "it is cheaper to transport freight to Utah by wagon than by rail to the end of the railroad and then load on wagons."[25] Evidently Perry was a man of singular convictions.

While Nebraska Citians enviously watched Omaha and regretted their own paucity of freighters, they must have derived great satisfaction from the political victory of the region south of the Platte River, which had long begrudged Omaha, a city north of the Platte, its territorial capital. Using the opportunity provided by statehood, those south of the Platte advanced the argument that a capital should be located near the geographic center of the population, and succeeded in having Lincoln named as capital.

Lincoln, nothing more than a name at the time it was chosen and derisively called the "paper town" by the Omaha press, had no agriculture or trades; nearly everything had to be imported by wagon. Nebraska City and Plattsmouth freighters generally shared this business with many farmers and merchants, who sometimes ran only a single wagon. The roads were good and safe and the distance short. For a time during 1867 and 1868 the Lincoln business was a temporary stimulant to Nebraska City and Plattsmouth business. In the fall of 1867 most of the Lincoln freight was general provisions and construction material for the new capitol. Passenger and express service was provided by the tri-weekly coaches of the Western Stage Company from Nebraska City. The trade increased throughout the winter and spring with Nebraska City sending out "trains of wagons" every day and Plattsmouth averaging from three to ten wagonloads daily. By late 1868 the cargo was usually government records and office furniture, which indicated that the end of this "boom" was near. Within a short time, as Lincoln became more self-sufficient, its dependence on Nebraska City and Plattsmouth ended.[26]

The Lincoln business provided temporary employment for a few of the lesser traders, but most freighters had to look elsewhere. Those who preferred to stay in the business moved along ahead of the railroad. The most venturesome, such as James R. Porter and W. B. Weston, worked as government contractors on the Bozeman Trail. Porter became a central figure in the famed Wagon Box Fight, one of the chief skirmishes of Red Cloud's War.[27] Most of the Bozeman Trail freighters and contractors were Nebraskans. This employment proved to be of short duration when the government abandoned the trail fortifications in 1868 and the area reverted to Indian control. Many other freighters went to work for Wells Fargo, and still others sold out to the company. A good many freighters worked for the Union Pacific, carrying railroad supplies from the end of the track points along the graded roadbed. Many men returned to their previous occupations—usually farming. A few of the freighters moved on out of Nebraska and continued freighting in Colorado and Wyoming; some of these later returned to Nebraska to participate in the Sidney trade.

As the freighters moved out, Nebraska City changed from a bustling small city to a rather quiet little river town. Things were not happening there any more. The wholesale merchants went the way of the freighter. There was no justification for extensive wholesaling in a community which served only an adjacent farming area. The once large outfitters, who had traded with an empire stretching away to Utah and Montana, were replaced by small town merchants. Many others who had drawn on freighting for their livelihood—the blacksmiths, the wagon and harness makers, the livery operators, and the saloon keepers—felt the end of freighting. Fond reminiscing took the place of progress.

In 1867 it seemed to Nebraskans that overland freighting, which had been so basic in the pioneer economy, was ended. There was certainly no way for them to foresee that in the not-too-distant future gold discoveries would revive freighting briefly in western Nebraska.

VIII

The Sidney–Black Hills Trade

By the 1870's overland freighting in the Platte Valley seemed relegated to the pages of history. Beginning in 1874, however, there was a brief but dramatic revival of freighting in the western part of Nebraska. For a few years Sidney was a significant frontier town because of her importance as a supply point for Indian agencies and for the Black Hills gold rush.

During the generation following the Mexican War, the trans-Mississippi West was affected radically by an influx of emigrants, gold seekers, freighters, soldiers, and others. The transcontinental railroads and the buffalo hunters were the final agents in the long process of reducing the Indians to complete dependence on the government. The railroads and the hunters greatly reduced the movement of both the great buffalo herds and the Indian tribes, leaving the broad regions between railroad lines as the only unsettled West. Northern plains tribes in their survival struggle clung desperately to the area between the Union Pacific and the projected route of the Northern Pacific. The determination of these tribes was evidenced by Red Cloud's War, which caused the government to remove its troops from the Bozeman Trail and Powder River country. After the end of Red Cloud's War in 1868, one of the last great Indian strongholds was the region bounded roughly by the Missouri River on the east and north, the Big Horns on the west, and the Union Pacific on the south. Near the center of the area lay the traditionally sacred grounds of the western Sioux— the Black Hills. White men also came to think of these hills as precious, but not for the same reasons.

In August, 1874, news of gold discoveries in the Black Hills flashed throughout the nation. Coming as it did on the heels of a panic, it had an interesting parallel to the Pike's Peak discoveries. Gold in the Black Hills was news to thousands of people, but it was merely confirmation to a handful of schemers who had long believed there was gold there. There is reason to believe that the Sioux knew of gold but for obvious reasons kept it a secret. It has been ascertained through skeletal remains, diggings, and an inscription in stone that gold seekers visited the Hills as early as 1833. Later parties, including that of army explorer James Mullan, reported gold. As early as 1861 an exploring and mining association was organized in the small town of Yankton, then capital of Dakota Territory. This group was instrumental in causing a private scientific expedition to go into the Hills, led by the well-known geologist Dr. F. V. Hayden, who later reported enthusiastically about the potential natural riches of the area. However, the association's intentions to reconnoiter the Hills in 1866–1867 were thwarted when military authorities forbade the expedition to enter Indian land. In spite of the ferocity of the Sioux in defending their sacred grounds, and in spite of the government's determination to keep the white man out of the Hills, gold seekers persisted. Even after the Laramie Treaty of 1868 officially included the Hills as part of a great Sioux reservation, demands still were made to open the area.

Sioux Citians, who had tried vainly to make Sioux City the emporium for the Northwest through the Niobrara Trail, schemed to open the Hills so that they could become the suppliers for thousands of miners. Some of Sioux City's leading men, notably editor Charlie Collins, the publicist of the group, organized the Black Hills Exploring and Mining Association in 1872. The association's contemplated expedition to the Hills was forbidden by the military commander of the Department of Dakota and was subsequently given up.[1]

Ironically, the army whose avowed purpose was to keep whites out of the Hills was responsible for the official discovery of gold. The military had the unenviable task of keeping the Teton Sioux on reservations in northwestern Nebraska from wandering northward to the Powder River country where one of the last sizeable buffalo herds grazed. Gen. Philip H. Sheridan, commander of the Division of the Missouri, believed that a military post somewhere in the Black Hills was the key to stabilizing the itinerant Sioux.

Accordingly, Lt. Col. George A. Custer was ordered to lead a reconnaissance party of over 1,000 men into the area. The group included a number of scientists, which indicates plainly that the location of a military post was not the sole mission of the expedition. Late in July members of the expedition discovered gold in French Creek near present-day Custer, and the news was rapidly circulated after the expedition's return to Fort Abraham Lincoln, Custer's home base.[2]

The cry of gold stirred not only the Sioux City boosters but also rivals in Cheyenne, Sidney, Yankton, and Bismarck. Sioux City was first in the field with the Gordon party. The party won the distinction of safely crossing northern Nebraska and building a fort near the spot of the gold discovery. The Gordon party did not discover any great quantity of gold. It survived the winter of 1874–1875, and then military authorities forced the group to evacuate. These trespassers, evaluated by frontier mores, became heroes of a sort for their defiance of the government. Their historic image was undoubtedly greatly enhanced by a reminiscent history later written by Annie D. Tallent, a member of the group.[3]

Military dedication was put to the acid test in 1875 when several hundred miners invaded the southern Hills. The government, in the uncomfortable and politically inexpedient position of having to defend the Indians from the whites, decided that the handiest solution would be to purchase the Black Hills and legally open the region. After forcing perhaps as many as 600 white men out of the southern Hills in the late summer of 1875, the government negotiated with the Sioux near Fort Robinson. When the talks broke down, so did frontier patience and government determination. Prospectors invaded the Hills with renewed vigor and increased numbers. Many of the disillusioned Sioux left the reservations to resist the government in what came to be called the Sioux War of 1876. The Indians won one major battle, in which Custer's entire command was wiped out. Ironically, the Indians' one major, decisive victory was their swan song. The Battle of the Little Big Horn completely undercut what support and sympathy the Indians had from government officials. After this episode the government and the army moved ahead decisively to conquer and capture Sioux renegades. The malcontents such as Sitting Bull and Crazy Horse ruined any possibility of Indians such as Red Cloud and Spotted

Tail negotiating to keep sacred grounds. The Sioux signed away their rights to the Black Hills in October, 1876, thereby legalizing the presence of the thousands of miners in the Hills.[4]

The early stages of a gold rush offered the greatest opportunity for the individual. In the Black Hills during 1875 and 1876 the placer miners reigned. Initially they worked in the southern Hills where the town of Custer was the main community. Then in 1876 the action shifted to the northern Hills because of sizeable strikes in Deadwood Gulch. Deadwood became the chief town, rivaled and envied by settlements such as Rockerville, Pactola, Rochford, and Rapid City. By 1877 the rush had worn off and Black Hills mining stablized considerably. Organized mining companies, especially those backed by California capitalists, turned to quartz mining, which involved deep shafts revetted with lumber, mining machinery, including heavy quartz mills, and extensive wooden sluices to carry water for washing from mountain streams. Quartz mining was not for the man of limited funds. Once this phase was reached, and it was reached quite rapidly on all mining frontiers, the inexperienced tended to stay out or go elsewhere. Thus, in the Black Hills the greatest activity was during the first few years, and then as new discoveries became less frequent the rush slowed perceptibly.[5]

While the Black Hills gold rush lacked the richness of California and Montana and did not attract as many people as Colorado, by regional standards it was very important. An increase in population from nothing to thousands within a few years cannot help but have economic impact upon a region. As in other mining areas the population of the Black Hills during the rush period fluctuated considerably, but available statistics accurately portray the approximate population. Contemporary newspapers commonly claimed that population on July 1, 1876, was 8,000, about 7,000 of whom were in the Deadwood area. The 1879 estimates ranged from 15,000 to as high as 25,000. The official 1880 census reported 16,487 residents in the three-county mining area, with about 80 per cent of these in Lawrence County, where Deadwood was located.[6]

The gold yield of the Black Hills was small compared to that of the California rush, but it was not greatly less than that of the highly advertised Pike's Peak rush. The estimated yield of 1876 from countless placers was $1,500,000. The 1877 take was estimated at between $2,000,000 and $2,500,000, which increased to $3,000,000 for each of the next two years. The high point of the rush was reached in 1880 with a return of $5,000,000. Production for the next five years averaged about $3,500,000 per year.[7]

An economy with a fluctuating population and miner's luck as its base was both unstable and unpredictable. As in other mining areas the Black Hills miners were close to the hard reckonings of supply and demand. A heavy rain, a blizzard, a delay, or someone cornering the limited market could send prices skyrocketing. By the same token good conditions that might favor the purchaser could ruin shippers. Generally speaking, prices stayed high. In the spring of 1876 when "grub" was reported scarce, flour was selling for from $16 to $22 a hundred, and corn, which could "hardly be had for money," was 50¢ a pound.[8] At another time when rains made roads impassable, flour rose from $12 to $25 per hundred in a week.[9] Flour prices were always reported, since it was such a basic item, but all commodities bore inflated prices. Eggs were always in short supply. At a time when flour was down to $8 it was said that "fresh state eggs are retailing in Deadwood at 75 cents and ranch eggs at $1.00, and are very scarce at these figures."[10] There is no reason to doubt the price, but there is some question about how fresh "fresh" state eggs were, considering the distance they were hauled by wagon.

Every ambitious town within striking distance had plans to open roads to the Black Hills. Initially, Cheyenne and Sidney on the Union Pacific were in advantageous positions. They were on a direct line from the major supply centers of Omaha and Chicago. They were closest to the mines when Custer was the metropolis, and they had a number of freighters hauling Indian and military supplies who were eager and willing to extend their operations into the Hills. Furthermore, these two towns could easily attract Colorado and Wyoming freighters.

Sidney became a major freighting town in 1874 because of government policies which placed numerous Indians and soldiers within easy traveling distance of the town. The government, seeking to locate the western Sioux in an area suitable for agriculture, in 1873 moved the Oglala from their old reservation on the North Platte in Wyoming to a site on the White River near present-day Crawford, Nebraska. This site, Red Cloud Agency, became the home at times of over 10,000 Oglala and their Cheyenne and Arapaho allies. While Indian numbers fluctuated greatly from year to year, and even season to season, there were always at least several thousand red men at the agency. They, of course, were almost totally dependent on the government and all supplies had to be imported by wagon. When the agency was on the Platte, it was supplied from Cheyenne, only 132 miles distant. Supplies initially were carried from Cheyenne to the new agency, a distance estimated at 170 miles. For some reason known possibly only to officials in the scandal-ridden Grant administration, the government paid for 212 miles over the route.[11]

The year after Red Cloud Agency was established, a military post, Fort Robinson, was started nearby, and a road was laid out from Sidney. The road was meant to benefit the Red Cloud Agency and Fort Robinson, but it was also of service to a second major agency, that of the Brule Sioux located about forty miles from Fort Robinson or about twelve miles east of present-day Chadron. Spotted Tail Agency had a population of nearly 10,000 in 1875. Since this agency was off the main trail, it was not as convenient to supply from the south as was Red Cloud Agency. Apparently some of the Spotted Tail supplies were shipped from Fort Randall, despite a distance that was roughly double that of the Sidney route. The Brule were supervised by soldiers at nearby Camp Sheridan.[12]

Sidney's most serious challenge for the Indian and military trade came from Cheyenne. The shift of Red Cloud Agency to Nebraska did not totally remove Cheyenne from the market of supplying the agencies, and the trade was coveted by both towns. It was during this fight for the government business that Sidney and Cheyenne boosters began enthusiastically panning each other's town, starting a journalistic feud that carried over into the gold rush. The commonest jibe, reminiscent of the earlier battles between Nebraska City and Omaha, was about the dull times in the other town and how all of her freighters were moving to the rival burg. The Indian trade whetted the Sidney and Cheyenne appetites and made freighters of both cognizant of the potential of the carrying trade. When the first gold seekers ventured into the Black Hills in 1875, the freighters were poised to move.

Perhaps Sidney's biggest boosters were not her own freighters but rather powerful merchant and transportation groups in Omaha who hoped to become the main suppliers of the Black Hills. Aside from the direct benefits to Omaha, such a business would enhance western Nebraska, and the popularization of a trail north of the Union Pacific would probably hasten the opening of this entire section of the state. It was with these many motives that Omaha planners thought of routing their trade through Sidney, then a placid little town some 400 miles west of the Missouri. The advantages of Sidney were well advertised by Omaha papers, especially the *Bee,* which reported the standard cliches for outfitting points. Sidney had "an abundance of water, grass, camping places, and guides who know the trail." Furthermore, the gold fields were reported to "lie on an 'airline' NW of Sidney." The road was, of course, good, said the *Bee.*[13]

While the Omaha and Sidney promoters were reluctant to admit it, they had to recognize that the trail had one serious drawback—the North Platte was unbridged. The North Platte during low water when it could be forded was, at best, a nuisance. But during high water periods, the river was an impassable barrier. Richard B. Hughes, who traveled from Sidney to the Hills in the spring of 1876, recalled seeing a Pratt & Ferris bull train wait two days before the river receded enough to permit a risky fording. The heavy wagons loaded with flour for Red Cloud Agency were using seven yoke of oxen on the trail, but during fording twenty-one yoke were used on each wagon. Crossing the river took this particular outfit most of a day.[14] Lt. Col. Richard Dodge, commander of a military escort for a geologic survey group that reconnoitered the Hills in 1875, when comparing the Cheyenne and Sidney trails, highly recommended the Cheyenne route, noting that north of Sidney "there is no bridge on the North Platte, and the crossing is a bad one."[15]

If Sidney freighters wanted a bridge crossing, they had two choices, both inconvenient: Fort Laramie or North Platte. During the spring of 1875 some Sidney freighters went by way of North Platte so they could use the wagon bridge there.[16] Sidney freighters were forced to ford the river for two seasons. Then in 1876 the route was streamlined with the construction of a substantial bridge. The bridge was the result of the ambition and enterprise of Omaha merchants, railroad personnel, and Henry T. Clarke.

During the winter of 1875–1876, Clarke, a veteran freighter and bridge builder, was contacted by some Omaha merchants who asked him to reconnoiter the Sidney Trail with the object of determining the feasibility of bridging the North Platte. Clarke complied and reported that such a bridge could be built although it would have to be nearly half a mile long—certainly a major enterprise. Inadequate capital nearly ruined the venture, but Clarke agreed to accept an initial fee and then charge tolls. The Chicago & Rock Island and Union Pacific railroads were interested enough in the project to haul materials free from lumberyards in Moline, Illinois, and Davenport, Iowa, to Sidney. At Sidney they hired freighters to transship the materials to the bridge site at the traditional fording place. Only the piles were secured locally. These were cut into the hills southwest of the bridge location.[17]

Clarke's bridge, a solid, sixty-one-truss span about two thousand feet long, was completed in June, 1876. Clarke prided himself with building enduring structures. Twenty-five years later he boasted that this monument to civilization, which had so changed the country and the future of Sidney, was still standing. The bridge, about nine miles east of Chimney Rock and about three miles west of present-day Bridgeport, immediately popularized the "Sidney Short Route," as it was widely advertised throughout the frontier. Clarke constructed toll houses at the smooth, well-engineered bridge approaches. The rates were $2 for an outfit consisting of two animals, a vehicle and a man, and 50¢ extra for each additional animal and man. A single freighter's wagon pulled by five yoke of oxen would be charged $6. On the south side of the river Clarke constructed a store, a hotel, a blacksmith shop, and a corral stocked with grain and hay. Taking advantage of the improved trail, Clarke also began freighting from Sidney.

The army was vitally interested in the route because of the necessity for rapid movement during the campaigns of 1876. Accordingly, a company of troops in Camp Clarke, a little blockhouse fortification on the north side of the river, guarded the bridge. The Sidney trail was also protected by men from Fort Sidney and Fort Robinson. The trail was heavily used, especially in 1876 and 1877, and travelers were comparatively free from molestation by Indians or white outlaws.[18]

Clarke later reminisced that while the toll bridge and its attendant mercantile enterprises were good investments, he was probably better known for a much less remunerative but grandly dramatic small-scale pony express from Sidney to the mines. Influenced by the Philadelphia Centennial commemorating the one hundredth anniversary of the Declaration of Independence, Clarke called his line the Centennial Express. Clarke's riders, who started weekly from both ends of the trail with only three stops from Sidney to Custer, were carrying letters and newspapers into the Hills by August. The service was good, sometimes only four days from Omaha and only five from Chicago. With numerous little post offices in the mining camps, Clarke advertised a regular five-day service from Omaha to Deadwood. He continued to operate the line into 1877 despite poor returns due to high operating costs, then contracted with a stage company to carry his mail.[19]

Travelers on the "Sidney Short Route" covered about 167 miles to Custer and about 260 to Deadwood. By 1876 the entire route was well defined with numerous road ranches where emigrants and freighters could obtain provisions and protection. Omaha, Sidney, and Black Hills newspapers as a service to emigrants commonly published detailed descriptions of the trail.[20]

The trail ran about a mile due west of Sidney before turning north through a small canyon, then ascended to a tableland where the Water Hole Ranch was located about twelve miles out. This ranch was marked by a "round rock, upon a lofty mound, where it was placed by the Indians."[21] The road crossed the divide of the South and North Platte and descended to the little station of Greenwood Creek, picturesquely situated in an elm grove—a place where travelers were advised to take on wood. From Greenwood to Clarke's Bridge, only about fifteen miles, Court House Rock and Chimney Rock were in continual view of the travelers. The trail crossed Pumpkin Creek just west of Court House Rock. From there it was only nine miles to the North Platte and the bridge.

Across the river the route ascended through long low hills that rose from the narrow valley. Red Willow, where abundant fuel and water were available, was only twelve miles from the bridge. E. Morton & Company operated the ranch there. Then the trail ran slightly northwest through the Snake Creek Ranch operated by J. W. Dear, the Red Cloud Agency trader, through Point of Rocks, Running Water, and White Clay Creek before reaching Red Cloud Agency and Fort Robinson, the rendezvous of the northern and southern divisions of the stage line.

The area around the agency arrested the attention of even

impassive travelers. Pine woods cast deep shadows across the hills and Crow Butte rose to the east of the trail. The agency itself was overshadowed by white sandstone bluffs that rose sharply just to the north. From the highest points of these bluffs Harney Peak, the greatest elevation in the Black Hills a hundred miles to the north, was visible.

Just over twenty miles north of the agency the trail left Nebraska and entered Dakota Territory. There were several variations in the approaches to the mining communities. The main road went to Buffalo Gap, a great natural opening into the mountains from the plains on the southeast. It was also possible to swing west several miles south of the state line and pick up the Cheyenne Trail to Custer. Buffalo Gap, about ten miles north of the Cheyenne River, was sometimes hard to reach because of the treacherous Cheyenne which had to be forded. Once the North Platte had been bridged, the Cheyenne became the freighters' major obstacle. Certainly its contrariness contributed to the success of outfitters and freighters at Bismarck and Fort Pierre.

The way station at Buffalo Gap was at the juncture of two trails—one leading to Custer in the interior, and the other staying outside the mountains to Rapid City. When the boom passed from Custer to Deadwood, most freighters and emigrants took the outside trail through Rapid City enroute to Deadwood. It was also possible to reach Deadwood by taking an interior route from Custer, but the narrow mountainous roads were not to the liking of time-conscious freighters.[22]

For about five years after the construction of Clarke's bridge, the Sidney Trail was lively. Hundreds of emigrants trekked along it, most of them on their way to the Hills. Passengers and express parcels were moved by stage while the methodical freighters handled the heavy goods. Several stage lines were opened during this period. J. W. Dear, the Red Cloud agency trader and owner of several road ranches, began running stages in 1876. Before the year was out two of Clarke's Omaha acquaintances, Capt. Marsh and Jim Stephenson, started a line usually called the Sidney & Black Hills Stage Line but officially named the Western Stage Line. Marsh and Stephenson opened service with stages from both ends of the trail twice a week. In March, 1877, Stephenson sold his interest to John Gilmer and Monroe Salisbury, owners of the Cheyenne & Black Hills Stage Company, who wanted to divert some of their heavy

Cheyenne traffic to an alternate route. Soon after acquiring Stephenson's interest, the new managers, who were experienced in frontier transportation and who were doing well with the Cheyenne stages, extended the Sidney service to daily coaches. They then turned their efforts to making the service more efficient and economical. By operating night coaches and improving roads they were able to reduce travel time to a degree. By 1878 even during bad weather the stages were making the Sidney to Rapid City run in only forty-six hours. Railroads in Chicago and Omaha promoted the stages by offering through tickets to the Hills. Tickets from Chicago to Deadwood via Sidney ranged from $32 to $55, depending on the class of travel. The trip was reported to have been made in as little as three and one-half days, but this was the extraordinary not the routine time. Stage tickets from Sidney to Deadwood were about $30 and about $20 to Custer. Each passenger was allowed fifty pounds of baggage free. Anything over that could be expressed for about 12¢ a pound to Custer and 20¢ to Deadwood. These rates were not fixed. They changed somewhat from season to season and tended to be reduced as service was improved, but they generally reflect approximate travel costs during the gold rush.[23]

Stagecoaching was but a narrow facet of Sidney's trade. The real business was done by the freighters who hauled millions of pounds to Indian agencies, military posts, and mining towns.

It is impossible to make a quantitative distinction between Sidney's Black Hills civilian trade and its Indian agency and military business. Freighters who carried mining supplies usually also supplied the agencies and posts. There is a fair chance that in any given year, and particularly in 1876, the Indian and military business exceeded the Black Hills trade. Hills freighting was fairly lively in 1876 with the completion of Clarke's bridge and the rush of miners, and it showed a sharp increase the next year, when quartz mills became a regular trade item. The *Sidney Telegraph* of January 6, 1877, reported "an immense amount of machinery arriving in Sidney for the Northern mines. Two engines and three ten-stamp mills were shipped this week." During the last week in June nine quartz mills were shipped and seven engines and boilers were awaiting transportation. A quartz mill included a mammoth steam engine, a boiler, and a great metal wheel with numerous steel stamps and could easily weigh several hundred thousand pounds. Cherry & Boyle of Chicago sent a 120,000 pound mill by way of Sidney, and on another occasion Pratt & Ferris transported two sixty-stamp mills with a combined weight of over 800,000 pounds to the Homestake Mine. Pratt & Ferris' freight bill would have been $40,000 if figured at 5¢ a pound, and there is a good chance that the bill was even higher considering that the machinery was difficult to handle. Even though the mills were disassembled, individual parts often weighed several tons. It is known that on one occasion the Homestake Mining Company paid Pratt & Ferris $33,000 for moving a single mill.[24]

While the mills were an important trade item, especially in the period 1877–1879, when machinery from both California and Chicago was sent to the Hills, the normal cargoes were the everyday provisions required by the burgeoning Black Hills population. Usually the wagons made the return trip empty except for a few passengers who paid about $10 each for the rough ride in a wagon box. The freighting business reflected the beginning of the Black Hills lumber business. In the fall of 1877, A. J. Haskell, a Sidney lumber dealer, began importing lumber via Pratt & Ferris trains. Haskell was reported to have contracted for a quarter million board feet which he intended to ship east on the Union Pacific. This was the first time Black Hills products other than gold were exported by Union Pacific.[25]

While the Black Hills business remained fairly constant, the Indian trade was subject to uncertainties because of the government's difficulty in permanently locating the Oglala and Brule Sioux. Red Cloud Agency was the center of one of the many scandals involving the Indian Bureau during the Grant administration. Along with the loud debate over malfeasance and incompetence on the part of agency employees there were complaints that freighters, particularly D. J. McCann, were failing to deliver government provisions to the Indians.[26] Officials of the incoming Hayes administration, especially Secretary of the Interior Carl Schurz, were eager to eliminate corruption and achieve government economy. Hence, Schurz and Hayes proposed that the Sioux would receive their 1877 annuities along the Missouri River, thereby saving the government the cost of overland transportation. The Indians agreed to move to the Missouri during the winter of 1877 and stay there until permanent reservations could be found outside of Nebraska, where their occupancy had been illegal and the subject of many complaints. When the tribes moved to their river locations in Dakota Territory, Sidney lost what had been a main facet of its trade for several years.[27]

In 1878 the Sioux were returned to the interior, finally to be settled in permanent homes after years of wandering. But the new reservations, Rosebud and Pine Ridge, were both in Dakota Territory, well off the Sidney Trail. The government, at first uncertain as to the best means of supplying the reservations, immediately after their establishment contracted with George H. Jewett of Sidney to carry 2,000,000 pounds of Indian goods to the sites. Government policy changed, however, when the Indian Bureau began using Indian teamsters to haul supplies from the Rosebud steamboat landing on the Missouri above Fort Randall to the agencies. This scheme to save money and gainfully employ reservation Sioux was adopted in October, 1878. During the next year the Indian freighters carried 2,000,000 pounds to the Pine Ridge Agency, and the Rosebud Agency was reported to have 255 wagons and an annual requirement of 3,400,000 pounds of supplies. From this time forward, supplies to these reservations were hauled from the east, first from the Missouri and then, beginning in 1882, from railheads in north central Nebraska. So, except for a brief revival with the Jewett contract of 1878 and an occasional rare shipment such as the quarter million pounds of Indian flour which came through Sidney in 1879, Sidney did not have any significant Indian trade after 1876. This, of course, forced the freighters to concentrate on the Black Hills trade, where they were challenged by numerous eager rivals.[28]

From 1876 through 1878, Sidney was a lively freighting town. In 1876 Pratt & Ferris, the ranking outfit in Sidney, shipped 9,230,560 pounds of freight, mostly to the Indian agencies. It had 70 wagons and 550 animals. By 1878, Pratt & Ferris and the second ranking outfit, Daugherty, Kelly & Company, had facilities to handle a million pounds of freight a week. This probably meant that the two firms combined had about two hundred wagons. Robert E. Strahorn, a Union Pacific publicist and frontier booster, after visiting Sidney reported the 1877 Black Hills trade as totaling 4,000,000 pounds. The total 1878–1879 trade over the Sidney trail was said to be from 22,000,000 to 25,000,000 pounds. This would have included Jewett's Indian freight as well as military and Black Hills freight. Most of this trade must have been in 1878. There is no reason to believe that 1879 compared favorably to the preceding three years. Lack of notices in Sidney and Black Hills papers clearly shows that the Sidney business was suffering badly from Fort Pierre competition.[29]

This impressive trade had definite salutary effects on the economy of Sidney and northwest Nebraska, but to put it in proper perspective it should be thought of in terms of ton miles rather than millions of pounds. Like freighting during the construction period of the Union Pacific, the Sidney trade was a short haul business. Wagons from Sidney made hauls ranging from 180 to 530 miles round trip, so each outfit could make numerous trips during a season that sometimes extended through an open winter. This short haul feature of Sidney freighting accounts for the comparatively few wagons carrying millions of pounds of freight.

The short hauls over a road unharassed by Indians enabled the Sidney freighters to charge comparatively stable rates, although rates were some higher during the coldest winter months. For most of the year, when the weather was favorable and the roads in good condition, the standard charges from Sidney to mining towns were 3¢ to 5¢ a pound, depending on the nature of the goods and the size of the consignment. In November or December the charges advanced to 5¢ or 6¢. Rates for express freight, which was carried through on an around the clock schedule, were naturally higher. W. S. Whiting, who offered seven-day parcel and passenger service to Deadwood, charged 7¢ a pound and $15 fare during the best seasons. Rates to the agencies and posts were generally about the same per hundred pounds per hundred miles as the Black Hills goods. In 1877 George H. Jewett, the supplier of Camp Sheridan, was paid $1.65 per hundred for the distance from Sidney during July through October and $2.24 during November and December.[30]

Sidney freighting was dominated by the firm of Pratt & Ferris. James Hervey Pratt and Cornelius Ferris were the key men in this company, which dealt in provisions, transportation, land, and cattle. For over a quarter century Colonel Pratt, as he was generally called, was one of the best-known men in Nebraska—mainly because of his extensive ranch holdings and his affiliation with Chicago capitalists. Born in Massachusetts, he was raised in Ohio and worked in Michigan before moving west to Fort Randall in 1870 at the age of forty-five after a varied career as a merchant, lieutenant in a Michigan infantry regiment during the Civil War, and flour miller. During his Fort Randall years Pratt became associated

The Sidney—Black Hills Trail

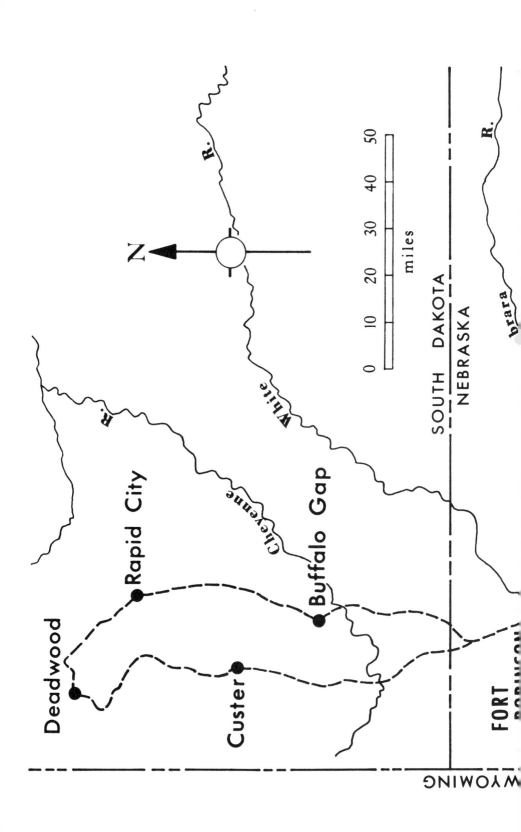

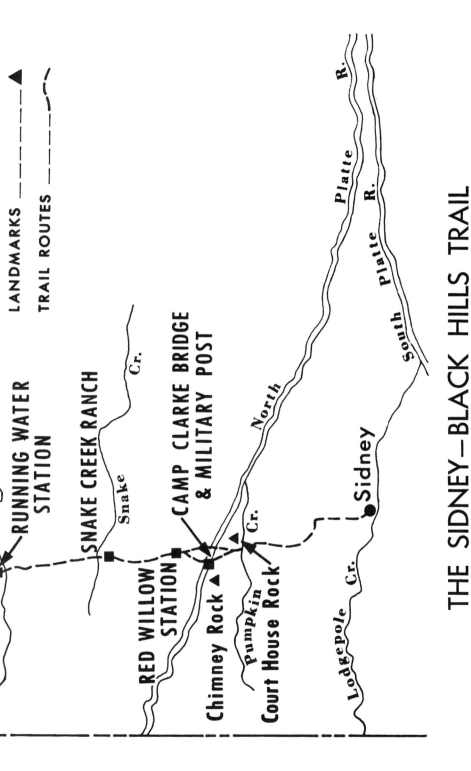

HISTORIC PLACES ————

LANDMARKS ————

TRAIL ROUTES ————

RUNNING WATER STATION

SNAKE CREEK RANCH

Snake Cr.

CAMP CLARKE BRIDGE & MILITARY POST

RED WILLOW STATION

Chimney Rock

Pumpkin Cr.

Court House Rock

North Platte R.

South Platte R.

Platte R.

Sidney

Lodgepole Cr.

THE SIDNEY–BLACK HILLS TRAIL

Scott's Bluffs, a massive promontory located south of present-day Scottsbluff, Nebraska, lay astride the Oregon Trail just south of the North Platte River. The photo was taken about 1960.

—Nebraska State Historical Society

Robidoux Pass, the longer of two routes through Scott's Bluffs, carried traffic on the Oregon Trail. The pass is located about five miles south of the North Platte River. The photo was taken in 1938.

—U.S. Department of the Interior

Fort Laramie, Wyoming, a major military installation on the approaches to the Rocky Mountains, is located at the confluence of the North Platte and Laramie rivers. The latter stream is in the foreground. This sketch was drawn by Frederick Piercy in about 1853.

—Nebraska State Historical Society

The Platte River Bridge carried the Oregon Trail north across the river at Fort Caspar, Wyoming. Here the freighters left the river valley and moved onto the highlands toward South Pass. William H. Jackson painted this picture in 1927 from his original sketch of 1866.

—Nebraska State Historical Society

The grave of Private Bennett Tribbett, Company B, 11th Ohio Cavalry, is located at the Three Crossings of the Sweetwater near South Pass in Wyoming. Photo was taken in 1870 by William H. Jackson.

—U.S. Geological Survey

The D & B Powers Trains freighted between Leavenworth and Denver, Colorado Territory. Photo shows a Powers train assembled on June 20, 1868, on Market Street in Denver between the 14th and 16th Street intersections.

—State Historical Society of Colorado

Fort Bridger, Wyoming, acquired an enlarged military role during the bloodless Mormon War of 1857. These partially restored installations were photographed in 1927 by Emil Kopac.

—Nebraska State Historical Society

Wagon trains bringing goods to merchants in Salt Lake City were operated both by Mormon Church authorities and professional freighters. Photo was taken in 1868 on Main Street in Salt Lake City.

—Utah State Historical Society

Sidney, Nebraska, a division point on the Union Pacific Railroad, in 1874 became the southern terminal of the Sidney–Black Hills overland freight route. The round-house is at the left of the photo, taken about 1880.

—Cheyenne County, Nebraska, Historical Society

Warehouses to store goods for the Black Hills trade were built on sidings of the Union Pacific Railroad in Sidney. Lettering on the roof of the building reads: "Pratt & Ferris, Black Hills Freight House and Out-fitting Depot."

—Cheyenne County, Nebraska, Historical Society

A Pratt & Ferris mule train on the trail north of Sidney. James H. Pratt and his partner Cornelius Ferris dominated the Sidney trade between 1875 and 1879. Business declined due to competition of the Pierre route, and the firm disbanded in 1879.

—Nebraska State Historical Society

Camp Clarke in 1876 contained a store and postoffice. At right in the photo is the southern approach to the vital Clarke Bridge carrying the Sidney–Black Hills route over the North Platte River.

—Nebraska State Historical Society

Supplies for the Red Cloud Agency, which served over 10,000 Indians being reset-tled on reservations, were freighted from Sidney. J. W. Dear's trading post is at center. Location of the agency was just east of present-day Fort Robinson, Nebraska. This photo was taken in 1876.

—Nebraska State Historical Society

Women were not known to have been employed as bullwhackers, and the female in this picture may only have been temporarily assisting—if, indeed, the photo was not posed. Male attendants stand near the lead oxen and by the first wagon. The photo, date unknown, lists the destination of the wagon train as Deadwood, Dakota Territory.

—Nebraska State Historical Society

Merchants in Deadwood, Dakota Territory, the main trade center in the Black Hills during the gold-strike years, obtained their goods chiefly over the trail from Sidney. Photograph was taken about 1880.

—Nebraska State Historical Society

One of the freighting routes into the Black Hills had its eastern terminus at Fort Pierre, Dakota Territory, a Missouri River port. This route had cut heavily into the trade via Sidney by 1879. Date of photo is about 1876.

—Nebraska State Historical Society

with Ferris in the Pratt & Ferris Cattle Company, a company which contracted to supply beef for Fort Randall and nearby Indian agencies. The post tradership also provided Pratt with his first experience with plains wagon transportation. With this background he and Ferris moved to Sidney in July, 1875, to take part in the expanding trade to the Red Cloud and Spotted Tail agencies.[31]

The gold rush offered new opportunity for expansion, and Pratt and Ferris moved rapidly. In 1877, in association with George H. Jewett, the partners organized the Sidney & Black Hills Transportation Company and entered the merchant and outfitting trade for miners and ranchers. They constructed a 30 by 120 foot warehouse with a full stone basement on the Union Pacific and began offering regular wagon service to the Hills. The company dominated the trade by advertising extensively. In Omaha and all major eastern cities agents arranged for through bills of lading to the mines, and the company hired agents in the important mining towns. Most importantly, it could assure shippers that it regularly dispatched large trains so goods would not be delayed.[32]

Throughout their freighting career Pratt and Ferris expanded their cattle holdings and began making large shipments of stock from Sidney to Chicago in 1878. Pratt and Ferris, after a realistic appraisal of the future of Sidney freighting, sold out in August, 1879, to their partner Jewett and to Harvey Dickinson, who had been the Deadwood agent for the company.[33]

Pratt & Ferris did not have a monopoly of the Sidney business. In 1878 John W. Daugherty of Sidney and R. D. Kelly of Deadwood entered the trade as Daugherty, Kelly & Company, freighters, wholesale and retail grocers, and commission and forwarding merchants. The firm purchased a warehouse from Henry Gantz, a Sidney merchant, and advertised that it could handle 500,000 pounds every thirty days.[34] Kelly & Daugherty operated just one year out of Sidney and then moved its trains to the increasingly popular Fort Pierre route.

For a brief time Dwight J. McCann, the Nebraska City banker and freighter and controversial government contractor, was a major Sidney trader. McCann, with years of experience in the Nebraska City–Colorado business, had a 40 by 120 foot warehouse in Sidney and operated a general wholesale and retail store. Like Pratt & Ferris he offered through bills of lading from Omaha and eastern cities to the Hills. During three days in February, 1877, McCann's teams carried 900,000 pounds of Black Hills provisions. He also offered a fast freight service and once contracted to take a party of over two hundred Bostonians into the Hills. After 1877, McCann turned his attention to the development of a large ranch on the Niobrara—an enterprise backed in part by Chicago capital. [35]

There were dozens of other freighters. Most of them were small-scale operators of only a few wagons who were in the business for just a few trips. They included A. S. Van Tassel, a Sidney merchant; H. T. Clarke, the bridge builder who was in the business for a year or so; John Cessena; John Pantenburg; Steve Smith; Frank Wilson; William Coltharp; Robert Smith; F. D. Dickinson; C. Welsh; "Hawk" Thompson; Frank Griffin; and "Arkansas John," who worked out of Sidney for several years. In spite of being in the trade for several seasons, Arkansas John was known by no other name. Fred T. Evans, who later developed the Fort Pierre trail, also operated out of Sidney for a short time in 1876.[36]

The Black Hills trade and the freighters gave Sidney a few years of regional significance as an outfitting and transportation center. The boom dramatically changed the town from a quiet Union Pacific division station to a bustling community where the business and social life reflected the rough, informal manners of the miner and the cowboy.

The town lay on flat ground just south of a rocky bluff about sixty to seventy feet high that paralleled the settlement and provided a marvelous overlook of the plains stretching away to distant horizons. From here the visitor could see the great seas of buffalo grass, green in early spring but otherwise greyish brown. Clumps of sometimes brightly blooming cactus could be found without difficulty on the plains, and the abundance of rock and stone revealed a country initially too challenging to the farmer but inviting to cattlemen.

Sidney was laid out with regular streets, some of them lined with cottonwoods. These sparsely leaved trees and the grass along the irrigation ditches fed by a dam on Lodgepole Creek provided fingers of vegetation that contrasted with and magnified the bleakness of the plains.[37]

A glance from the bluff revealed the Union Pacific depot with shops and a roundhouse nearby. Usually the clanging of bells announced the approach of a train. Trains at this stage of their history carried no diners. They all stopped for breakfast and supper. A contemporary observer noted that in Sidney "the amount of eating done is simply enormous."[38] The brown barracks at Fort Sidney, established in 1867 to protect the railroad and later used for overland trail security, were always in view. The largest buildings were the warehouses, stores, and two hotels described by Strahorn as the best "in the state outside of Omaha."[39] There were some frame houses and other neat, solid homes with exteriors of softly colored field stone. The stone was used in its original state, not cut or altered, and set in concrete or mortar which left broad margins of contrasting white about the stones. Most of the residences were not so substantial; dugouts and earth-covered cabins were a common sight. The great number of dugouts on the bluff with their dirty, bewhiskered dwellers were constant reminders of the new frontier. An 1876 observer noted that "there were no churches, but there was a schoolhouse wherein a young lady wields the birch, with a salary of $75 per month."[40]

While churches were non-existent and schools rare, saloons were abundant. Visitors always noted this fact and were amazed that the excessive alcohol consumption did not lead to high crime rates. The incidence of capital crimes was evidently low, but the saloons and dance halls, featuring liquor, girls, and gambling round the clock, kept the town alive. There were frequent brawls, principally involving freighters, soldiers, and transient Texas cowhands, all of whom had little toleration for one another.[41]

To some who longed for established society, Sidney was a fray in the social fabric. It, like Cheyenne, was oftentimes criticized for its morality, or lack of it. However, the *Weekly Bee,* Sidney's foremost defender, explained frontier mores as follows:

> Talk about the morality and virtue of Sidney and Cheyenne is simply silly bosh, of course there are many nice families in both places, but on the other hand the *nymph du paue* are numerous, drinking, gambling, and kindred vices cannot long remain unfamiliar to a settler here in the present status of society. These are characteristic features of all new western towns, and especially so from a great outfitting point. Still, ladies are just as safe in Sidney as in other places, and are treated with the utmost respect.[42]

This then was Sidney, a young town where "new buildings, new men, and ceaseless activity are the order of the day."[43] The numerous wagons and animals attested to its place as a freighting town, and the heavy influx of tramps passing through to the gold fields was stark testimony of the appeal of gold to the down-and-outers.[44]

In such an environment lawlessness was bound to exist. Charles Reed, a Texan, shot and killed a young man and was jailed for his crime. A vigilante group of about four hundred removed Reed from jail after overpowering his guards and forced him to climb a ladder slung against a telegraph pole. With the rope around his neck, Reed, outwardly cool, jumped from the ladder after a terse farewell statement: "Good bye, gentlemen."[45] This single episode later led to greatly exaggerated tales about vigilante mobs in Sidney.

Sidney well illustrated the effect of the gold rush upon population centers. An Omaha correspondent reported Sidney's population early in 1877 at 1,200 to 1,600. It was but days later that the same paper reported that "with a fair count, in our estimation, Sidney contains 2,800 people. One thing is certain, there are two hundred and seventy-one females in Sidney."[46]

The base of Sidney's economy, of course, was the freighter and the large outfitter. Nearly everyone in Sidney from the butchers and bakers through the liquor vendors and the wholesale merchants had a finger in the Black Hills trade, but it was the merchandise firms that prospered spectacularly with the gold rush. These firms, in turn, led to the success of the freighters.

The most important outfitters and suppliers were H. T. Clarke, D. Carrigan, G. W. Dudley, Dwight J. McCann, C. A. Moore, and C. A. Morian. Clarke, who started his business in June, 1876, engaged in a general merchandise trade including lumber, wagons, and farm machinery. Carrigan, one of Sidney's first citizens, started business the year of the town's founding. He dealt in general merchandise and was reported to have considerable financial interests in the mining towns. Dudley, the young postmaster, had an extensive general merchandise store and regularly furnished supplies to the traders at the agencies and posts. McCann, after building his warehouse in December, 1876, handled groceries grains, lumber, coal, and other items in wholesale lots, which he generally forwarded to the mines in his own wagons. Like Carrigan, Moore was a Sidney veteran, having started his business during the winter of 1867–1868. His company was reported to be "the largest wholesale and retail mercantile house in Sidney."[47] Morian came to Sidney with the gold rush in October, 1876. Like his rivals he handled general merchandise, and a large portion of his goods were sold in the Hills. He planned to extend his business into the northern mining camps by starting a store in either Crook City or Deadwood.[48]

Sidney sales during the gold rush reflected the town's new role. Merchants handled everything from groceries and clothing through mining tools—picks, shovels, and gold pans. Hardware and camping equipment were always in heavy demand, as were wagons and animals. The draft animals, oxen and mules, were not nearly as easy to obtain as they had been when overland freighting started on the Missouri near farming communities where these animals could be readily purchased. Sidney was far from farming areas, and the price of mules and oxen shows the effect of this. Mules sold for from $100 to $300 each and oxen from $65 to $100 a head. Horses, on the other hand, which were probably numerous because of the influx of Texas cattle herds and cowboys, sold from $25 to $100.[49]

During Sidney's three good years in the Black Hills trade her merchants and freighters engaged in a relentless competition with ambitious rivals. Cheyenne was Sidney's primary enemy because she and Sidney vied for the business originating on the Union Pacific. Bismarck and Fort Pierre on the Missouri were dismissed by Sidney freighters as unavoidable competition. It was easy to reason that a great share of the goods were bound to enter the Hills from the Missouri, and Sidney could not hope to control this. She should, instead, aim to dominate the trade from the south. In the end it was not Cheyenne but a more distant rival which prevailed at Sidney's expense.

Before the completion of Clarke's bridge, when mining was still mainly in the southern Hills, Cheyenne was the king of the trade. Beyond Fort Laramie there were several main branches of the Cheyenne Trail, so Deadwood could be reached by at least three routes. Distances varied slightly, but the federal Post Office Department listed it as 271 miles from Cheyenne to Deadwood, which was quite close to the general estimates which ranged from 267 to 275. The postal department called the Sidney–Deadwood distance 275 miles, but the *Black Hills Journal* consistently reported it as 267 miles.[50] The distinction between distances from Cheyenne and Sidney to Deadwood was narrow; neither town could make truthful claims for having a decidedly shorter trail. Thus, the benefit in shipping from one or the other had to depend in large part on the source of the goods, since the rates were usually competitive. As a general rule Cheyenne controlled business from California and Colorado. Mining machinery was commonly moved by California investors eastward to Cheyenne, and Denver merchants shipped their Black Hills goods through Cheyenne. Sidney, on the other hand, got the bulk of her business from Omaha, Chicago, and points east.

While Sidney and Cheyenne spokesmen boasted of the advantages and superiority of their towns, there is no reason to believe that one was more prominent than the other in the Black Hills trade during 1876 and 1877. Strahorn in 1877 reported Cheyenne freighters as having a total of about four hundred wagons, held by about twenty companies and a number of small operators. There is good reason, however, to believe that by 1878 Cheyenne freighting was running behind that of Sidney, Bismarck, and Fort Pierre. The *Black Hills Pioneer,* Deadwood's main newspaper, consistently reported the arrival of trains, many times indicating the number of wagons and always naming the home base. During the spring of 1878 little mention was made of Cheyenne trains.[51]

Sidney and Cheyenne almost monopolized the Union Pacific–Black Hills trade, but many other towns aspired to benefit from the gold rush. North Platte businessmen surveyed and staked a road from their town, which was advertised as the shortest to the Hills but which never developed. A group in Kearney raised $800 to hire a surveying party to locate a northwest trail. This route was announced as being opened by May, 1877, and at least one train of twenty-five wagons and some stagecoaches soon used it. Parties from as far east as Fremont and Blair shipped small quantities of selected goods to the mines, usually butter, lard, and eggs, during the winter and early spring when the demand and prices were high and speculation inviting. North Platte, Kearney, and the other towns never developed systematic or extensive freighting. They are of interest primarily because they show the far-reaching effects of the gold rush.[52]

Bismarck, the northernmost of the Black Hills supply points, did not become an important factor in the business until 1877. The town was advantageously located on the Missouri at the end of the Northern Pacific Railroad, which had been temporarily halted by bankruptcy since 1873. Bismarck's railroad promoters were among the first to obtain first-hand gold strike reports from

Custer's troops, who were stationed at Fort Abraham Lincoln just across the river. For one reason or another, mostly due to lack of leaders and money, schemes for an overland stage and freight connection from Bismarck did not materialize in 1875 or 1876. Then in 1877, through a combination of the Northern Pacific, the Minnesota Stage Company, and several businessmen, the Northwestern Express & Transportation Company was organized and Bismarck was ready to move into the Deadwood business. The Northern Pacific arranged for through freight shipments from Chicago by way of St. Paul, and the Minnesota Stage Company was the overland carrier. This veteran outfit had started in Minnesota Territory in 1851 and successfully operated throughout the frontier period in that area, first before the railroads and then later as an ally and feeder of various railroads.[53] The company shifted west with the advancing railroads and entered Dakota Territory with the Northern Pacific. Russell Blakeley and Cephas W. Carpenter, long-time leaders of the Minnesota Stage Company, became president and secretary-treasurer, respectively, of the Northwestern Express & Transportation Company. With a capital of $200,000, the company soon built ten stations on the 210-mile Deadwood Trail and began running stages and freight wagons. By mid-June, 1877, after only two months of operation, the firm had 26 Concord coaches and 200 freight wagons in service on a trail which closely followed the path of Custer's 1874 expedition.[54]

The company and the trail had three highly profitable years before being badly hurt by the shorter Fort Pierre route in 1880. The Chicago–Deadwood connection through Bismarck was nearly 1,100 miles long: 410 miles from Chicago to St. Paul, then 469 from the Minnesota capital to Bismarck, then over 200 miles more to Deadwood.[55] The *Black Hills Daily Pioneer* of February 9, 1879, reported the arrival of goods by Northwestern wagons in "unusually quick time"—twenty-three days from Chicago and seventeen days from St. Paul.

While there was initially widespread reluctance to use the northern trail, especially during the winter months, the close coordination of railroads and stage and freight lines ultimately made it popular, and the company before a year was out expanded its freighting to 250 wagons. The Northwestern Express & Transportation Company competed successfully as long as the Fort Pierre route depended on a railroad-steamboat-wagon combination. However, once Fort Pierre was reached by rail it soon dominated all rivals.[56]

Fort Pierre and Deadwood, only 200 miles apart, were connected by a good wagon road that was generally passable year round and free from any major stream crossing. However, to the east the closest railroad was at Yankton, capital of Dakota Territory, with connections to Sioux City and Chicago by the Chicago & Northwestern. So Fort Pierre freighters depended on three types of transportation necessitating involved and carefully coordinated arrangements between different companies.

Yankton, benefiting from her position at the end of track, was the steamboat capital of the upper Missouri and the home base for the Coulson Line, the leading company on the river and consistently the successful bidder for large government contracts to supply Indians and the army. Yankton was still rivaled by Sioux City, where up-river steamboating had been centered during the late sixties and early seventies. Sioux City remained the base for some boats, notably those of the Peck Line, Coulson's chief competitor. Yankton controlled most of the Fort Pierre freight, but Sioux City had enough to cause a steamboating revival there in the late seventies, probably because Yankton simply did not have the boats and warehouses to handle all of the freight despite her commanding up-river position.[57]

Use of the Fort Pierre route was sporadic in 1876, first because the government closed the trail because of Indian hostilities. Secondly, after reopening it the government refused to provide military escorts, thereby leaving trains at the mercy of renegade Indians. The army roundup of hostiles following the Sioux War of 1876 and the cession of the Black Hills removed any question about the legality and security of the Fort Pierre trail. Beginning in 1877 it was again used regularly.[58]

Fort Pierre freighters were the last of four links in a cooperative transportation arrangement providing through freight service from Chicago to the Black Hills. They worked with the Chicago & Northwestern Railroad serving Sioux City, the Dakota Southern Railroad connecting Sioux City and Yankton, and the Missouri River Transportation Company (i.e. Coulson Line) that ran steamboats from Yankton. Charles Woolworth, representing all interested carriers, made his headquarters in Deadwood, where he supervised the detailed scheduling and forwarding of freight. The railroads and steamboat line worked principally with two large freighting companies, the Fort Pierre & Black Hills Transportation Company of Fred T. Evans and the Merchants Transportation Company of Bramble, Miner & Company.[59]

Evans of Sioux City had trouble with the army in 1876 when one of his trains was destroyed for traveling illegally on Indian land, but the next year he was fully engaged in the trade as "Evans & Hornick, Forwarders, Freighters and General Outfitters for the Black Hills."[60] When Hornick left the company in 1878, Evans brother-in-law Edwin Loveland, who managed the firm's general merchandise store in Rapid City, became his partner. Evans, Fort Pierre's leading freighter, expanded his business to the point of transporting 10,000,000 pounds in 1879, using about 200 wagons. He worked with the Coulson Line into the summer of 1879 and then for some unapparent reason began cooperating with the Peck Line, whose half dozen steamers made regular trips from Sioux City.[61]

The extensiveness of Evans' freighting made him the best-known shipper in the Hills, and he was consistently and favorably reported by the area newspapers. The *Black Hills Journal* of July 20, 1878, noted that "there were 199,000 pounds of freight shipped on July 6 from Fort Pierre to the Hills by Fred T. Evans. This is the largest shipment made in one day to the Black Hills, over any of the different routes."

The Merchants Transportation Company was an outgrowth of the mercantile careers of Downer T. Bramble and his junior partner William Miner, who had a general merchandise store, a steam elevator, and a flour mill in Yankton. For several years Bramble, Miner & Company had been one of the leading outfitters for the upper Missouri trade. Hence, they were in a good position to enter the Black Hills business, which provided a great opportunity to distribute their own goods, particularly flour. They established a branch store at Fort Pierre and ran both mule and ox teams on the Black Hills trail. During 1880 they employed 2,000 animals and 300 men to ship 8,000,000 to 10,000,000 pounds to the mines.[62]

Shipping through Fort Pierre had one serious drawback. The steamboat connection from Yankton or Sioux City was seasonal, and during the winter months supplies had to be hauled overland all the way from Yankton to Fort Pierre and then on to the Hills.

When the river was open, Evans always advertised that he could carry goods for 50¢ a hundred less from Chicago to Deadwood than could a freighter from any rival route. During the winter, because wagon transportation was more costly than steamboat, rates increased, probably to the point of causing Fort Pierre to lose the advantage it had during the steamboat season. Nonetheless, quantities of freight were shipped overland from Yankton, especially during the winter of 1878–1879, when a surplus of feed in the farming area west of Yankton enabled freighters to inexpensively provide for their animals.[63]

Because of Evans and Bramble & Miner, Fort Pierre became the major freighting point for the Black Hills trade. It is not possible to determine exactly or even very closely how the trade was divided among the four rival towns. It is apparent that Bismarck and Fort Pierre were not important until 1877, and that by late 1878 Fort Pierre had the lead over Cheyenne, Sidney, and Bismarck. Since shippers would naturally seek the least expensive route, one can only surmise that the Fort Pierre way was somewhat cheaper, probably because it had the shortest overland section and because the Chicago & Northwestern and the steamboat companies were willing to more than meet the competition from the Union Pacific and the Northern Pacific. A common estimate, first reported in the *Black Hills Journal* of March 22, 1879, and then repeated by other newspapers, was that the total Hills imports for 1878 amounted to 46,000,000 pounds with an expectation of 70,000,000 during 1879. Fred T. Evans claimed that two-thirds of the 1878 freight was shipped from Fort Pierre.[64] No one, of course, kept an accurate statistical record of these imports, so later historians are in part at the mercy of contemporary estimators. Numerous news items in the Black Hills papers, however, seem to indicate that Fort Pierre's claims are generally true.

The movement to Fort Pierre became a full scale runaway in 1880, when the extension of railroads to the Missouri removed the steamboat middlemen. Early that spring the Milwaukee Road reached the river at Running Water, about fifty miles above Yankton, and the steamboat companies shifted most of their operations there. John W. Daugherty, onetime Sidney freighter who ran the Fort Pierre Freight Line, brought in most of his goods by railroad to Running Water and from there by steamboat to Fort Pierre. When Running Water replaced Yankton as the railroad terminus, the river phase of the Chicago-Deadwood trade was reduced nearly 20 per cent, thereby cutting time and expense. This slight shift was enough to give Fort Pierre a definite advantage, and much to her rivals' dismay yet another railroad was being extended across the Dakota prairies to the Missouri opposite Fort Pierre. During the summer and fall the Chicago & Northwestern speedily constructed its track to the river, and on November 4 the first train arrived at the new townsite of Pierre. For all practical purposes this was the end of any serious threat from Fort Pierre's rivals. The Northwestern Express & Transportation Company moved from Bismarck to Fort Pierre, and freighting ceased to be a significant activity at Sidney and Cheyenne.[65]

During 1880 the departure of wagon trains from Sidney was anything but commonplace. A few of the small freighters hung on, and while they may have profited as individuals, they did not contribute greatly to the community's business. Even after the railroad reached Pierre, there was still some freighting from Sidney. The *Black Hills Journal* of May 7, 1881, noted that "several freight outfits came in from Sidney during the past week." The complete withering of the trade is indicated by a story in the *Sidney Plaindealer-Telegraph* of December 9, 1882. It seems that Fort Pierre freighters had problems. They had too much freight, too few wagons, and poor weather, so an inquiry was received in Sidney asking if any goods could be transferred by the old Sidney Trail. Sidney had warehouses, but the press regretfully reported that "the freighters might be harder to get as the large number who used to be engaged between here and the Black Hills are scattered about and could not readily be gotten together."

The wheels again stopped rolling. For a second time Nebraska grass would grow over a famous trail, and nothing would remain of the overland freighter traffic except a great heritage and a prominent place in the history of a plains region where the story of the bullwhacker, the wagon, and the ox were vital to its frontier beginnings.

Biographical Sketches
APPENDIX I

The following brief sketches were written with the aim of providing personal information about some of the people involved in overland freighting from Nebraska towns. This is not intended to be a comprehensive directory but rather sketches of representative freighters. Generally, these are men who were involved in freighting for some time as entrepreneurs, although some wagonmasters and bullwhackers are included, as are some others who had very brief freighting careers.

It is noteworthy that, as a general rule, the freighters were young men with comparatively meager education, and freighting was but a brief phase in their careers. Most of them came from the New England, Middle Atlantic, and Great Lakes states, and many of them spent some years in Iowa or Missouri before moving west of the Missouri. After engaging in freighting, a surprising number of these people became men of substance in merchant, banking, ranching, and transportation activities. Many others returned to farming—their pre-freighting occupation. One became a United States senator. To most of these men freighting was an opportunity to secure capital, which became the basis for investments outside of transportation.

The biographical information was drawn from a variety of sources, but three were of particular significance. They were: J. Sterling Morton and Albert Watkins (eds.), *Illustrated History of Nebraska*, 3 vols. (Lincoln: Jacob North & Co.; Western Publishing & Engraving Co., 1905–1913); Raymond E. Dale, "Otoe

County Pioneers, a Biographical Dictionary," unp. MS. in the Nebraska State Historical Society; and *Portrait and Biographical Album of Otoe and Cass Counties, Nebraska* (Chicago: Chapman Brothers, 1889). The *Illustrated History of Nebraska* is generally cited as Morton-Watkins, so this reference is used in the documentation following the sketches. This history contains a wealth of information, but its organization leaves much to be desired. The main problem occurs because there are three versions of Volume III. The text for all versions is essentially the same, but the biographical sections are entirely different. One version has sketches of those whose surnames begin with A through G. Another version contains, generally, H through N, and still another, O through Z. There are, however, some exceptions to this general classification. The three versions, in keeping with the alphabetical arrangement of the biographies, are usually labeled as III A, III B, and III C.

Another, but minor, problem in using Morton-Watkins is locating portraits. A few of the biographical sketches are accompanied by portraits, which are usually located near the sketch. Some portraits, however, were placed pages away from the subject. Only references to these misplaced portraits have been made in the following citations.

Dale's "Otoe County Pioneers" is a series of many hundreds of unpublished sketches about first generation settlers of Otoe County. These were compiled from a great variety of sources, and the late Mr. Dale spent many years extracting minute references from census rolls and newspapers. These are arranged alphabetically in bound volumes. This source is referred to in the following text as "Dale, 'Otoe County Pioneers.'" *The Portrait and Biographical Album of Otoe and Cass Counties* is referred to simply as *Otoe and Cass Counties*.

ADKINS, JAMES. Adkins was born in Kentucky about 1831 and lived in Missouri for some time before moving to Nebraska City, where he was a full-time freighter in 1865 and 1866. In 1865 he ran ten wagons from Nebraska City to Julesburg and Denver, and the following year he had twenty-five wagons in the Nebraska City–Bozeman Trail trade. By late 1866 he and his family had moved to Platte County, Missouri. (Dale, "Otoe County Pioneers." *Nebraska City News,* June 10, July 22, 1865; June 30, 1866.)

ARENDS, JOHN HENRY. b. Hanover, Germany, April 15, 1843; d. November 18, 1924. The Arends family moved to the United States in 1854 and farmed in Illinois for five years before moving to a farm near Talmage, Nebraska. During 1860 and 1861 Arends freighted to Colorado from Nebraska City. He then engaged in mercantile activities, first at Nebraska City and then at Syracuse, where he opened a general store in 1877. Arends also had financial interests in a mill, a lumber company, and a bank. He was active in civic affairs, and as a Republican was elected to the State Senate in 1898 and reelected in 1900. (Morton-Watkins, I, 580. *Otoe and Cass Counties*, 540-41. Dale, "Otoe County Pioneers.")

ASHTON, TALBOT. b. about 1822; d. Dunbar, Nebraska, April 19, 1898. Talbot Ashton moved to Nebraska City from Brown County, Ohio, in about 1859 and began a general merchandise business. In association with James N. Tait he operated one of Nebraska City's major general mechandise firms, acted as a commission and forwarding agent, packed pork, and engaged in overland freighting. Throughout the freighting period Ashton and Tait sent trains of their own goods to Colorado. They were especially important in freighting during the early 1860's. Ashton withdrew from his business with Tait in 1868 and two years later moved to a farm near Nebraska City. He was also president of the Otoe County National Bank for some years and served as a Republican in the 1869 State Senate. (Morton-Watkins, III A, 502. Dale, "Otoe County Pioneers.")

BARTON, GUY CONGER. b. Carlisle, Lorain County, Ohio, July 1, 1839; d. Walnut Lodge, Nebraska, June 15, 1909. Barton was raised in a poor farm family and after acquiring only a common school education was employed as a clerk in a Monmouth, Illinois, store in 1856. He then moved to St. Joseph, Missouri, and worked as a store clerk for five years before entering overland freighting in 1862. His lively freighting business during the Civil War years was conducted in partnership with Charles D. Woolworth, a brother of the famous Omaha financier James M. Woolworth. Barton and Woolworth dispatched many trains from all of the major freighting towns and shifted their operations westward with the construction of the UPRR. After moving from St. Joseph to Omaha in 1869, Barton handled construction contracts for the UPRR but soon moved to North Platte to engage in ranching. While living at North Platte, he was treasurer of Lincoln County in 1870 and state senator in 1872 and 1874. After his return to Omaha in 1882, he became one of the city's major capitalists with financial holdings in a smelting company, a bridge company, a street railway line, an electric light company, and a bank. He had a luxurious country estate, Walnut Lodge, at Gilmore just outside of South Omaha, where he was living at the time of his death. (Morton-Watkins, I, 586. *Omaha World Herald,* January 5, 1958, p. 12 G. *Omaha Morning World Herald,* June 16, 1909.)

BAILEY, GEORGE. Bailey was born in Kentucky about 1819 and lived in Indiana and Iowa before moving to a farm near Nebraska City in 1856. During the next several years he bought over a section of land and served as county commissioner. In 1860 and 1861 in association with Sylvester Hollister, he freighted from Nebraska City to Denver. He evidently left Nebraska City in 1862, since no local records of him exist after that time. (Dale, "Otoe County Pioneers.")

BEAUVIS, GEMINIAN PIERRE (JAMES PETER) b. St. Genevieve, Missouri, December 6, 1815; d. St. Louis, November, 1878. Throughout the period of overland freighting Jim Beauvais was one of the most important men in western Nebraska because of his famous ranche, his freighting, and his work as an interpreter in government negotiations with the Indians. A graduate of a Jesuit college, Beauvais taught school for a time before entering the services of Pierre Chouteau, Jr. & Company, successor of the American Fur Company. In 1849 he establised a trading post at the Lower California Crossing, called the Star Ranche, but normally referred to in emigrant guides as simply "Beauvais' Ranche." He operated a second ranche near Fort Laramie and dealt extensively in the Indian trade. Because of his ranches and buffalo robe trade, he consistently freighted, usually with one large annual train, from St. Joseph or Atchison. When the UPRR reached the vicinity of the Lower California Crossing, Beauvais quit and returned to St. Louis with a reported capital of nearly $1,000,000. At the time of his death in 1878, he was preparing to move to Frontier County, Nebraska, where his son Edward had just purchased a ranch. (Morton-Watkins, II, 583-84. "Beauvais Genealogy" in G. P. Beauvais Papers, Nebraska State Historical Society.)

BRATT, JOHN. b. Leek, Staffordshire, England, August 9, 1842. By the time Bratt emigrated to the United States in 1864, he had served five years as an apprentice to a merchant, and had another five years' experience in business on his own. From 1864 to 1866 he gradually worked his way from New York to Nebraska City by speculating in merchandise, serving as purchasing agent for a construction camp, and hiring out as a freight checker on a Mississippi River steamboat. His brief freighting career was highlighted by his first venture as a bullwhacker on the long trip from Nebraska City to Fort Phil Kearny in 1866. This trip became the basis for his *Trails of Yesterday,* one of the best descriptions of the bullwhackers' daily life, posthumously published. After this initial trip he worked several years in western Nebraska as a foreman for Coe & Carter, the well-known freighting company which was then transporting military supplies and providing ties and wood for the UPRR. In 1869 Bratt entered a partnership with Coe & Carter in the cattle business under the firm name John Bratt & Company. Working out of his home in North Platte, Bratt stayed in the cattle business for nearly three decades and participated in some of the celebrated long drives from Texas. The partners were also interested in irrigation and pioneered several projects in western Nebraska. Bratt had a long-standing interest in local history and was reputed to be a highly effective story teller, as is evidenced by his autobiography. His wife Elizabeth was a daughter of John Burke, the Cottonwood Springs rancheman. He died at his home in North Platte, June 15, 1918. Bratt was well known regionally and was one of the first Nebraskans to be chosen to the "Hall of Great Westerners" of the National Cowboy Hall of Fame and Western Heritage Center. (Morton-Watkins, I, 596, portrait, 567. *Nebraska History and Record of Pioneer Days,* I, Nos. 3 & 4 [April and May, 1918], 5. John Bratt, *Trails of Yesterday* [Lincoln: University Publishing Co., 1921]. "Hall of Fame Will Depict an Authentic Story of the West," *Nebraska Cattleman,* XVIII, No. 3 [November, 1961], 12.)

BROWN, JAMES JAY. b. Stephentown, New York, January 12, 1832; d. Omaha, February 9, 1901. When only eighteen, Brown became manager of his father's store in Stephentown. After disposing of the business he moved to Omaha in 1856 and organized a general merchandise business with his brother Randall A. The firm of J. J. and R. A. Brown freighted quantities of its own goods to

Denver, and James Jay made several of these trips himself. After the freighting era he and his brother operated a wholesale dry goods house until 1884. He organized the Omaha Loan and Trust Company in 1885 and from then until his death was mainly concerned with banking, real estate investment, and street railway promotion in Omaha and Council Bluffs. Brown also invested in the National Bank of Ashland and was its president when he died. (Arthur C. Wakeley [ed.], *Omaha: The Gate City and Douglas County, Nebraska* [Chicago: S. J. Clarke Publishing Co., 1917], II, 12-16.

BUETER, HERMAN. b. Kingdom of Hanover, Germany, 1823; d. Nebraska City, September 23, 1888. Bueter moved to Nebraska City in 1856 and managed a brickyard before entering the grocery business. While a grocer, he engaged in overland freighting to Colorado and in 1861 was one of the incorporators of the Nebraska City, Fort Kearny, and Denver City Freight and Express Company. In 1864 Bueter left the grocery business but resumed it three years later and continued as a grocer for most of the remainder of his life. (Dale, "Otoe County Pioneers." *Nebraska City News*, September 28, 1888.)

BUETER, JOHN (brother of Herman). b. Kingdom of Hanover, Germany, 1831. John Bueter moved to Nebraska City as a merchant in 1855 and during the freighting days of the 1860's was associated with Arnold F. Mollring and Herman H. Petring in a general merchandise company. The company transported quantities of its goods to Colorado. He served one term (1865) in the Nebraska Territorial Legislature. He moved to the Black Hills in 1876 to establish a store in Deadwood. Bueter died at Hot Springs, South Dakota, November 19, 1904, and was buried at Deadwood. (Dale, "Otoe County Pioneers.")

BURKE, JOHN. In 1852 at age twenty-six, Burke moved from Germany with his wife and young son to a farm at Nauvoo, Illinois, where they remained for eight years before moving to a Tecumseh, Nebraska, farm. After four years at Tecumseh, Burke started out to relocate in Colorado, but threats from hostile Indians caused him to abandon the trip near Fort McPherson. He stayed there and built a road ranche several miles west of the fort. The place was later destroyed by Indians, but Burke and his family escaped to Fort McPherson. Burke then relocated his ranche so as to be in a position to benefit from the great overland migrations immediately prior to the construction of the UPRR. In addition to operating the ranche, Burke farmed, worked as a government contractor, and was said to have constructed the first irrigation ditch in Nebraska. After the construction of the UPRR, Burke built a wagon bridge across the North Platte near the fort in order to deliver his contract goods. In June, 1872, the rampaging Platte swept away several spans of the bridge and Burke resorted to moving military supplies by boat. He was drowned when the boat sank during one of these hazardous crossings. (Morton-Watkins, I, 606-7, portrait, 563. *Nebraska City News* [Weekly], July 8, 1910.)

BYRAM, AUGUSTUS. b. Kentucky, 1822. Byram had prior freighting experience, probably in the Santa Fe trade, before coming as Majors' agent to Nebraska City when it was designated as the military depot. He and his brother Peter succeeded Majors, and for several years they were the ranking freighters on the plains. The Byrams built a large warehouse on the Nebraska City levee in 1862 and actively explored the possibilities of salt mining in Lancaster County. In 1864 they moved to Atchison, Kansas, and after that time were no longer important freighters in the Platte Valley. In Kansas Augustus had a brief political career, serving in the state House of Representatives in 1868. Evidently much of his time was devoted to managing extensive investments in Utah silver mines; he was reported to have realized $6,000,000 through the sale of his interest in a single mine. He died in Chicago where he made his home after leaving Atchison sometime during the 1880's. (*Nebraska City News,* August 30, 1862. Dale, "Otoe County Pioneers." "Biographies of Members of the Legislature of 1868," *Transactions of the Kansas State Historical Society,* X [Topeka, 1908], 269.)

BYRAM, PETER. b. Bath County, Kentucky, August 21, 1824. In 1845 Peter Byram moved to Westport, Missouri, and farmed for eight years before entering Santa Fe freighting in 1853. During this time he and his brother no doubt became well acquainted with Alexander Majors. His Nebraska City career paralleled that of his brother, and they moved to Atchison at the same time. He did some freighting to New Mexico until 1868 and then became an extensive farmer by purchasing a thousand acres of land five miles west of Atchison. In a biographical sketch published in 1883, he was listed as a "stock dealer and farmer." He was married in 1859 to Emma Meeker, daughter of the well-known Indian missionary, Jotham Meeker. (A. T. Andreas [compiler], *History of the State of Kansas* [Chicago: Western Historical Company, 1883], 385.)

CALDWELL, ALEXANDER. b. Drakes Ferry, Huntingdon County, Pennsylvania, March 1, 1830; d. May 19, 1917, Kansas City, Missouri. As the most important military contractor on the plains from 1861 through 1866, Caldwell operated mainly out of Leavenworth, Kansas, but also did considerable business from Nebraska City, Plattsmouth, and Omaha, all of which were military depots at various times. Caldwell's father James was a charcoal and iron furnace operator until he enlisted in the army during the Mexican War. Alexander accompanied his father into the army and with him participated in several engagements, including the Battle of Chapultepec, where the elder Caldwell was fatally wounded. After the war young Caldwell worked as cashier in a Columbia, Pennsylvania, bank until moving to Leavenworth in the spring of 1861 and beginning his freighting career with Irwin, Jackman & Company. With the end of overland freighting, Caldwell became a railroad contractor and promoter. He had the contract for building the Missouri Pacific from Kansas City to Leavenworth and later extended the line to Atchison and became its president. He also organized the Kansas Central Railroad Company, which constructed a 170-mile line from Leavenworth to Miltonvale. During this time Caldwell had become a key figure in state Republican circles and was chosen as United States senator by the Kansas Legislature for the term starting March 4, 1871. Caldwell's opponents, however, charged that bribery had been used in securing his selection, which led to an investigation by both the Kansas Legislature and the United States Senate. When it became obvious that some of Caldwell's supporters without his knowledge or consent had acted illegally in his behalf, Caldwell resigned March 24, 1873, and turned his attention to business activities in Leavenworth.

He soon organized the Kansas Manufacturing Company headquartered at Leavenworth and was its president from 1874 to 1888. The company was mainly devoted to building farm wagons and was reported to have manufactured as many as 7,000 "Caldwell" wagons annually. He also headed the Idaho and Oregon Land

Improvement Company, which located towns and constructed irrigation ditches. From 1897 to 1915 Caldwell was president of the First National Bank of Leavenworth, one of the largest Kansas financial institutions. He lived in obscure retirement for many years. His death, occurring just after the United States entry into World War I, was not widely noticed. He was interred in Mount Muncie Cemetery, Leavenworth. (William E. Connelley, *A Standard History of Kansas and Kansans* [Chicago: Lewis Publishing Company, 1918], V, 2403-4. Thomas LeGrand Harris, "Caldwell, Alexander," *Dictionary of American Biography,* ed. Allen Johnson [New York: Charles Scribner's Sons, 1929], III, 405. *Biographical Directory of the American Congress* [Washington: Government Printing Office, 1928], 775.)

CARLYLE, HENRY. Henry Carlyle was born in Kentucky about 1830 and lived for years in western Missouri where he became well acquainted with Ben Holladay. From 1863 until 1865 Carlyle and his younger brother Alexander worked out of Nebraska City, mainly as freighters of supplies for the Overland Stage Company. In this capacity they worked in partnership with Holladay, then owner of the overland line. When the Byrams moved to Atchison in 1864, the Carlyles became Nebraska City's largest freighting company. After freighting, Henry Carlyle moved to a fruit farm in Orange County, California, where he was still living at the turn of the century. ALEXANDER CARLYLE moved from Nebraska City to Waverly, Missouri, during the winter of 1866–1867 to engage in farming. (Frank A. Root and William Elsey Connelley, *The Overland Stage to California* [Topeka, 1901], 312, 358-59. Dale, "Otoe County Pioneers.")

CARTER, LEVI. b. 1830. In 1857 Carter, a native of Belknap County, New Hampshire, moved to Nebraska City as an experienced carpenter. For seven of his ten years in Nebraska City he engaged in freighting in partnership with Isaac Coe. Coe & Carter was consistently one of the leading freighting companies from 1860 until 1867. Carter moved to Omaha in 1867 and continued with Coe and later John Bratt in the railroad contracting and cattle businesses. In 1888 he bought the Omaha White Lead Company and then incorporated it as the Carter White Lead Company, which became one of the largest concerns of its kind in the nation. During the 1890's he discontinued his cattle and railroad interests but remained active in the lead company until his death in Omaha, November 7, 1903. (Morton-Watkins, I, 611. *Omaha World-Herald,* November 8, 1903.)

CHIVINGTON, JOHN M. b. Ohio, January 27, 1821; d. Denver, Colorado, October 4, 1894. Chivington is one of the best known and most controversial figures in Great Plains history because of his role as commander of the forces that penetrated the Sand Creek Massacre. After entering the ministry of the Methodist Episcopal Church, he preached in Illinois and Missouri from 1848 until 1855, when he moved to Nebraska. During his five years in Nebraska he lived at Omaha and Nebraska City and in 1859 was appointed presiding elder of a church district which included much of eastern Nebraska. In 1860 Chivington went to Colorado as the presiding elder of the Rocky Mountain district. He was soon widely known for his evangelistic fervor, a fervor evident not only in religion but in politics as well, for he was a militant Republican abolitionist. In 1861 he enlisted in the Colorado militia and as a major in this service played a vital role in repulsing the Confederate Sibley Expedition that threatened southern Colorado in 1862. Because of this he became a great regional hero, and, continuing in the military, he fulfilled the frontier ideal by advocating stern handling of Indians. After the Battle of Sand Creek, Chivington was generally praised by frontiersmen and damned by eastern humanitarians, who immediately called the episode the "Chivington Massacre." Despite his loss of military command, he retained great prestige throughout the West, where, at least, his efforts during the Sibley invasion were remembered. After his forced resignation from the army, he entered overland freighting and continued in it until June, 1867, when he sold out to Wells, Fargo & Company. (Morton-Watkins, II, 196-97.)

CHIVINGTON, THOMAS (son of John M.). Thomas Chivington was born in 1841 and came to Nebraska with his parents. When they moved to Colorado in 1860, he stayed on in Nebraska City, where he became one of the town's best known freighters. Chivington never became a major entrepreneur, but he did operate small trains throughout the year and, largely because of his winter freighting to Colorado, was frequently mentioned by Nebraska City newspapers. He continued in freighting until his death by drowning on June 23, 1866, in the North Platte. (Dale, "Otoe County Pioneers."

Nebraska City News, July 7, 1866. *Nebraska Republican* [Omaha], July 13, 1866.)

CLARKE, HENRY TEFFT. b. Greenwich, Washington County, New York, April 26, 1834; d. Excelsior Springs, Missouri, February 3, 1913. After some experience as a store clerk, Clarke moved to Bellevue in 1856, where he became the steamboat agent and dealt in general merchandise. In 1862 in partnership with his brother Artemus M. he began contracting to supply grain to Fort Kearny. After several years as a government contractor, Clarke & Company engaged in private freighting to Colorado. In the meantime Clarke worked stenuously but futilely to have the UPRR started at Bellevue rather than Omaha. After the construction of the UPRR, he surveyed railroad routes from Bellevue to Sioux City and Lincoln. Still in partnership with his brother, he began constructing railroad and highway bridges, including seven across the Platte, the last and best known being the bridge on the Sidney Trail. After his venture in the Black Hills gold rush trade, he returned to Omaha and engaged in numerous mercantile activities including a finance company, a wholesale hardware firm, and a wholesale drug house. Clarke was active in civic affairs and in politics as a Republican. In 1862 he was elected to the state House of Representatives and in 1863 to the Senate. He actively participated in the affairs of the Nebraska State Historical Society and was chosen as its president in 1905. During his last years Clarke worked to revive commercial navigation on the Missouri River and was a leader in convening several Missouri River congresses, which were composed of representatives of civic and political groups who wanted river improvement. (Morton-Watkins, I, 614. *Omaha Morning World Herald,* February 4, 1913. Henry Tefft Clarke, "Freighting–Denver & Black Hills," *Proceedings and Collections of the Nebraska State Historical Society,* 2nd series [Lincoln, 1902], V, 299-312.)

CLASBY, WILLIAM F. b. Missouri, 1838. Clasby freighted out of Nebraska City during the 1864–1865 boom in association with A. B. Daniels and F. J. McConnell. In February, 1866, he sold out to McConnell and probably returned to his native Missouri. (Dale, "Otoe County Pioneers.")

CLAYTON, JOHN D. b. Virginia, about 1835. Clayton freighted out of Nebraska City from 1862 to 1866, and in 1867 moved to

Denver to carry on freighting in that region. By 1870 he was again living in Nebraska City. (Dale, "Otoe County Pioneers.")

COAD, JOHN F. b. County Wexford, Ireland, December 5, 1842; d. Omaha, October 15, 1910. John F. Coad was generally associated with his older brother Mark M. in freighting and the cattle business. He worked from 1871 to 1873 as an Indian Department contractor with Dwight J. McCann and for some six more years as a military contractor in western Nebraska and Wyoming. While ranching in the North Platte Valley, he resided in Cheyenne and served in the Wyoming Territorial Legislature in 1878 and 1884. In 1883 the Coads sold their ranch land and stock to the Bay State Livestock Company. John later moved to Omaha where he accrued a considerable fortune as president of the Packers' National Bank and president of the Coad Real Estate Company. He held farm land in Iowa, Nebraska, Texas, and Oklahoma. (Morton-Watkins, I, 620-21. *Omaha Sunday Bee,* October 16, 1910. A. B. Wood, "The Coad Brothers: Panhandle Cattle Kings," *Nebraska History,* XIX, No. 1 [January-March, 1938], 28-43. Ralph G. Coad, "Irish Pioneers of Nebraska," *Nebraska History,* XVII, No. 3 [July-September, 1936], 171-77.)

COAD, MARK M. b. Davis Township, County Wexford, Ireland, 1832. In 1850 Coad moved with his parents from Ireland to Albany, New York. After seven years there they moved to Dubuque, Iowa, and after the death of the father in 1858 the widow and her children moved to Nebraska City. In about 1861 Coad and his brother John F. began freighting to Denver on a small scale, and within several years they had expanded to over 50 wagons and 400 oxen. While continuing freighting, the brothers established two road ranches in 1862, one at Julesburg and the other midway between Julesburg and the beginning of the Denver cut-off road. They shifted west with the Union Pacific and in 1871 started cattle ranching on the North Platte. The brothers acquired many thousands of acres in the area of Scottsbluff, and by the time they sold out to the Bay State Livestock Company in 1883 the Coads reportedly had 25,000 head of range stock. Mark Coad was the resident manager for a time of the Bay State Company, which was comprised of English, Scottish, and eastern American capitalists. He then moved to a farm near Fremont, where he bred Percheron horses from stock acquired in Ireland. He was also one of the important stockholders in the Merchants National Bank of Omaha, had mining and land interests in California, and a ranch on Horse Creek in Wyoming. His long and colorful career ended tragically; on January 4, 1911, he was shot to death by a sheepherder in the lobby of the Normandie Hotel in Cheyenne, Wyoming. (Morton-Watkins, I, 621-22. *Omaha World Herald,* January 6, 15, 1911. Wood, "The Coad Brothers." Coad, "Irish Pioneers in Nebraska.")

COE, ISAAC. b. Middletown, Connecticut, May 15, 1816; d. Columbus, Ohio, January 16, 1899. After working as a farmer, traveling salesman, and merchant, Coe moved to Nebraska City in 1858 and invested in land and freighting. In partnership with Levi Carter, Coe was one of Nebraska City's major freighters. After the completion of the UPRR Carter and Coe engaged in government contracting, railroad construction, ranching, and mining in Colorado. While his business career was significant, Coe was much better known for his participation in the territorial militia. In 1861 he was chosen as brigadier general in the militia by the officers of various volunteer units and after that time was usually referred to, at least in the newspapers, as General Coe. (Morton-Watkins, I, 622. *Otoe and Cass Counties,* 696. Andreas [compiler], *History of the State of Nebraska* [Chicago: Western Publishing Co., 1882], 1218.)

CORBIN, DANIEL CHASE. b. Newport, New Hampshire, October 1, 1832; d. Spokane, Washington, June 29, 1918. At nineteen, after having acquired some common school education, Corbin received a government contract to survey land in Iowa. Several years later he was granted a similar contract for Nebraska land, which afforded him an opportunity to successfully engage in land speculation. In 1856 Corbin moved to Nebraska City as a land and insurance agent, and three years later established a trading post west of Fort Kearny and began freighting. From 1859 until 1865 he was one of Nebraska City's most constant freighters, hauling both to his ranche and to Colorado. During much of this time he was evidently residing in Denver. In 1865 he moved to Helena, Montana, where he spent nearly a decade as a merchant, cashier, and part owner of a bank. He moved to New York City in 1876 and for six years he was associated with his brother Austin in financing and managing the Manhattan Beach Railway. He then turned his interests to the silver-lead mining region about Coeur d'Aléne, Idaho, and in 1886 headed a group that constructed one of the first concentrating plants in the area. Corbin also organzied the Coeur d'Aléne Railroad and Navigation Company, which operated steamboats and constructed a railroad. In 1889 he moved to Spokane and constructed the Spokane Falls & Northern Railway. After the turn of the century he built the Spokane International Railway connecting Spokane and the Canadian Pacific. While transportation was his main concern, Corbin also organized the Washington State Sugar Company, which operated a beet sugar factory, promoted the Spokane Valley Land & Water Company to irrigate eastern Washington land, and directed the Old National Bank and Union Trust Company of Spokane. He was also president of the Corbin Coal & Coke Company, which owned coal lands in British Columbia. (William A. Robinson, "Corbin, Daniel Chase," *Dictionary of American Biography* [1930], IV, 437. *National Cyclopaedia of American Biography* [New York: James T. White & Co., 1932], XXII, 120. *Nebraska City News*, July 30, 1859; June 16, 1860.)

COWLES, CHARLES H. b. Genesee County, New York, May 20, 1818; d. Nebraska City, April 14, 1888. Charles Cowles was raised on an Ohio farm, then spent seven years in Indiana and six more in Missouri before moving to Nebraska in 1854 to establish a trading post in Otoe County. Cowles and his brothers Henry Clinton and James H. had divergent careers before they moved to Nebraska, but they no doubt coordinated their movement to the new territory. After selling the trading post in 1856, Cowles turned to farming near Nebraska City. This occupied the rest of his life except for his freighting experience. From 1860 until 1863 he and his brothers ran wagons from Nebraska City to Denver, and judging from newspaper coverage they were among the best known of the small operators. A Republican, Cowles represented Otoe County in the First Territorial Legislature. (Morton-Watkins, I, 220-21. *Otoe and Cass Counties*, 624-26.)

COWLES, HENRY CLINTON. Cowles was born on a farm in Genesee County, New York, August 22, 1815, and spent his youth on an Ohio farm before gradually working westward as a farmer, cabinetmaker, and millwright. He moved to land near the site of Nebraska City in 1853. As one of the first squatters in the area, he presumed the opening of the territory and legally claimed land as soon as it was possible. Cowles farmed and operated a grist mill and in 1857 represented Otoe County in the Territorial Legislature. In 1860 he moved to Empire, Colorado, where he lived until his death in 1890. During the early 1860's he and his brothers Charles H. and James H. ran freighting trains from Nebraska City, and his role was evidently that of distributing and selling the supplies in the mining camps. (Morton-Watkins, I, 305)

COWLES, JAMES HARVEY. b. Trumball County, Ohio, October 21, 1821. Like his brothers, James Cowles was among the first pioneers in Otoe County. He had earlier lived in Iowa and was reported to have constructed the first house in Sidney, Iowa. In 1855 he was elected to the Territorial Legislature. He evidently farmed before entering the freighting business. In 1863 he moved to Hamburg, Iowa, and died in Omaha, July 30, 1867. (Morton-Watkins, I, 255.)

CREIGH, THOMAS A. b. Mercersburg, Pennsylvania, October 6, 1840; d. May 16, 1909. Creigh attended Franklin and Marshall College and clerked in a drugstore before serving in combat with a Pennsylvania infantry regiment during the Civil War. After his discharge Creigh moved to Omaha in 1864, working first as chief clerk in the army commissary department and then as an assistant to the Pawnee Indian agent. In 1866, as managing clerk for a wagon train carrying mining machinery from Nebraska City to Virginia City, Montana, Creigh kept an interesting diary of the trip. He stayed at Virginia City until 1869, and the next year in partnership with Henry C. Lett started a drugstore in Brownville. He stayed there three years, then spent two more in Lincoln before moving to Omaha in 1875, where he stayed the remainder of his life. He worked for a drug company until 1883 and then entered the real estate business. He was active in the Grand Army of the Republic and was chosen as the Nebraska departmental commander in 1907. (Morton-Watkins, III A, 645. Thomas Alfred Creigh, "From Nebraska City to Montana, 1866: The Diary of Thomas Alfred Creigh," ed. James C. Olson, *Nebraska History*, XXIX, No. 3 [September, 1948], 208-37.)

CREIGHTON, EDWARD. b. Barnesville, Belmont County, Ohio, August 31, 1820; d. Omaha, November 5, 1874. As a youth Creighton worked on his father's farm and as a cart-boy on pike roads, where Phil Sheridan of Civil War fame was one of his companions.

At twenty-one he began freighting in Ohio and combined it with farming until approximately 1847, when he began constructing telegraph lines. In 1858–1859, when he already had a considerable reputation as a telegraph line builder, he assisted in the construction of a line from St. Joseph to Omaha. At the instigation of telegraph magnate Hiram Sibley, he made a survey of the overland route to explore the feasibility of a transcontinental line from Omaha to California. Creighton was general superintendent of the company that built the line from Omaha to Salt Lake City in 1861, and for the next six years he was the general superintendent and a major stockholder of the Pacific Telegraph Company, as the firm came to be called. Using returns from his telegraph investments, Creighton turned to overland freighting, working actively with his brother John A. and his cousin James, who operated many of the trains. During the period 1863–1866 they worked mainly in shipping private freight to Colorado, Utah, and Montana. One of their Montana trains, consisting of forty mule-drawn wagons, was reported to have made $52,000. Creighton also worked as a grading contractor for the UPRR, installed telegraph lines for the company, and constructed a telegraph line from Utah to Montana. In 1869 he helped organize the Omaha & Northwestern Railroad. He may have been Omaha's wealthiest man by the time of his death. A devout Roman Catholic, Creighton made extensive donations to the Catholic church and before his death indicated that he desired to make a donation for the formation of a college. His widow then provided an endowment which served as the foundation for a new school, Creighton University, incorporated in 1879 and assigned to the Jesuit order. Creighton is remembered as one of Nebraska's greatest figures, and he was chosen to represent the state in the "Hall of Great Westerners" of the National Cowboy Hall of Fame and Western Heritage Center located near Oklahoma City. (Morton-Watkins, I, 627-29. Victor Rosewater, "Creighton, Edward," *Dictionary of American Biography* [1930], IV, 534. *National Cyclopaedia of American Biography* [1932], XXII, 169-70. Alfred Sorenson, "Biographical Sketch of Edward Creighton," *Nebraska History*, XVII, No. 3 [July-September, 1936], 163-69. *Nebraska Cattleman*, XVIII, No. 3 [November, 1961], 12.)

CREIGHTON, JAMES. b. March 1, 1822; d. June 8, 1903. With his cousins, Edward, John, and Joseph Creighton, James Creighton moved from his native Ohio to Omaha in 1856 and thereafter was closely identified with the activities of Edward and John in telegraph construction and freighting. He was one of Edward's principal aides during the construction of the overland telegraph line and managed most of the Creighton freighting interests. He was oftentimes mentioned in Omaha newspapers as he embarked or returned from one of his numerous plains treks. After freighting he spent most of his time in the cattle business and was also active in Omaha civic and political affairs. He served a term in the State Legislature, was a delegate to several national Democratic conventions, and also had terms on the Omaha City Council and school board. (Morton-Watkins, III A, 647.)

CREIGHTON, JOHN A.　b. Licking County, Ohio, October 15, 1831; d. February 7, 1907. Although overshadowed by his much better known older brother, John A. Creighton had a remarkable career in his own right. After working with Edward on telegraph lines, he moved to Omaha in 1856, where he farmed and clerked in the store of J. J. and R. A. Brown, who were among the first significant Omaha suppliers of the Colorado miners. In 1860, while working with the Browns, Creighton took two trains to Denver. He worked with his brother before moving to Virginia City, Montana, in 1863, where he spent five years as a grocer. In Montana he acted as the distributor for freight shipped by his brother and cousin. After returning to Omaha in 1868, he amassed a fortune in a long business career, which included investing in banks, real estate, and mines, operating a forwarding business at Corinne, Utah, and helping form the Omaha Nail Works Company and the Union Stock Yards Company. He contributed liberally to Creighton University and is noted for building the Creighton Medical College. In recognition of his philanthropy, Pope Leo XIII in 1895 made John A. Creighton a knight of the Order of St. Gregory and conferred on him the title of Count of the Papal Court. He was a lifelong enthusiastic Democrat and in 1896 was one of Bryan's ardent supporters. (Morton-Watkins, I, 629-31. J. D. Hicks, "Creighton, John Andrew," *Dictionary of American Biography* [1930], IV, 535-36. *National Cyclopaedia of American Biography* [1909], XI, 369.)

DANIELS, ALVIN B.　b. Pennsylvania, 1836. In 1860 Daniels was living in Nebraska City as an attorney, real estate agent, farmer, and member of the Nebraska City Quartz Mining Company. He later freighted to Colorado, first in association with Levi Carter, then as a partner of William T. Clasby. He was one of the comparatively few freighters consistently mentioned in the Nebraska City newspapers. After the end of freighting, he established a loan business in Nebraska City. (Dale, "Otoe County Pioneers.")

DAUCHY, JEROME H. b. Rochester, New York, February 2, 1834; d. Stockville, Frontier County, Nebraska, March 9, 1897. Dauchy moved to Nebraska City as a carpenter in 1855 and then to Colorado three years later. In 1862 he was operating a ranche near Alkali Station. He freighted out of Nebraska City for several years in the 1860's, both to his ranche and Colorado. When the UPRR was being constructed, he freighted ahead of it and in 1867 worked mainly in the trade from Julesburg to the Bozeman Trail posts. Dauchy moved to Johnson County in 1868; after six years there he moved to Frontier County to develop a large cattle ranch. He was also Frontier County treasurer and a county commissioner for nine years. (Dale, "Otoe County Pioneers." Jerome H. Dauchy Papers, Nebraska State Historical Society. [This includes an obituary and a Russell, Majors & Waddell leatherbound Train Book, which includes printed instructions to wagonmasters. Dauchy used this as an account book in 1866].)

DAUGHERTY, JOHN W. b. Venango County, Pennsylvania, January 1, 1841; d. Omaha, September 10, 1902. After moving with his family to Epworth, Dubuque County, Iowa, Daugherty served three years in the Union army, and then worked for his brother William E., who had the surveying contract for the area of present Perkins County, Nebraska. The Daughertys had a narrow escape in 1869 when the surveying party was attacked by a group of Sioux. After holding the Indians off for a day they escaped by nightfall, ultimately making their way to Fort McPherson where they obtained military assistance to recover their tools and notes. Daugherty was injured slightly during the skirmish, but soon resumed surveying. In about 1872 Daugherty moved his wife and child from Epworth to Fremont, Nebraska, where he continued living until he began freighting out of Sidney in 1878. After his freighting experience from Sidney and in the Fort Pierre–Deadwood trade, Daugherty moved to Omaha and later did railroad surveying in South Dakota and Canada. (Paul D. Riley, research associate, Nebraska State

Historical Society, letter to the author, September 15, 1971. Leonard P. McCoun, Fairmont, Minnesota, letters to Paul D. Riley, June 13, 30, 1970. *Fremont Semi-weekly Herald,* September 12, 1902.)

EVANS, CHARLES EDWARD. b. Philadelphia, Pennsylvania, July 21, 1843. Evans moved with his father to Fontanelle, Nebraska, in 1855. During the 1860's he worked as a freighter and stage driver. Later, he was employed in a grocery business and as a painting contractor. In 1906 he was living in St. Joseph, Missouri. (Morton-Watkins, III A, 696.)

FOWLER, SAMUEL HORTON. b. Westfield, Massachusetts, September 6, 1825. In 1849 Fowler moved to Michigan, where he lived for a decade before moving to a farm on the Platte east of Columbus. While farming, Fowler freighted for five years between Omaha and Fort Kearny, then moved to Fremont, where he operated the Fremont House and established stage lines between Fremont and Lincoln, and Fremont and West Point. He died in Fremont in November, 1870. (Morton-Watkins, I, 654-55 Daniel M. Carr [ed.], *Progressive Men of Nebraska: A Book of Portraits, Dodge County Edition* [Fremont, Nebraska: Progress Publishing Company, 1902], 80.)

FULTON, WILLIAM. b. Allegheny County, Pennsylvania, October 10, 1836; d. Kansas City, Missouri, April 9, 1908. Fulton obtained a common school education in St. Louis before moving to Nebraska City in 1859. After clerking in a store for a year, he returned to St. Louis, then came back to Nebraska City in 1861 to embark on a short career in general merchandising and freighting. In these businesses he worked closely with E. W. Terry, Rollin M. Rolfe, and Nathan L. Simpson. In 1863 Fulton accompanied the Sully Expedition as the quartermaster because he had the expedition's supply contracts. He later freighted and sent a twelve-wagon train from Nebraska City to Salt Lake City in May of 1867. After quitting freighting he became active in organizing the Midland Pacific Railroad. He was one of its incorporators and supervised its construction from Nebraska City to Lincoln. He went on to spend over thirty years as an adjustor for an insurance company. He and his wife moved to Kansas City in 1892. (Dale, "Otoe County Pioneers." Morton-Watkins, II, 653-54. *Nebraska City News,* May 24, 1867. William Fulton, "Freighting and Staging in Early Days,"

Proceedings and Collections of the Nebraska State Historical Society, 2nd series [1902], V, 261-64.)

GARROW, ERNEST DONALD. b. Abelour, Bannfshire, Scotland, February 17, 1851; d. Nebraska City, November 2, 1909. After leaving Scotland in 1855 Garrow and his family lived for a time in Canada and Illinois before moving to an Otoe County farm in 1859. His freighting career was brief, evidently consisting of an 1866 trip as a bullwhacker for Smith & Galbraith from Nebraska City to Fort C. F. Smith on the Bozeman Trail. Later he worked with an Indian trader and as a transporter of ties for the UPRR. After years of mining, prospecting, and odd jobbing in the West, he finally returned to Nebraska City in 1884 and entered the livestock commission business with his brother. (Morton-Watkins, III A, 742. *Otoe and Cass Counties,* 373-75. Dale, "Otoe County Pioneers.")

GARSIDE, JOSHUA. b. Cheshire, England, December 16, 1821; d. Atchison, Kansas, December 24, 1902. After emigrating to the United States in 1847, Garside first settled in Canton, Illinois, where he worked in banks for nine years before moving to Nebraska City as the cashier in Stephen F. Nuckolls' Platte Valley Bank. In 1864 he moved to Atchison, Kansas, where he worked in the firm of A. S. Parker & Company, wholesale and forwarding merchants who dealt in both steamboat and overland freight. Garside was also employed as accountant and cashier by Augustus and Peter Byram during their Atchison freighting in 1864-1866. In 1866 he succeeded the Byrams and continued in freighting and the transfer business for a time. He then worked for many years as an accountant and cashier for a railroad company. (Morton-Watkins, II, 658-59, portrait, 778.)

GILMAN, JEREMIAH C. b. Bartlett, New Hampshire, November 8, 1834; d. University Place, Lincoln, October 24, 1904. Until he was twenty Jerry Gilman worked on his father's farm. Then he and his brother John moved to Iowa, where they speculated in a townsite and operated a steam sawmill for three years before moving to Nebraska City in 1857. After two years in the livery business, they moved out on the trail and started a road ranche west of Fort Kearny. During 1861 and 1862 the brothers, in addition to managing the ranche, ran two full trains in the Nebraska City to Denver trade. In late 1863 they had the contract to construct the main buildings of what became Fort McPherson. With his brother, Gilman continued the ranche until 1868; then he returned to Nebraska City, investing in a section of land and engaging in general farming. *(Otoe and Cass Counties,* 381-83. Dale, "Otoe County Pioneers.")

GILMAN, JOHN K. (brother of Jeremiah C.). b. Bartlett, New Hampshire, July 3, 1829; d. Nebraska City, January 21, 1887. John Gilman left New Hampshire with his younger brother in 1854 and after three years in Iowa moved on to Nebraska City. He was associated with his brother until 1868, when he moved briefly to Wyoming Territory and unsuccessfully ran as the Democratic candidate for congressional delegate. He soon returned to Nebraska City, where he bought a large farm, which was worked by others since he continued his activities in the West. He mined in the Wasatch Mountains, probably in association with S. F. Nuckolls, and in 1876 established a store in the Black Hills in partnership with Robert Hawke. By 1880 Gilman had returned to Nebraska City. (Dale, "Otoe County Pioneers." *Otoe and Cass Counties,* 273-74.)

GILMORE, JOHN D. b. Washington County, Pennsylvania, November 12, 1824; d. July 15, 1892. As a youth Gilmore rafted produce on the Ohio and Mississippi, then in 1851 settled on a farm near Red Oak, Iowa. In 1853 Gilmore crossed the Missouri and squatted on land about ten miles south of the mouth of the Platte River. During the freighting period he was both a farmer and a freighter and made many trips across the plains from Nebraska City and Plattsmouth. After 1866 he devoted full time to farming and stock raising and came to own a good deal of land in Cass County. (Morton-Watkins, II, 661-62.)

GILMORE, JOSEPH C. b. Harrisville, Mercer County, Pennsylvania, December 17, 1832; d. Omaha, February 14, 1907. Joseph Gilmore migrated to Plattsmouth in 1858 and farmed for a time before entering overland freighting in 1860. He freighted from Omaha, Plattsmouth, and Nebraska City and was credited with pioneering several new trails, including a direct route from Plattsmouth to Fort Kearny which ran through present Lincoln. In surveying this trail, Gilmore marked the line of what became O Street in Lincoln. He also pioneered the portion of the Sidney Trail south of the North Platte. He continued in Platte Valley freighting until 1868, then shifted to the Bozeman Trail during the construction of the UPRR. After some hazardous experiences during Red Cloud's War, Gilmore resumed the more mundane business of farming in Cass County seven miles west of Plattsmouth. He remained there until 1891, when he began a ranch in Dundy County. He retired from this business in 1904 and moved to Omaha. He was quite active in local politics, representing Cass County for two terms in the Nebraska House of Representatives and participating in Farmers' Alliance activities. *(Plattsmouth Evening Journal,* February 16, 1907. Morton-Watkins, II, 663.)

GREGG, JOHN E. b. Indiana, 1835. In 1858 Gregg was operating a stove and tinware business with John Garside in Nebraska City. Two years later he went to the Colorado mines to manage a similar business. Still in the same trade, he returned to Nebraska City in 1861 and became a partner of John A. Goodlet. During their association, 1861–1862, they freighted their own merchandise to Colorado. (Dale, "Otoe County Pioneers.")

HARVEY, AUGUSTUS FORD. Although he was not a freighter, Harvey did much to promote freighting in Nebraska City by surveying the direct line to Fort Kearny and boosting the town through the *Nebraska City News.* Harvey was born at Watertown, New York, January 19, 1830, and before moving to Nebraska City at age twenty-six had worked as a school teacher, civil engineer, and railroad surveyor. In Nebraska City he first worked as an insurance agent and city engineer. It was while serving in the latter capacity that he was commissioned to lay out the new trail to Fort Kearny. For four years, 1861–1865, he was the editor of the *Nebraska City News.* During his last five years in Nebraska, 1865–1870, Harvey surveyed and platted the townsite of Lincoln, edited the *Statesman* in Lincoln, worked as secretary of the University of Nebraska, and served in the State Legislature. He died August 28, 1900, in Kirkwood, Missouri, where he had spent his last thirty years as an actuary in the insurance field. (Morton-Watkins, II, 68-69.)

HAWKE, ROBERT. b. Waynesburg, Stark County, Ohio, January 25, 1826; d. Nebraska City, May 2, 1887. After a brief stint at blacksmithing, Hawke established a store at Hemmes Landing, Missouri, and operated it successfully for just over a decade before moving to Nebraska City in 1859 to form a partnership with Stephen F. Nuckolls. Hawke & Nuckolls was one of the first Nebraska City general merchandise firms to ship its own goods to the Colorado mines. Hawke managed the western end of the business, selling goods in various mining camps from 1860 through 1862. He then returned to Nebraska City and formed a merchandise firm, Robert Hawke & Company, with his brothers Jacob and George. The brothers continued freighting and worked as freighters and outfitters for the UPRR during its construction period. During the last twenty years of his life, Hawke continued operating a retail store and was also concerned with banking and meat packing in Nebraska City. A Democrat, he served in the State Senate in 1870–1871. (Morton-Watkins, I, 673-74. Andreas, *History of Nebraska*, 1220. *Otoe and Cass Counties*, 427-28.)

HAWLEY, EZRA S. b. Deposit, Delaware County, New York, October 10, 1833; d. Schenectady, New York, May 19, 1908. Hawley lived in Deposit, New York, until 1856. He came to Nebraska City in 1859 as an agent of the United States Express Company, a position he had held in Kansas City and St. Joseph for two years previously. He soon became a steamboat agent and merchant as well as an express agent. By September, 1863, Hawley had formed a partnership with Francis A. White. They were commission dealers in general merchandise and farm machinery and also freighted extensively to Colorado in 1864–1866. After his freighting experience he had financial interests in railroads and entered a partnership with J. M. Burks to deal in grain and farm implements. He and Burks were among the first important landowners in Lincoln. Hawley later moved to Lincoln and expanded the business, which by 1882 included branch stores in twelve eastern Nebraska towns and one Iowa community. After his wife's death in 1898, Hawley lived with a daughter in Schenectady. (Dale, "Otoe County Pioneers." *Otoe and Cass Counties*, 646-48.)

HETH, JOHN. b. Richmond, Virginia, January 6, 1834; d. Omaha, January 14, 1890. After attending Hampden-Sidney College in Virginia and working as a civil engineer in West Virginia, Heth moved to Fort Riley in 1854 to join his brother Gen. Henry Heth. He soon was employed by Dyer & Company, post traders at Fort Kearny, and during the period 1855–1864 lived at or near the post, where he became a well-known trader. In 1864 Heth moved to

Nebraska City and freighted from there until 1866. After freighting he operated a store in Nebraska City and a mill in Syracuse until he moved to Lincoln in 1876 as a representative of the Union Pacific. He moved to Omaha several years before his death and was employed by the Union Stock Yards Company. *(Transactions and Reports of the Nebraska State Historical Society* [Lincoln, 1892], IV, 236-38.)

HOLLISTER, SYLVESTER. This New York native (b. 1811) moved to a farm near Nebraska City in 1856. However, he soon opened a dry goods and clothing store, and by May, 1860, was in partnership with George W. Bailey. They freighted some of their merchandise to Colorado; then Hollister left the firm to become a full-time freighter for a short time. In 1862–1863 he served in the Second Nebraska Cavalry and participated in the Dakota campaign against the Sioux in 1863. (Dale, "Otoe County Pioneers.")

HOOK, H. M. b. Pennsylvania, 1831. By 1863 Hook was the owner and operator of a road ranche at Dogtown (i.e. Valley City) and a Nebraska City freighter. "Old Beaver," as he was nicknamed, freighted to Colorado in 1865 and then to Montana the next year. He shifted west with the Union Pacific and was living in Cheyenne by August, 1867, where he operated a hotel, stable, and corral with James Moore. He also served as town mayor. In 1868 he was one of the founders of Green River, Wyoming. On June 18, 1869, Hook was drowned in Lodore Canyon while accompanying a party that was attempting to raft down the Green River and on to the Gulf of California. (Dale, "Otoe County Pioneers." *Nebraska City News,* March 17, 1866. I. S. Bartlett [ed.], *History of Wyoming* [Chicago: S. J. Clarke Publishing Co., 1918], I, 621.)

HORTON, HOSEA B. b. Vermont, about 1819; d. Nebraska City, November 19, 1884. A shoemaker, Hosea Horton moved to Nebraska City in 1858. He was a member of the Nebraska City Quartz Mill Company and as such went to Colorado in 1860. Two years later he formed a partnership with S. B. Sibley in the shoemaking trade in Nebraska City. He did some freighting from Nebraska City and was a full-time freighter from 1866 to 1868, working most of this time in Wyoming and Utah. In 1869 he bought land near Nebraska City and farmed for the remainder of his life. (Dale, "Otoe County Pioneers." Morton-Watkins, II, 685. *Nebraska City News,* March 16, 1867.)

HUMPHREY, OLIVER NORRIS. b. Richfield, Ohio, November 26, 1840; d. Lincoln, April 28, 1901. At nineteen, Humphrey and his brother Austin moved to a farm south of Nebraska City. He enlisted in the Second Nebraska Cavalry Regiment and participated in the Sully campaign in Dakota Territory in 1863. He freighted from Nebraska City for three years, 1864–1866, and then entered a commission business with his brothers Austin and Decius. They dealt mainly in construction supplies for the UPRR. After moving to Lincoln in 1869, Humphrey was principally involved in managing an agricultural implement and hardware store—Humphrey Brothers Hardware Company—which he owned with Austin. (Morton-Watkins, I, 680-81. "Freighting to Denver," *Nebraska History*, XV, No. 2 [April-June, 1934], 121.)

KELLY, WILLIAM D. b. Johnstown, County Kilkenny, Ireland, 1831; d. Lancaster County, Nebraska, January 31, 1896. Kelly migrated to the United States in 1850 and lived in New York and Illinois before moving to Minnesota, where he had his first freighting experience and participated in one of the Fisk expeditions. In about 1863 he moved to Omaha and, until the completion of the UPRR, freighted to Denver. After leaving freighting he moved to Council Bluffs, where he worked for some years as a construction contractor before retiring and moving to a Lancaster County farm. (Morton-Watkins, III C, 495.)

KING, JACOB. b. Sangamon County, Illinois, September 3, 1831; d. South Omaha, January 19, 1910. King moved to Omaha in 1856 and farmed in the vicinity. During the early 1860's he freighted from Omaha to Colorado and way points and judging from newspaper coverage, was one of Omaha's best known shotgun freighters. In 1864 he moved to a farm near Genoa and then worked variously as a grader for the UPRR, a stable manager, a carpenter, and a farmer before retiring to Omaha. (Morton-Watkins, I, 684-86. *Omaha Bee*, April 21, 1912.)

KOUNTZE, AUGUSTUS. b. November 19, 1826, Osnaburg, Ohio; d. April 30, 1892, New York City. Kountze is primarily remembered as the eldest of four brothers who established banking houses in Omaha, Denver, and New York City. He was much more interested in railroads than in overland freighting, but he was one of the founders of the Western Transportation Company, which combined rail and wagon freighting during the construction period of the UPRR. After working in his father's store and as a real estate agent, he moved to Omaha in 1856 where he and his brother Hermann soon opened a bank. He lived there for the next sixteen years, then moved to New York to take charge of the eastern branch of the Kountze Brothers bank. In addition to banking in Omaha he was active in the affairs of the UPRR, serving on its first board of directors. He and his brothers invested in other railroads, including some lines in Texas. He served as territorial treasurer and also for a time as state treasurer. (Morton-Watkins, II, 315-17, portrait, 311.)

KOUNTZE, HERMAN. b. Osnaburg, Ohio, August 21, 1833. With his brother Augustus, Herman established a bank and real estate business in Omaha in 1856. In 1863 this firm was chartered as the First National Bank of Omaha, which had the distinction of being the first Nebraska bank organized under the provisions of the National Bank Act. Kountze succeeded Edward Creighton, the National Bank's first president, in 1874 and after that time managed the Kountze Brothers affairs in Omaha. He was very active in overland freighting, especially as a government contractor. He had a number of grain and forage contracts from 1863 through 1866, and in 1866 during the construction of the UPRR held several major supply contracts. He was probably the principal organizer and manager of the Western Transportation Company. After his freighting experience, Kountze was financially involved in the South Omaha Land Company, in the South Omaha Stockyard Company, and in banking. He died in Watkins Glen, New York, November 20, 1906. (Morton-Watkins, II, 317. *National Cyclopaedia of American Biography* [1922], XVIII, 159-60.)

LABOO, PETER. In 1859 this thirty-one-year-old Ohio native moved to a farm near Nebraska City. In 1860 he went to Colorado and two years later opened a bowling alley and bar in Nebraska City. Laboo was a wagonmaster in the Second Nebraska Cavalry during the Dakota campaign of 1863. He was a freighter during the boom period and after that time operated a boarding house and saloon in Nebraska City. (Dale, "Otoe County Pioneers.")

LACEY, JESSE. b. Cadiz, Ohio, July 8, 1826; d. Omaha, September 29, 1899. Lacey was postmaster in Laceyville, Ohio, and a bookman and publisher in Cincinnati before 1859, when he moved to Omaha and established a partnership with John McCormick (who was married to Lacey's wife's sister) in a wholesale grocery business. They freighted quantities of their merchandise to Denver and other Colorado towns. In the spring of 1861 Lacey left the firm and moved to Cincinnati. He later returned to Omaha and re-entered business with McCormick for a time. He served on the Omaha City Council during 1869–1870, was a retail grocer and railroad ticket agent, and finally worked for twelve years as custodian of the First National Bank Building. (Morton-Watkins, III B, 607-8. *Omaha Republican*, April 10, 1861. *Omaha Evening Bee*, September 30, 1899.)

LEE, HENRY J. b. Bradford County, Pennsylvania, August 27, 1837; d. Fremont, January 30, 1923. While not an important or long-standing freighter, Lee is interesting because he typifies the amateurs who entered the business during the boom period. He freighted only during 1865, his first year in Nebraska, and as a newcomer was no doubt drawn into the most promising business of the time in the hopes of obtaining working capital. In 1870 he started a hardware business in Fremont and was also one of the founders of an Omaha wholesale hardware firm of which Henry T. Clarke was also a partner. At the time of his death, Lee was said to be Fremont's wealthiest man, having made a fortune in the hardware business and in farms and other real estate. (Morton-Watkins, I, 692. *Nebraska History and Record of Pioneer Days*, VII, No. 2 [April-June, 1942], 40.)

McCANN, DWIGHT J. b. Erie County, Pennsylvania, March 3, 1827. McCann grew up on his father's farm and attended Erie Academy, where he also taught part time. In 1849 he went to New Orleans as a principal in a large public school and studied medicine at the University of Louisiana. He moved to Philadelphia as a merchant in 1857 and the next year formed a partnership in Nebraska City with Julian Metcalf, his brother-in-law. They engaged in private banking and also worked as land agents and dealers in land warrants. Throughout the 1860's McCann was involved in freighting as an entrepreneur who hired others to manage his trains. In 1865 he bought out Metcalf and as D. J. McCann & Company continued in banking and land speculation. He also went into pork packing and cattle contracting. McCann was a prominent member of the

Republican Party and in 1868 was suggested as a possible United States senator. He served as a regent for the University of Nebraska in 1871 and as a member of the constitutional convention of that year. He was mentioned as a prospective candidate for governor in 1871. In about 1873 McCann became a contractor for Indian annuities in Wyoming and Nebraska. He later freighted from Sidney to the agencies and the Black Hills and operated a general merchandise store in Sidney. His controversial handling of Indian supply contracts caused the government to press a fraud suit. He was found guilty in a federal court trial in Cheyenne in 1878, but the decision was reversed in a re-trial in 1880. McCann died on a train at Savanna, Illinois, in August, 1888. (Morton-Watkins, III, 51, 186. Dale, "Otoe County Pioneers." *Nebraska City News,* August 17, 1888. A. C. Edmunds, *Pen Sketches of Nebraskans* [Lincoln, Omaha: R. & J. Wilbur, 1871], 480-81.)

McComas, Rufus. b. Cabell County, West Virginia, February 14, 1834; d. January 21, 1891. At twenty-two McComas moved to Bellevue, Nebraska, where he speculated in real estate before moving to Nebraska City in 1858. For nearly a decade, until the completion of the Union Pacific, McComas freighted from Nebraska City and was one of the few Nebraska Citians who stayed with the business during the city's entire freighting era. After freighting he was a merchant in Nebraska City and was also active in railroad construction and banking. (Andreas, *History of Nebraska,* 1225. Dale, "Otoe County Pioneers.")

McCormick, John. b. Johnstown, Pennsylvania, September 12, 1822; d. Omaha, June 2, 1884. After some general country store experience in Ohio, McCormick moved to Omaha in 1856 to engage in banking and real estate speculation. In 1859 with Jesse H. Lacey, he formed Lacey & McCormick, Omaha's first wholesale grocery firm. Lacey & McCormick was no doubt Omaha's major supplier of Colorado during the first few years of the gold rush. The partners organized numerous trains for the purpose of shipping their own goods. Later McCormick organized the firm of John McCormick and Company with two of his brothers. This company continued in overland freighting until its end. In addition to merchandizing and freighting, McCormick did some government contract work, dealt in city real estate, and built a grain elevator, said to be Omaha's first. After 1869 he devoted most of his attention to the grain business. He served on the Omaha City Council and in the Territorial Legislature. (Morton-Watkins, II, 22. *Transactions and Reports of the Nebraska State Historical Society* [1885], I, 139-40.)

McDONALD, CHARLES.   b. Morristown, Jefferson County, Tennessee, October 25, 1826; d. North Platte, April 22, 1919. McDonald was raised on a farm and briefly farmed for himself before coming to Nebraska in 1855, where he farmed for four years at various places. During this time he served as a representative in the Second Territorial Legislature, from 1855 to 1856. In 1859 he moved to Cottonwood Springs and established a road ranche, which he continued throughout the period of overland emigration and freighting. The McDonald Ranche was one of the best known on the overland trail, and McDonald worked closely with freighters as well as freighting some of his own ranche supplies. He maintained a store at Cottonwood Springs until 1872. The next year he moved to North Platte, establishing a general merchandise store and a private bank. He continued in banking for the rest of his life after abandoning the general merchandise business in 1899. (Morton-Watkins, I, 696. *Nebraska History and Record of Pioneer Days,* I, No. 7 [November, 1918], 1; II, No. 2 [April-June, 1919], 8.)

McMAKEN, HENRY CLAY.   b. Fort Wayne, Indiana, January 21, 1850; d. Plattsmouth, January 17, 1912. At seventeen McMaken settled on a claim near Plattsmouth and farmed for two years before entering freighting. For three years, 1859–1861, he freighted with just a few wagons, first to the Pawnee Indians on the Loup Fork and then to Denver. During 1862–1863 he served with a Nebraska cavalry unit and participated in the one major engagement of the 1863 Sully expedition—the Battle of White Stone Hill in present North Dakota. In 1864 he returned to farming but after six years went to work with a government surveying party. In 1877 he went to the Black Hills and for the next five years worked as a freighter and mica miner. He then returned to Plattsmouth and entered the ice business. (Morton-Watkins, II, 710-11. *Nebraska State Journal* [Lincoln] January 18, 1912.)

McMECHAN, JOHN.   b. Belfast, Ireland, October 10, 1800; d. Nebraska City, November 3, 1883. At the age of ten McMechan moved to the United States with his parents. He had merchant experience in West Virginia and Ohio before moving to Glasgow, Missouri, in 1842 where he operated a store and packing plant until 1846. He then opened a wholesale grocery business in St. Louis. In 1853 he moved to Council Bluffs to operate a wholesale grocery and outfitting store. The next year he moved to Nebraska City, where he first operated a hotel and farmed. He was also one of the proprietors of Kearny City, later absorbed by Nebraska City. During the 1860's he combined farming and freighting, although most of the actual freighting was done by his son John Henry, referred to as "Young John" by the Nebraska City newspapers. After freighting he devoted full attention to his farm Headwood, near Nebraska City. (*Otoe and Cass Counties*, 177-79. *Transactions and Reports of the Nebraska State Historical Society* [1887], II, 332-35.)

McMECHAN, JOHN HENRY. b. Zanesville, Ohio, February 22, 1839; d. Nebraska City, July 26, 1897. In the fall of 1859 the younger McMechan began freighting to Denver, hauling corn that had been raised on the McMechan farm. From 1860 until 1863 he managed the freighting business operated with his father. He was also in partnership with his brother David in the wholesale grocery business in Denver. Their Denver store burned in 1863, and they then entered the hardware business in Nebraska City that same year. Six years later he left the firm and took over the management of his father's farm. (Dale, "Otoe County Pioneers." *Otoe and Cass Counties*, 177-81.)

MAJORS, ALEXANDER. b. Franklin, Simpson County, Kentucky, October 4, 1814; d. Chicago, January 13, 1900. (For Majors' pre-Nebraska and Nebraska career see text, especially p. 48 and Chapter III.) Majors concluded his Nebraska freighting career with the dispatching of two trains from Nebraska City to Utah and Montana in 1865. In the spring of 1867 he sold his equipment and stock to Edward Creighton and that fall moved with his family from their Nebraska City home to Salt Lake City. He lived for a decade in Utah, working first as a railroad grading contractor and then as an independent silver prospector. After 1879 he lived in various places, including St. Louis, Denver, and Kansas City. Reduced to poverty, Majors attempted to earn money by writing his autobiography. *Seventy Years on the Frontier,* published in 1893 and edited by Colonel Prentiss Ingraham, one of the most prolific of the dime novelists, is really a poor tribute to Majors' remarkable career. The work is poorly organized and contains great sections of non-pertinent material, such as descriptions of western animals, and does not deal, except in a remote sense, with the key activities of Russell, Majors & Waddell. The book brought Majors neither fame nor fortune. He was physically active in his late years and made a public speech in Denver as late as 1899. He died as a result of pneumonia contracted on a business trip to Chicago. (Stella M. Drumm, "Majors, Alexander," *Dictionary of American Biography* [1933], XII, 214-15. Morton-Watkins, I, 92. Raymond and Mary Lund Settle, *Empire on Wheels* [Stanford: Stanford University Press, 1949], 118-20. Herman R. Acton, caretaker, Union Cemetery, Kansas City, Missouri, letter to the author, August 9, 1967.)

MARVIN, GEORGE PENDLETON. b. Shullsburg, Wisconsin, March 24, 1851; d. Beatrice, March 4, 1908. Marvin moved to Nebraska with his family in 1859 and, after living briefly in Falls City and Rulo, went to work in the office of the *Nebraska Advertiser* in Brownville. For five years beginning in 1865 he worked as a bull-whacker and muleskinner, first in regular overland freighting, then in grading and freighting for the UPRR. The experiences of these early years, about which he later reminisced, included his witnessing the driving of the last spike linking the Union Pacific and Central Pacific at Promontory Point, Utah, in 1869. In 1879 he began a long journalistic career by founding the *Gage County Democrat*. This became his weekly paper, and he also published the *Beatrice Daily Sun*. An active Democrat and supporter of J. Sterling Morton, he was Beatrice postmaster during Cleveland's second term. (Morton-Watkins, I, 701. George Marvin "Bull-Whacking Days," *Proceedings and Collections of the Nebraska State Historical Society*, 2nd series [1902], V, 226-30. *Portrait and Biographical Album of Gage County, Nebraska* [Chicago: Chapman Brothers, 1888], 565-66. *Beatrice Daily Sun*, March 5, 1908.)

MAXON, JOHN H. b. New York, 1844; d. St. Louis, Missouri, July 16, 1903. Maxon moved to Nebraska City in 1856 and first worked as a surveyor, land agent, and insurance agent. By 1860 he was a cashier in the Platte Valley Bank. In partnership with John B. Boulware, he freighted from 1864 until 1866. Their business was quite extensive; in 1864 they sent a forty-wagon train to the Montana mines. Maxon served in the 1866 Territorial Legislature and shortly thereafter moved to St. Louis, where he had a long and successful career as president of a street railway company. (Dale, "Otoe County Pioneers.")

MOHRENSTECHER, GEORGE. b. Gueterstoh, Westphalia, Germany, March 1, 1829; d. Lincoln, April 2, 1895. On moving to the United States in 1847, Mohrenstecher became a saddler in St. Louis. He became a captain in the Missouri infantry during the early years of the Civil War and moved to Nebraska City in 1863 after being discharged. He first worked for C. Vogt, a grocer, and then in 1865 took over the business, which became George Mohrenstecher & Company. He operated a general merchandise store and engaged in freighting, which was really a delivery service for the store. He was quite active in civic affairs and in the Republican Party. At the time of his death he was doorkeeper of the Senate gallery of the Nebraska Legislature. (Dale, "Otoe County Pioneers.")

MOLLRING, ARNOLD F. In 1856 this twenty-four-year-old native of Prussia moved to Nebraska City where he formed a merchant partnership with John Beuter and Herman H. Petring. During the freighting era Mollring worked mainly with these men but was also in business for himself for a time. He freighted to Colorado when he was associated with Beuter and Petring and also when he was in business for himself. After 1870 he operated his own Nebraska City store. Mollring is credited with perfecting a machine used for measuring cloth and reportedly sold the patent for a large amount of money. He moved to Alliance, Nebraska, about 1900 and four years later to Newcastle, Wyoming, where he died January 14, 1905. (Dale, "Otoe County Pioneers.")

MUNN, EUGENE. b. Wayne County, Ohio, December 28, 1836; d. Bellingham, Washington, May 19, 1919. After two years of freighting experience in Iowa, Munn moved to Nebraska City in 1856 and two years later went to work for Russell, Majors & Waddell. Munn first worked as a wagonmaster for the firm, later worked closely with his friend Alexander Majors, and still later operated his own wagon trains. His freighting career covered nine years and included numerous trips across the plains. Some of these experiences Munn later recalled in an interesting memoir published in 1902. In 1867, rather than trail west ahead of the Union Pacific, he quit freighting and bought a section of land near Nebraska City, where he farmed until 1894. He then moved to University Place, near Lincoln. He served three terms in the Nebraska Legislature and in 1898 was elected president of the Farmers' Mutual Insurance Company, a position he held eight years. Munn moved to Colorado in 1906 and later to Bellingham, Washington. (Morton-Watkins, I, 719-20, portrait, 237. Edmunds, *Pen Sketches of Nebraskans*, 100-101. Dale, "Otoe County Pioneers." Eugene Munn, "Early Freighting and Claims Club Days in Nebraska," *Proceedings and Collections of the Nebraska State Historical Society*, 2nd series, [1902], V, 313-17.)

NUCKOLLS, STEPHEN FRIEL. b. Grayson County, Virginia, August 16, 1825; d. Salt Lake City, February 14, 1879. Nuckolls is known first of all as the "Founder of Nebraska City." In 1854, after seven years of merchant experience in Iowa and Missouri, he laid out the town of Nebraska City and as president of the Nebraska City Town Company promoted the place by constructing buildings, establishing a sawmill and bank, and finally giving the community a meaningful economic base by obtaining its designation as a military depot in 1858. In association with Robert Hawke, he became one of the significant suppliers of Colorado miners, and the partners operated branch stores, sawmills, and quartz mills in the mining areas. From 1864 to 1867 Nuckolls lived in New York and was reported to have made a large fortune through mining speculations. In 1867 he moved to the new town of Cheyenne and became one of its leading merchants. With the organization of Wyoming Territory in 1869, Nuckolls, a Democrat, was elected as territorial delegate to Congress and served from December 6, 1869, through March 3, 1871. He was defeated in a reelection bid in 1870, but in 1871 was elected to the Council of the Wyoming Legislature and served as its presiding officer. Nuckolls was also a delegate to the National Democratic Conventions in 1872 and 1876. He spent his last seven years in Salt Lake City, where he was in the milling business. (Morton-Watkins, I, 106-107. *Biographical Directory of the American Congress* [1928], 1364. *Weekly Bee* [Omaha], February 19, 1879.)

OVERTON. JOHN H. b. Pike County, Delaware, April 2, 1835; d. Holt County, Nebraska, May 4, 1913. When an infant, Overton was moved to Pennsylvania, where he was raised. He first worked as a carpenter for a canal company. In 1859 Overton went to Colorado, where he speculated and mined. From 1862 through

1867 he freighted from Nebraska City to Colorado, much of the time in partnership with his brothers Martin and Nelson. After freighting he participated in cattle drives from Texas and farmed in Otoe County. He left Otoe County in about 1902 for a ranch in Holt County. He was active in farmers' protest groups and was elected to the State Legislature in 1870 as the candidate of dissatisfied farmers. (Dale, "Otoe County Pioneers." Edmunds, *Pen Sketches of Nebraskans,* 105.)

OVERTON, MARTIN V. b. Pennsylvania, about 1841; d. Nebraska City, on May 25, 1902. Martin Overton served in a Pennsylvania artillery unit during the Civil War. About 1864 he moved to Nebraska City and went into freighting with his brothers. He later settled on a farm south of Nebraska City. (Dale, "Otoe County Pioneers.")

OVERTON, NELSON. b. Bradford County, Pennsylvania, April 16, 1840; d. about June 1, 1912. Nelson Overton moved to Nebraska City in 1862 and engaged in freighting with his brothers John and Martin. He later drove cattle with John, then became a farmer near Nebraska City. He served two terms in the lower house of the State Legislature and helped organize the Otoe County Grange. (Dale, "Otoe County Pioneers.")

PADDOCK, JOSEPH WILLIAMSON. b. Massina, St. Lawrence County, New York, 1825; d. Omaha, January 20, 1895. Paddock freighted independently in 1865 and then worked with the Western Transportation Company, of which he was a founder and secretary. During 1866 and 1867 he was closely affiliated with the Kountzes and the Creightons. He was one of Omaha's earliest residents, arriving in 1854. He served as chief clerk of the First Territorial Legislature and as clerk of the federal district court in Nebraska from April, 1855, to July, 1858. In 1861 he was appointed captain in the Nebraska Volunteers and during his brief military career served as adjutant general on the staff of Gen. Fred Steele. After 1867 Paddock was employed mainly as a claim agent for the UPRR. He was named a director of the UPRR in 1891 and also served as a Douglas County commissioner. (Morton-Watkins, III C, 506. *Nebraska State Journal,* January 21, 1895. J. Sterling Morton, "Sketch of Major J. W. Paddock, Chief Clerk of the First House of Representatives," *Proceedings and Collections of the Nebraska State Historical Society,* 2nd series [1898], II, 110-15.)

PARMALEE, SAMUEL NEWELL. This native of Twinsburg, Ohio, arrived in Omaha in 1857 and with the Smith brothers established the firm of Smith & Parmalee, which became involved in merchandising, banking, and mining. They established supply depots in Colorado to facilitate their merchant sales and mining. Parmalee was generally in charge of the supply trains. He suffered severely from exposure on one of the trips and died in 1864 while attempting to recuperate at Twinsburg, Ohio. (Morton-Watkins, III C, 509.)

PAXTON, WILLIAM A. b. Springfield, Kentucky, January 26, 1837; d. July 18, 1907. After working as a farmer and foreman for a bridge contractor in Missouri, William A. Paxton moved to Omaha in 1860 and began freighting to Denver. For the next seven years he did considerable freighting but also worked on a farm, in a livery stable, and on a telegraph construction crew. From 1867 to May, 1869, he was a major grading contractor for the UPRR, which enabled him to earn enough to lay the base to future fortunes. He then invested in cattle and railroads and did beef contracting for the government. He quit the cattle business in 1883, then turned his attention to numerous business pursuits in Omaha, including real estate, the Omaha Savings Bank, and the Union Stock Yards Company. In partnership with Ben Gallagher, he formed the wholesale house of Paxton and Gallagher. During his business career Paxton was considered to be one of Omaha's most significant financiers, and his building projects contributed markedly to the city's growth. In recognition of his importance in pioneering range cattle in western Nebraska, Paxton was enshrined in the "Hall of Great Westerners" of the National Cowboy Hall of Fame and Western Heritage Center. Politically, he served one term in the state House of Representatives. (Morton-Watkins, I, 731. Alfred Sorenson, *The Story of Omaha from the Pioneer Days to the Present Time* [3rd ed.; Omaha: National Printing Co., 1923], 551-53. J. R. Johnson, *Representative Nebraskans* [Lincoln: Johnsen Publishing Co., 1954], 142-46. *Nebraska Cattleman*, XVIII, No. 3 [November, 1961], 12.)

PECK, JAMES PORTER. b. Summit County, Ohio, October 11, 1821; d. Omaha, February 20, 1887. As a youth Peck worked for a Columbus, Ohio, newspaper and then studied medicine, graduating from the Cleveland Medical College in 1850. After practicing for six years in Akron, in 1856 he moved to Omaha, where he continued in general practice nearly to the time of his death. From 1860 until 1866 Peck engaged in freighting from Omaha to Denver. His freighting was neither large nor extensive, consisting of several small trains annually. He evidently owned equipment but hired others to do the actual work. During 1864 and 1865 he was associated in freighting with Reuben Wood, who probably managed the business. *(Transactions and Reports of the Nebraska State Historical Society* [1892], IV, 241-43.)

PETRING, HERMAN H. b. Kingdom of Prussia, February 13, 1824; d. Nebraska City, January 29, 1879. Petring moved from his native land to St. Louis in 1847 and lived there for a decade before moving to Nebraska City. For the next ten years he was usually associated with John Bueter and A. F. Mollring in a general merchandise firm. The company freighted most of its own goods to Colorado. Petring, while outside of the concern in 1861–1862, also freighted independently. In 1867 he started his own clothing and grocery business. He served as a captain of the Nebraska City Guards in 1862 and as a major in the First Nebraska Militia Regiment the next year. (Dale, "Otoe County Pioneers.")

PORTER, JAMES RALSTON. b. Steubenville, Ohio, February 11, 1828; d. Haigler, Nebraska, March 5, 1911. After attending college for over two years, Porter went to California during the gold rush and stayed there three years before returning to Ohio. In 1856 he moved to Plattsmouth, where he filed a preemption claim and started farming. From 1860 through 1868 he freighted from Plattsmouth, first to Denver and then to the Bozeman Trail forts. During 1864 and 1865 as head of J. R. Porter & Company, he was Plattsmouth's leading freighter and one of the most important on the river. By 1864 he owned thirty-six wagons, and his equipment holdings no doubt increased the following year. In 1866 and 1867, in association with Joseph C. Gilmore and Moses Dodge, Porter had an army wood contract for Fort Phil Kearny. His group became involved in the famed Wagon Box Fight, an important skirmish during Red Cloud's War, and played a key role in repulsing the Indians. In 1868 J. R. Porter & Company was dissolved, but Porter freighted independently for the army in Arizona for three more years. Porter had political aspirations and was the Democratic candidate for governor in 1868, but he was defeated by David Butler. During the 1870's he invested in Omaha real estate but sustained losses. In 1881 Porter homesteaded at Haigler and with his sons opened a general merchandise business there the next year. (Morton-Watkins, II, 182-84. *Nebraska State Journal,* March 12, 1911. *Omaha Weekly Herald,* August 22, 1867.)

PRATT, JAMES HERVEY. b. Plainfield, Hampshire County, Massachusetts, December 27, 1825; d. Bennington, Nebraska, November 12, 1910. (For Pratt's pre-freighting and freighting activities see text, pp. 201-03.) After Pratt and his partner Cornelius Ferris sold out their freighting interests in 1879, they plunged full time into the cattle business. They brought Marshall Field and Levy Leiter, two of Chicago's most prominent merchants and financiers, into their cattle company. Over its eighteen-year history, 1880–1898, the company expanded its capitalization to $400,000 and had vast land holdings in Nebraska, Wyoming, and Texas. Pratt alone drew over $111,000 in dividends during these years and was commonly believed to be a millionaire. After 1898 he continued his interests in western ranch land and also owned the Omaha Anchor Fence Company, of which he was president. He served as president of the Arlington, Nebraska, National Bank and as director of the Union Stockyards in South Omaha. He died in 1910 at his ranch near Bennington, where he had lived in semi-retirement for some years. (Morton-Watkins, II, 752. *Omaha Bee, Omaha News, Omaha World Herald,* November 13, 1910. "Pratt & Ferris Cattle Company Statements, 1898," p. 15 in J. H. Pratt Papers, Nebraska State Historical Society.)

QUINLAN, PATRICK. b. County Cork, Ireland. Quinlan moved to Omaha from St. Joseph, Missouri, in 1856 and later freighted for several years before the construction of the UPRR. He then worked on the construction of the railroad. (Morton-Watkins, III C, 537.)

RANKIN, BENJAMIN P. Rankin was born in Indiana in about 1827 and by profession was a physician. Throughout his Nebraska political career he was referred to as Dr. Rankin. He was living on a farm in Sarpy County by the spring of 1855, when he was named as the first territorial treasurer. He later served as United States marshal for Nebraska Territory from 1856 to 1858 and as a member of the Territorial Legislature in 1858 but was narrowly defeated in an attempt to become the Democratic candidate for territorial delegate in 1859. He was active in townsite speculation, laying out Central City with two partners in 1858 and later establishing Kearney City. In 1859 he did some freighting to Fort Kearny, and the next year, having moved to Nebraska City late in 1859, freighted to Colorado. Rankin apparently left Nebraska soon after, and in 1870 he was living in San Jose, California. (Morton-Watkins, I, 256, 434. Dale, "Otoe County Pioneers.")

REYNOLDS, WILSON. b. Virgi*l* Corners, Cortland County, New York, December 25, 1825; d. May 9, 1909. When Reynolds was twelve, his family moved to Racine, Wisconsin, where he lived until 1857, with the exception of a trip to California during the gold rush. He moved to a farm north of Fremont in 1857 and stayed in that area the remainder of his life. During the 1860's he worked in overland freighting and then as a grading contractor for the UPRR. (Morton-Watkins, III C, 552.)

ROLFE, DEFOREST P. b. Cooper's Plains, Steuben County, New York, July 20, 1839; d. November 14, 1902. Rolfe worked for a weekly newspaper in Bath, New York, and as a clerk in a St. Louis commission firm before joining his brother Rollin M. in Nebraska City in 1860. The brothers had operated a grocery business for about two years when DeForest P. joined William Fulton in a clothing and outfitting store. Rolfe had freighting experience while working with both his brother and Fulton, and wrote a significant memoir about trail life. After dissolving his business with Fulton in 1867 Rolfe lived in Chicago for two years, then returned to Nebraska City to work variously in the lumber and farm machinery businesses, finally settling on the management of a lumber yard by 1879. A politically active Democrat, he served as county treasurer, as a member of the last Territorial Legislature, and was elected mayor of Nebraska City in 1885 and again in 1888. *(Otoe and Cass Counties, 143-45. Nebraska City News, November 18, 1902. DeForest P. Rolfe, "Overland Freighting from Nebraska City," Proceedings and Collections of the Nebraska State Historical Society, 2nd series [1902], V, 279-93.)*

ROLFE, ROLLIN M. b. Bath, Steuben County, New York, October 12, 1830; d. Nebraska City, May 10, 1913. After considerable experience as a store clerk, Rolfe left New York in 1857 and resided for brief periods at Keokuk, Iowa, Memphis, Tennessee, and St. Louis,

Missouri, before arriving in Nebraska City in the fall of 1860, where he entered the general merchandise business. As the first wholesale jobber south of the Platte, he was vitally interested in the western trade and was one of the leaders in developing the direct route to Fort Kearny. He formed a partnership with E. W. Terry in 1862 and for the next four years they freighted extensively and operated stores in both Nebraska City and Denver. Most of their trains were managed by W. L. Simpson. After the UPRR ruined freighting, Rolfe quit merchandising and engaged in banking and land speculation. He was a member of a syndicate which bought quantities of land in Lincoln at the time of the capital relocation. In 1875 he again entered the grocery business with Terry, but after four years the partnership was dissolved and he acted alone as R. M. Rolfe & Company. During his merchandising career, Rolfe continued his interest in land and lived on a luxurious country estate called Boscobel near Nebraska City. (Andreas, *History of Nebraska,* 1227-28. Morton-Watkins, I, 741-42. *Nebraska City News,* May 10, 1913.)

SAUNDERS, JOSEPH. b. England, 1836; d. Reynolds, Nebraska, March 10, 1912. Saunders' family moved to Ohio when he was only four, and he was living in Nebraska City by 1855, working as a carpenter. In 1860 he was given a mail contract for the Nebraska City–Beatrice service. He opened a general store in Beatrice in 1862, but probably returned to Nebraska City during the Indian scare of 1864. With J. B. Weston, also of Beatrice, Saunders freighted out of Nebraska City in 1866 and continued freighting to the Bozeman Trail posts the next year. In 1868 he returned to Beatrice and in 1880 moved to Reynolds, where he was first a merchant and then a banker. (Dale, "Otoe County Pioneers." *Fairbury News,* March 15, 1912.)

SCHINDLER, DIETRICH. b. Canton of Glarus, Switzerland, July 10, 1843; d. Nebraska City, December 5, 1916. Schindler came to Otoe County with his family in 1857, and after living on a claim for two years they moved to Arkansas. He served with the Confederate Army from 1861 to 1863, but after his unit was captured went over to the Union cause and returned to Nebraska City, where he became a teamster in a freighting outfit. In 1864 he obtained a position as supervisor of transportation for a military unit in eastern Colorado. In this capacity he was present at the Chivington

Massacre. Shortly thereafter he quit freighting and became a full-time farmer in Otoe County. (Morton-Watkins, I, 748-49. *Otoe and Cass Counties*, 720-23. Dale, "Otoe County Pioneers.")

SIMPSON, NATHAN L. b. Madison County, Kentucky, July 31, 1831; d. about March 1, 1897. When only seven, Simpson moved to Jackson County, Missouri, wth his family. In 1851 he married Maria Meeker, daughter of Rev. Jotham Meeker, the well-known Kansas missionary. They lived in Wisconsin for five years, and then after a time in Kansas moved to Nebraska City in 1859, where he was employed as a clerk by Russell, Majors & Waddell. During 1860–1867 Simpson freighted from Nebraska City to Colorado and Montana and also owned an eighty-acre farm near Nebraska City. After freighting he continued farming and was a stockholder and director of the Midland Pacific Railroad. He served as Otoe County treasurer and sold farm machinery for a time. He later moved to western Kansas. (Dale, "Otoe County Pioneers." Andreas, *History of Nebraska*, 1241.)

SIMPSON, RICHARD D. (brother of Nathan L.). b. in Kentucky. At twenty, Richard D. Simpson moved to Nebraska City in 1858 and accompanied one of the Russell, Majors & Waddell trains to Utah. He then worked for several years as a wagonmaster for the firm and after its collapse formed the freighting outfit of R. D. Simpson & Company. In 1864 he married Missouri A. Majors, daughter of Alexander. He continued freighting until 1867, part of the time in association with his father-in-law. After freighting he had a lumber business and farm at Nebraska City and worked as a railroad supply contractor; then, prior to 1874, he moved to Jefferson County, Kansas. In 1878, he was living in Valley Falls, Kansas, where he was in the real estate business. (Dale, "Otoe County Pioneers.")

SMITH, PETER. b. New York, about 1834; d. Nebraska City, October 12, 1895. After living for a time at Madison, Wisconsin, Smith moved to Denver about 1860. He later operated a road ranche on the overland route to Denver and managed a mule freighting business between Nebraska City and Denver. In October, 1865, he and his family moved to Nebraska City, where he continued freighting for a brief time and opened a butcher shop. He later expanded his trade to include a livestock commission business and in 1869 helped promote the construction of a railroad branch line from Red Oak, Iowa, to Nebraska City. (Dale, "Otoe County Pioneers.")

STREET, ALEXANDER.   b. Shawano County, Wisconsin, about 1820; d. Nebraska City, September 15, 1877. Street's first business was that of Indian trader in Iowa. After moving to Westport, Missouri, he became associated with Russell, Majors & Waddell and moved to Nebraska City in 1862 as a court-appointed trustee to liquidate the property of the bankrupt firm. He then freighted independently for several years out of Nebraska City and with the extension of the UPRR was employed as the Omaha manager for Wells Fargo. He later returned to Nebraska City, where he served several terms as city treasurer. He was chosen mayor in 1875. (Morton-Watkins, III C, 631. Dale, "Otoe County Pioneers.")

SWIFT, THOMAS.   b. Kentucky, 1836; d. Omaha, March 25, 1911. At twenty Swift moved to Omaha and became an active freighter in the 1860's. He crossed the plains four times and made numerous short trips. Later, he fulfilled grading contracts for the UPRR and for several years had a contract to ferry Union Pacific freight from Council Bluffs to Omaha. Afterwards he bought a farm in Douglas County and also invested in Omaha real estate. (Morton-Watkins, III C, 642.)

TAIT, JAMES NELSON.   b. Springfield, Massachusetts, December 19, 1816; d. Nebraska City, May 1, 1869. Tait lived in New York City before moving to Brown County, Ohio, where he kept stores in Clermont County and Marathon, Ohio. In 1858 he and his family moved to Nebraska City, where, two years later, he formed a wholesale and commission business with Talbot Ashton. Their main concern was forwarding freight and outfitting freighters, but they also owned trains and hauled goods to their Colorado store. Because of their forwarding business they were vitally concerned with steamboat transportation. They leased the levee from the city, collected wharfage fees, and kept the levee in repair. Tait continued the business after Ashton withdrew in 1868. He died as a result of injuries caused by falling off a high embankment in the dark. (*Otoe and Cass Counties,* 311-12.)

TERRY, EDWARD W.   b. Hartford, Connecticut, February 3, 1835; d. Long Beach, California, January 28, 1890. In 1862 Terry, after wholesale merchant experience in Muscatine, Iowa, moved to Ne-

braska City, where he was first briefly associated with William
Fulton in the grocery business. Then from 1862 until 1865 he
worked with Rollin M. Rolfe in wholesaling and freighting.
They sold and transported general merchandise to mining camps
and ranches. After the dissolution of the partnership in 1867, Terry
spent five years in New Orleans, where he worked with his brother
in the cotton commission trade. He returned to Nebraska City in
1874 and for five years operated a wholesale grocery house with
Rolfe. He was then an officer in the James Sweet National Bank
of Nebraska City from 1880 until he moved to California in 1885.
(Dale, "Otoe County Pioneers." Andreas, *History of Nebraaska,*
1230.)

WARD, SETH E. b. Virginia, about 1820; d. Kansas City, Missouri,
December, 1903. After a long career as a trapper in the Rockies,
Ward by 1860 operated a trading post at Fort Laramie and was
also post sutler. As sutler he freighted supplies from various river
towns, and in 1863 he moved to Nebraska City and devoted more
time to freighting while apparently still continuing his Fort Laramie store. After freighting through 1866, Ward moved to Nebraska
City and bought a farm at Nursery Hill. In 1872 he moved to a
farm near Westport, Missouri, and began raising purebred cattle.
(Dale, "Otoe County Pioneers.")

WESTON, JEFFERSON B. b. Bremen, Maine, March 3, 1831; d.
Beatrice, September 15, 1905. Weston graduated from Union College, Schenectady, New York, in 1856 and moved to Nebraska City
in April, 1857, but almost immediately moved inland as one of a
group that founded Beatrice. He stayed there for seven years, working as a carpenter and attorney before moving to Nebraska City
when Beatrice was evacuated during the Indian scare of August,
1864. He did some freighting out of Nebraska City in 1865, and in
1866–1867 had government wood and supply contracts for the Bozeman Trail posts. The Plattsmouth *Nebraska Herald* of September
5, 1867, reported that it was Weston who rode swiftly through
masses of Indians to bring relief to the beleaguered woodcutters at
the Wagon Box Fight. After returning to Beatrice in 1868 he conducted a real estate business and had an interest in the Beatrice
National Bank. He was a prominent Republican and was mentioned in 1868 both as a gubernatorial possibility for Wyoming

Territory and as a Congressional candidate. He was twice elected state auditor and served in that position from January 13, 1873, through January 9, 1879. (Morton-Watkins, I, 499. Hugh J. Dobbs, *History of Gage County, Nebraska* [Lincoln: Western Publishing & Engraving Co., 1918], 409-11.)

WILCOX, SAMUEL. b. Vergennes, Vermont, about 1809; d. Nebraska City, April 9, 1897. Wilcox moved to Nebraska City in about March, 1860, engaging in the produce business and in freighting to Colorado. After discontinuing freighting in 1865, he worked for many years as a lightning rod salesman. (Dale, "Otoe County Pioneers.")

WHITE, FRANCIS A. b. Unadilla, Delaware County, New York, July 19, 1823; d. Omaha, January 24, 1904. White was educated at the Delaware Literary Institute and then studied medicine. Instead of going into practice, however, he entered the general merchandise business at twenty-one. He moved to Bellevue, Nebraska in 1857 and to Nebraska City the next year. He farmed briefly and operated a livery stable before moving to Colorado in 1859. On returning to Nebraska City in 1863, he joined Ezra S. Hawley in the firm of Hawley & White, commission merchants. They freighted to Colorado and expanded their business to include a general merchandise store. He left the company in 1867 and became a railroad promoter, serving as the president of the Midland Pacific in the late 1860's. In about 1870 he moved to New York, where he reportedly became quite wealthy. He later lived in Everett, Washington. (Dale, "Otoe County Pioneers." Edmunds, *Pen Sketches of Nebraskans*, 261-62.)

WOODS, JAMES M. b. about 1836. A Missouri native, Woods was twenty-nine when he moved to Nebraska City in 1865 to engage in freighting with his brother. They continued freighting until 1868, and then Woods bought a farm near Factoryville, Nebraska. In 1888 he moved to the Black Hills, where he had mining interests and a large cattle ranch. He served as mayor of Deadwood and was also a bank president in Custer. Woods amassed a fortune and was considered to be a millionaire. He died on May 13, 1908, in Des Moines, Iowa, where he had hotel property. He was buried at Nebraska City. (Dale, "Otoe County Pioneers." *Nebraska City News*, April 20, 1868.)

List of Freighters
APPENDIX II

The following listed individuals or their companies also freighted from Missouri River towns during the period 1857–1867. Each person is listed under the town from which he most commonly freighted. The list was compiled from numerous newspaper references, and is provided with the hope that it may help others to identify the activities of these men.

Atchison

Antoine, C.
Auld, David
Barbee, Elias
Barnard, John P.
Blair, Edward K.
Branham, C. C.
Broadwell, J. M.
Brown, Junius
Brown, W. E.
Clayton, Curtis
Connard, C. J.
Cook, W. W.
Coons, B. F.
Copeland, T. J.
Davis, T.
Dennison, M. B.
Digby, T. M.

Dold, John
Dyer, R. H.
Ewing, R. C.
Ferrier, J.
Fisher, T. M.
Galbraith, J. S.
Gaylord, L. B.
George, Jacob
Gillespie, W. A.
Goodale, Tim
Gratiot, C. H.
Green, J. Y.
Griffith, W. W.
Guthrie, J. M.
Hannere, A.
Hays, A.
Hilton, Joseph

Hinkley, J. W.
Kneidson, S.
Knite, S.
McCleary, H. H.
Manion, C.
Marshall, F. J.
Mason, S. G.
Marten, M.
Murdock, Hugh
Perry, C. A.
Rallston, J.
Roper, Joseph
Samuels, J.

Slatter, Thomas
Thompson, James
Trimmer, M. M.
Turgeon, Joseph
Van Etten, E. W.
Walker, James E.
Watson, R. S.
White, D. D.
Williams, H. D.
Wilson, Richard D.
Wood, S. E.
Young, W. L.

Brownville

Beane, J. N.
Crow, J. E. & Barrett
Gentry, ———
Hill, J. H.

Martin, D. J. & Company
Melvin, J. G.
Rogers & Brothers

Nebraska City

Barnes, ———
Bischof, William
Boulware, John B.
Bradford, R. B.
Brattle, ———
Campbell, John
Campbell, William
Carter, William A.
  (sutler at Fort Bridger)
Chinn, William H.
Davidson, J. L.
  (rancheman on Big Blue)
Delany, John
Dillon, W. E.
Doyle, James B.
Dunham, Samuel
Dunn, William
Evans, B. W.
Evans, Daniel T.

Evans, Townsend
Ewing, Finis Y.
Fox, ——— (rancheman at
  Cottonwood Springs)
Fraker, Peter
Fraker, Daniel
Frost, L.
Graham & Gregory (ranchemen
  near Fort Kearny)
Hadley, C. B.
Hanauer, Solomon &
  Company of Denver
Hanover, A.
Hays, William
Helvey, Frank
Helvey, Quitman
Higgins, M. W.
Horton, Charles B.
Hosford, J. W.

Howe, George W.
Ingham, S. A.
Johnson, B. S.
Jones & Kerr
Knight, Joseph
Lamar, ———
Langford, Henry
Larton, Robert
Livingston, Bell & Company
Lobb & Company
Maddox, Porter
Mason, E. C.
Mayhew, A. B.
Moffit, Joseph
Monahan Boys
Moore, James A. (rancheman)
Newsom, B. J.
Otaway, Charles
Payne, Moses U.
Phelphs, Major ———
Pinney, M. E.
Pope, James
Potts, J. C.
Raley, Jonathan
Randall, Sloan & Company
Reed, John

Repime, A.
Rockett, ———
Ryan, Mat
Scroggins, Henry
Shelden, Henry
Sloan, William T.
Smith & Galbreth
Squire & Hutchins
Stodden & Benham
Street, Anthony W.
Sydenham, Moses
Syfcus, Jacob
Taylor, Jesse
Tunley, Ben
Vallandra, ———
Walters, ———
Ware, N. M.
White, Fred
Williams, Robert (rancheman
    at O'Fallon's Bluffs)
Williams, W. C. (rancheman
    at O'Fallon's Bluffs)
Willis & Claggett
Windsor & Lytton
Withee, Francis
Wyatt, C. W.

Omaha

Baldwin & Dodge
Brown, S. R.
Clopper, Reagan &
    Coffman, J. F.
Curley, J. E.
Dallon, S.
Evans, Charles Turner
Forbes, George W.
Marshall, George
Martin, W.
Morrow, Jack

Nichols, S. R.
O'Banion, James
Pegram & Warner
Ruth, William
Shepherd, J.
Smith, F.
Tilton, A. E.
Tilton, C. E.
Willard, R. H.
Willis, R. H.
Wood, Reuben

Plattsmouth

Allinson, John
Buttery & White
Davidson, William A.
Fallis, ———
Fuller, A. B.
Hendrie, ———
Hurd, C.
Kelpser, Capt. ———

Murphy, Pat
Nesbit, ———
Orr, ———
Parmalee, C. H.
Porter, William B.
Squires & McDonald
Tyson, T. K.

Notes to the Text

NOTES TO CHAPTER I

1. Alexander Majors, *Seventy Years on the Frontier,* ed. Col. Prentiss Ingraham (reprint; Minneapolis: Ross & Haines, 1965 [1893], 103.

2. Randolph B. Marcy, *The Prairie Traveler, a Hand-Book for Overland Expeditions* (New York: Harper & Brothers, 1859), 28.

3. *Freedom's Champion* (Atchison), September 14, 1865.

4. Marcy, *The Prairie Traveler,* 28. *Freedom's Champion,* January 4, 1866. *Nebraska City News,* March 31, 1866.

5. *Senate Exec. Doc. No. 1, Pt. 2,* 31 Cong., 2 Sess. (Serial 587), 321. *Nebraska News* (Nebraska City), March 13, 20, 1858. *Nebraska City News,* March 31, 1866. *Freedom's Champion,* January 4, 1866.

6. Dwight Bennett Newton, "Techniques of Overland Freighting in the Trans-Missouri West" (Master's thesis, University of Kansas City, 1940), 45–46.

7. Marcy, *The Prairie Traveler,* 28. Newton, "Techniques of Overland Freighting," 33. William Henry Jackson, *Time Exposure, the Autobiography of William Henry Jackson* (New York: G. P. Putnam's Sons, 1940), 109.

8. *Senate Exec. Doc. No. 1, Pt. 2,* 31 Cong., 2 Sess. (Serial 587), 320–21. William Chandless, *A Visit to Salt Lake* (London: Smith, Elder & Co., 1857), 55.

9. John Bratt, *Trails of Yesterday* (Lincoln: University Publishing Co., 1921), 52.

10. Chandless, *A Visit to Salt Lake,* 16. Charles E. Young, *Dangers of the Trail in 1865* (Geneva, N.Y., 1912), 26. Thaddeus S. Kenderdine, *A California Tramp and Later Footprints* (Newtown, Pa.: 1888), 16, 100.

11. William Francis Hooker, *The Bullwhacker: Adventures of a Frontier Freighter,* ed. Howard R. Driggs (New York: World Book Co., 1924), 120. DeForest P. Rolfe, "Overland Freighting from Nebraska City," *Proceedings and Collections of the Nebraska State Historical Society,* 2nd series, V (Lincoln, 1902), 281–82.

12. Hooker, *The Bullwhacker,* 12. Jackson, *Time Exposure,* 112. Jesse Brown and A. M. Willard, *The Black Hills Trails,* ed. John T. Milek (Rapid City: Rapid City Journal Co., 1924), 64.

13. Chandless, *A Visit to Salt Lake,* 52–54. Hooker, *The Bullwhacker,* 11–12. Jackson, *Time Exposure,* 112. Kenderdine, *A California Tramp,* 35. George P. Marvin, "Bull-Whacking Days," *Proceedings and Collections of the Nebraska State Historical Society,* 2nd series, V, 227–28.

14. Bratt, *Trails of Yesterday,* 53. Marvin, "Bull-Whacking Days," 228.

15. Majors, *Seventy Years on the Frontier,* 103–4. Kenderdine, *A California Tramp,* 36.

16. Jackson, *Time Exposure,* 112.

17. Newton, "Techniques of Overland Freighting," 46. George Shumway, Edward Durell, and Howard C. Frey, *Conestoga Wagon 1750–1850* (York, Pa.: George Shumway, 1964), 132.

18. Nick Eggenhofer, *Wagons, Mules and Men* (New York: Hastings House, 1961), 52, 95, 118. Oscar Osburn Winther, *The Transportation Frontier: Trans-Mississippi West 1865–1890* (New York: Holt, Rinehart & Winston, 1964), 36. Newton, "Techniques of Overland Freighting," 47.

19. Eggenhofer, *Wagons, Mules and Men,* 51, 118.

20. Newton, "Techniques of Overland Freighting," 47–48. Winther, *The Transportation Frontier,* 36.

21. For a full description of the Conestoga, see Shumway, Durell, and Frey, *Conestoga Wagon 1750–1850.*

22. Winther, *The Transportation Frontier,* 32. Eggenhofer, *Wagons, Mules and Men,* 55. Rolfe, "Overland Freighting from Nebraska City," 281. Emily Ann O'Neil Bott, "Joseph Murphy's Contribution to the Development of the West," *Missouri Historical Review,* XLVII, No. 1 (October, 1952), 18. Lloyd Espenschied, "Louis Espenschied and his Family," *Bulletin of the Missouri Historical Society,* XVIII, No. 2 (January, 1962), 96–97.

23. Newton, "Techniques of Overland Freighting," 52–53. William B. Napton, *Over the Santa Fe Trail 1857,* introduction by Donald C. Cutter (Santa Fe: Stagecoach Press, 1964), 12. Dora Cowan, "St. Joseph, Missouri, as a Starting Point for Western Emigration, Freight, and Mail" (Master's thesis, University of Missouri, 1939), 73.

24. *Nebraska City News,* January 21, 1865.

25. Kenderdine, *A California Tramp,* 35, 38.

26. Newton, "Techniques of Overland Freighting," 54. Shumway et al., *Conestoga Wagon,* 186. Capt. Eugene F. Ware, *The Indian War of 1864,* ed. Clyde C. Walton (New York: St. Martin's Press, 1960), 102. Henry Pickering Walker, *The Wagonmasters: High Plains Freighting from the Earliest Days of the Santa Fe Trail to 1880* (Norman: University of Oklahoma Press, 1966), 96–97.

27. *Nebraska Advertiser* (Brownville), November 15, 1860.

28. Marcy, *The Prairie Traveler*, 30–31. Newton, "Techniques of Overland Freighting," 89. C. B. Hadley, "The Plains War in 1865," *Proceedings and Collections of the Nebraska State Historical Society*, 2nd series, V, 274.

29. *Deseret News* (Salt Lake City), August 15, 1860.

30. *Ibid.*, April 20, 1864.

31. Ware, *The Indian War of 1864*, 6. Jackson, *Time Exposure*, 114. Eggenhofer, *Wagons, Mules and Men*, 91–92. H. M. Kemp to Jay Amos Barrett, September 19, 1899, MS in Nebraska State Historical Society.

32. *Freedom's Champion*, August 18, 1860.

33. Bratt, *Trails of Yesterday*, 51. Jackson, *Time Exposure*, 107. Kenderdine, *A California Tramp*, 36. Marvin, "Bull-Whacking Days," 229.

34. Julie Beehrer Colyer, "Freighting Across the Plains: True 1858 Experiences of George W. Beehrer from His Diary and as Related to a Friend," *Montana, the Magazine of Western History*, XII, No. 4 (Autumn, 1962), 3–4.

35. Jackson, *Time Exposure*, 110–11.

36. Kenderdine, *A California Tramp*, 45–46.

37. Chandless, *A Visit to Salt Lake*, 20.

38. Bratt, *Trails of Yesterday*, 52–53.

39. Kenderdine, *A California Tramp*, 35.

40. *Nebraska City News*, August 13, 1865.

41. Richard F. Burton, *The City of the Saints*, ed. Fawn M. Brodie (New York: Alfred A. Knopf, 1963), 29.

42. Kenderdine, *A California Tramp*, 36. Jackson, *Time Exposure*, 107. Marvin, "Bull-Whacking Days," 229.

43. Kenderdine, *A California Tramp*, 120. *Nebraska City News*, May 14, 1859. Henry Ernst Dosch, "Reminiscences of Colonel Henry Ernst Dosch," ed. Fred Lockley, *The Quarterly of the Oregon Historical Society*, XXV, No. 1 (March, 1924), 55. *Freedom's Champion*, June 20, 1863. Henry Tefft Clarke, "Freighting—Denver & Black Hills," *Proceedings and Collections of the Nebraska State Historical Society*, 2nd series, V, 300. Porter Maddox, "Freighting Reminiscences," *ibid.*, V, 296. Marvin, "Bull-Whacking Days," 228–29. Jackson, *Time Exposure*, 107.

44. Jackson, *Time Exposure*, 108. Ware, *The Indian War of 1864*, 101.

45. Kenderdine, *A California Tramp*, 34. Newton, "Techniques of Overland Freighting," 70.

46. Jackson, *Time Exposure*, 109.

47. Chandless, *A Visit to Salt Lake*, 14. Colyer, "Freighting Across the Plains," 17.

48. Raymond W. and Mary Lund Settle, *War Drums and Wagon Wheels: The Story of Russell, Majors and Waddell* (Lincoln: University of Nebraska Press, 1966), 44, 50. *Freedom's Champion*, March 10, Novem-

ber 3, 1860; January 4, 1866. *Nebraska City News,* March 31, 1866. Additional information on wagon prices is available from the records of Louis Espenschied. In 1861, for example, he contracted with the army to construct 200 freight wagons of 5,000 to 6,000 pounds capacity for $125 each. (Espenschied, "Louis Espenschied and His Family," 96.)

49. *Nebraska City News,* July 19, 1862.

50. Alexander Caldwell, "Address of Hon. Alexander Caldwell," *Transactions of the Kansas State Historical Society,* III (Topeka, 1886), 452.

51. *Daily Times* (Leavenworth), August 6, 1862. Cowan, "St. Joseph, Missouri," 84.

52. Chandless, *A Visit to Salt Lake,* 19.

53. Walker, *The Wagonmasters,* 101.

54. Bratt, *Trails of Yesterday,* 54. Hooker, The Bullwhacker, 37–38. Jackson, *Time Exposure,* 111. Kenderdine, *A California Tramp,* 31. Marvin, "Bull-Whacking Days," 227.

55. Bratt, *Trails of Yesterday,* 54. Jackson, *Time Exposure,* 112. Kenderdine, *A California Tramp,* 22, 33–34, 38. Rolfe, "Overland Freighting," 282.

56. Brown and Willard, *The Black Hills Trails,* 66. Jackson, *Time Exposure,* 115. Kenderdine, *A California Tramp,* 18, 38. Rolfe, "Overland Freighting," 283. Young, *Dangers of the Trail in 1865,* 25.

57. Caldwell, "Address," 454.

58. Kenderdine, *A California Tramp,* 39–40.

59. Shumway *et al., Conestoga Wagon,* 174, 185–86. Eggenhofer, *Wagons, Mules and Men,* 42–44.

60. Eggenhofer, *Wagons, Mules and Men,* 44.

61. J. Sterling Morton and Albert Watkins, *Illustrated History of Nebraska,* 3 vols. (Lincoln: Jacob North & Co., 1905), I, 80. Merrill J. Mattes, *The Great Platte River Road: The Covered Wagon Mainline Via Fort Kearny to Fort Laramie (Nebraska State Historical Society Publications,* XXV) (Lincoln, 1969), 282, 294–95. Mattes writes that windlasses were not used at Ash Hollow during the period of overland migrations and freighting and doubts that they were ever used. Windlass Hill, he concludes, "seems to be a bit of folklore superimposed in later years." (282).

62. Julius C. Birge, *The Awakening of the Desert* (Boston: Gorham Press, 1912), 133–41. Thomas Alfred Creigh, "From Nebraska City to Montana, 1866: The Diary of Thomas Alfred Creigh," ed. James C. Olson, *Nebraska History,* XXIX, No. 3 (September, 1948), 221. Jackson, *Time Exposure,* 120–21. Kenderdine, *A California Tramp,* 56–58.

63. Birge, *The Awakening of the Desert,* 76. Bratt, *Trails of Yesterday,* 54. Clarke, "Freighting," 300. A. W. Haygood, "The Freighting Business," *Annals of Wyoming,* III, No. 1 (July, 1925), 85–86. Hooker, *The Bull-*

whacker, 25. Kenderdine, *A California Tramp,* 33. Rolfe, "Overland Freighting," 282. T. K. Tyson, "Freighting to Denver," *Proceedings and Collections of the Nebraska State Historical Society,* 2nd series, V, 259.

64. Brown and Willard, *The Black Hills Trails,* 66. Kenderdine, *A California Tramp,* 33.

65. Brown and Willard, *The Black Hills Trails,* 66. Chandless, *A Visit to Salt Lake,* 20. Jackson, *Time Exposure,* 112. Rolfe, "Overland Freighting," 282. Clarke, "Freighting," 301. Bratt, *Trails of Yesterday,* 60.

66. Jackson, *Time Exposure,* 113.

67. Kenderdine, *A California Tramp,* 33.

68. Chandless, *A Visit to Salt Lake,* 21. Birge, *The Awakening of the Desert,* 58. Kenderdine, *A California Tramp,* 41.

69. Birge, *The Awakening of the Desert,* 59–60.

70. Clarke, "Freighting," 301.

71. *Ibid.* Marcy, *The Prairie Traveler,* 73. Newton, "'Techniques of Overland Freighting," 60.

72. Marvin, "Bull-Whacking Days," 230.

73. Louise Pound, *The Folk-Song of Nebraska and the Central West, a Syllabus (Nebraska Academy of Sciences Publications,* IX, No. 3) (Lincoln, 1915), 32–33.

74. Richard E. Lingenfelter, Richard A. Dwyer, and David Cohen, eds. and compilers, *Songs of the American West* (Berkeley and Los Angeles: University of California Press, 1968), 58.

75. Alan Lomax, *The Folk Songs of North America in the English Language* (Garden City, N.Y.: Doubleday & Co., 1960), 326–27.

76. Lingenfelter, Dwyer, and Cohen, *Songs of the American West,* 58–59. The Nebraska State Historical Society has a portion of a somewhat different version. (T. K. Tyson to Jay Amos Barrett, October 24, 1899 [MS]).

77. Chandless, *A Visit to Salt Lake,* 41. Kenderdine, *A California Tramp,* 33, 42–43.

NOTES TO CHAPTER II

1. *House Exec. Doc. No. 2,* 35 Cong., 1 Sess. (Serial 943), 529–30. Hiram Martin Chittenden, *The American Fur Trade of the Far West,* 2 vols. (Stanford: Academic Reprints, 1954), II, 770. Merrill J. Mattes, *The Great Platte River Road: The Covered Wagon Mainline Via Fort Kearny to Fort Laramie (Nebraska State Historical Society Publications,* XXV) (Lincoln, 1969), 6.

2. W. J. Ghent, *The Road to Oregon* (New York: Longmans, Green & Co., 1929), 129.

3. David Lavender, *Westward Vision: The Story of the Oregon Trail* (New York: McGraw-Hill, 1963), 217.

4. Ghent, *The Road to Oregon,* 129. Irene D. Paden, *The Wake of the Prairie Schooner* (New York: Macmillan, 1944), 100–101.

5. Chittenden, *The American Fur Trade,* I, 463–64. Paden, *The Wake of the Prairie Schooner,* 20.

6. Ghent, *The Road to Oregon,* 125–27.

7. This description is based on the author's impressions of the area formed during the summer of 1963 when he traveled over the path of the Oregon Trail in Nebraska.

8. Paden, *The Wake of the Prairie Schooner,* 105–6. Thaddeus S. Kenderdine, *A California Tramp and Later Footprints* (Newtown, Pa., 1888), 56. Henry Villard, *The Past and Present of the Pike's Peak Gold Regions,* ed. LeRoy R. Hafen (Princeton: Princeton University Press, 1932), 167. Mattes, *The Great Platte River Road,* 264.

9. Ghent, *The Road to Oregon,* 130–32. J. Sterling Morton and Albert Watkins, *Illustrated History of Nebraska,* 3 vols. (Lincoln: Jacob North & Co., 1905), I, 79.

10. Author's impressions. Earl R. Harris, *History of Scotts Bluff National Monument* (Gering, Nebr.: Oregon Trail Museum Association, 1962), 8. Mattes, *The Great Platte River Road,* 436.

11. Wallace Stegner, *The Gathering of Zion: The Story of the Mormon Trail* (New York: McGraw-Hill, 1964), 10.

12. LeRoy R. Hafen and Francis Marion Young, *Fort Laramie and the Pageant of the West, 1834–1890* (Glendale: Arthur H. Clark Co., 1938), 137–38.

13. Lyle E. Mantor, "Fort Kearny and the Westward Movement," *Nebraska History,* XXIX, No. 3 (September, 1948), 175. Charles Boyd Mapes, "The Nebraska City–Fort Kearny Cut-Off as a Factor in the Early Development of Nebraska and the West" (Master's thesis, University of Nebraska, 1931), 13–14.

14. *House Exec. Doc. No. 1,* 30 Cong., 2 Sess. (Serial 537), 235.

15. Mapes, "The Nebraska City–Fort Kearny Cut-Off," 15–16. Mantor, "Fort Kearny and the Westward Movement," 176. *House Exec. Doc. 5,* 31 Cong., 1 Sess. (Serial 569), 225.

16. *House Exec. Doc. 1,* 30 Cong., 2 Sess. (Serial 537), 184d. *House Exec. Doc. 5,* 31 Cong., 1 Sess. (Serial 569), 188d. *Senate Exec. Doc. 1,* 32 Cong., 1 Sess. (Serial 611), 196. *House Exec. Doc. 1,* 32 Cong., 2 Sess. (Serial 674), 56. *House Exec. Doc. 1,* 33 Cong., 2 Sess. (Serial 778), 116.

17. Hafen and Young, *Fort Laramie,* 141–42.

18. *Senate Exec. Doc. 1, Pt. 2,* 31 Cong., 2 Sess. (Serial 587), 148–49.

19. *Deseret News* (Salt Lake City), June 29, 1850. Hafen and Young, *Fort Laramie,* 164.

20. *Senate Exec. Doc. 1,* 32 Cong., 1 Sess. (Serial 611), 109.

21. *Ibid.,* 289.

22. *Ibid.*

23. *House Exec. Doc. 38,* 31 Cong., 1 Sess. (Serial 576), 19, 24.

24. *Senate Exec. Doc. 1,* 32 Cong., 1 Sess. (Serial 611), 295–97.

25. *House Exec. Doc. 68,* 33 Cong., 2 Sess. (Serial 788), 11.

26. Hafen and Young, *Fort Laramie,* 220–30 *passim. House Exec. Doc. 1,* 33 Cong., 2 Sess. (Serial 778), 38–40.

27. Hafen and Young, *Fort Laramie,* 233. *House Exec. Doc. 1,* 33 Cong., 2 Sess. (Serial 778), 55–57.

28. *Senate Exec. Doc. 7,* 34 Cong., 1 Sess. (Serial 815), 9.

29. *Ibid.,* 8–9.

30. Raymond W. and Mary Lund Settle, *Empire on Wheels* (Stanford: Stanford University Press, 1949), 5–16 *passim.*

31. Alexander Majors, *Seventy Years on the Frontier,* ed. Col. Prentiss Ingraham (reprint; Minneapolis: Ross & Haines, 1965 [1893], 76.

32. *House Exec. Doc. 1,* 34 Cong., 1 Sess. (Serial 841), 134–35. *Senate Exec. Doc. 5,* 34 Cong., 3 Sess. (Serial 876), 107–12.

33. U.S. Bureau of the Census, *Seventh Census of the United States: 1850; Statistics,* 993. *Eighth Census: 1860; Population,* 575–76.

34. Henry Pickering Walker, *The Wagonmasters: High Plains Freighting from the Earliest Days of the Santa Fe Trail to 1880* (Norman: University of Oklahoma Press, 1966), 157. "Utah's Commerce and Co-operation," *Tullidge's Quarterly Magazine,* I, No. 3 (Salt Lake City, April, 1881), 354. William E. Connelley, *A Standard History of Kansas and Kansans,* 5 vols. (Chicago: Lewis Publishing Co., 1918), I, 170. *Deseret News,* June 22, July 6, 1850. J. V. Frederick, *Ben Holladay The Stagecoach King: A Chapter in the Development of Transcontinental Transportation* (Glendale: Arthur H. Clark Co., 1940), 28–30.

35. *Deseret News,* July 6, August 31, 1850.

36. Connelley, *A Standard History of Kansas and Kansans,* I, 170.

37. *Deseret News,* September 28, 1850.

38. *Ibid.,* August 24, September 7, 1850.

39. *Ibid.,* June 14, 28, August 19, 1851; July 6, 13, 1854.

40. *Kansas Weekly Herald* (Leavenworth), March 22, 1856.

41. *Ibid.,* February 23, May 11, October 13, 1855.

42. *Ibid.,* January 12, May 25, June 8, 1855.

43. *Ibid.,* January 26, 1856.

44. *Deseret News,* November 21, December 19, 1855.

NOTES TO CHAPTER III

1. James C. Olson, *History of Nebraska* (Lincoln: University of Nebraska Press, 1955), 83–85. Everett Dick, *The Sod-House Frontier, 1854–1890* (Lincoln: Johnsen Publishing Co., 1954), 40–54.

2. *Kansas Weekly Herald* (Leavenworth), March 2, 1855.

3. For a full account of the causes of the Mormon War, see Norman F. Furniss, *The Mormon Conflict, 1850–1859* (New Haven: Yale University Press, 1960).

4. *Ibid.*, 63.

5. *House Exec. Doc. 2*, 35 Cong., 1 Sess. (Serial 943), 58, 172–73.

6. *Missouri Republican* (St. Louis), July 4, 1857, as quoted in the *Kansas Weekly Herald,* July 11, 1857.

7. *Kansas Weekly Herald,* January 10, 1857. *Senate Exec. Doc. 31,* 35 Cong., 1 Sess. (Serial 924), 8.

8. Raymond W. and Mary Lund Settle, *Empire on Wheels* (Stanford: Stanford University Press, 1949), 17–18.

9. *House Exec. Doc. 2,* 35 Cong., 2 Sess. (Serial 998), 46–47.

10. Settle and Settle, *Empire on Wheels,* 19. *House Exec. Doc. 2,* 35 Cong., 1 Sess. (Serial 943), 25–30, 59.

11. Settle and Settle, *Empire on Wheels,* 19–20. *House Exec. Doc. 2,* 35 Cong., 1 Sess. (Serial 943), 29. *Nebraska News* (Nebraska City), February 27, 1858.

12. *Kansas Weekly Herald,* August 22, 1857. Settle and Settle, *Empire on Wheels,* 23.

13. *House Exec. Doc. 2,* 35 Cong., 2 Sess. (Serial 998), 31.

14. *House Exec. Doc. 50,* 35 Cong., 2 Sess. (Serial 1006), 4.

15. *Ibid.* Alexander Majors, *Seventy Years on the Frontier,* ed. Col. Prentiss Ingraham (reprint; Minneapolis: Ross & Haines, 1965 [1893]), 76. Randolph B. Marcy, *The Prairie Traveler: A Hand-Book for Overland Expeditions* (New York: Harper & Brothers, 1859), 326.

16. *Nebraska Advertiser* (Brownville), March 4, 1858.

17. *Omaha Times,* July 15, 1858.

18. Addison Erwin Sheldon, *Nebraska, the Land and the People,* 3 vols. (Chicago: Lewis Publishing Co., 1931), I, 217.

19. William E. Connelley, *A Standard History of Kansas and Kansans,* 5 vols. (Chicago: Lewis Publishing Co., 1918), II, 979.

20. *Nebraska News,* February 27, 1858.

21. *Ibid.*

22. *House Exec. Doc. 50,* 35 Cong., 2 Sess. (Serial 1006), 5.

23. *Ibid.*, 9.

24. *Nebraska News,* March 13, 20, 1858. *Nebraska Advertiser,* March 18, 1858.

25. *Nebraska News,* March 20, 1858.

26. Majors, *Seventy Years on the Frontier,* 72.

27. *Nebraska News,* February 27, 1858.

28. Alexander Caldwell, "Address of Hon. Alexander Caldwell," *Transactions of the Kansas State Historical Society,* III (Topeka, 1886), 454.

29. *Nebraska News,* May 22, August 21, 1858.

30. *House Exec. Doc. 2,* 35 Cong., 2 Sess. (Serial 999), 782–83. *Omaha Nebraskian,* May 12, 1858. *Omaha Times,* May 13, 1858. *Nebraska News,* May 22, June 12, 1858.

31. *Nebraska Advertiser,* August 19, 1858.

32. Wm. [William] N. Byers and Jno. [John H.] Kellom, *Hand Book to the Gold Fields of Nebraska and Kansas* (Chicago: D. B. Cooke & Co., 1859), 55–56. W. B. Horner, *The Gold Regions of Kansas and Nebraska* (Chicago: W. H. Tobey & Co., 1859), 49.

33. *Ibid. Nebraska News,* April 2, 1859.

34. Byers and Kellom, *Hand Book to the Gold Fields,* 56–57. Horner, *The Gold Regions of Kansas and Nebraska,* 49–50.

35. Marcy, *The Prairie Traveler,* 326. O. Allen, *Allen's Guide Book and Map to the Gold Fields of Kansas & Nebraska* (Washington, D.C.: R. A. Waters, 1859). Horner, *The Gold Regions of Kansas and Nebraska,* 50. Byers and Kellom, *Hand Book to the Gold Fields,* 57. For the survey descriptions of the route by range and township, see J. Sterling Morton and Albert Watkins, *Illustrated History of Nebraska,* 3 vols. (Lincoln: Jacob North & Co., 1906), II, 73–74.

36. *Nebraska Advertiser,* September 30, 1858. Settle and Settle, *Empire on Wheels,* 26. "Notes of various sub-contractors to Russell, Majors & Waddell," Office of the Quartermaster General, Consolidated Correspondence File, 1794–1915, Box 949, Old Army Division, National Archives.

37. *House Exec. Doc. 2,* 35 Cong., 2 Sess. (Serial 999), 780–81.

38. *Omaha Times,* September 9, 1858.

39. *Nebraska Advertiser,* December 2, 23, 1858.

40. Peter Beckman, "The Overland Trade and Atchison's Beginnings," *Territorial Kansas, Studies Commemorating the Centennial (University of Kansas Publications, Social Science Studies)* (Lawrence, 1954), 150–53.

41. *Freedom's Champion* (Atchison), April 3, 10, May 29, 1858.

42. *Ibid.,* June 5, 1858.

43. *Ibid.,* August 21, 1858.

44. *Ibid.*

45. *Ibid.,* April 3, 1858.

46. *Ibid.,* June 12, 1858.

47. *Ibid.,* October 30, 1858.

48. *Ibid.,* August 14, 1858.

49. *Ibid.,* July 31, October 30, 1858.

50. *Ibid.,* July 24, 1858.

51. *House Exec. Doc. 2,* 35 Cong., 2 Sess. (Serial 999), 797.

52. *St. Joseph Gazette,* May 12, 1858, as reported in the *Nebraska City News,* May 22, 1858. For further comment on the economic benefits of the Mormon War, see George L. Anderson, "Some Phases of Currency and Banking in Territorial Kansas," *Territorial Kansas,* 111–12.

53. *House Exec. Doc.* 2, 35 Cong., 2 Sess. (Serial 999), 797. The *Deseret News* of October 6, 1858, reported that Russell, Majors & Waddell had sent 4,004 wagons to Utah. There is a considerable disparity between this figure and the official report when one considers that Jesup's figure included Fort Kearny and Fort Laramie freight. The *Deseret News* probably accidentally exaggerated by erroneously crediting many army wagons to the contractors.

54. *Nebraska News,* September 25, 1858.

55. *Nebraska Advertiser,* December 2, 1858.

56. *Ibid.*

57. *Ibid.,* January 13, 1859. Thaddeus S. Kenderdine, *A California Tramp and Later Footprints* (Newtown, Pa., 1888), 94.

58. Alexander Toponce, *Reminiscences of Alexander Toponce, Pioneer, 1839–1923* (Ogden, 1923), 38.

59. *Senate Exec. Doc.* 2, 36 Cong., 1 Sess. (Serial 1024), 608–9. *House Exec. Doc.* 22, 36 Cong., 1 Sess. (Serial 1047), 9.

60. *Nebraska News,* May 14, 21, June 25, 1859. *Daily Times* (Leavenworth), May 21, 1859.

61. LeRoy R. Hafen and Francis Marion Young, *Fort Laramie and the Pageant of the West, 1834–1890* (Glendale: Arthur H. Clark Co., 1938), 302. *Nebraska News,* August 13, 1859; May 5, 1860.

62. *Nebraska News,* April 30, May 21, 1859.

63. *Freedom's Champion,* July 2, 1859.

64. This quoted population was evidently an approximation which included transients. The official census of 1860 showed 1,922 residents. (U.S. Bureau of the Census, *Eighth Census of the United States: 1860; Population,* 559).

65. *Nebraska News,* October 22, 1859.

NOTES TO CHAPTER IV

1. Ray Allen Billington, *The Far Western Frontier, 1830–1860* (New York: Harper & Brothers, 1956), 259–60. Rodman Wilson Paul, *Mining Frontiers of the Far West, 1848–1880* (New York: Holt, Rinehart & Winston, 1963), 111–13.

2. LeRoy R. Hafen (ed.), *Colorado Gold Rush: Contemporary Letters and Reports 1858–1859 (Southwest Historical Series,* X) (Glendale: Arthur H. Clark Co., 1941), 30.

3. *Ibid.,* 48–49.

4. *Daily Times* (Leavenworth), April 29, 1859

5. *Nebraska News* (Nebraska City), April 30, 1859.

6. Billington, *The Far Western Frontier,* 261–64. Paul, *Mining Frontiers of the Far West,* 113–14.

7. U.S. Bureau of the Census, *Eighth Census of the United States: 1860; Population,* 548.

8. *Daily Rocky Mountain News* (Denver), October 26, 1860.

9. *Ibid.*

10. *Omaha Nebraskian,* April 9, 1859. *Nebraska News,* March 10, 1860.

11. Charles E. Young, *Dangers of the Trail in 1865* (Geneva, N.Y., 1912), 67. Henry Villard, *The Past and Present of the Pike's Peak Gold Regions,* ed. LeRoy R. Hafen (Princeton: Princeton University Press, 1932), 169. LeRoy R. Hafen, "Map of Early Trails, Forts, and Battlefields of Colorado," prepared for *Municipal Facts Magazine,* Denver, May, 1925 (MS, Colorado Historical Society, Denver). Margaret Long, *The Smoky Hill Trail* (2nd ed.; Denver: W. H. Kistler Stationery Co., 1947), 191–99.

12. *Omaha Times,* September 30, 1858. *House Exec. Doc. 2,* 35 Cong., 2 Sess. (Serial 999), 1031–32, 1288–91.

13. *Omaha Times,* December 9, 1858.

14. *House Exec. Doc. 2,* 35 Cong., 2 Sess. (Serial 999), 1291. LeRoy R. Hafen (ed.), *Overland Routes to the Gold Fields, 1859, from Contemporary Diaries (Southwest Historical Series,* XI) (Glendale: Arthur H. Clark Co., 1942), 113.

15. *Rocky Mountain Herald* (Denver), May 5, 1860.

16. *Omaha Times,* September 30, 1858.

17. Hafen, *Overland Routes,* 123–25.

18. *Nebraska News,* April 16, 1859. *Republican* (Omaha), January 18, July 18, 1860.

19. *Nebraska News,* November 6, 1858.

20. *People's Press* (Nebraska City), February 3, 1860.

21. [Nathan Howe] Parker and [D. H.] Huyett, *The Illustrated Miners' Hand-Book and Guide to Pike's Peak* (St. Louis, 1859), 57–58.

22. Charles Boyd Mapes, "The Nebraska City–Fort Kearny Cut-Off as a Factor in the Early Development of Nebraska and the West" (Master's thesis, University of Nebraska, 1931), 34.

23. *Nebraska News,* December 24, 1859. W. Turrentine Jackson, *Wagon Roads West* (Berkeley: University of California Press, 1952), 134–35.

24. *People's Press,* February 17, 1860.

25. *Ibid.,* March 30, 1860. Author's impressions of the area, formed during the summer of 1962 when he traveled over the route of the new Nebraska City trail to Fort Kearny.

26. DeForest P. Rolfe, "Overland Freighting from Nebraska City," *Proceedings and Collections of the Nebraska State Historical Society,* 2nd series., V (Lincoln, 1902), 281. Mapes, "The Nebraska City–Fort Kearny Cut-Off," 35.

27. *People's Press,* March 30, April 27, 1860. Mapes, "The Nebraska City–Fort Kearny Cut-Off," 47. A. E. Fuller, cartographer, map entitled "Geographical and Historical Points of Interest in Nebraska," Nebraska State Historical Society, copyright 1937.

28. *Nebraska News,* April 28, 1860.

29. *People's Press,* March 30, April 27, 1860.

30. *Ibid.,* February 12, June 25, 1859. *People's Press,* March 9, 17, August 23, 1860.

30. *Nebraska News,* December 22, 1860.

31. *Ibid.,* February 12, June 25, 1859. *People's Press,* March 9, 17, August 23, 1860.

32. *Nebraska News,* March 17, 1860. *People's Press,* March 13, August 23, 1860.

33. *Nebraska News,* April 7, 1860.

34. Raymond W. and Mary Lund Settle, *Empire on Wheels* (Stanford: Stanford University Press, 1949), 42–44. LeRoy R. Hafen, *The Overland Mail, 1849–1869* (Cleveland: Arthur H. Clark, 1926), 150.

35. Hafen, *The Overland Mail,* 156–57.

36. For a complete account of the Pony Express, see Raymond W. and Mary Lund Settle, *Saddles and Spurs, the Pony Express Saga* (Harrisburg, Pa.: The Stackpole Co., 1955).

37. *Nebraska News,* July 16, 1859; April 10, 28, May 4, November 24, 1860.

38. *People's Press,* April 10, July 19, 1860.

39. *Nebraska News,* November 24, 1860.

40. *Daily Rocky Mountain News,* August 27, 1860.

41. *Nebraska News,* April 21, 1860.

42. *Ibid.,* July 28, 1860.

43. *Rocky Mountain Herald,* September 3, 1860. *Daily Rocky Mountain News,* August 27, 1860.

44. *Nebraska News,* April 21, June 16, September 1, 1860.

45. *Ibid.,* December 15, 1860.

46. *Ibid.,* March 24, 1860. *Rocky Mountain News,* February 29, 1860.

47. *Nebraska News,* June 16, 23, 1860. *People's Press,* June 21, August 23, 1860.

48. *Nebraskian & Times* (Omaha), April 23, 1859. *Daily Omaha Nebraskian,* October 27, 1860. *Republican,* April 11, May 2, July 11, August 15, 1860.

49. *Republican,* July 11, September 26, 1860. *Daily Omaha Nebraskian,* September 22, 25, 1860.

50. *Republican,* February 15, May 9, August 8, 1860. *Rocky Mountain Herald,* June 23, 1860.

51. *Republican,* September 26, 1860.

52. *Freedom's Champion* (Atchison), July 2, 1859; November 3, 1860.

53. *Rocky Mountain News,* September 22, 1859. *Daily Rocky Mountain News,* December 22, 1860. *Daily Times* (Leavenworth), June 15, 1860.

54. *Rocky Mountain News,* November 17, 1859. *Nebraska Advertiser* (Brownville), November 15, 1860.

55. *Rocky Mountain Herald,* May 12, October 22, 1860. *Rocky Mountain News,* August 13, 1859. *People's Press,* July 19, 1860.

56. *Rocky Mountain Herald,* May 12, 1860. *Daily Rocky Mountain News,* September 28, 1860.

57. Capt. Eugene F. Ware, *The Indian War of 1864,* ed. Clyde C. Walton (New York: St. Martin's Press, 1960), 31, 71.

58. Samuel Bowles, *Across the Continent* (New York: Hurd & Houghton, 1865), 21.

59. Albert D. Richardson, *Beyond the Mississippi* (Hartford: American Publishing Co., 1867), 330. Bowles, *Across the Continent,* 21.

60. Ware, *The Indian War of 1864,* 71.

61. *Ibid.,* 52. Everett Dick, *The Sod-House Frontier, 1854–1890* (Lincoln: Johnsen Publishing Co., 1954), 107. John Bratt, *Trails of Yesterday* (Lincoln: University Publishing Co., 1921), 61–62.

62. "Account Book for 1862–64," in Charles McDonald Papers, Nebraska State Historical Society.

63. *Ibid.;* receipt of Eugene Munn, October 8, 1863; account of T. Ewing; Alexander Majors to Charles McDonald, October 28, 1863.

64. *Omaha Telegraph,* April 9, May 1, 1861. *Nebraska News,* February 25, 1860. *Rocky Mountain Herald* (weekly), May 5, 1860.

65. Frank A. Root and William E. Connelley, *The Overland Stage to California* (Topeka, 1901), 206–207.

66. *Rocky Mountain Herald* (weekly), May 5, 1860. J. Sterling Morton and Albert Watkins, *Illustrated History of Nebraska,* 3 vols. (Lincoln: Jacob North & Co., 1905), I, 98n. *People's Press,* September 29, 1862. Ware, *The Indian War of 1864,* 51–52.

67. Root and Connelley, *The Overland Stage to California,* 210.

68. Bratt, *Trails of Yesterday,* 61. Julius C. Birge, *The Awakening of the Desert* (Boston: Gorham Press, 1912), 93. Ware, *The Indian War of 1864,* 70–71.

69. Ware, *The Indian War of 1864,* 70. Bratt, *Trails of Yesterday,* 61.

70. *Nebraska News,* July 7, 1860.

71. *Senate Exec. Doc. 1,* 36 Cong., 2 Sess. (Serial 1079), 216–23.

72. *Nebraska News,* July 16, 1859.

73. Settle and Settle, *Empire on Wheels,* 48–50. Horace Greeley, *An Overland Journey: From New York to San Francisco in the Summer of 1859* (New York: C. M. Saxton, Barker & Co., 1860), 253.

74. *Nebraska News,* January 14, 1860.

75. *Freedom's Champion,* April 7, 1860.

76. *Ibid.,* November 3, 1860.

77. *Deseret News* (Salt Lake City), October 10, 1860.

78. *Ibid.,* September 26, October 31, 1860. *Republican,* June 20, 1860.

79. *Freedom's Champion,* November 3, 1860. *Nebraska News,* July 21, 1860.

80. *Rocky Mountain News,* May 28, October 18, December 1, 1859. *Daily Rocky Mountain News,* October 11, December 13, 1860.

81. A Kansas City newspaper, the *Western Journal of Commerce* of December 20, 1860, reported freight totals in pounds from the following points as: Kansas City 16,439,134; Atchison 6,097,943; Leavenworth 5,656,082, Nebraska City 5,496,000; St. Joseph 1,672,000; and Omaha 713,000. (James C. Malin, *Grassland Historical Studies: Natural Resources Utilization in a Background of Science and Technology, Geology and Geography* [Lawrence, 1950], I, 223–24.) These statistics are questionable. Since none of the towns save Atchison compiled detailed summaries, there is a logical question about the basis of the Kansas City summary. Then, too, the extremely detailed study done by the *Freedom's Champion* of Atchison is two million pounds over the *Journal's* figure. The Omaha figure is probably low, but the Leavenworth amount is greatly exaggerated and the Nebraska City figure is somewhat high.

82. U.S. Bureau of the Census, *Eighth Census of the United States: 1860; Population,* 554–55.

NOTES TO CHAPTER V

1. *Nebraska City News,* February 16, April 20, 1861.

2. *People's Press* (Nebraska City), July 17, 21, 24, 28, August 25, September 1, 1862; January 1, February 23, March 19, 1863. Warren Upham and Rose Barteau Dunlap (compilers and eds.), *Minnesota Biographies 1655–1912 (Minnesota Historical Society Collections,* XIV), (St. Paul. 1912), 84.

3. *Nebraska City News,* April 6, 1861. Charles Boyd Mapes, "The Nebraska City–Fort Kearny Cut-Off as a Factor in the Early Development of Nebraska and the West" (Master's thesis, University of Nebraska, 1931), 42–43, 46–47, 49–59.

4. *Nebraska City News,* April 6, June 8, 1861; February 8, 22, June 7, 1862. *People's Press,* June 26, September 18, 1862; April 20, 1863.

5. *People's Press,* September 18, December 4, 1862.

6. *Nebraska City News,* April 27, May 25, 1861.

7. *People's Press,* May 15, 1862.

8. *Rocky Mountain News* (Denver), October 2, 1862; April 2, 1863. *Commonwealth and Republican* (Denver), March 26, 1863.

9. *Nebraska City News,* June 29, 1861; July 12, 1862.

10. *Ibid.,* July 19, 1862.

11. *Ibid.,* February 9, 23, April 20, 1861; May 1, August 16, 1862. *People's Press,* June 12, 1862.

12. Rodman Wilson Paul, *Mining Frontiers of the Far West, 1848–1880* (New York: Holt, Rinehart & Winston, 1963), 115.

13. *Colorado Republican and Rocky Mountain Herald* (Denver), May 25, August 17, 1861.

14. *Ibid.,* June 22, 1861. *Commonwealth and Republican,* November 13, 1862.

15. *Colorado Republican* and *Rocky Mountain Herald,* May 1, 1862. *Rocky Mountain News,* May 3, 1862.

16. *People's Press,* July 10, September 22, 1862.

17. *Ibid.,* July 3, 7, 1862. *Rocky Mountain News,* June 14, 1862; May 21, 1863. *Commonwealth and Republican,* November 20, 1862; January 1, 1863. *Commonwealth,* September 10, 1863.

18. *Commonwealth and Republican,* November 27, 1862.

19. *Ibid.,* November 13, 1862. *Rocky Mountain News,* November 20, 1862.

20. *People's Press,* April 27, 1863. Neil M. Clark, "When the Turkeys Walked," *American Heritage,* XV, No. 1 (December, 1963), 92.

21. LeRoy R. Hafen, *The Overland Mail, 1849–1869* (Cleveland: Arthur H. Clark Co., 1926), 208–23.

22. Raymond W. and Mary Lund Settle, *War Drums and Wagon Wheels: The Story of Russell, Majors and Waddell* (Lincoln: University of Nebraska Press, 1966), 163–69. J. V. Frederick, *Ben Holladay The Stagecoach King: A Chapter in the Development of Transcontinental Transportation* (Glendale: Arthur H. Clark Co., 1940), 63–66.

23. Hafen, *The Overland Mail,* 230–35. Frank A. Root and William E. Connelley, *The Overland Stage to California* (Topeka, 1901), 224, 320–21, 588–89.

24. *Nebraska City News,* April 13, May 18, 1861.

25. *People's Press,* April 20, 1863.

26. *Ibid.,* June 12, 1862; April 27, 1863.

27. *Nebraska Republican* (Omaha), September 12, 1861.

28. *Ibid.,* May 21, 1862.

29. *Daily Telegraph* (Omaha), May 23, 1861. *Nebraska Republican,* June 18, 1862.

30. *Daily Telegraph,* July 12, 1861.

31. *Nebraska Republican,* August 8, 1861.

32. *Rocky Mountain News,* December 25, 1862.

33. *Daily Telegraph,* March 5, 1861.

34. *Ibid.,* April 3, June 2, 13, 1861.

35. *Ibid.,* April 9, May 9, June 25, 1861. *Nebraska Republican,* April 10, 1861; March 23, May 11, 1863.

36. Leonard J. Arrington, *Great Basin Kingdom: An Economic History of the Latter-day Saints, 1830–1900* (Cambridge, Mass.: Harvard University Press, 1958), 208. *Deseret News* (Salt Lake City), September 25, 1861.

37. *Deseret News,* May 14, 1862.

38. *Ibid.,* November 26, 1862.

39. James C. Olson, *History of Nebraska* (Lincoln: University of Nebraska Press, 1955), 117. LeRoy R. Hafen and Carl Coke Rister, *Western America* (2nd ed.; Englewood Cliffs, N.J.: Prentice-Hall, Inc., 1950), 464.

40. *Daily Telegraph,* May 29, 1861.

41. *Ibid.,* May 29, June 1, 2, 6, 1861.

42. Olson, *History of Nebraska,* 117.

43. Paul, *Mining Frontiers of the Far West,* 138–40.

44. James H. Bradley, "Affairs at Fort Benton from 1831 to 1869. From Lieut. Bradley's Journal," *Contributions to the Historical Society of Montana,* III (Helena, 1900), 277; "Bradley Manuscript—Book II and Book F," *ibid.* VIII (Helena, 1914), 127.

45. *Nebraska Republican,* April 24, June 15, 1863.

46. Irwin, Jackman & Company, to Joseph E. Johnston, quartermaster general, USA, March 23, 1861 (Records of the Office of the Quartermaster General, Record Group 94, Old Army Division, National Archives).

47. Settle and Settle, *War Drums and Wagon Wheels,* 131–55 *passim.*

48. Contract between Irwin, Jackman & Company and Capt. Stewart Van Vliet, assistant quartermaster, USA, March 30, 1861 (Quartermaster Records, Group 94, Old Army Division, National Archives). *House Exec. Doc. 101,* 37 Cong., 2 Sess. (Serial 1136), 5.

49. Contract between Irwin, Jackman & Company and M. C. Meigs, quartermaster general, USA, March 10, 1862 (Quartermaster Records, Group 94, Old Army Division, National Archives).

50. Norman F. Furniss, *The Mormon Conflict, 1850–1859* (New Haven: Yale University Press, 1960), 230. *House Exec. Doc. 101,* 37 Cong., 2 Sess. (Serial 1136), 14.

51. *Senate Exec. Doc. 1,* 37 Cong., 2 Sess. (Serial 1118), 54. LeRoy R. Hafen and Francis Marion Young, *Fort Laramie and the Pageant of the West, 1834–1890* (Glendale: Arthur H. Clark Co., 1938), 303.

52. Hafen and Young, *Fort Laramie,* 307. Furniss, *The Mormon Conflict,* 230–31.

53. Hafen and Young, *Fort Laramie,* 308.

54. *Daily Times* (Leavenworth), May 22, June 7, 26, 1861.

55. *Ibid.,* May 22, June 7, 1861; August 6, 1862.

56. *Ibid.,* June 9, 1861.

57. *Ibid.,* June 11, 1861.

58. *Morning Herald* (St. Joseph), May 16, 1863.

59. *Nebraska City News*, April 25, 1863. *Nebraska Republican*, May 4, 1863.

60. *Nebraska Republican*, May 4, 1863.

61. *Ibid.*, April 1, May 11, 18, June 17, 1863. *Morning Herald*, May 29, 1863.

62. W. W. Watson, "Early History of Jefferson County Overland Route," *Proceedings and Collections of the Nebraska State Historical Society*, 2nd series, V (Lincoln, 1902), 219. *Nebraska Advertiser* (Brownville), December 30, 1858.

63. *Nebraska Advertiser*, January 10, March 7, June 13, 20, July 11, 1861.

64. *Ibid.*, August 16, 1862.

65. *Ibid.*, March 13, August 16, 1862.

66. *Ibid.*, June 13, 1861.

67. *Rocky Mountain News*, June 21, 1862.

68. *Ibid.*, September 25, 1862.

69. *Freedom's Champion* (Atchison), February 9, December 14, 1861; January 10, 1863.

70. *Commonwealth and Republican*, November 27, 1862.

71. *Deseret News*, August 5, 1863. *Daily Missouri Republican* (St. Louis), May 1, 1863.

72. *Freedom's Champion*, July 11, 1863; March 23, 1865.

73. *Daily Times*, May 18, June 2, 1861.

74. *Leavenworth Conservative* as quoted in the *Rocky Mountain News*, December 11, 1862, and the *Nebraska Republican*, December 18, 1862.

75. *Morning Herald*, June 14, 1863. *Nebraska Advertiser*, February 28, 1861.

76. *Nebraska City News*, May 17, June 28, 1862. *People's Press*, July 7, 1862. *Commonwealth and Republican*, June 4, 1863. *Rocky Mountain News*, May 14, 1863. Arrington, *Great Basin Kingdom*, 217–20.

77. *People's Press*, July 3, 1862; March 30, 1863.

78. *Commonwealth*, September 10, 1863.

NOTES TO CHAPTER VI

1. George E. Hyde, *Spotted Tail's Folk: A History of the Brule Sioux* (Norman: University of Oklahoma Press, 1961), 83–84.

2. The best account of the Sioux Uprising is in William Watts Folwell's *A History of Minnesota*, Vol. II (St. Paul: Minnesota Historical Society, 1924).

3. Hyde, *Spotted Tail's Folk,* 82–88. James C. Olson, *Red Cloud and the Sioux Problem* (Lincoln: University of Nebraska Press, 1965), 10. James C. Olson, *History of Nebraska* (Lincoln: University of Nebraska Press, 1955), 140–41.

4. Hyde, *Spotted Tail's Folk,* 88. LeRoy R. Hafen and Francis Marion Young, *Fort Laramie and the Pageant of the West, 1834–1890* (Glendale: Arthur H. Clark Co., 1938), 316–17. *Nebraska Advertiser* (Brownville), August 4, 1864.

5. Hafen and Young, *Fort Laramie,* 317. Hyde, *Spotted Tail's Folk,* 88. For a detailed account of the early raids in 1864, see Leroy W. Hagerty, "Indian Raids Along the Platte and Little Blue Rivers, 1864–1865," Part I, *Nebraska History,* XXVIII, No. 3 (July-September, 1947), 176–86.

6. Hafen and Young, *Fort Laramie,* 317–18.

7. Hagerty, "Indian Raids," Part II, *Nebraska History, XXVIII,* No. 4 (October-December, 1947), 239–41. *Nebraska City Press,* August 16, 1864.

8. *Nebraska City Press,* August 15, 1864. Hyde, *Spotted Tail's Folk,* 91. George P. Marvin, "Bull-Whacking Days," *Proceedings and Collections of the Nebraska State Historical Society,* 2nd series, V (Lincoln, 1902), 227. T. K. Tyson, "Freighting to Denver," *ibid.,* 258. The order by Capt. E. B. Murphy was printed in *Nebraska History,* XV, No. 2 (April–June, 1934), 121, under the heading "Freighting to Denver."

9. Olson, *History of Nebraska,* 141–42. Hafen and Young, *Fort Laramie,* 325.

10. *Nebraska Republican* (Omaha), August 26, 1864.

11. *Ibid.* Hyde, *Spotted Tail's Folk,* 92.

12. For full accounts of Fort McPherson, see Louis A. Holmes' *Fort McPherson, Nebraska, Fort Cottonwood, N.T.: Guardian of the Tracks and Trails* (Lincoln: Johnsen Publishing Co., 1963) and Capt. Eugene F. Ware's *The Indian War of 1864,* ed. Clyde C. Walton (New York: St. Martin's Press, 1960).

13. Agnes Wright Spring, "The Founding of Fort Collins, United States Military Post," *Colorado Magazine,* X, No. 2 (March, 1933), 47–55. "Fort Collins" in Information File, Colorado Historical Society, Denver.

14. Grace Raymond Hebard and E. A. Brininstool, *The Bozeman Trail,* 2 vols. (Glendale: Arthur H. Clark Co., 1960), I, 82, 160.

15. Merrill J. Mattes, "A History of Old Fort Mitchell," *Nebraska History,* XXIV, No. 2 (April–June, 1943), 71–82.

16. *Rocky Mountain News* (Denver), July 7, 1865. C. M. Rolfson interview, February 20, 1934 (CWA Pamphlet 341, Doc. 31, Colorado Historical Society).

17. "Fort Morgan" and M. B. Gill interview (CWA Pamphlet 351, Doc. 45, Colorado Historical Society). Francis Paul Prucha, *A Guide to*

the Military Posts of the United States, 1789–1895 (Madison: State Historical Society of Wisconsin, 1964), 93.

18. Mattes, "Old Fort Mitchell," 73. Ware, *The Indian War of 1864*, 226. Report of Maj. George M. O'Brien, May 25, 1865, in Fort McPherson Letters Sent, February 28, 1865 to August 25, 1866 (War Department Records, USA Commands, National Archives, 1954). Microfilm copy in the Nebraska State Historical Society.

19. Hafen and Young, *Fort Laramie*, 326–30. Hyde, *Spotted Tail's Folk*, 92–97. *Nebraska Republican*, January 20, 1865.

20. *Nebraska Advertiser*, May 11, 1865. *Nebraska Republican*, November 17, 1865.

21. *Nebraska Republican*, January 20, 1865.

22. *Nebraska City News*, October 28, 1865.

23. Raymond Leo Welty, "The Western Army Frontier, 1860–1870" (Ph.D. dissertation, University of Iowa, 1924), 385–90.

24. Contract between Alexander Caldwell & Company and Capt. Henry C. Hodges, acting quartermaster, Fort Leavenworth, July 18, 1864 (Records of the Office of the QM General, Old Army Division, National Archives).

25. *Senate Exec. Doc. 31*, 38 Cong., 2 Sess. (Serial 1209), 2. Contract between Henry S. Bulkley and Col. J. A. Potter, quartermaster, Fort Leavenworth, March 21, 1865 (Records of the Office of the QM General, Old Army Division, National Archives).

26. *Senate Exec. Doc. 31*, 38 Cong., 2 Sess. (Serial 1209), 6.

27. *House Exec. Doc. 84*, 38 Cong., 2 Sess. (Serial 1230), 79, 95. Contracts between Henry S. Bulkley and Col. J. A. Potter, quartermaster, Fort Leavenworth, April 10, 1865 (Records of the Office of the QM General, Old Army Division, National Archives).

28. *House Exec. Doc. 1*, 39 Cong., 1 Sess. (Serial 1249), 112–14, 251.

29. *Nebraska City Press*, March 17, 1864. Contract between Julian Metcalf and William P. Dole, commissioner of Indian affairs, April 29, 1864 (Contract Book 9, pp. 23–25, Bureau of Indian Affairs, National Archives).

30. Contract between William McLennan and William P. Dole, commissioner of Indian affairs, May 1, 1865 (Contract Book 9, pp. 181–83, Bureau of Indian Affairs, National Archives). The "old Fort Atkinson" mentioned in the contract was not officially known by that name. The reference is obviously to the military camp on the Arkansas River that evolved into Fort Dodge, which was formally established September 9, 1865. Fort Dodge was located just east of the site of Fort Atkinson, which had been maintained as a Santa Fe trail bastion from August, 1850 to October, 1854. (Prucha, *Guide to Military Posts*, 57, 72.)

31. Rodman Wilson Paul, *Mining Frontiers of the Far West, 1848–1880* (New York: Holt, Rinehart & Winston, 1963), 120–25.

32. *Rocky Mountain News,* January 13, 1864. *Commonwealth* (Denver), June 1, 8, 15, 1864.

33. *Rocky Mountain News,* September 21, October 12, 1864.

34. *Ibid.,* November 30, 1864.

35. *Nebraska City News,* December 14, 1864.

36. *Ibid.,* October 14, 1865. *Rocky Mountain News,* April 26, 1865.

37. Leonard J. Arrington, *Great Basin Kingdom: An Economic History of the Latter-day Saints, 1830–1900* (Cambridge, Mass.: Harvard University Press, 1958), 208. Andrew Jenson (ed.), "Latter-Day Saints Emigration from Wyoming, Nebraska—1864–1866," *Nebraska History,* XVII, No. 2 (April–June, 1936), 113–27.

38. *Ibid.* Helen Roberta Williams, "Old Wyoming," *Nebraska History,* XVII, No. 2 (April–June, 1936), 85–86.

39. *Nebraska City News,* April 1, 1865.

40. *Deseret News* (Salt Lake City), September 7, 1864; September 6, 1865.

41. *Ibid.,* November 9, 1864.

42. For summaries of the Colorado River scheme, see Milton R. Hunter, "The Mormons and the Colorado River," *American Historical Review,* XLIV, No. 3 (April, 1939), 549–55, and Andrew Love Neff, *History of Utah, 1847 to 1869* (Salt Lake City, 1940), 808–12. The most complete account is Leonard J. Arrington's "Inland to Zion: Mormon Promotion of the Colorado River Trade," an unpublished ms. loaned to the author by Dr. Arrington.

43. James H. Bradley, "Bradley Manuscript—Book II and Book F," *Contributions to the Historical Society of Montana,* VIII (Helena, 1917), 127. Paul, *Mining Frontiers,* 144. H. A. Trexler, "Missouri-Montana Highways: II. The Overland Route," *Missouri Historical Review,* XII (April, 1918), 146.

44. For a full account of the use of steamboats, see William E. Lass, *A History of Steamboating on the Upper Missouri River* (Lincoln: University of Nebraska Press, 1962).

45. Trexler, "Missouri-Montana Highways," 153.

46. *Ibid.,* 154–55. Eugene Munn, "Early Freighting and Claims Club Days in Nebraska," *Proceedings and Collections of the Nebraska State Historical Society,* 2nd series, V, 314. Robert E. Strahorn, *Montana and Yellowstone National Park* (Kansas City, Mo.: Ramsey, Millet & Hudson, 1881), 19.

47. Trexler, "Missouri-Montana Highways," 148.

48. Hebard and Brininstool, *The Bozeman Trail, I,* 214–20.

49. *Ibid.,* 237–61.

50. C. G. Coutant, *The History of Wyoming from the Earliest Known Discoveries* (Laramie, 1899), I, 506.

51. Hebard and Brininstool, *The Bozeman Trail,* I, 81; II, 119–21.

52. *Nebraska Republican,* May 25, 1866.

53. *Ibid.,* June 3, October 28, 1864; May 12, June 2, 1865. *Omaha Herald,* November 17, 1865.

54. Albert D. Richardson, *Beyond the Mississippi* (Hartford: American Publishing Co., 1867), 482.

55. For a complete account of the Niobrara road, see W. Turrentine Jackson, *Wagon Roads West* (Berkeley: University of California Press, 1952), 281–95. A good firsthand account of the 1865 expedition is Albert M. Holman's "Niobrara–Virginia City Wagon Road," *Pioneering in the Northwest* (Sioux City, Ia.: Deitch & Lamar Co., 1924), 1–50.

56. *Nebraska City News,* April 15, May 6, 1865.

57. *Ibid.,* July 22, 1865.

58. *Ibid.,* March 31, 1866.

59. *Ibid.,* April 20, 1865.

60. *Ibid.,* February 15, May 20, 1865; March 31, 1866.

61. *Ibid.,* January 17, 1865.

62. *Ibid.,* March 23, July 22, 1865; March 31, 1866.

63. *Nebraska Herald* (Plattsmouth), July 19, August 16, 1865.

64. *Ibid.,* June 21, August 16, 1865; March 21, 1866. *Daily Mining Journal* (Black Hawk, Colorado), March 17, 1866.

65. *Nebraska Republican,* December 23, 1864.

66. *Ibid.,* January 13, 20, 1865.

67. *Ibid.,* May 26, 1865.

68. *Ibid.*

69. *Ibid.,* June 16, 1865.

70. *Ibid.,* December 8, 1865.

71. *House Exec. Doc. 1,* 39 Cong., 1 Sess. (Serial 1249), 113.

72. *Freedom's Champion* (Atchison), February 18, 1864.

73. *Ibid.,* October 5, 1864. *Rocky Mountain News,* December 14, 1864. Peter Beckman, "The Overland Trade and Atchison's Beginnings," in *Territorial Kansas, Studies Commemorating the Centennial (University of Kansas Publications, Social Science Studies)* (Lawrence, 1954), 156.

74. *Freedom's Champion,* March 23, 1865.

75. *Ibid.,* January 5, 1865.

76. *Ibid.,* January 5, March 23, 1865.

77. *Ibid.,* July 6, 1865. For a good account of emigrant use of the Smoky Hill Trail, see Calvin W. Gower, "The Pike's Peak Gold Rush and the Smoky Hill Route, 1859–1860," *Kansas Historical Quarterly,* XXV, No. 2 (Summer, 1959), 158–71.

78. *Freedom's Champion,* July 20, 26, 1865. *Rocky Mountain News,* July 26, August 9, 1865.

79. Richardson, *Beyond the Mississippi,* 329. *House Exec. Doc. 1,* 39 Cong., 1 Sess. (Serial 1248), 885. *Nebraska Republican,* November 16, 1866.

NOTES TO CHAPTER VII

1. James C. Olson, *History of Nebraska* (Lincoln: University of Nebraska Press, 1955), 119. Robert Edgar Riegel, *The Story of the Western Railroads* (Lincoln: University of Nebraska Press, 1964), 74.

2. *Nebraska Republican* (Omaha), February 2, March 30, 1866.

3. Contract between Alexander Caldwell and Bvt. Col. Alexander Bliss, assistant quartermaster, USA, March 12, 1866 (Records of the Office of the QM General, Old Army Division, National Archives).

4. Contract between Harrison H. Moulton and D. N. Cooley, commissioner of Indian affairs, April 3, 1866 (Contract Book 9, pp. 334–35, Bureau of Indian Affairs, National Archives). *Nebraska Republican,* June 1, 1866.

5. *Nebraska City News,* June 22, 30, 1866.

6. *Nebraska Republican,* April 20, 1866.

7. *Nebraska Herald* (Plattsmouth), June 20, 1866. *Nebraska City News,* June 30, 1866.

8. Grace Raymond Hebard and E. A. Brininstool, *The Bozeman Trail,* 2 vols. (Glendale: Arthur H. Clark Co., 1960), I, 265–79 *passim.*

9. Contracts between Herman Kountze and Bvt. Brig. Gen. William Myers, assistant quartermaster, USA, June 6, June 11, 1866 (Records of the Office of the QM General, Old Army Division, National Archives).

10. Miscellaneous abstracts and vouchers, September 14 to December 15, 1866 (Herman Kountze file, Records of the Office of the QM General, Old Army Division, National Archives).

11. *House Exec. Doc. 28,* 39 Cong., 2 Sess. (Serial 1289) , 3–7.

12. *Nebraska Republican,* August 31, 1866. J. Sterling Morton and Albert Watkins (eds.), *Illustrated History of Nebraska,* 3 vols. (Lincoln: Jacob North & Co., 1906), II, 123. Riegel, *Western Railroads,* 85. *Weekly Herald* (Omaha), August 1, 1867.

13. *Nebraska City News,* January 23, 1867.

14. Silas Seymour, *Incidents of a Trip Through the Great Platte Valley, to the Rocky Mountains and Laramie Plains, in the Fall of 1866* (New York: D. Van Nostrand, 1867), 124.

15. *Weekly Herald,* August 1, 1867.

16. *Ibid.,* November 30, 1866. *Nebraska Republican,* April 20, 1866.

17. *Rocky Mountain News* (Denver), December 19, 1866. *Weekly Herald,* January 5, 1867. Seymour, *Incidents of a Trip,* 126. Riegel, *Western Railroads,* 114. Morton and Watkins, *Illustrated History,* II, 109, 119.

18. *Nebraska City News,* January 19, 1867.

19. Riegel, *Western Railroads,* 114. Nelson H. Loomis, "Kansas and the Union Pacific," *Twenty-Sixth Biennial Report of the Board of Directors, Kansas State Historical Society, 1926–1928* (Topeka, 1929), 99–101.

20. C. G. Coutant, *The History of Wyoming from the Earliest Known Discoveries* (Laramie, 1899), I, 594. Raymond Leo Welty, "The Western Army Frontier, 1860–1870" (Ph.D. dissertation, University of Iowa, 1924), 378. *House Exec. Doc. 1*, 40 Cong., 2 Sess. (Serial 1324), 41.

21. *Nebraska City News,* February 1, March 18, 1867.

22. *Ibid.,* April 10, 1867.

23. *Ibid.*

24. *Ibid.,* April 26, 1867.

25. *Ibid.,* August 28, 1868.

26. *Ibid.,* October 25, 1867; February 17, 1868. *Nebraska Herald,* April 23, December 24, 1868.

27. *Weekly Herald,* August 22, 1867.

NOTES TO CHAPTER VIII

1. Harold E. Briggs, *Frontiers of the Northwest: A History of the Upper Missouri Valley* (New York: D. Appleton–Century Co., 1940), 26–29. Herbert S. Schell, *Dakota Territory During the Eighteen Sixties* (Vermillion: Governmental Research Bureau, University of South Dakota, 1954), 42–43. Herbert S. Schell, *History of South Dakota* (Lincoln: University of Nebraska Press, 1961), 125–26.

2. Schell, *History of South Dakota,* 126–29.

3. *Ibid.,* 129–30. Briggs, *Frontiers of the Northwest,* 33–34.

4. Briggs, *Frontiers of the Northwest,* 34. Schell, *History of South Dakota,* 139.

5. Briggs, *Frontiers of the Northwest,* 37–38. Rodman Wilson Paul, *Mining Frontiers of the Far West, 1848–1880* (New York: Holt, Rinehart & Winston, 1963), 180. Schell, *History of South Dakota,* 140–52 *passim.*

6. *Black Hills Journal* (Rapid City), March 22, 29, 1879. U.S. Bureau of the Census, *Tenth Census of the United States: 1880; Population,* 52–53.

7. *Black Hills Journal,* March 22, 1879. *Resources of Dakota* (Pierre: Department of Immigration and Statistics, Territory of Dakota, 1887), 178.

8. *Weekly Bee* (Omaha), May 10, 1876.

9. *Ibid.,* May 23, 1876.

10. *Ibid.,* March 26, 1879.

11. George E. Hyde, *Red Cloud's Folk: A History of the Oglala Sioux Indians* (Norman: University of Oklahoma Press, 1937), 201–202. J. W. Daniels, U.S. Indian inspector, to Edward S. Smith, commissioner of Indian affairs, August 1, September 1, 1873 (Letters Received, Red Cloud Agency, Bureau of Indian Affairs, National Archives). *Report of the Commissioner of Indian Affairs for 1875,* 25. Bill of lading, January 4, 1873 (Letters Received, Red Cloud Agency). Vouchers to D. J. McCann, August 19, 26, September 10, 17, 1873 (Letters Received, Red Cloud Agency).

12. James C. Olson, *Red Cloud and the Sioux Problem* (Lincoln: University of Nebraska Press, 1965), 168–69. *Annual Report of the Commissioner of Indian Affairs for 1875*, 254.

13. *Weekly Bee*, April 14, 1875.

14. Richard B. Hughes, *Pioneer Years in the Black Hills*, ed. Agnes Wright Spring (Glendale: Arthur H. Clark Co., 1957), 37–39.

15. Richard Irving Dodge, *The Black Hills* (reprint; Minneapolis: Ross & Haines, Inc., 1965 [1876]), 144.

16. *Weekly Bee*, May 12, 1875.

17. Henry Tefft Clarke, "Freighting—Denver & Black Hills," *Proceedings and Collections of the Nebraska State Historical Society*, 2nd series, V (Lincoln, 1902), 299–309 *passim*.

18. *Ibid.*, 309. *Sidney Telegraph*, January 6, 1877; August 17, 1878. Robert J. Casey, *The Black Hills and Their Incredible Characters* (Indianapolis: Bobbs–Merrill, 1949), 233–34.

19. Clarke, "Freighting," 308–10. *Weekly Bee*, August 16, 1876. *Black Hills Pioneer* (Deadwood), March 3, 1877.

20. On the Sidney Trail the English spelling of *ranch* was used. Evidently during the decade-long freighting interregnum, the Spanish spelling that had been used on the Oregon Trail fell into disuse.

21. *Sidney Telegraph*, January 6, 1877.

22. *Ibid.*, July 15, 1876; January 6, 1877. *Weekly Bee*, August 2, November 15, 1876; April 18, 1877. Casey, *The Black Hills*, 229.

23. Agnes Wright Spring, *The Cheyenne and Black Hills Stage and Express Routes* (Lincoln: University of Nebraska Press, 1965), 195–96. Norbert R. Mahnken, "The Sidney–Black Hills Trail," *Nebraska History*, XXX, No. 3 (September, 1949), 213–14. *Weekly Bee*, September 20, 27, 1876; March 28, 1877. *Black Hills Journal*, December 28, 1878. *Sidney Telegraph*, January 6, 1877.

24. *Black Hills Pioneer*, July 14, 1877. *Weekly Bee*, October 17, 1877; July 31, 1878. Mahnken, "The Sidney–Black Hills Trail," 224.

25. *Weekly Bee*, October 31, November 14, 1877. *Sidney Telegraph*, July 15, 1876.

26. *Weekly Bee*, September 8, 1875; July 25, 1877.

27. For detailed accounts of this phase of Teton Sioux history, see Hyde's *Spotted Tail's Folk, Red Cloud's Folk: A History of the Oglala Sioux Indians* (Norman: University of Oklahoma Press, 1937), and *A Sioux Chronicle* (Norman: University of Oklahoma Press, 1956) and Olson's *Red Cloud and the Sioux Problem*.

28. *Sidney Telegraph*, June 22, 29, 1878; March 15, 1879. *Report of the Commissioner of Indian Affairs for 1879*, 39, 41. Hyde, *A Sioux Chronicle*, 84.

29. *Sidney Telegraph*, January 6, 1877; August 17, 1878. Robert E.

Strahorn, *To the Rockies and Beyond* (2nd ed.; Omaha: New West Publishing Co., 1879), 13. Mahnken, "The Sidney–Black Hills Trail," 224.

30. *Weekly Bee,* June 27, December 26, 1877. *Sidney Telegraph,* December 7, 1878. *Black Hills Pioneer,* June 27, 1877. *Black Hills Journal,* December 7, 1878.

31. *Omaha World Herald,* November 13, 1910. *Sidney Telegraph,* January 6, 1877.

32. *Weekly Bee,* March 7, 1877. *Black Hills Pioneer,* June 17, 1877. *Sidney Plaindealer,* October 10, 1878.

33. *Weekly Bee,* July 17, 1878. *Sidney Telegraph,* August 9, 1879. *Black Hills Journal,* July 26, 1879.

34. *Black Hills Pioneer,* March 20, 1878. *Western Enterprise* (Deadwood), July 23, 1878. *Sidney Telegraph,* August 17, 1878.

35. *Weekly Bee,* March 7, 14, 1877. *Black Hills Pioneer,* June 27, 1877. *Sidney Telegraph,* June 15, 1878.

36. *Sidney Telegraph,* January 6, 1877; June 7, 1879. *Black Hills Journal,* April 20, 1878.

37. *Weekly Bee,* August 23, 1876.

38. *Ibid.*

39. Strahorn, *To the Rockies and Beyond,* 13.

40. *Weekly Bee,* August 23, 1876.

41. *Ibid.,* February 28, March 7, 1877.

42. *Ibid.,* February 28, 1877.

43. *Ibid.*

44. *Ibid.,* April 18, 1877.

45. *Ibid.,* May 14, 1879.

46. *Ibid.,* February 28, March 21, 1877.

47. *Sidney Telegraph,* January 6, 1877.

48. *Ibid.*

49. *Ibid.*

50. *Black Hills Times* (Deadwood), June 11, 1878. *Black Hills Journal,* April 12, 1879.

51. Strahorn, *To the Rockies and Beyond,* 17.

52. *Weekly Bee,* March 21, April 18, May 16, 1877; February 19, April 15, 1879.

53. Arthur J. Larsen, "The Northwestern Express and Transportation Company," *North Dakota Historical Quarterly,* VI, No. 1 (October, 1931), 42–57 *passim.*

54. *Daily Champion* (Deadwood), June 2, 1877. Larsen, "The Northwestern Express and Transportation Company," 59.

55. *Black Hills Pioneer,* May 31, 1878.

56. Larsen, "The Northwestern Express and Transportation Company," 60.

57. For a detailed account of Yankton and Sioux City steamboating, see William E. Lass, *A History of Steamboating on the Upper Missouri River* (Lincoln: University of Nebraska Press, 1962).

58. Harold E. Briggs, "Early Freight and Stage Lines in Dakota," *North Dakota Historical Quarterly*, III, No. 4 (July, 1929), 245.

59. *Daily Champion*, June 8, 1877. William E. Lass, "Steamboating on the Missouri: Its Significance on the Northern Great Plains," *Journal of the West*, VI, No. 1 (January, 1967), 64–65.

60. *Daily Champion*, June 2, 1877.

61. Lass, *Steamboating*, 133. *Black Hills Journal*, July 12, 1879.

62. Lass, *Steamboating*, 133–34. *Black Hills Pioneer*, April 26, 1878. *Black Hills Journal*, July 19, 1879.

63. *Black Hills Journal*, January 4, 1879.

64. *Ibid.*, March 29, 1879.

65. *Ibid.*, March 27, 1880. Schell, *History of South Dakota*, 162.

Bibliography

BOOKS

Allen, O. *Allen's Guide Book and Map to the Gold Fields of Kansas & Nebraska.* Washington, D.C.: R. A. Waters, 1859.

Andreas, A. T. (compiler). *History of the State of Kansas.* Chicago: Western Historical Co., 1883.

―――― (compiler). *History of the State of Nebraska.* Chicago: Western Publishing Co., 1882.

Arrington, Leonard J. *Great Basin Kingdom: An Economic History of the Latter-day Saints, 1830–1900.* Cambridge, Mass.: Harvard University Press, 1958.

Bartlett, I. S. (ed.). *History of Wyoming,* Vol. I. Chicago: S. J. Clarke Publishing Co., 1918.

Billington, Ray Allen. *The Far Western Frontier, 1830–1860.* New York: Harper & Brothers, 1956.

Biographical Directory of the American Congress. Washington, Government Printing Office, 1928.

Birge, Julius C. *The Awakening of the Desert.* Boston: Richard C. Badger, Gorham Press, 1912.

Bowles, Samuel. *Across the Continent.* New York: Hurd & Houghton, 1865.

Bratt, John. *Trails of Yesterday.* Lincoln: University Publishing Co., 1921.

Briggs, Harold E. *Frontiers of the Northwest: A History of the Upper Missouri Valley.* New York: D. Appleton-Century Co., 1940.

Brown, Jesse, and A. M. Willard. *The Black Hills Trails,* ed. John T. Milek. Rapid City: Rapid City Journal Co., 1924.

Burton, Richard F. *The City of the Saints,* ed. Fawn M. Brodie. New York: Alfred A. Knopf, 1963.

Byers, Wm. [William] N., and Jno. [John H.] Kellom. *Handbook to the Gold Fields of Nebraska and Kansas.* Chicago: D. B. Cooke & Co., 1859.

Carr, Daniel M. (ed.). *Progressive Men of Nebraska, a Book of Portraits, Dodge County Edition.* Fremont, Nebr.: Progress Publishing Co., 1902.

287

Casey, Robert J. *The Black Hills and Their Incredible Characters.* Indianapolis: Bobbs-Merrill, 1949.

Chandless, William. *A Visit to Salt Lake.* London: Smith, Elder & Co., 1857.

Chittenden, Hiram Martin. *The American Fur Trade of the Far West.* 2 vols. Stanford: Academic Reprints, 1954.

Connelley, William E. *A Standard History of Kansas and Kansans.* 5 vols. Chicago: Lewis Publishing Co., 1918.

Coutant, C. G. *The History of Wyoming from the Earliest Known Discoveries,* Vol. I. Laramie, 1899.

Dick, Everett. *The Sod-House Frontier, 1854–1890.* Lincoln: Johnsen Publishing Co., 1954.

Dictionary of American Biography, Vols. III, IV, and XII. New York: Charles Scribner's Sons, 1929, 1930, 1933.

Dobbs, Hugh J. *History of Gage County, Nebraska.* Lincoln: Western Publishing & Engraving Co., 1918.

Dodge, Richard Irving. *The Black Hills.* Reprint. Minneapolis: Ross & Haines, Inc., 1965 [1876].

Edmunds, A. C. *Pen Sketches of Nebraskans.* Lincoln, Omaha: R. & J. Wilbur, 1871.

Eggenhofer, Nick. *Wagons, Mules and Men.* New York: Hastings House, 1961.

Folwell, William Watts. *A History of Minnesota.* 4 vols. St. Paul: Minnesota Historical Society, 1921–1930.

Frederick, J. V. *Ben Holladay The Stagecoach King: A Chapter in the Development of Transcontinental Transportation.* Glendale: Arthur H. Clark Co., 1940.

Furniss, Norman F. *The Mormon Conflict, 1850–1859.* New Haven: Yale University Press, 1960.

Ghent, W. J. *The Road to Oregon.* New York: Longmans, Green & Co., 1929.

Greeley, Horace. *An Overland Journey: From New York to San Francisco in the Summer of 1859.* New York: C. M. Saxton, Barker & Co., 1860.

Hafen, LeRoy R. (ed.). *Colorado Gold Rush: Contemporary Letters and Reports, 1858–1859 (Southwest Historical Series,* eds. R. P. Bieber and LeRoy R. Hafen, Vol. X). Glendale: Arthur H. Clark Co., 1941.

———. *The Overland Mail, 1849–1869.* Cleveland: Arthur H. Clark Co., 1926.

——— (ed.). *Overland Routes to the Gold Fields, 1859, from Contemporary Diaries (Southwest Historical Series,* eds. R. P. Bieber and LeRoy R. Hafen, Vol. XI). Glendale: Arthur H. Clark Co., 1942.

Hafen, LeRoy R., and Carl Coke Rister. *Western America.* 2nd ed. Englewood Cliffs, N.J.: Prentice-Hall, 1950.

Hafen, LeRoy R., and Francis Marion Young. *Fort Laramie and the Pageant of the West, 1834–1890*. Glendale: Arthur H. Clark Co., 1938.

Harris, Earl R. *History of Scotts Bluff National Monument*. Gering, Nebr.: Oregon Trail Museum Association, 1962.

Hebard, Grace Raymond, and E. A. Brininstool. *The Bozeman Trail*. 2 vols. Glendale: Arthur H. Clark Co., 1960.

Holmes, Louis A. *Fort McPherson, Nebraska, Fort Cottonwood, N. T.: Guardian of the Tracks and Trails*. Lincoln: Johnsen Publishing Co., 1963.

Hooker, William Francis. *The Bullwhacker: Adventures of a Frontier Freighter*, ed. Howard R. Driggs. New York: World Book Co., 1924.

Horner, W. B. *The Gold Regions of Kansas and Nebraska*. Chicago: W. H. Tobey & Co., 1859.

Hughes, Richard B. *Pioneer Years in the Black Hills*, ed. Agnes Wright Spring. Glendale: Arthur H. Clark Co., 1957.

Hyde, George E. *Red Cloud's Folk: A History of the Oglala Sioux Indians*. Norman: University of Oklahoma Press, 1937.

——. *A Sioux Chronicle*. Norman: University of Oklahoma Press, 1956.

——. *Spotted Tail's Folk: A History of the Brule Sioux*. Norman: University of Oklahoma Press, 1961.

Jackson, William Henry. *Time Exposure: The Autobiography of William Henry Jackson*. New York: G. P. Putnam's Sons, 1940.

Jackson, W. Turrentine. *Wagon Roads West*. Berkeley: University of California Press, 1952.

Johnson, J. R. *Representative Nebraskans*. Lincoln: Johnsen Publishing Co., 1954.

Kenderdine, Thaddeus S. *A California Tramp and Later Footprints*. Newtown, Pa., 1888.

Lass, William E. *A History of Steamboating on the Upper Missouri River*. Lincoln: University of Nebraska Press, 1962.

Lavender, David. *Westward Vision: The Story of the Oregon Trail*. New York: McGraw-Hill, 1963.

Lingenfelter, Richard E., Richard A. Dwyer, and David Cohen (eds. and compilers). *Songs of the American West*. Berkeley and Los Angeles: University of California Press, 1968.

Lomax, Alan. *The Folk Songs of North America in the English Language*. Garden City, N.Y.: Doubleday & Co., 1960.

Long, Margaret. *The Smoky Hill Trail*. 2nd ed. Denver: W. H. Kistler Stationery Co., 1947.

Majors, Alexander. *Seventy Years on the Frontier*, ed. Col. Prentiss Ingraham. Reprint. Minneapolis: Ross & Haines, Inc., 1965 [1893].

Malin, James C. *Grassland Historical Studies: Natural Resources Utilization in a Background of Science and Technology, Geology and Geography*, Vol. I (Lawrence, 1950).

Marcy, Randolph B. *The Prairie Traveler: A Hand-Book for Overland Expeditions.* New York: Harper & Brothers, 1859.

Mattes, Merrill J. *The Great Platte River Road: The Covered Wagon Mainline Via Fort Kearny to Fort Laramie. (Nebraska State Historical Society Publications,* Vol. XXV). Lincoln, 1969.

Morton, J. Sterling, and Albert Watkins (eds.). *Illustrated History of Nebraska.* 3 vols. Lincoln: Jacob North & Co., Western Publishing & Engraving Co., 1905–1913.

Napton, William B. *Over the Santa Fe Trail 1857.* Introduction by Donald C. Cutter. Santa Fe: Stagecoach Press, 1964.

National Cyclopaedia of American Biography, Vols. XI, XVIII, and XXII. New York: James T. White & Co., 1909, 1922, 1932.

Neff, Andrew Love. *History of Utah, 1847 to 1869.* Salt Lake City: Deseret News Press, printer, 1940.

Olson, James C. *History of Nebraska.* Lincoln: University of Nebraska Press, 1955.

———. *Red Cloud and the Sioux Problem.* Lincoln: University of Nebraska Press, 1965.

Paden, Irene D. *The Wake of the Prairie Schooner.* New York: Macmillan, 1944.

Parker [Nathan Howe] and [D. H.] Huyett. *The Illustrated Miners' Hand-Book and Guide to Pike's Peak.* St. Louis, 1859.

Paul, Rodman Wilson. *Mining Frontiers of the Far West, 1848–1880.* New York: Holt, Rinehart & Winston, 1963.

Portrait and Biographical Album of Gage County, Nebraska. Chicago: Chapman Brothers, 1888.

Portrait and Biographical Album of Otoe and Cass Counties, Nebraska. Chicago: Chapman Brothers, 1889.

Pound, Louise. *The Folk-Song of Nebraska and the Central West, a Syllabus (Nebraska Academy of Sciences Publications,* Vol. IX, No. 3). Lincoln, 1915.

Prucha, Francis Paul. *A Guide to the Military Posts of the United States, 1789–1895.* Madison: State Historical Society of Wisconsin, 1964.

Resources of Dakota. Pierre: Department of Immigration and Statistics, Territory of Dakota, 1887.

Richardson, Albert D. *Beyond the Mississippi.* Hartford: American Publishing Co., 1867.

Riegel, Robert Edgar. *The Story of the Western Railroads.* Lincoln: University of Nebraska Press, 1964.

Root, Frank A., and William Elsey Connelley. *The Overland Stage to California.* Topeka, 1901.

Schell, Herbert S. *Dakota Territory During the Eighteen Sixties.* Vermillion: Governmental Research Bureau, University of South Dakota, 1954.

——. *History of South Dakota.* Lincoln: University of Nebraska Press, 1961.

Settle, Raymond W., and Mary Lund Settle. *Empire on Wheels.* Stanford: Stanford University Press, 1949.

——. *Saddles and Spurs, the Pony Express Saga.* Harrisburg, Pa.: Stackpole Co., 1955.

——. *War Drums and Wagon Wheels: The Story of Russell, Majors and Waddell.* Lincoln: University of Nebraska Press, 1966.

Seymour, Silas. *Incidents of a Trip Through the Great Platte Valley, to the Rocky Mountains and Laramie Plains, in the Fall of 1866.* New York: D. Van Nostrand, 1867.

Sheldon, Addison Erwin. *Nebraska, the Land and the People.* 3 vols. Chicago: Lewis Publishing Co., 1931.

Shumway, George, Edward Durell, and Howard C. Frey. *Conestoga Wagon 1750–1850.* York, Pa.: George Shumway, 1964.

Sorenson, Alfred. *The Story of Omaha from the Pioneer Days to the Present Time.* 3rd ed. Omaha: National Printing Co., 1923.

Spring, Agnes Wright. *The Cheyenne and Black Hills Stage and Express Routes.* Lincoln: University of Nebraska Press, 1965.

Stegner, Wallace. *The Gathering of Zion: The Story of the Mormon Trail.* New York: McGraw-Hill, 1964.

Strahorn, Robert E. *Montana and Yellowstone National Park.* Kansas City, Mo.: Ramsey, Millet & Hudson, 1881.

——. *To the Rockies and Beyond.* 2nd ed. Omaha: New West Publishing Co., 1879.

Toponce, Alexander. *Reminiscenses of Alexander Toponce, Pioneer, 1839–1923.* Ogden, 1923.

Transactions and Reports of the Nebraska State Historical Society, Vols. I, II, and IV. Lincoln: 1885, 1887, 1892.

Upham, Warren, and Rose Barteau Dunlap (compilers and eds.). *Minnesota Biographies 1655–1912 (Minnesota Historical Society Collections, Vol. XIV).* St. Paul, 1912.

Villard, Henry. *The Past and Present of the Pike's Peak Gold Regions,* ed. LeRoy R. Hafen. Princeton: Princeton University Press, 1932.

Wakeley, Arthur C. (ed.). *Omaha: The Gate City and Douglas County, Nebraska,* Vol. II. Chicago: S. J. Clarke Publishing Co., 1917.

Walker, Henry Pickering. *The Wagonmasters: High Plains Freighting from the Earliest Days of the Santa Fe Trail to 1880.* Norman: University of Oklahoma Press, 1966.

Ware, Capt. Eugene F. *The Indian War of 1864,* ed. Clyde C. Walton. New York: St. Martin's Press, 1960.

Winther, Oscar Osburn. *The Transportation Frontier: Trans-Mississippi West, 1865–1890.* New York: Holt, Rinehart & Winston, 1964.

Young, Charles E. *Dangers of the Trail in 1865.* Geneva, N.Y.: W.F. Humphrey, printer, 1912.

ARTICLES AND PERIODICALS

Anderson, George L. "Some Phases of Currency and Banking in Territorial Kansas," *Territorial Kansas, Studies Commemorating the Centennial (University of Kansas Publications, Social Science Studies)* (Lawrence, 1954), 103–47.

Beckman, Peter. "The Overland Trade and Atchison's Beginnings," *Territorial Kansas, Studies Commemorating the Centennial (University of Kansas Publications, Social Science Studies)* (Lawrence, 1954), 148–63.

"Biographies of Members of the Legislature of 1868," *Transactions of the Kansas State Historical Society,* X (Topeka, 1908), 265–79.

Bott, Emily Ann O'Neil. "Joseph Murphy's Contribution to the Development of the West." *Missouri Historical Review,* XLVII, No. 1 (October, 1952), 18–28.

Bradley, James H. "Affairs at Fort Benton from 1831 to 1869. From Lieut. Bradley's Journal," *Contributions to the Historical Society of Montana* (Helena), III (1900), 201–87.

———. "Bradley Manuscript—Book II" and "Bradley Manuscript—Book F," *Contributions to the Historical Society of Montana* (Helena), VIII (1917), 127–250.

Briggs, Harold E. "Early Freight and Stage Lines in Dakota," *North Dakota Historical Quarterly,* III, No. 4 (July, 1929), 229–61.

Caldwell, Alexander. "Address of Hon. Alexander Caldwell," *Transactions of the Kansas State Historical Society* (Topeka), III (1886), 451–58.

Clark, Neil M. "When the Turkeys Walked," *American Heritage,* XV, No. 1 (December, 1963), 92–93.

Clarke, Henry Tefft. "Freighting—Denver and Black Hills," *Proceedings and Collections of the Nebraska State Historical Society,* 2nd series (Lincoln), V (1902), 299–312.

Coad, Ralph G. "Irish Pioneers of Nebraska," *Nebraska History,* XVII, No. 3 (July-September, 1936), 171–77.

Colyer, Julie Beehrer. "Freighting Across the Plains: True 1858 Experiences of George W. Beehrer from His Diary and as Related to a Friend," *Montana, the Magazine of Western History,* XII, No. 4 (Autumn, 1962), 2–17.

Creigh, Thomas Alfred. "From Nebraska City to Montana, 1866: The Diary of Thomas Alfred Creigh," ed. James C. Olson, *Nebraska History,* XXIX, No. 3 (September, 1948), 208–37.

Dosch, Henry Ernst. "Reminiscences of Colonel Henry Ernst Dosch," ed. Fred Lockley, *Oregon Historical Society Quarterly,* XXV, No. 1 (March, 1924), 53–71.

Espenschied, Lloyd. "Louis Espenschied and His Family," *Bulletin of the Missouri Historical Society*, XVIII, No. 2 (January, 1962), 87–103.

"Freighting to Denver," *Nebraska History*, XV, No. 2 (April-June, 1934), 121.

Fulton, William. "Freighting and Staging in Early Days," *Proceedings and Collections of the Nebraska State Historical Society*, 2nd series (Lincoln), V (1902), 261–64.

Gower, Calvin W. "The Pike's Peak Gold Rush and the Smoky Hill Route, 1859–1860," *Kansas Historical Quarterly*, XXV, No. 2 (Summer, 1959), 158–71.

Hadley, C. B. "The Plains War in 1865," *Proceedings and Collections of the Nebraska State Historical Society*, 2nd series (Lincoln), V (1902), 273–78.

Hagerty, Leroy W. "Indian Raids Along the Platte and Little Blue Rivers, 1864–1865," *Nebraska History*, XXVIII, No. 3 (July-September, 1947), 176–86; XXVIII, No. 4 (October-December, 1947), 239–60.

"Hall of Fame Will Depict an Authentic Story of the West," *Nebraska Cattleman*, XVIII, No. 3 (November, 1961), 12–14.

Haygood, A. W. "The Freighting Business," *Annals of Wyoming*, III, No. 1 (July, 1925), 85–86.

Holman, Albert M. "Niobrara–Virginia City Wagon Road," *Pioneering in the Northwest* (Sioux City, Ia.: Deitch & Lamar Co., 1924), 1–50.

Hunter, Milton R. "The Mormons and the Colorado River," *American Historical Review*, XLIV, No. 3 (April, 1939), 549–55.

Jenson, Andrew (ed.). "Latter-Day Saints Emigration from Wyoming, Nebraska–1864–1866," *Nebraska History*, XVII, No. 2 (April-June, 1936), 113–27.

Larsen, Arthur J. "The Northwestern Express and Transportation Company," *North Dakota Historical Quarterly*, VI, No. 1 (October, 1931), 42–62.

Lass, William E. "Steamboating on the Missouri: Its Significance on the Northern Great Plains," *Journal of the West*, VI, No. 1 (January, 1967), 53–67.

Loomis, Nelson H. "Kansas and the Union Pacific," *Twenty-Sixth Biennial Report of the Board of Directors, Kansas State Historical Society, 1926–1928* (Topeka, 1929), 94-102.

Maddox, Porter. "Freighting Reminiscences," *Proceedings and Collections of the Nebraska State Historical Society*, 2nd series (Lincoln), V (1902), 296–97.

Mahnken, Norbert R. "The Sidney–Black Hills Trail," *Nebraska History*, XXX, No. 3 (September, 1949), 203–25.

Mantor, Lyle E. "Fort Kearny and the Westward Movement," *Nebraska History*, XXIX, No. 3 (September, 1948), 175–207.

Marvin, George P. "Bull-Whacking Days," *Proceedings and Collections of the Nebraska State Historical Society*, 2nd series (Lincoln), V (1902), 226–30.

Mattes, Merrill J. "A History of Old Fort Mitchell," *Nebraska History*, XXIV, No. 2 (April-June, 1943), 71–82.

Morton, J. Sterling. "Sketch of Major J. W. Paddock, Chief Clerk of the First House of Representatives," *Proceedings and Collections of the Nebraska State Historical Society*, 2nd series (Lincoln), II (1898), 110–15.

Munn, Eugene. "Early Freighting and Claims Club Days in Nebraska," *Proceedings and Collections of the Nebraska State Historical Society*, 2nd series (Lincoln), V (1902), 313–17.

Nebraska History and Record of Pioneer Days (later *Nebraska History*), I, Nos. 3–4 (April-May, 1918); I, No. 7 (November, 1918), 1; II, No. 2 (April-June, 1919), 8; VII, No. 2 (April-June, 1924), 40.

Rolfe, DeForest P. "Overland Freighting from Nebraska City," *Proceedings and Collections of the Nebraska State Historical Society*, 2nd series (Lincoln), V (1902), 279-93.

Sorenson, Alfred. "Biographical Sketch of Edward Creighton," *Nebraska History*, XVII, No. 3 (July-September, 1936), 163–69.

Spring, Agnes Wright. "The Founding of Fort Collins, United States Military Post," *Colorado Magazine*, X, No. 2 (March, 1933), 47–55.

Trexler, H. A. "Missouri-Montana Highways: II. The Overland Route," *Missouri Historical Review*, XII (April, 1918), 145–62.

Tyson, T. K. "Freighting to Denver," *Proceedings and Collections of the Nebraska State Historical Society*, 2nd series (Lincoln), V (1902), 256–60.

"Utah's Commerce and Co-operation," *Tullidge's Quarterly Magazine*, I, No. 3 (April, 1881), 353–432.

Watson, W. W. "Early History of Jefferson County Overland Route," *Proceedings and Collections of the Nebraska State Historical Society*, 2nd series (Lincoln), V (1902), 217–22.

Williams, Helen Roberta. "Old Wyoming," *Nebraska History*, XVII, No. 2 (April-June, 1936), 79–90.

Wood, A. B. "The Coad Brothers: Panhandle Cattle Kings," *Nebraska History*, XIX, No. 1 (January-March, 1938), 28–43.

GOVERNMENT PUBLICATIONS AND RECORDS

PUBLISHED DOCUMENTS

House Exec. Doc. 1, 30 Cong., 2 Sess. (Serial 537).

—— *5*, 31 Cong., 1 Sess. (Serial 569).

—— *38*, 31 Cong., 1 Sess. (Serial 576).

—— *1*, 32 Cong., 2 Sess. (Serial 674).

—— *1*, 33 Cong., 2 Sess. (Serial 778).

—— *68*, 33 Cong., 2 Sess. (Serial 788).

—— *1*, 34 Cong., 1 Sess. (Serial 841).

—— *2*, 35 Cong., 1 Sess. (Serial 943).

—— *2*, 35 Cong., 2 Sess. (Serial 998–99).

—— *50*, 35 Cong., 2 Sess. (Serial 1006).

—— *22*, 36 Cong., 1 Sess. (Serial 1047).

—— *101*, 37 Cong., 2 Sess. (Serial 1136).

—— *84*, 38 Cong., 2 Sess. (Serial 1230).

—— *1*, 39 Cong., 1 Sess. (Serial 1249).

—— *28*, 39 Cong., 2 Sess. (Serial 1289).

—— *1*, 40 Cong., 2 Sess. (Serial 1324).

Senate Exec. Doc. 1, Pt. 2, 31 Cong., 2 Sess. (Serial 587).

—— *1*, 32 Cong., 1 Sess. (Serial 611).

—— *7*, 34 Cong., 1 Sess. (Serial 815).

—— *5*, 34 Cong., 3 Sess. (Serial 876).

—— *31*, 35 Cong., 1 Sess. (Serial 924).

—— *2*, 36 Cong., 1 Sess. (Serial 1024).

—— *1*, 36 Cong., 2 Sess. (Serial 1079).

—— *1*, 37 Cong., 2 Sess. (Serial 1118).

—— *31*, 38 Cong., 2 Sess. (Serial 1209).

U.S. Bureau of the Census. *Eighth Census of the United States: 1860. Population.*

——. *Seventh Census of the United States: 1850. Statistics.*

——. *Tenth Census of the United States: 1880. Population.*

U.S. Bureau of Indian Affairs, *Annual Report of the Commissioner of Indian Affairs,* 1875, 1879.

CONTRACTS

Contract between Irwin, Jackman & Company and Capt. Stewart Van Vliet, assistant quartermaster, USA, March 30, 1861. Quartermaster Records, Group 94, Old Army Division, National Archives.

Contract between Irwin, Jackman & Company and M. C. Meigs, quartermaster general, USA, March 10, 1862. Quartermaster Records, Group 94, Old Army Division, National Archives.

Contract between Alexander Caldwell & Company and Capt. Henry C. Hodges, acting quartermaster, Fort Leavenworth, July 18, 1864. Records of the Office of the Quartermaster General, Old Army Division, National Archives.

Contracts between Henry S. Bulkley and Col. J. A. Potter, quartermaster, Fort Leavenworth, March 21, April 10, 1865. Records of the Office of the Quartermaster General, Old Army Division, National Archives.

Contract between Julian Metcalf and William P. Dole, commissioner of Indian affairs, April 29, 1864. Contract Book 9, pp. 23–25, Bureau of Indian Affairs, National Archives.

Contract between William McLennan and William P. Dole, commissioner of Indian affairs, May 1, 1865. Contract Book 9, pp. 181–83, Bureau of Indian Affairs, National Archives.

Contract between Alexander Caldwell and Bvt. Col. Alexander Bliss assistant quartermaster, USA, March 12, 1866. Records of the Office of the Quartermaster General, Old Army Division, National Archives.

Contract between Harrison H. Moulton and D. N. Cooley, commissioner of Indian affairs, April 3, 1866. Contract Book 9, pp. 334–35, Bureau of Indian Affairs, National Archives.

Contracts between Herman Kountze and Bvt. Brig. Gen. William Myers, assistant quartermaster, USA, June 6, 11, 1866. Records of the Office of the Quartermaster General, Old Army Division, National Archives.

CORRESPONDENCE

Fort McPherson Letters Sent, February 28, 1865–August 25, 1866. War Department Records, USA Commands, National Archives, 1954. Microfilm copy in the Nebraska State Historical Society.

Irwin, Jackman & Company to Joseph E. Johnston, quartermaster general, USA, March 23, 1861. Records of the Office of the Quartermaster General, Record Group 94, Old Army Division, National Archives.

Kountze, Herman. "File," abstracts and vouchers, September to December, 1866. Records of the Office of the Quartermaster General, Old Army Division, National Archives.

"Notes of various sub-contractors to Russell, Majors and Waddell," 1858 to 1859. Office of the Quartermaster General, Consolidated Correspondence File, 1794–1915, Box 949, Old Army Division, National Archives.

Red Cloud Agency, Letters Received, 1873. Bureau of Indian Affairs, National Archives.

UNPUBLISHED MANUSCRIPTS AND MISCELLANY

Acton, Herman R., caretaker, Union Cemetery, Kansas City, Missouri. Letter to the author, August 9, 1967.

Arrington, Leonard J. "Inland to Zion: Mormon Promotion of the Colorado River Trade," MS. loaned to the author.

Beauvais, Geminian Pierre. Papers, Nebraska State Historical Society.

Dale, Raymond E. "Otoe County Pioneers, a Biographical Dictionary," MS, Nebraska State Historical Society.

Dauchy, Jerome H. Papers, Nebraska State Historical Society.

"Fort Collins," Information File, Colorado Historical Society, Denver.

"Fort Morgan," CWA Pamphlet 351, Colorado Historical Society, Denver.

Fuller, A. E., cartographer. Map entitled "Geographical and Historical Points of Interest in Nebraska," Nebraska State Historical Society, copyright 1937.

Gill, M. B. Interview, CWA Pamphlet 351, Doc. 45, Colorado Historical Society, Denver.

Hafen, LeRoy R. "Map of Early Trails, Forts, and Battlefields of Colorado," prepared for *Municipal Facts Magazine,* Denver, May, 1925. Colorado Historical Society, Denver.

Kemp, H. M. Letter to Jay Amos Barrett, September 19, 1899. MS, Nebraska State Historical Society.

McCoun, Leonard P., Fairmont, Minnesota. Letters to Paul D. Riley, research associate, Nebraska State Historical Society, June 13, 30, 1970. Copies in possession of the author.

McDonald, Charles. Papers, Nebraska State Historical Society.

Pratt, J. H. Papers, Nebraska State Historical Society.

Riley, Paul D., research associate, Nebraska State Historical Society. Letter to the author, September 15, 1971.

Rolfson, C. W. Interview, February 20, 1934. CWA Pamphlet 341, Doc. 31, Colorado Historical Society, Denver.

Tyson, T. K. Letter to Jay Amos Barrett, October 24, 1899. MS, Nebraska State Historical Society.

NEWSPAPERS

Beatrice Daily Sun (Nebraska), March 5, 1908.

Black Hills Journal (Rapid City), 1878–1881.

Black Hills Pioneer (Deadwood), 1877–1878.

Black Hills Times (Deadwood), 1877–1878.

Colorado Republican and Rocky Mountain Herald (Denver), May, 1861–June, 1862.

Commonwealth and Republican (Denver), July, 1862–August, 1863.

Daily Champion (Deadwood), 1877–1878.

Daily Mining Journal (Black Hawk, Colorado), March 17, 1866.

Deseret News (Salt Lake City), June 15, 1850–1866.

Fairbury News (Nebraska), March 15, 1912.

Freedom's Champion (Atchison), 1858–1866.

Fremont Semi-Weekly Herald (Nebraska), September 12, 1902.

Kansas Weekly Herald (Leavenworth), September 15, 1854–1857.

Leavenworth Daily Times, 1859–1863.

Leavenworth Weekly Times, 1857–1859.

Missouri Republican (St. Louis), 1863.

Morning Herald (St. Joseph), 1863.

Nebraska Advertiser (Brownville), 1858–1867.

Nebraska City News, 1858–1868; August 17, September 28, 1888; November 18, 1902; July 8, 1910; May 10, 1913.

Nebraska City Press, 1859–1868. Originally named the *People's Press,* then *People's Press and Herald,* and finally the *Nebraska City Press.*

Nebraska Herald (Plattsmouth), April, 1864–1867.

Nebraska Republican (Omaha), May 12, 1858–1867.

Nebraska State Journal (Lincoln), January 21, 1895; March 12, 1911; January 18, 1912.

Omaha Bee, 1873–1882 (weekly); September 30, 1899; October 16, November 13, 1910; April 21, 1912.

Omaha Nebraskian, May 12, 1858; 1859–1863. Originally named the *Nebraskian and Times.*

Omaha News, November 13, 1910.

Omaha Telegraph, 1861.

Omaha Times, 1858–1859.

Omaha Weekly Herald, August 22, 1867.

Omaha World Herald, November 8, 1903; June 16, 1909; November 13, 1910; January 6, 15, 1911; February 4, 1913; January 5, 1958.

Plattsmouth Evening Journal, February 16, 1907.

Rocky Mountain Herald (Denver), 1860.

Rocky Mountain News (Denver), 1859–1867.

Sidney Plaindealer, 1878–1882.

Sidney Telegraph, 1877–1879.

Weekly Commonwealth (Denver), August-December, 1863; May-June, 1864.

Western Enterprise (Deadwood), 1878.

UNPUBLISHED THESES AND DISSERTATIONS

Bresee, Floyd Edgar. "Overland Freighting in the Platte Valley, 1850–1870," Master's thesis, University of Nebraska, 1937.

Cowan, Dora. "St. Joseph, Missouri, as a Starting Point for Western Emigration, Freight, and Mail," Master's thesis, University of Missouri, 1939.

Mapes, Charles Boyd. "The Nebraska City–Fort Kearny Cut-Off as a Factor in the Early Development of Nebraska and the West," Master's thesis, University of Nebraska, 1931.

Newton, Dwight Bennett. "Techniques of Overland Freighting in the Trans-Missouri West," Master's thesis, University of Kansas City, 1940.

Welty, Raymond Leo. "The Western Army Frontier, 1860–1870," Ph.D. dissertation, University of Iowa, 1924.

Index